TENEMENT
CITIES

FROM 19TH CENTURY BERLIN
TO 21ST CENTURY NAIROBI

MARIE HUCHZERMEYER

AFRICA WORLD PRESS
TRENTON | LONDON | CAPE TOWN | NAIROBI | ADDIS ABABA | ASMARA | IBADAN

AFRICA WORLD PRESS
541 West Ingham Avenue | Suite B
Trenton, New Jersey 08638

Cover design: Rochelle Mawona
Book design: Charlene Bate

Library of Congress Cataloging-in-Publication Data

Huchzermeyer, Marie.
Tenement cities: from 19th century Berlin to 21st century Nairobi /
by Marie Huchzermeyer. p. cm.
Includes bibliographical references and index.
ISBN-13: 978-1-59221-857-8
ISBN-10: 1-59221-857-1
ISBN-13: 978-1-59221-858-5 (pbk.)
ISBN-10: 1-59221-858-X (pbk.)
1. Tenement houses–Kenya–Nairobi. 2. Tenement houses–Germany–
Berlin–History. 3. Urbanization–Kenya–Nairobi. 4. Urbanization–
Germany–Berlin–History. 5. Population density–Kenya–Nairobi.
6. Population density–Germany–Berlin–History. 7. Nairobi (Kenya)–
Social conditions. 8. Berlin (Germany)–Social conditions. I. Title.
HD7287.6.K4N354 2011
307.3'360943155–dc23

2011018121

Contents

Nairobi as a contemporary tenement city in Africa

Reason across time and space

List of figures and tables

List of acronyms

ADAV	*Allgemeiner Deutscher Arbeiterverein* (General German Workers' Association)
ASK	*Arbeitersanitätskommission* (Workers' Health Commission)
COHRE	Centre on Housing Rights and Evictions
EU	European Union
Ford	Forum for the Restoration of Democracy (Kenya)
GDP	Gross Domestic Product
GIS	Geographic Information System
HABRI	Housing and Building Research Institute (Nairobi)
HDD	Housing Development Department (Nairobi)
HFCK	Housing Finance Corporation Kenya
ILO	International Labor Organization
IMF	International Monetary Fund
JAM	Journal of African Marxists
KACC	Kenya Anti-Corruption Commission
KADU	Kenya African Democratic Union
KANU	Kenya African National Union
KPD	*Kommunistische Partei Deutschlands* (German Communist Party)
KPU	Kenya People's Union
Kshs	Kenya Shillings
m	meter
MKP	Map Kibera Project
NARC	National Alliance Rainbow Coalition
Nazi	National Socialist (Germany)
NGO	Non-Government Organization
NHC	National Housing Corporation (Kenya)
ODM	Orange Democratic Movement (Kenya)
PNU	Party of National Unity (Kenya)
SAP	Sozialistische Arbeiterpartei
SDAP	*Sozialdemokratische Arbeiterpartei* (Social Democratic Workers' Party) (Germany)
SDI	Slum/Shack Dwellers International
SPD	*Sozialdemokratische Partei Deutschlands* (Social Democratic Party of Germany)
SERAC	Social and Economic Rights Action Centre (Nigeria)
UN	United Nations
UNCHS (HABITAT)	United Nations Centre for Human Settlements (Habitat)
UN-HABITAT	United Nations Human Settlements Programme
UIC	Umoja Inner Core (Nairobi)
US	United States
USA	United States of America
USAID	United States Agency for International Development
USSR	Union of Soviet Socialist Republics
WWI	World War One
WWII	World War Two

Acknowledgements

Private multi-story tenement investment is a neglected topic in contemporary housing research. Visiting Nairobi for the first time in 2004, I stumbled across its prevalence with great surprise. I already knew about individual cases of such investment through my PhD student Alfred Omenya's case studies of self-help housing networks. When Alfred took me to his case study areas, I was dumbfounded by the apparent boom in such investment, particularly in multi-story rooming establishments. This triggered a series of questions, at a time when I was formulating a research theme for my first academic sabbatical at the University of the Witwatersrand, Johannesburg.

Escaping the often antagonistic environment of housing and informal settlement research in South Africa, I relished the opportunity to spend a few weeks in Berlin in the *Staatsbibliotek* and the library of the Technical University, and talking to urban scholars and historians. My intention of combining Berlin's 19th century tenements with a study of multi-story private rental investment in Kenya elicited surprise, but support nevertheless. At the Berlin Technical University I'm particularly indebted to Astrid Ley and Peter Herrle both for discussions and for logistics, and to Harald Bodenschatz for a valuable consultation. Urban Geographer Christoph Haferburg accompanied me on cycle tours through Berlin's 19th century tenement districts, while my longstanding friends Andrea Staack and Kirsten Twelbeck each saw to my accommodation in different tenement districts and, though working in non-urban fields, gave me important (but not mainstream) literature on Berlin's tenements; Andrea Sperk kept me abreast of all manner of media information and events. At the University of the West of England in Bristol, Peter Malpass generously provided pointers on urban history.

In Nairobi, I initially had difficulty convincing my counterparts that I was not equating contemporary Kenya with 19th century Prussia or Germany, but rather that my interest lay in understanding the emergence of a phenomenon – massive private multi-story rental housing investment – at different times and on different continents, and what this might mean for a discourse on such development. The fieldwork in Nairobi would not have materialized if architect Andrew Kimani, a friend and colleague of Alfred Omenya, had not embraced this approach and taken time out of his architectural practice (FNDA Architecture (K) Ltd.) to assist in the research. Andrew's Toyota took us on potholed roads deep into areas with towering tenements, abuzz with trade and building activity. Mostly these were new to him too. Once we had chosen two case study areas, Andrew's draughtsman at the time, Kevin Osodo, who resided in one of the areas, became an invaluable guide, interpreter, assistant and long-term friend who has continued to share the housing trajectory of his young family within Nairobi's tenement market. Andrew, meanwhile, ably navigated the bureaucracy, building the necessary trust for us to conduct key interviews and gain access to maps and data. His questions and explanations helped shape my research. Former University of Cape Town colleagues Christopher Nyongesa and Crispino Ochieng, and University of the Witwatersrand PhD students at the time Grace Lubaale and Luke Obala, enjoyed debating my interim findings and, alongside Andrew Kimani, ensured I had caring friends in Nairobi. I'm also indebted to staff in the disciplines of Architecture, Planning, Land Economics and Sociology at the University of Nairobi for taking time to share their thoughts on my research. Jane Oluoch assisted with literature searches in the valuable collection of the Housing and Building Research Institute (HABRI) at the same university. I had the opportunity to present interim findings to an academic audience in Nairobi in 2005 and again in 2008, and disseminated an interim report among academics and my interviewees in 2006. I'm grateful for the insightful comments I received.

The research and compilation of this book would not have been possible without funding support from the Anderson Capelli Fund and the School of Architecture and Planning Research Fund of the University of the Witwatersrand and, from 2009 to 2011, the National Research Foundation. However, the views expressed in this book are those of the author and do not necessarily represent the official views of these funders. To the University of the Witwatersrand I'm particularly grateful for an eight-month sabbatical in 2005 and a further four months in 2009. Thanks are due to supportive Heads of School Alan Mabin and Randall Bird and my Dean Beatrice Lacquet.

In writing the book I'm indebted to a long list of people, most of whom I hope to mention here. For maps and graphics: Andrew Kimani and Kevin Osodo, Wendy Job and Jacob Mamabolo. For a photograph of Edinburgh's tenements: Harry Smith; for a photograph of terraced housing in Liverpool: Andrea Sperk. For assistance in a tenement count on aerial photographs: Andre Mengi Yengo. For reading and commenting on parts of the early manuscript: Kevin Osodo, Alfred Omenya, Christoph Haferburg, Marcelo Lopes de Souza, Richard Pithouse, Harald Bodenschatz, Mary-Alice Farquharson and Alan Mabin. For detailed scrutiny of the entire manuscript, at different stages: my colleague Claire Benit-Gbaffou and my father Fritz Huchzermeyer. For reviewing both an early and a later version of the manuscript and for invaluable guidance: Bill Freund. For insightful and invaluable comments on the submitted manuscript: an anonymous reviewer for Africa World Press. For reading and commenting on the Kenyan chapters: Steve Ouma Akoth. For trusting me with her unpublished manuscript on Nairobi: Janet Bujra. For meticulous copy editing: Karen Press; for typesetting: Charlene Bate; for indexing: Hannalie Knoetze; for the cover design: Rochelle Mawona. For a supportive publishing process with Africa World Press: Kassahum Checole and Angela Ajayi. From the literature, I would like to acknowledge particular inspiration from Jared Day, Harald Bodenschatz, Anja Nevanlinna and Michael Chege. I relied on encouragement and support from both my parents, from my wider family, from Hans Kohlmeyer and from other friends and colleagues, many already mentioned above.

I owe my interest in qualities of urban space within history and urban society to my lecturers and fellow students in City Planning and Urban Design at the University of Cape Town, where I studied in 1993 and 1994, and my PhD supervisor in Sociology (1998–2000) at the same university, Owen Crankshaw. I owe the formation of my urban political concerns to friends and colleagues in Brazil and more recently the emerging network in South Africa surrounding the social movement *Abahlali baseMjondolo* and similar grassroots formations, in particular Richard Pithouse. Lastly, this book expands on a 2007 publication of my Nairobi findings in the *International Journal of Urban and Regional Research* 31 (4): 741–732.

Chapter 1

Introduction

It will take imagination and political guts, a surge of revolutionary fervor and change (in thinking as well as in politics) to construct a requisite poetics of understanding for our urbanizing world... In this regard... there is much to learn from our nineteenth century predecessors... (Harvey 2001, 22)

Over the past 20 years, tenement construction has transformed large parts of Nairobi. Areas intended for owner occupation, with some lodging at the most, today are neighborhoods of almost exclusively multi-story buildings. Defying modernist and largely suburban planning and building regulations, Nairobi's housing investors amass residential units to maximum capacity in up to eight-story walk-ups. They provide no elevators. In many cases, rental agents let the units on behalf of the private landlords who own one or more such buildings, in addition to pursuing a commercial, entrepreneurial, political or professional livelihood.

In many ways, this housing is equivalent to the 'tenements' of 19th century cities such as New York, Glasgow, Stockholm or Berlin – individually owned buildings designed to stack as many rental units as possible, motivated by the extraction of rental profit. For many housing investors in Nairobi, these multi-story buildings are a safe retirement income, earned through small-scale saving and accumulation. Landlords themselves seldom live in their own rental blocks. In designing their buildings, they are motivated primarily by the ambition to capitalize on rental profit. In order to exploit space to the maximum, they attach one multi-story block to the next, lining streets in a continuous front. In this process, a dense city is built. With density comes convenience due to shorter travel distances. In that sense Nairobi's tenement development as a built form has relevance for the future. However, it is largely unregulated and in many instances poses a threat to the health and safety of tenants.

Where 19th century tenements in the west were poorly regulated and managed, with individual units overcrowded and living conditions deteriorating,

1

officials and reformers labeled them as 'slums'. In the modern town planning terminology that evolved in the first half of the 20th century, this label paved the way for demolition and redevelopment, as did a more general condemnation of the building form, density and standards. The term 'slum' has a different meaning today, largely referring to unplanned and insecure or 'informal' settlements of the poor (UN-HABITAT 2003b). But as debated then, the dilemma resurfaces in Nairobi today: should such housing be condemned? Should it be tolerated, or can it be regulated and improved? Do tenements have a future in a city like Nairobi?

In this book I argue that tenements must be taken seriously as an urban form that has relevance for fast-growing cities over many centuries, from ancient Rome and industrializing cities of the 19th century to cities in 21st century Africa. My intention is to bring contemporary African cities such as Nairobi into the tenement literature, which is largely confined to the historical period of the 19th and early 20th century. Berlin's 19th century tenements are typical of continental Europe (Forsell 2006, 6), though unique in some important ways. These include the density achieved despite the extent to which they conformed to planning and regulation, the intensity of the debate about this building type at the time, which 'nowhere else' was as 'heated' (Bodenschatz 2010, 20), and the epic trajectory that the city's historic tenements have followed over the past century. Today, 19th century tenements in western cities are largely adapted to lifestyles of the 21st century, provide access to urban amenities, in some cases provide for luxurious living, and are of particular interest to real estate developers. In Berlin, '[t]hey belong to the urban design heritage of European standing' (Bodenschatz 2010, 120).

Private tenancy in Nairobi has roots in the land dispossessions and neglect of housing provision by the colonial rulers. Lucrative landlordism, mostly providing single-room accommodation, emerged across Nairobi in the early 20th century, but with strong concentrations in the Indian 'bazaar' and in the segregated African settlements (Hake 1977; White 1990; Nevanlinna 1996). Since the second half of the 20th century, Nairobi has shown an interesting though unregulated progression to multi-story tenements as a dominant housing type for people who can afford not to live in what today are referred to as 'slums'. Accommodation in Nairobi's 'slums' is largely single-roomed and made of wattle and daub (or mud and pole) and rusted corrugated iron, and is often let by wealthier individuals to a vast population with limited financial means.

Berlin's historical tenement market and that of present-day Nairobi share an interesting similarity in scale. A building count based on 2009 aerial photography revealed over 10 000 multi-story tenement buildings in Nairobi, quite possibly housing 740 000 people (see Table 7.1 in Chapter 7). By 1871, Berlin had a total of 14 478 tenements housing 845 000 people (Wietog 1981, 129–130), 90 per cent of the city's population (Bodenschatz 2010, 14). These figures for Berlin more than doubled in the following decades. Social differentiation increased over that period, so that by the start of the First World War (WWI) in 1914, almost as much land was taken up by tenements as by 'exclusive suburban residential areas' (*ibid.*). In Nairobi, multi-story tenements (based on an estimated number of units per building) account for only 23 per cent of the city's population. A smaller, more affluent percentage is housed in suburbia or gated estates, and the largest percentage lives in the city's 'slums'. In different parts of Nairobi, multi-story tenements are displacing (and perhaps absorbing the tenants of) single-story 'slums', replacing freestanding houses in estates designed for owner occupation, or expanding onto under-utilized and often contested land. Any tenement market of the scale of that of Nairobi today, even if curbed in future, has a lasting legacy in urban space.

Other African cities, for instance Abidjan in Côte d'Ivoire, parts of Lagos and Ibadan in Nigeria and Dar es Salaam in Tanzania, may well be following suit (in Chapter 2, I present interesting accounts of tenements in these cities). While multi-story tenements do not as yet dominate non-'slum' housing in any other African city as they do in Nairobi, tenements need to be embraced in urban strategies that seek a more dense and sustainable urban future. However, they come about through deeply entrenched practices that are often corrupt (while also pragmatic) and defy regulation. In cities like Nairobi, there is no easy path into regulated tenement development and management. The accumulated body of Third World urban planning and housing literature today provides little if any guidance for negotiating this complex reality. It is therefore relevant to look in some depth into the literature on the history of the densest and historically most debated tenement concentration in the west, and the interpretation and treatment of its spatial legacy to date, as a starting point for examining the 21st century context of Nairobi.

Nairobi, shaped both through the racial and socio-economic partitioning of the city by the colonial state and through subsequent land market dynamics, is segregated (K'Akumu and Olima 2007), as is its multi-story tenement market. Some districts provide predominantly single-room or 'rooming' accommodation, some provide small self-contained units with internal bathrooms and cooking space, and others multi-roomed apartments. The smaller the units, the higher the residential density and, exactly as Harvey (1985a, 83–84) observed for 19th century Paris, the higher the return for the landlord. Nevertheless, landlords in Nairobi take risks when investing in the lower income tenement market. As in the late 19th and early 20th century tenements of Europe and the US, mobility among low income tenants in Nairobi, and with it the tenant turnover, is high. Leases seldom last longer than a year. The probability of rent default is high, as is that of tenants absconding before the infamous auctioneers and their dreaded youths can evict them and seize their assets. In this market tenants are always on the lookout for a better or cheaper deal, depending on their circumstances. Landlords of newly erected tenements, for their part, lure tenants from older buildings, in the same fashion that Day (1999, 46) records for 19th century New York.

Landlords in Nairobi's tenement market seldom perceive the enforcement of building and zoning regulations as a risk to their investment. At the time of my main fieldwork in Nairobi in 2005, the unauthorized residential density in one multi-story rooming district already outstripped by far the highest tenement densities recorded during industrialization in the west. A part of Huruma in the centrally located Mathare Valley had reached more than 1 500 dwelling units on each hectare (including streets) (see Figures 7.1, 7.2 and 7.5 in Chapter 7). In this part of Huruma, single-room or 'rooming' tenements predominate. Given that these rooms provide mainly small family accommodation, this means there were more than a staggering 5 000 people on every hectare of this area at that time, quite possibly among the highest population densities on the African continent.[1]

The residential density of African cities is poorly researched. Informally developed settlements in Cairo are generally referred to as 'the most densely populated areas in Africa' (UN-HABITAT 2008, 58). According to a 2003 study for UN-HABITAT (Sims 2003), the highest density within Cairo is a mere 3 500 people per hectare, lower than that of Huruma. Three years after my initial fieldwork in Nairobi, investors had increased the building density in Huruma, inserting new tenement buildings and adding further floors. This brought about an even higher number of units per hectare. Over the same period, ethnic clashes were escalating the demand for accommodation or refuge in Huruma and had swelled the rates of occupation.

This stands in contrast to late 19th century Berlin. By 1900 this city was considered the densest tenement city in Europe, with around 1 350 people per hectare in its most densely populated neighborhoods (Leyden 1933/1995). At the time and up to today, these are thought to be staggering densities. The most densely populated or most crowded tenement neighborhood in late 19th century New York reached 1 294 people per hectare, whereas the overall density of Manhattan averaged 282 people per hectare (Day 1999, 8).[2] New York's tenements consisted of five to six floors above a basement. In order to finance the rent, tenant families often took in lodgers, resulting in occupation rates above five people per unit (Day 1999). A similar practice existed in Berlin and Edinburgh (Wietog 1981; Robinson 2005). Berlin's so-called 'Building Police' restricted working class tenements to a height of five stories. However, they allowed exceptionally generous plots to reach deep into the large street blocks. Therefore, on every hectare very little land was used up by roads. Landlords could fill entire plots with five-story buildings, save for courtyards. As a fire safety precaution, the Building Police insisted on minimum courtyard dimensions (Geist and Kürvers 1984). Yet in Berlin, the high residential density mentioned above was generated by high occupation levels or overcrowding, in addition to the dense stacking of units. The officially sanctioned level of occupation was already alarmingly high by today's standards, as was the figure of close on a quarter of Berlin's population living in 'overcrowded' conditions (Wietog 1981).

4

In Nairobi, dense multi-story tenement districts such as Huruma exist alongside single-story 'slums' accommodating those whom development experts term the 'urban poor'. Nairobi's Kibera has long been considered the famous 'largest slum' on the African continent, with wildly inflated population estimates ranging from 600 000 to 1 million people (Government of Kenya 2004; Gendall 2008). Kenya's 2009 census, released in September 2010, put Kibera's population at a mere 170 070 (Warah 2010).[3] The multi-story rooming tenements represent a distinct step up from accommodation in Kibera and Nairobi's other 'slums'. Households renting a room in a formally constructed, usually multi-story tenement are not forced to resort to overcrowding of individual units to afford the rent – they have a lower cost option in the 'slums'. In 19th century Berlin, authorities tolerated no lower cost option; they applied force to stamp out the occasional eruption of shack settlements in Berlin's years of greatest housing need (Richie 1998, 165).

In Huruma, the lower middle class continues to demand rooming accommodation, in part due to its convenient location. The spatial structure of the city and increased ethnic partitioning of space intensifies this demand. In Huruma, the residential density has already overburdened the infrastructure designed for single-story development. The heavy flow of people moving back and forth congests the streets. During my visits in 2005 and 2008, once the early morning and evening tide of people leaving and returning to Huruma had ebbed, severe erosion of roads would meet the eye, as would piles of uncollected refuse and sewage spilling from blocked or overburdened pipes. But the varied use of street-facing ground floor units generates an uplifting buzz.[4] Commercial activity thrives on the high residential density, and includes an occasional internet cafe, restaurant or video cinema, while privately run schools shed neatly uniformed children into the streets. This appeal is weaker in districts with self-contained flats, such as Umoja Inner Core. There, ground floor shop owners struggle to survive on the lower residential densities, although these are still high by international standards. The tenants, who are largely employed outside of these districts, also have the financial means to shop in bulk at the city's supermarket stores.

My return to Huruma in May 2008 revealed a more unsettling transformation. Earlier that year, the area had become one of the epicenters of the post-election ethnic violence orchestrated by the Kenyan leadership. In 2006, Nyairo (2006, 75) referred to Nairobi as 'a cosmopolitan city hosting a varied mix of indigenous ethnic groups, including those of either Asian or European decent'. However, the enduring result of the violent aftermath of the 2007 elections is a stronger ethnic division by street and building. Residents in Huruma, when asked about the post-election clashes, gave accounts of barricades ethnically separating one half of the neighborhood from the other, of forced participation in the fighting, and of shops eventually looted to stave off hunger behind the barricades. As often before, landlord-tenant tensions had been exploited in the election campaign (Waki 2008). Therefore, in one section Luo tenants withheld rent from Kikuyu landlords and prevented landlords or rental agents from entering the area they controlled. Four months after the post-election violence, an intensified ethnic awareness continued to determine occupation of the tenements, and indeed consumer behavior. A year later this was still the case. A cosmopolitan urbanism, to the extent that it had existed in Huruma's streets before the elections, has now been reversed.

Tenement history and the present

In this book I draw parallels between present-day tenements in Nairobi and those of late 19th and early 20th century Europe and the US. I focus in particular on the tenement trajectory in Berlin, the city which, as already mentioned, was the densest tenement agglomeration in Europe by 1900, also outstripping residential densities in rapidly growing North American cities, including New York. While tenements were uncommon in England, they dominated most continental European cities at the time. The series of provocative photographs and captions which conclude this chapter (Figures 1.1–1.6) illustrate striking similarities across Berlin's and Nairobi's tenement stock, particularly where the tenement ensemble is no longer complete (in the case of Berlin) or not yet fully densified (in the case of Nairobi). Later, I also explore the role of ground floor commercial activity in both Berlin's and Nairobi's tenement streets. Yet in some ways Nairobi's low income tenement typology has more in common with that of New York, particularly in terms of plot size, building form and defiance of officially intended building type – I expand on this in the next chapter. Urban scholars have also written more on various actors in the late 19th/early 20th century tenement market in New York, Chicago or Glasgow (Morgan and Daunton 1983; Dennis 1995; Day 1999) than on their equivalent in Berlin. However, it is the particular puzzle of how high urban densities and excesses in building typology came to dominate Berlin's housing market over many decades, and the debate that this triggered, that makes for an interesting and, I would argue, important comparison with present-day Nairobi. In addition, the regulated nature of the Berlin tenement, and the process and approach of reform which eventually succeeded in challenging these regulations, provide a fascinating counterpoint to the unregulated, largely ignored and undebated tenement situation in Nairobi.

It was the German reformers of the late 19th century that Friedrich Engels addressed in his *Housing Question*, which he penned in 1872 (Engels 1887/1935). The alternative that these reformers promoted by selectively using the ideas of the French anarchist thinker Proudhon, and with reference to the English model housing, all of which Engels rigorously criticized, informed the early planning movement (Hall 1990, 3). It also formed the basis of modern-day physical planning and regulation. In Berlin, the 1925 Building Ordinance represented the first victory for the reformers. It summarily halted investment in Berlin's tenement typology (Geist and Kürvers 1984). In Nairobi an accepted informality, greased in part by entrenched corruption, enabled landlords to override modern zoning, physical planning and building regulations at scale. Day (1999, 59) records a similar situation for 19th century New York which enabled tenement investors to override plans and regulations. In Nairobi, the unfolding of this informality and landlord practice in the late 1970s can be read as a counter-victory half a century after tenement production was halted in Berlin. But we cannot interpret it as a counter-victory for Engels, for whom industrial-era tenements held the potential for working class mobilization and 'intellectual emancipation' towards a social revolution that would end the 'the exploitation and oppression of the working class by the ruling class' (Engels 1887/1935, 21, 28). In Nairobi, the victory is for those benefiting from the economic logic of tenement investment, and for urbanizing households in need of mobility and convenience as they enter the urban economy. In that sense, it is a victory over modern town planning and over the chronological determinism that modernism seeks to inscribe into space.

It is not a new approach to examine the past in order to understand the present. Harvey (1974, 1985a, 2001, 2008) and Lefebvre (1974/1991) draw extensively on 19th century Paris. To my frustration, they and the English-language literature, including that translated from French, say little about the tenement market in Paris. However, as I show in more detail towards the end of the next chapter, Harvey's, Lefebvre's and others' arguments on legitimacy and justification help us understand the tenement situation in Europe and the US in the late 19th and early 20th centuries. Whether these arguments help us understand the situation in Nairobi today is a question I ask in the later chapters of this book.

How tenements came to dominate urban development in Nairobi is a complex and puzzling question. Unregulated tenancy emerged and expanded in Nairobi in response to unmet housing demand throughout its colonial past. Since the 1980s, multi-story tenements have mushroomed literally outside the offices of development control officials, who willingly turn a blind eye or accept a bribe. While it is hard to find conclusive evidence, my assumption is that the planning and building control officials were and are complicit, not only because of the bribes that supplement their meager municipal salaries and quite likely help them invest in a tenement of their own, but for a more complex reason. Modern western planning education, whether in Kenya or other countries, has been unsuccessful in indoctrinating the would-be officials, thus allowing them to recognize some logic in the tenement boom, which on the one hand responds to an enormous housing demand and on the other hand provides a secure form of investment and source of income.[5] While official data do not exist and landlords avoid disclosure, rumor and anecdotes hold that some municipal officials, alongside pastors, politicians, lawyers and university professors, and those with stakes in the taxi or grain industry (some of whom consented to being interviewed), own an unauthorized tenement or two as a safe source of retirement income. And who can blame them, in the absence of a developed insurance and pension fund industry in Kenya? Harvey (1985a, 82) explains that the 'speculative binge' in the first half of the 19th century in Paris emerged 'in part because property was one of the few secure forms of investment open to [these investors]'. In the context of the current global economic crisis, as I write, the equivalent investments of Nairobi's landlords are far more secure than stakes in any globally invested fund.

Nairobi's unauthorized tenements must be seen as a subversion of the norm imposed by planning and regulation. Thus we could argue with Lefebvre (1974/1991, 23) that 'the rationality of the state, of its techniques, plans and programs, provokes opposition. The violence of power is answered by the violence of subversion... State-imposed normality makes permanent transgression inevitable.' But in the Kenyan case, urban planning and regulation have never been imposed more than half-heartedly. The state seldom makes its real rationality, including its determination to maintain the *status quo* of elite rule and indeed of transgression, transparent through plans or programs.

In the 1980s, as the tenement logic took root and gained legitimacy in Nairobi, as the first districts began to 'shoot up' and as officials met the investors' bold transgression of the zoning schemes with tolerance and encouraged others to follow suit, West Germans began to re-evaluate Berlin's 19th century tenement typology. This arose out of extensive opposition to the destructive urban renewal that was underway (Bodenschatz 1990). The purpose of the re-evaluation was not to inform renewed tenement construction, but to halt the urban renewal that saw tenement demolition and its replacement with modernist monstrosities. These were to become the real 'slums' and ghettos of Berlin (Häußermann and Kapphan 2000). Two decades later, global capital discovered the charm and convenience inherent in tenement districts. By settling two forms of restitution claim, the state unwittingly triggered the large-scale release of tenement buildings into the open market in East Berlin. One type of claim related to tenements which the East German state (1945–1989) had expropriated in East Berlin;[6] the other to Jewish-owned tenements which the Nazi regime (1933–1945) had expropriated across Berlin (Häußermann and Kapphan 2000).[7] In East Berlin, through the restitution process in the 1990s, and where heirs could be identified, properties fell into the hands of a generation which had no interest in being landlords. They chose instead to sell. Profit-extracting companies continue to sweep up the offerings, turning the erstwhile tenements into modernized sectional title apartments (condominiums) and marketing entire streets with an up-market café industry to young globalized professionals (Häußermann and Kapphan 2000; Levine 2004).

While the rediscovery of quality in Berlin's tenements in the 1980s is generally acknowledged as a triumph over large-scale modernist urban development, Nairobi's defiance of modern town planning through the proliferation of dense multi-story tenement construction is itself an important critique of modern planning. The literature recognizes defiance of modern planning as a characteristic of 'developing country' cities in general, and African cities in particular (Rakodi 2001, 212; Potts 2006, 271; Watson 2009, 157). However, in Nairobi this defiance takes the form of densely developed tenements, very similar to those which in the 19th century occasioned the search for an alternative 'modern' urban form in continental Europe. Reformers legitimized this modern alternative with reference to its antithesis, namely tenements (Taut 1920). Nineteenth century tenements, in turn, were delegitimized with reference to the emerging alternative provided by the modern town planning movement (Hegemann 1930). Given the legitimacy that modern town planning continues to enjoy in sub-Saharan Africa (UN-HABITAT 2009; Watson 2009), it is relevant to ask what legitimizes the opposite, namely tenements as an urban form, in Nairobi today. Towards that end, it is relevant to explore shifts in tenement legitimacy more broadly across time and space.

An uneasy future

In this book I ask how the future may treat Nairobi's tenements, and those emerging in other African cities or elsewhere on the globe. Some officials that I interviewed in the Development Control Department of the Nairobi City Council in 2005 insisted on a return to the official physical planning and building regulations. Their strategy is one of legal action against non-compliant landlords, followed by demolition of the unauthorized structures or parts thereof. However, they admit to a very slow and disrupted pace of rolling this out – Okpala (1984) discusses a similar dilemma experienced by Nigerian officials in Ibadan in the 1980s. If taken to scale, this course of action would result in massive homelessness, the loss of urban qualities, and – perhaps of sole political importance to the elitist rulers of Kenya – the loss of tenement investment which is widespread among Nairobi's moneyed population.

Nairobi's planners and development controllers are faced with a dilemma which western planning, regulation and off-the-shelf Third World housing policy are not helping them to resolve: what to do with large-scale, unauthorized private investment that accommodates a substantial proportion of Nairobi's population in a typology that modern town planning schemes have long rejected. The 2004 *National Housing Policy for Kenya* (Ministry of Lands and Housing 2004) aims to expand homeownership, and makes no mention of the predominance of private multi-story tenancy at extreme densities in Kenyan cities, its problems or the urban and economic opportunities it presents. There is no logic in inserting homeownership for poor households into the rent-dominated market of Nairobi, where even the middle class has no opportunity to own a home in the city. Inevitably, poor beneficiaries of homeownership schemes trade this privilege to the better-off, and usually into the hands of experienced or aspirant landlords (Huchzermeyer 2008).

What is to be done about tenements? With silence on this matter in contemporary research literature and policy documents, and planning or development control officials largely turning a blind eye, one may ask: does anyone know and care about conditions on the seventh floor of a rooming tenement in

Nairobi, where toddlers crawl on a narrow balcony whose railing has rusted from the heavy load of daily washing and where a gloomy corridor or threatening void allows hardly any light and air to enter many of the rooms? Does anyone care that in the mornings and evenings people coming or going congest the streets in these districts to the extent that one can hardly move, and yet defiant landlords add more floors? Or that children play in large piles of refuse and sewers are regularly blocked, while a landlord expanding his or her stock grabs or is corruptly allocated another piece of open space? And who should care?

A recurring theme in the literature on urban history is that the conditions of the working class occupied the minds of the 19th century housing reformers less than the threat of a working class revolution. In *The Housing Question*, Engels (1887/1935) argued that the tenement environment, with its high mobility, was conducive to an intellectual emancipation of the working class, not excluding possibilities of its radicalization. But it was conducive to emancipation and perhaps radicalization as much as it was to neighborliness and solidarity, which were keys to survival amidst poverty, periodic strikes and unemployment. The tenement was also conducive to the spread of epidemics, another threat to the bourgeoisie from among whom stemmed the reformers and the first modern urban planners.[8] And ever since, planners have in practice been anti-urban, in as far as they have made sure that tenements would never again lead urban development into high density residential and mixed use districts. Instead, at least in sub-Saharan Africa, planners sought and continue to seek carefully zoned, mono-functional, either standardized modern (tower-block or suburban) (UN-HABITAT 2009; Watson 2009) or medieval (pre-industrial) typologies.[9] With very few exceptions, in Nairobi actors have collectively defied these ideals.

Engels' view was that with the promotion of homeownership and the English 'cottage system', much of which was subsequently incorporated into modern and suburban town planning, the reformers at the time were forcing a return to pre-industrial relations. It was from these very relations that industrialization and urbanization had freed the former peasant, allowing for his/her emancipation. To further paraphrase Engels, tenements contributed to this freedom in that they enabled the mobility and flexibility required for participation in mass industrial action. They provided the necessary context for such action to eventually lead to the working class revolution to which Marx and Engels aspired. The bourgeoisie recognized this aspiration as a threat, and translated it into proposals for reform which brought tenement production to an end, thereby turning away from a housing typology thought to be highly conducive to revolution.[10]

What then is the future of Nairobi's tenements? The recent post-election upheavals suggest that these tenements pose no threat of working class emancipation to the moneyed class and political elite. Instead, they have provided a convenient theatre for the deepening of ethnic antagonisms and playing out of elite political differences. Tenant mobilization is weak; where it erupts it is politically orchestrated. The extensive violence in Nairobi's rooming-tenement districts that followed the December 2007 general election exemplified this most starkly (Waki 2008). Tenant agency is restricted to the exercise of choice in the tenement market, and even this is curtailed by ethnic division. There is no explicit debate about reform, no lobby for or against tenements. New York's history shows that landlord mobilization only emerges when threats appear (Day 1999). While enforcement of regulations still seems unlikely in Nairobi's unauthorized tenement districts, the trajectory in African countries to the north and south of Kenya suggests that real threats to unauthorized investments can evolve, and that governments can issue – and act on – them with authoritarianism and violence, leaving no space for mobilization.[11] Investor and/or community defiance of inappropriate modern urban plans can undermine the sense of legitimacy of undemocratic regimes.

It is generally accepted in Nairobi that the city's 1948 Master Plan and the 1973 Nairobi Growth Strategy are out of date, and remain as unlikely to be implemented now as they have been since their inception. In December 2008, Kenya's new Ministry of Nairobi Metropolitan Development launched a document, *Nairobi Metro 2030*, with the subtitle *A World Class African Metropolis* (Ministry of Nairobi Metropolitan Development 2008). Essentially a vision for a city region, it projects images of highways, high-speed trains, skyscrapers and industry. The media contrast the strategy with real 'problems bedeviling Nairobi' (Kiberenge 2009), and highlight unanswered questions over funding as well as the fears these images conjure among ordinary citizens (Aluanga 2009). The vision covers 15 municipalities, including Nairobi. However, its intention to attract substantial foreign investment to the 'core', namely the unevenly congested urban nucleus of Nairobi, would require corridors to be opened up, therefore necessitating eviction and demolition. 'Slums' and unauthorized low income tenements would be first in the queue. With this possibility looming, Nairobi urgently needs strong but cautious and progressive proposals that can ensure a future for its tenements, if only as a lesser evil.

There are other threats to the tenement stock and its inhabitants that progressive proposals for Nairobi ought to consider with care. The threat of epidemics resulting from lack of infrastructure and municipal services seems most immediate in relation to those living in the unserviced 'slums'. But earthquakes (resulting from the city's proximity to the tectonically active Rift Valley) certainly pose a greater threat to those living in multi-story tenements than to 'slum' dwellers. While earthquakes are rare in Nairobi, it experienced tremors measuring up to 6.1 on the Richter Scale as recently as July 2007 (Mwangi 2007). The Meteorological Services warn that tremors exceeding 6.5 would place Kenyan cities at 'high risk' (*ibid.*).

In Kenya's capitalist urban society, tenants of private multi-story rooming establishments to a large extent earn their livelihood in the '*jua kali*', Kenya's unique version of the informal sector with its clusters of manufacturing and trading activities. Here it is unlikely that economic emancipation or a revolution of a 'working class' will emerge. Souza (2009, 28) uses the concept of a 'hyperprecariate… to describe the workers who depend on (and often were excluded to) the informal sector in semi-peripheral countries, and who work and live under very vulnerable conditions'. In Nairobi, this class shares the status of tenant and occupies Nairobi's 'slums', where rents are lowest. But it also occupies the low end of the multi-story tenement market. According to Souza's line of argument, the question is whether this category of urban dwellers can be mobilized into an emancipatory social movement. With regard to the Brazilian context, he points to limits imposed by 'the culture of violence, consumerism and individualism' (*ibid.*, 45) on this possibility. In the Kenyan context, ethnic division is an added limitation, because of the country's complex colonial and post-independence political trajectory, and its economy of patronage which has reinforced ethnic identity. Kenyan society must avoid creating further ethnic tension at all costs, and nurture a cosmopolitan solidarity. What seems most likely to succeed is an approach in which, to use Harvey's (2001, 22) words, 'tensions' are not 'repressed, but liberated in socially exciting ways – even if this means more rather than less conflict, including contestation over socially necessary socialisation of market processes for collective ends'. In a later work, Harvey (2008, 40) articulates his vision as the need to 'adopt the right to the city as both working slogan and political ideal'.

The concept of a right to the city was first articulated by Lefebvre in 1968. Though not explicitly referring to a 'right to the city' approach, Day (1999) illustrates what this could mean in the context in which the majority of city inhabitants are tenants in inadequate tenement housing. Day shows how tenant mobilization gradually transformed New York from a 'property owners' city' (1999, 29) in the 19th century to a 'tenant city' (*ibid.*, 191) by 1943. This exemplifies the process of tenants gaining the right to participation and decision-making. Lefebvre, who by the time of writing *Le Droit à la Ville* in 1968 had been expelled from the French Communist Party after 'tense confrontation with the Party's resurgent Stalinism' (Harvey 1991, 427), envisioned this process going much further: 'Only the taking charge by the working class of planning and its political agenda can profoundly modify social life and open another era: that of socialism in neo-capitalist countries' (Lefebvre 1968/1996, 179). In Lefebvre's conception this 'planning oriented towards social needs and democratic control of the State through self-management' (1968/1996, 180) is only one aspect of the right to the city. Another addresses 'the poverty of the habitat' (*ibid.*, 178). It entails the right 'to urban life, to renewed centrality, to places of encounter and exchange, to life rhythms and time uses, enabling the full and complete *usage* of these moments and places' (*ibid.*, 179, emphasis in the original). With this right to 'appropriation', Lefebvre implied use value and not property or exchange value (Kofman and Lebas 1996, 20). Purcell (2002, 103) explains that this 'stands against… [t]he conception of urban space as private property, as a commodity to be valorized (or used to valorize other commodities) by the capitalist production process'. Purcell refers to this as a vision of 'radical transformation of urban social and spatial relations' (*ibid.*). However, this transformation may address itself to 'an array of social and spatial structures of which capitalism is only one' (*ibid.*, 106).

In the case of the occupants of Nairobi's single-story 'slums' and multi-story rooming tenements, it is perhaps not possible to predict outcomes, were these tenants actually to take charge of planning and its political agenda. Whether induced by tenant mobilization or by other forms of lobbying, pragmatic interventions will have to balance the protection of the positive attributes of urban life that Lefebvre articulates (including centrality and encounter), which are currently enabled by Nairobi's tenement market, with the amelioration of conditions and reduction of threats that undermine the enjoyment of these values. However, each intervention, unless supported by a strong political bearer (as eventually was the case in Berlin) would be blocked because it threatens existing economic stakes. It would foster new social and political tension that would require a legitimate outlet. The continued political centralization and only very recent (2010) introduction of a democratic constitutional dispensation in Kenya pose a further challenge and suggest that democratic outlets for contestation at city level may only emerge from below. However, such spaces in Nairobi are increasingly occupied by urban vigilantism, providing only violent outlets for contestation.

To complicate matters, the history of tenements shows us that tenement markets are volatile, can be undermined by regulation and may produce perverse and unanticipated responses even to well intentioned intervention. One purpose of this book is to sensitize those who would lead such interventions (in Nairobi and in cities with emerging tenement markets elsewhere), whether from the position of the state, expert or other lobby groups, or that of landlords or tenants. The 19th century west, and in particular the case of Berlin, provides sensitization on several fronts: firstly, regarding the urban qualities that a tenement market can produce; secondly, with respect to the destruction of such qualities and of tenants' 'lived experience of space' (Lefebvre 1974/1991, 316) through reform proposals whose implementation was aided by the necessity of reconstruction after World War Two (WWII); and, thirdly, the rediscovery of these qualities first by the grassroots, then by the state and finally (with renewed detrimental effects) by capital.

Up to the early 1980s, 'urban planning and policy debates' tended not 'to move much beyond their boundaries to question or engage in the broader debates about the future of cities' (Amin and Graham 1997, 412). However, there has been a recent surge of Anglophone publications dedicated to the future of cities (e.g. Robinson 2004; Read Rosemann and Eldijk 2005; Pieterse 2008), mostly with a global focus. Part of my purpose in this book is more pragmatic and perhaps naive. I seek to inform a localized urban discourse in cities with growing tenement markets like Nairobi, while I also hope to shed new light on urban trajectories more broadly.

In writing this book, I was driven by a realization that is seldom articulated, namely that there exists a growing trend towards rental tenancy as the only option for the poor and the slightly better-off across rapidly urbanizing parts of the globe. Linked to globalization, and the increasing privatization of public land and its release into a profit-seeking residential market, there is increasing scarcity of urban land for owner-occupied low income housing, in particular self-help 'squatting'. This trend has been reported for cities such as Kigali in Rwanda, Phnom Penh in Cambodia (Durand-Lasserve 2006) and Kuala Lumpur in Malaysia (Bunnell and Nah 2004). In Istanbul even people whose incomes have improved as a result of the selective economic benefits of globalization are increasingly housed as tenants (Özüekren 1995; Keyder 2005). A more extreme trend is documented for rapidly growing industrial towns in China, where villagers respond to a massive housing need from a floating population of migrant workers by transforming their semi-rural traditional settlements into so-called 'urban villages', where unregulated, poor quality rental units are stacked at high densities (Ji and Yang 2008; Wang, Wang and Wu 2009; Liu, He, Wu and Webster 2010).

As I began writing, the impact of the global economic recession had triggered media reports on a rise in tenement-type living conditions in the USA, with entire families sharing a single rented room and landlords illegally renting out 'basement rooms' or 'closets under stairways' (Sacchetti 2009). The scale of foreclosures has resulted in a renewed interest in rented housing, with statements such as 'Hey, it's OK to rent' (Tuhus-Dubrow 2009). In Nairobi, it is certainly acceptable to rent. Owner-occupation is low, and in the 'slums' or informal settlements it is almost entirely absent. According to the Central Bureau of Statistics (2004), only 1.4 per cent of Nairobi's households are in the tenure category of 'no rent, squatting'. A staggering 84.7 per cent, by contrast, are tenants.

To briefly provide some comparison, a table in UN-HABITAT (2003a, 10), which is not comprehensive, lists Kisumu (Kenya) with 82 per cent, followed by Cairo (Egypt) with 63 per cent, as the African cities with the highest percentages of tenant households. An earlier report (UNCHS 1996) indicates that in 1984, 88 per cent of households in Port Harcourt (Nigeria) were tenants. In the UN-HABITAT (2003a) report, the highest tenancy figure for Asian cities is 41 per cent for Bangkok (Thailand), the highest for Latin America is 46 per cent for Quito (Ecuador), whereas the highest for 'developed countries' is 89 per cent for Berlin (Germany). The high percentage of rental accommodation for Berlin stems to a large extent from its tenement history of the 19th and early 20th century.

The land scarcity and associated growth in rental tenancy among Nairobi's poor may be less related to processes of globalization that have shaped Istanbul, Cambodia and Kuala Lumpur than to the internal workings of capital in Kenya.

Gatabaki-Kamau and Karirah-Gitau (2004) describe the complex land speculation process on the eastern outskirts of Nariobi, and Obala (forthcoming) examines the often violent conflict that takes place over land in Nairobi. Although my tenement case studies are in less contested parts of Nairobi than those examined by these authors, I return to their studies when I discuss Nairobi in detail later in this book. Whether caused by liberalization and globalization or by internal economic processes, low income tenancy in peripheral or so-called 'developing' countries deserves attention in any engagement with the future of the city. Through the extreme case of Nairobi, I seek to make a contribution to the wider urban literature on cities in Africa and the 'developing world' city more broadly, while at the same time contributing to a largely historical literature on private tenements as a form of housing. I hope to steer readers away from policy proposals which simplistically assume that owner-occupation and small-scale lodging, which is always underpinned by the selective promotion of asset accumulation through homeownership for some, provide the answers in rapidly urbanizing and unevenly developed contexts.

In bringing the past into the present and future, this book does not provide answers to all the questions it raises. Instead, it intends to provide a comparative lens through which to begin engaging with urban reality across time and space. The aim is to attract attention to tenements as an urban form of the future, and therefore as an important and urgent area of contemporary research in urban studies. To this end, I provide a bridge to the German tenement literature (as Forsell (2006) does in comparing Stockholm and Berlin). The purpose here is also to raise awareness in the west that the built environment experience, in particular the 19th century tenement market, has relevance to cities such as Nairobi today. This book hopes to draw European readers to African cities, to discover complexities and urban realities that resonate with those that had to be overcome in the west and which, in terms of the spatial legacy, still hold positive qualities as well as challenges today. The hope is that those who have specialized in the tenement history of the west may be encouraged to contribute to a discourse on the future of cities like Nairobi.

A deeper collective exploration, which with hindsight avoids the bourgeois traps of the late 19th and early 20th century reformers, may trigger discussion and eventually lead to a nuanced, realistic and forward-looking treatment of this building form in practice. As a starting point, it must be recognized that the tenants of Nairobi's extremely dense tenement districts exercise a *de facto* right to inhabit the city through the existence of this form of housing within a relatively short radius of the city center. If existing regulations are enforced, this right will be eroded, with large-scale displacement from advantageous urban locations. To use the language of socio-economic rights: before being respected and promoted, this *de facto* right to the city in Nairobi must be protected.

A comparison across time and space

The approach taken by this book is a progression from past to present as well as a comparison between the two. The choice to focus on Berlin and Nairobi stems only marginally from my own experience of living in Berlin's tenements in the early 1990s and my encounter with Nairobi's tenements, through supervision from 2003 to 2005 of research on self-help housing networks in that city (Omenya 2006). Beyond the rapid growth of a tenement market with extreme densities over several decades, the conditions of society in 19th and early 20th century Berlin and mid-20th century to present-day Nairobi are very different. However, they do share high rates of urbanization, attempts at as well as obstacles to democratization, high levels of political patronage, and to some extent the formation and entrenchment of an upper middle class with interests in rental property over several decades. While this book does not contain a detailed comparative discussion of these aspects across the two cities, these broad parallels, despite many differences, allowed me to explore similar themes for each of the cities and thereby bring Berlin's tenement history, discourse and legacy into an argument about Nairobi's tenement future.

As already mentioned, Nairobi stands out among African cities through its extreme density and its increasing domination by tenement construction. Berlin's tenement history and legacy contain features that have relevance for a proper engagement with Nairobi's future as well as that of other cities that may be following suit. Berlin stands out as the largest and densest tenement city in late 19th century Europe. Tenement typology, and its underpinnings in terms of plot size (or the subdivision of land) and regulation in Berlin, played a role in both facilitating and curbing density. Since the decline and eventual termination of Berlin's tenement construction in the 1920s, the city's tenements have experienced close on a century marked by the widest possible range of different approaches to the existing built environment or tenement legacy. In no other city in the world have tenements witnessed such a combination and succession of neglect, destruction, physical division by means of the Iron Curtain, expropriation, both communist and social democratic determinism, demolition, modernist redevelopment, popular defense, illegal occupation, participatory renovation, revaluation, commodification and gentrification.

Before tenement construction was abandoned in Berlin, reformers for several decades debated and experimented with interventions in the tenement market. Late 19th century Berlin shows the real difficulties in impacting in any positive way on a private tenement market of this scale, whether through philanthropy or through governance structures in which vested interests are represented. There is no contemporary discussion about tenement markets that exist on the scale of that of Nairobi today. However, there are indirect parallels with present-day Nairobi in the strands of thinking on Berlin's tenements in the late 19th and early 20th century. Perhaps the strongest parallel is the refusal of all these strands of thinking to engage with the existing tenement stock, instead of wishing it away and projecting alternatives. There is an avoidance of the reality of tenements. And yet there are real disadvantages in the limited range of alternatives that continue to present themselves under the umbrella of modern town planning and the modern tenure form of individual homeownership which dominates development expertise today, and has also resurfaced in Berlin through a new wave of tenement capitalization.

In order to provide meaningful insight into both 19th to early 20th century Berlin and contemporary Nairobi, I dedicate a separate part of the book to each of these cities. To facilitate the discussion across time and space, I provide chronological diagrams towards the end of Chapter 3 (Figure 3.6) and Chapter 6 (Figure 6.2) for Berlin and for Nairobi respectively that set out the emergence and duration (and in Berlin's case decline and legacy) of the respective tenement markets within the context of political events and changes. The chapters that deal separately with Nairobi and Berlin are framed by chapters that spell out the theoretical and pragmatic questions that an engagement with tenements across two continents and across more than a century raises. Before I turn to Berlin, I draw, in Chapter 2, on the Anglophone literature on tenements in order to identify what tenement cities have in common, including typology, and how this is shaped by different contexts – mainly Glasgow, Edinburgh and New York. In that chapter, I make initial comparisons with Nairobi but also discuss the limited use (and recognition) of the concept of 'tenement' for that city. I explain the absence of tenements in England, where the 'terraced cottage' dominated instead. This was an influential, and some would argue fatalistic, counter-reality in the debates on reform at the time. Further, I examine key characteristics in tenement markets, their main players, and the hazards as well as regulation they entail. This allows me to explore the construction of legitimacy as well as justification (or not) of the largely inadequate tenement situation, a theme that is important for an understanding of the tenement situation in Nairobi today.

In Chapters 3 to 5, I base the analysis of 19th century Berlin and beyond on secondary sources. I identify some idiosyncrasies, myths and contradictions in this largely German urban studies and historical literature. This suggests a need for further archival research, which was beyond the scope of my research for this book. In Chapter 3 I set out distinct periods in the evolution of the industrial and tenement city of Berlin, including its political structures from 1800 through to the 1920s, and briefly sketch the epic trajectory up to the present. In Chapter 4 I discuss the planning process, plan and regulation in 19th century Berlin, and the land and tenement speculation that this enabled. I use the case of a particular tenement in the district of Wedding to provide some insight into the various actors in the speculative process, an aspect that the German tenement literature does not cover in depth. Chapter 5 deals with debates about Berlin's tenements in the late 19th century. To this end, I first set out the living conditions recorded at the time, both their inadequacies and their positive qualities. I then review a fascinating discussion about social and spatial integration of classes in Berlin's tenements, before turning to the politicized debates on urban reform as well as the more radical thrusts towards an urban revolution. I then review how Berlin's tenements were treated after their production was halted in the 1920s. Through an examination of shifts in thinking and action, this provides a snapshot of possible future trajectories of a tenement city.

The analysis of Nairobi in Chapters 6 to 8 draws on existing published and grey literature, supplemented by my fieldwork in 2005. This consisted of mapping sample areas in two case study districts (a low income rooming district and a middle income district of self-contained apartments) and of in-depth interviews with a small sample of officials, landlords, agents and tenants. In both the mapping and interviewing, I was assisted by Kenyan architect Andrew Kimani and draughtsman Kevin Osodo, also a tenant in the lower income case study area, Huruma. Andrew Kimani was familiar with the relevant authorities, and was able to navigate cultural barriers, secure access and interviews and translate where necessary. Kevin Osodo was able to negotiate access in the extremely dense rooming district both in 2005 and again in 2008, and helped make sense of much of what we observed and were told. The context of our fieldwork was one of largely unauthorized tenement investment, even in the middle income district. Interviewees were therefore deeply suspicious of any research. Our fieldwork approach, where it succeeded in securing interviews, allowed us to build the trust that was necessary to gain valuable qualitative insights. My intention from the outset was not to comprehensively present the tenement situation in Nairobi, but rather to expose key dimensions and raise awareness of this field so that other researchers could follow up and expand on our work. Our fieldwork was guided by an initial comparison with Berlin and other 19th century tenement cities, and we brought comparative aspects into the in-depth discussions with the interviewees.

For Nairobi, Chapter 6 examines the context in which multi-story tenements came to dominate the urban landscape. This takes us back to the end of the 19th century, from the policies of the colonial rulers to the unique dynamics of Kenyan society after its independence in 1964. I explain how a combination of political concepts and modernization, as well as a particular type of 'informal sector', nurtured large-scale urban tenancy that had already gained legitimacy among the indigenous population in colonial Nairobi. In Chapter 7 I explain the modern town planning principles that underpin Nairobi's official plans. I discuss their transgression and inversion at every level, through the production of tenement districts of the very kind that modern town planning sought to subvert. The collapse of development control is in part due to a set of regulations that have little relevance to the type of built environment that continues to manifest itself through large-scale investment in multi-story tenements. However, I point to attempts at adapting the regulatory framework to the built form, and a pragmatic approach by municipal officials. In this chapter, I introduce two case study areas by providing the unplanned development trajectory of low income Huruma, an extremely dense rooming district today, and the planned development trajectory of middle income Umoja Inner Core. In both cases, the City Council appears as an important agent in accommodating speculative tenement investment interests. In Chapter 8 I discuss density and living conditions, primarily in a sample area of the rooming district Huruma, but with the comparison of a sample area in Middle Class Umoja Inner Core. This provides a window on investor decision-making in the production of these living conditions, and helps to highlight the weakness of the discourse or official discussion on this reality. I observe that despite the limited acknowledgement of tenements in urban literature on Nairobi, there are parallels here with the discourse and interventions of late 19th and early 20th century reformers in Berlin.

In the concluding chapter, I make a case for the future of tenements in Nairobi and elsewhere. I draw on the arguments of critical urban theorists to explore the meaning of Nairobi's contemporary tenement market and to understand the use of history in responsibly reasoning about its future. This enables me to underline qualities in Nairobi's tenement environment and what these mean for a right to the city, while also pointing to changes in decision-making mechanisms in the city that will be indispensible for a right to the city to be given fuller meaning through relevant processes of planning and regulation.

Figure 1.1: Rear view: (*left*) a typical tenement in Kreuzberg, Berlin as seen from a courtyard; (*right*) the back of narrow rooming tenements in Huruma, Nairobi

Source: Author's photographs (2005)

Figure 1.2: Freestanding: (*left*) a lone tenement in Pankow, Berlin, having survived destruction in WWII and subsequent demolitions; (*right*) a lone tenement in Kawangware, Nairobi, awaiting investment on neighboring properties

Source: Author's photographs (2004, 2005)

Figure 1.3: Incomplete tenement ensemble with exposed windowless walls on property boundaries: (*left*) signs of tenement destruction in Wedding, Berlin; (*right*) signs of tenement growth in Huruma, Nairobi

Source: Author's photographs (2005)

Figure 1.4: Unintended open space? (*left*) greenery on a demolished tenement property in Wedding, Berlin; (*right*) multiple use of a future tenement property in Huruma, Nairobi

Source: Author's photographs (2005, 2008)

Figure 1.5: Representative façade of a middle class tenement: (*left*) restoration in Kreuzberg, Berlin; (*right*) construction in Umoja Inner Core, Nairobi

Source: Author's photographs (2005)

Figure 1.6: Fake façade exposed on a sharply angled property: (*left*) left over after tenement destruction in Wedding, Berlin; (*right*) awaiting concealment by neighboring tenement investment in Kawangware, Nairobi

Source: Author's photographs (2004, 2005)

Endnotes

1 'Rooming houses' in the west today provide accommodation primarily for single low income adults (Merrifield 2002, 136; Mifflin and Wilton 2005, 403).

2 Barbey (1984, 16) states that densities in New York exceeded 1 700 people per hectare, but does not cite a source. I therefore take Day's (1999, 18) figure as more reliable.

3 Independent survey data compiled by the Map Kibera Project, released early in 2009, already pointed to a much lower than assumed population density for Kibera (namely only 951 and not the usually cited 2 000 people per hectare) (MKP 2009; Nairobi News 2009).

4 I have adopted the Kenyan and UK convention when referring to building floors. 'Ground floor' therefore refers to what would be 'first floor' in US terminology. 'First floor above ground' in turn is the US 'second floor'.

5 My engagement with planning and architecture schools at universities in Nairobi in 2005 suggested that there was very little grappling with the city's dense tenement development, whether in research being undertaken or in the curriculum.

6 Marx and Engels had advocated for the 'abolition of bourgeois property' in *The Communist Manifesto* (Marx and Engels 1848/1964, 27).

7 In West Berlin, restitution relating to this second claim type was completed by the late 1960s (Lillteicher 2007).

8 In the case of New York, Day (1999, 24) refers to a 'profound social and economic gulf between reformers and tenants, a distance that complicated serious reform efforts'.

9 This refers to individual owner-built housing on small properties, extended vertically with a shop on the ground floor. Such housing types are promoted successfully in Brazilian cities (Wimpey 2004) but only serve households who have the means to invest in their own housing. Hall (1990, 242) refers to this paradigm in international housing policy as the 'city of sweat equity'.

10 Indirectly, the Russian revolution in 1917 that led to the formation of the USSR arguably gave greater control to East Berlin's working class for some 40 years following Germany's defeat in World War Two. However, Lenin's conceptualization of socialism, with its totalitarian form of implementation, was different from that of Marx and Engels (Chattopadhyay 1991). In Jackson's words (1957, 181), the Russians 'stretched' and 'twisted' Marxism, though the 'thread of Marxist tradition … was unbroken'.

11 Recent large-scale demolition on the African continent, to a large extent targeting unauthorized rental housing, has resulted from Operation *Murambatsvina* in Zimbabwe (Potts 2006), the restoration of the 1979 Abuja master plan in Nigeria (COHRE and SERAC 2008; Fowler 2008) and the modernization of Cameroon's capital Yaoundé (Teschner 2008).

Chapter 2

Cities shaped by tenements

A compelling reason for my comparison of tenement-dominated cities across two centuries is the physical similarity between multi-story rental housing in 21st century Nairobi and tenements of 19th century western cities. This similarity in urban form, captured in Figures 1.1–1.6 in Chapter 1, first drew my attention to this area of study. However, the case for a comparison does not rest merely on appearance. Tenement typologies are produced by a particular market with particular stakeholders and particular forms of operation or management. They also depend on legitimacy, which may be challenged over time. Tenement typologies have an important relationship with land subdivision and in some contexts with regulation. These underpinnings or preconditions help explain how this form of housing, with its excesses, was sustained in many cities of the west over several decades into the early 20th century. This provides us with a starting point for understanding the unchallenged existence of similar (and more extreme) excesses in Nairobi's tenement market today.

The literature in English on 19th and early 20th century housing in Anglophone cities that were dominated by tenements gives in-depth insight into tenement markets in New York, Glasgow and Edinburgh. When compared to those in Berlin and Nairobi, it becomes evident how the tenement typology is shaped differently in each city, yet is governed by common principles. The literature on which I draw for insight into Berlin is largely in German and therefore of a different tradition than the English readings on Scotland and the US, which I draw on in this chapter. It is the engagement with tenement form, the market and its actors, and the implication of regulation and lack thereof, that is best distilled from the Anglophone literature. My intention here is not to present a systematic review of this literature, but rather to extract common principles that apply to tenement markets. Critical urban theorists give insights on the justification or not of tenement markets. However, they tend to refer only to the example of 19th century Paris, rather than to the Anglophone or German, let alone African, tenement trajectory. They focus on the destruction (of the Parisian version of tenement districts) and urban restructuring through Haussmann's intervention after the mid-19th century, which was not paralleled in New York, Glasgow, Edinburgh or Berlin. These critical urban theorists give only indirect insights into the Parisian tenement market. The 19th century tenements of Paris, Vienna, Amsterdam, Barcelona, Eastern Europe and of German cities other than Berlin could provide further insights. However, the divergence of context across New York, the cities of Scotland and Berlin is sufficient to justify the claim that common principles and trends existed in western tenement markets of the 19th and early 20th century.

The dominant form of tenements in the 19th and early 20th century

The term 'tenement' is largely associated with 19th and early 20th century private rental housing in the industrializing and fast growing cities of Europe and the US. Housing literature about this period has a common definition of tenements, namely as a building containing individual units or dwellings for several tenants (Morgan and Daunton 1983; Homberger 1994; Robinson 2005). Implied is the maximization of returns by private investors through the subdivision and development of space into as many rental units as possible, with extensive plot coverage and usually several stories stacked one above the other. The English term 'tenement' is largely associated with rental accommodation for the lower income group, although in late 19th/early 20th century New York, as in Scotland, the term officially applied also to rental accommodation for the 'relatively well-off' (Robinson 2005, 104) or 'upper-class' (Montgomery 2003, 500). Investors in Berlin submitted the design of both middle class and working class tenements to the maximum exploitation of space. As a result, layouts even of middle class tenements were far from optimal in terms of health and comfort.

Cities characterized by a land and housing market dominated by large-scale private landlordism were typically referred to as 'tenement cities'. Examples are Glasgow (Robinson 2005), Stockholm (Forsell 2006) and Berlin (Hegemann 1930). The term 'tenement city' refers only to one dimension of the city, namely the housing market. Cities with this label were, at the same time, 'industrial cities'. Berlin up to 1918 was also an 'imperial city'. These city labels are not distinct, and I later weave them together to show how the industrial and imperial status of Berlin shaped tenement construction in that city.

In the literature, tenement landlordism is associated with a particular period in urban history. Despite extensive tenement demolitions throughout the 20th century, cities formerly dominated by tenements are today still physically characterized by relatively uniform districts of dense and now historic multi-story housing. Robinson (2005) therefore suggests that the term 'tenement city' can be applied to present-day Edinburgh, hitherto overshadowed in the literature by the formidable tenement history of nearby Glasgow.

Edinburgh's tenement suburbs are still dominant and important to the visual perception of the city. Their very solidity and coherence convey order. They are the uniform matrix that holds the town together – a regulated four-storey forest of chimney heads punctuated by spires...
(Robinson 2005, 124)

Robinson highlights positive qualities of the Edinburgh tenement. Referring to its interface with the street, he notes that 'the Edinburgh tenement street block has a well-defined public face' (*ibid.*, 122). He further describes a 'hierarchy of order from the public to the private, with the street door as demarcation point'. This quality was lost with the introduction in 1900 of 'English-inspired garden-city ideas that would challenge this hierarchy and lead to a move away from the regulated uniformity that gives Edinburgh's tenements their identity and character' (*ibid.*) (see Figure 2.1). Indeed, many subsequent forms of housing and development have shaped urban centers that had developed into tenement cities in the late 19th century. UN-HABITAT (2003b, 22) refers to the 'tenement city' as merely one of five city components distinguished by their 'class actors and economic functions'. In this typology,

Figure 2.1: Edinburgh street shaped by uniform tenements

Source : Photograph by Harry Smith (2009)

the 'tenement city' is characterized by 'immigrant enclaves, the lower paid wage workers and the "respectable poor"', and is distinct from the 'luxury', 'gentrified', 'suburban' and 'abandoned' cities (*ibid.*). In this definition, 'tenement city' refers only to dense districts with rental housing which private investors had constructed prior to the advent of modern town planning. Where these have been upgraded and traded to the not-so-poor, as in Berlin's historic tenement districts today, the term 'gentrified city' applies instead (*ibid.*).

While we can apply a uniform definition to the term tenement, it must be recognized that each city's tenement typology was shaped by local circumstances. Where legislation and regulations were ignored, partially enforced, or only introduced after a tenement market had established itself, the dimensions of land subdivided into individual plots were an important determinant of the multi-unit housing typology. It is therefore relevant in this chapter to expand on the technical underpinnings of the typology, in particular plot sizes, in addition to regulations where these were introduced and enforced. These underpinnings interacted with the urban land market. In Scotland, for example, a 'system of fixed payments in return for rights in perpetuity induced a reluctance to release developable land; and, when sites were released, superiors drove a hard bargain' (Robinson 2005, 228). The Scottish referred to this system as 'feuing'. Thus, '[c]ongestion bred congestion, as adjacent land values reflected the possibility of an equivalent density of development' (*ibid.*). The semi-rural surroundings of Glasgow were transformed from 'thatched cottages and hovels' into 'architecturally monumental, ashlar-faced ranges of four-storeyed tenements' (Horsey 1990, 3).

However, the varying local or regional predeterminations on their own cannot account for the conditions that were created. This is important, as it suggests that no easy intervention is possible to improve living conditions produced by a tenement market. A comparison between New York and Berlin, for instance, illustrates this well. Both cities were claimed to display the worst tenement conditions of their time (Hegemann 1930; Montgomery 2003). New York's reformers blamed the city's tenement conditions on the small plot size of approximately 8 m × 32 m, which a street plan in 1811 had determined for the whole of Manhattan (Montgomery 2003). This plan could not possibly anticipate the rapid urbanization and development that was to follow. Berlin's reformers blamed the equally extreme tenement conditions in Berlin on the excessively *large* plot size (20 m × 56 m). Thus clearly there are more than mere physical planning determinants at play in the private production of inadequate housing conditions.

The evolution of New York's tenement typology is interesting from two perspectives. As in Nairobi, tenements emerged on plots not originally designed for dense, multi-story accommodation. An attempted improvement in design of the tenement, once released into the market and (unintentionally) backed by legislation, allowed investors to improve their profits, but did not lead to substantial improvements in living conditions. Early tenements in New York replaced the shack settlements of poor immigrants, who were absorbed into the low income tenement market. The tenements also replaced single-family homes of the well-to-do for which the gridiron street layout and relatively small plots were originally designed (Barbey 1984; Montgomery 2003). 'By 1850, standard types of tenements began to proliferate based on the narrow parameters allowed by speculators' profit margins and New York's gridiron street pattern' (Day 1999, 16). Tenement investors developed the standard plots (8 m × 32 m) with a front house (8 m × 16 m) and a rear house (8 m × 8 m), leaving space for an 8 m × 8 m courtyard. This resulted in a plot coverage of 75 per cent (Figure 2.2). The front house had five to six stories in addition to a basement, and accommodated four families on each floor. Investors increased their profits by reducing backyards, adding additional floors and subdividing rooms. This earned tenement owners the label of 'mercenary landlords' shoving 'the greatest number of human beings into the smallest place' (Day 1999, 17, quoting from a 1834 report by the City Inspector's Department).

In 1879 the *Plumber and Sanitary Engineer* magazine 'sponsored a contest' for improved tenement designs for New York that would result in healthier conditions while also ensuring profit for the landlord (Day 1999, 25). The winning entry was a single building covering the entire plot in what was to become the 'dumbbell' typology (see Figure 2.2). It was not unlike the typology of Nairobi's rooming tenement (on plots of 7 m × 21 m, or 7.5 m × 17 m – see Figure 8.5 in Chapter 8), but had a narrow courtyard on each side. This doubled up with the side courtyard of the next-door tenement and allowed each room to have a window. Four units per floor shared sanitary facilities at the common stairwell. Reformers contested the adequacy of this design, and pressed instead for the adoption of legislation. An improved Tenement House Act (1879) was passed in the same year, limiting plot coverage to 65 per cent; however, by requiring windows in all bedrooms, the legislation unintentionally led to wide-scale adoption of the contested dumbbell design (Day 1999, 26). Overcrowding and inadequate conditions persisted. Any attempt at legislating against over-occupation of units did not take the economic reality of tenants into account. Where the authorities enforced such legislation, they merely displaced the overcrowding from one area to the next. The reformers 'tried to abolish the terrible byproducts of the tenement while leaving it fundamentally intact' (*ibid.*).

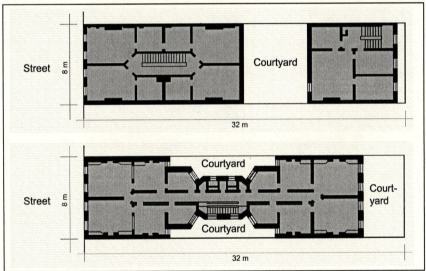

Figure 2.2: Early New York tenement type and later dumbbell tenement

Source: Redrawn from Day (1999, 16, 25)

Uniformity is a characteristic in all tenement markets. For the Victorian tenement in Scotland, those investing in new tenements preferred designs that were proven, thus 'their actions reinforced whatever local prejudices prevailed' (Robinson 2005, 117). My interviews with landlords in Nairobi revealed a similar logic of decision-making on tenement design. Victorian tenements were 'found almost everywhere in Scotland', mostly with three to four stories, but in Edinburgh 'sometimes with five storeys' (Robinson 2005, 103). Robinson articulates the characteristics of the Victorian/Scottish tenement, which was 'almost always built of stone with slate roofs and partitions of plastered brick, conveying an often grim solidity. They are durable and tend to be reasonably uniform within well-defined local traditions' (*ibid.*).

Tenements were not characteristic of 19th century England, and this exception made England an important reference point in not only the Anglophone but also continental European planning and housing discourse of the late 19th and early 20th centuries. It is therefore relevant to briefly expand on this English counterpoint. There, 'working class housing... was a variation on the theme of the self-contained cottage' – this was 'fundamentally different' from the Scottish 'high rise tenement block' (Horsey 1990, 51). In his early (1845) book T*he Condition of the Working Class in England* the young Friedrich Engels wrote, '[t]he houses in Scottish towns are generally four, five or six stories high. In this respect, Edinburgh is similar to Paris, but different from English towns, where as far as possible each family has its own house' (Engels 1845/1958, 42).[1] The distinction made between the English working class 'cottage' on the one hand and the tenement of Scotland and continental Europe on the other, though both were rented out by private landlords, is an important thrust in the reform debates that ultimately undermined the legitimacy of tenement production.

In England, a pre-industrial mix of residential types was replaced by 'the Georgian terrace' which 'became the generic house type in [the] nineteenth century' (Rodger 1989, 28). This new typology, in which 'each married worker occupies a little house of his own' (Engels 1887/1935, 33) shaped the English town into 'carefully delineated areas of homogenous housing... [B]y 1850 the tendency towards residential segregation was well established' (Rodger 1989, 28). The so-called 'cottage housing' first developed as 'ribbon development' along transport routes, with later infill in parallel rows resulting in a gridiron that matched the original shape of the agricultural fields (*ibid.*, 30). Richard Sennett (1974, 136), speaking of this urban form which 'was uniformly inhabited by the members of one class', deplores the implications of its fragmentation and low density, as 'London smeared itself across a larger and larger territory'.

The terminology here is a little confusing. What the English referred to as a 'cottage' was not a freestanding house, but rather a narrow unit attached on both sides in a long and monotonous 'terrace' (Figure 2.3). Horsey (1990, 38) describes it as a 'self-contained terraced house'. The so-called Scottish 'tenement block' is also attached on both sides, lending streets a continuous façade. As if in transition from cottage to tenement, working class housing in a small part of north-east England was dominated by the 'terraced flat', where the individual (attached) cottage consisted of two or more narrow units, one above the other. Whereas for the whole of England

and Wales in 1911 only 2.4 per cent of the population lived in 'flats', this figure was substantially higher at 25.4 per cent for the population in Northumberland (just south of Scotland) (Horsey 1990, 39–40).

Tenements in the late 19th and early 20th century did not only dominate working class housing in the industrializing cities of Europe and North America. To give just one example, in Sao Paulo, Brazil, around

Figure 2.3: Typical English street with working class row or cottage housing – Liverpool

Source: Photograph by Andrea Sperk (2009)

1900, an 'estimated one-third of all the dwellings… were *cortiços*' or tenements, and due to the high occupation rates, it is assumed that they housed the majority of the city's population (Kowarick and Ant 1994, 61). Tenements in this city consisted of 'deliberately constructed dwellings designed to house as many people as possible' as well as converted buildings, including family houses, stables and sheds, providing investment opportunities for a range of landlords (*ibid.*, 63). The *cortiço* is described as 'a long terrace of rooms opening onto a common courtyard or corridor, with a shared kitchen, bathroom, and washtub' (Rolnick 1994, 83). What the *cortiços* all had in common were small cubicles. Each cubicle housed 'a large number of people' (Kowarick and Ant 1994, 61). In Brazil, slavery was abolished only in 1888, after which 'the freed labourers had to fend for themselves' on wages that barely covered food. They therefore had no choice but to share very limited space with others in such tenements (*ibid.*). Brazilian working class *cortiços* existed side-by-side with middle class housing and were not segregated into working class districts. Eradication attempts having failed, '[t]here is no city district without its tenements' (*ibid.*, 71).

In a fascinating bridge between tenements in Brazil and those on the African continent, Mabogunje (1968, 240) explains how in Nigeria the family compound gave way to a new housing typology, introduced in the second half of the 19th century by ex-slaves from Brazil who had 'succeeded … in purchasing their freedom'. The new typology 'consisted simply of a central corridor on to which rooms opened on both sides' (*ibid.*, 119). It was rich in ornamental features and was 'known as Brazilian style' (*ibid.*). In 'north-eastern Lagos… the Brazilian Quarter stands out as a distinctive social area' (*ibid.*, 301) and in the late 1960s, Mabogunje observed that 'some impressive Brazilian-style storied buildings are still to be found in this area' (*ibid.*). From the 1920s, Nigerian cities saw 'increasing rent-seeking activities' in response to rural-urban migration (Chokor 2005, 82). 'Rooming houses' or 'tenement-type buildings... normally two or three storeys high' appeared as an individualized and distinct move away from the former compound housing (*ibid.*, 83), with the tenement corridor replacing the compound courtyard (*ibid.*, 85). In Ibadan in the 1950s, housing for better-off families was still 'being built in the new Brazilian style', and an individual household would rent 'one of the two rows of three or four rooms on the floor of a house', referred to as 'the "open apartment" system' (Mabogunje 1968, 231). Later designs provided for more family privacy (*ibid.*).

The city of Abidjan in Côte d'Ivoire shows a different progression from courtyard to corridor and then multi-story tenement. In Abidjan, courtyard housing continues to play an important role in private rental housing, to the extent that the city is referred to as 'a city of courtyards' (Dubresson 1997, 275). Nevertheless, with landlords' ambitions to maximize their rental income, '[b]uildings progress horizontally, plots becoming ever more densely occupied and some courtyards reduced to a corridor, then vertically, an additional floor being added on one side' (*ibid.*, 276). Okpala (1984, 77) mentions 400 such rooming houses ('mainly storeyed') in the Agbowo area of Ibadan (Nigeria), to the east of the university campus.

A last aspect of typology is whether or not the tenement included commercial units at its interface with the street. The Anglophone literature on tenements that I draw on in this chapter does not explicitly discuss shops on ground floors, although Robinson (2005, 104) mentions that the Victorian tenement in Scotland 'sometimes' had shops. Where they existed, it is not clear whether their rents differed from those of the residential units. As I show in the later chapters, the commercial activity in tenement districts in Berlin was a key characteristic of tenement life in that city, and one that is shared in Nairobi's tenement districts.

Limited use of the term 'tenement' in contemporary Nairobi

In Edinburgh, the terms 'tenement', 'house' and 'flat' are used interchangeably (Robinson 2005, 104). The term 'flat' (referring to an entire building made up of apartments), or earlier 'flet', originates from Scotland, to which 'its use was confined... well into the 19th century' (*ibid.*). Interestingly, and possibly through a British-colonial Scottish connection, Kenyans refer to the private multi-story rental buildings or tenements in Nairobi as 'flats'. This term applies both to private buildings with self-contained apartments (only the individual apartments are referred to as 'flats' in the English usage of the term), and to the buildings in predominantly rooming districts such as Huruma.

The urban research literature does not readily apply the term 'tenement' to housing in the Anglophone 'developing world'. This is not because of the irrelevance of the term, but rather due to a silence on, or only accidental mention of, the current production of large-scale private rental accommodation in cities of the south. Rakodi (1995), in her review of rental housing in the 'developing world', uses the term 'tenement' only in relation to inner-city rental buildings. She refers to the deterioration of tenements due to age, therefore implying that this term is applicable mainly to housing stock constructed in a past era. In a comprehensive review of literature on landlordism in the Third World, Kumar (1996, 761), notes that in the 1980s Philip Amis (1984) observed 'the production of rental units [in site-and-service areas in Nairobi], not dissimilar to those constructed in the inner city'. However, neither Kumar nor Amis expands on this phenomenon. Only in one instance does Amis (1987, 259), referring to the early rental housing (at the time still single-story) developed by housing companies in Mathare Valley, mention 'spectacular... capital investment in this tenement housing'. Shihembetsa (1991) uses the term 'private tenement' for the multi-story rooming blocks in Eastleigh, an area of the city originally established for Asian households in the 1920s.

This silence on the multi-story tenements of Nairobi can be explained by a strong bias in Nairobi's housing literature towards the city's so-called 'slums'. While researchers have documented large-scale landlordism for Nairobi, literature to date has focused primarily on landlordism in Nairobi's 'slums' (Amis 1984, 1987, 1988, 1996; Edwards 1990; Lee-Smith 1990; Syagga, Mithullah and Karirah-Gitau 2002; UN-HABITAT 2003a). UN-HABITAT (2003a, 43), in its review of private rental housing in developing countries, mentions the 'real exception [of] Kenya where renting seems to be dominated by larger, absentee landlords'. Edwards (1990, 262), in a review of rental housing for the urban poor in Africa and Latin America, observes that 'the case of Nairobi appears somewhat extreme'. Rents in Nairobi's 'slums' are a third of those in the multi-story rooming districts, which therefore enjoy a certain level of privilege in the housing market (Huchzermeyer 2008). This dominance of rental housing for the better-off in Nairobi is only indirectly acknowledged. UN-HABITAT (2003a, 43, quoting from Mwangi, 1997, 141, who also does not expand) merely mentions that in Nairobi 'rental housing' is 'the main form of housing for middle-income households and new urban residents of all income levels'.

The urban studies literature contains a further, though indirect, bias. It portrays 'tenements' only as a housing form of the past, with little relevance for present-day realities in the 'developing' world. I later explore in more detail the relationship between the orientation present in the urban history literature on Berlin and the treatment of the city's tenements in practice. Across the west, with very few exceptions, interest in tenements within urban studies declined in the 1990s, with very little literature appearing since then.[2] In Berlin, this trend in urban studies may be determined by the new and urgent urban challenges that reunification, and more recently new forms of segregation and commercialization in that city, have presented. This does not, however, explain the silence in the Anglophone urban studies literature.

With this book I demonstrate that current production of large-scale multi-story private rental establishments is shaping cities in the 'developing' world in much the same way that tenement production shaped late 19th and early 20th century cities of the west. While Nairobi is my case in point, there is evidence of a similar, though more localized, trend, and not only in the cities of Nigeria and Côte d'Ivoire. Kariakoo, a district bordering on the inner city of liberalizing Dar es Salaam, is rapidly being transformed from an environment of square, single-story Swahili houses to one of multi-story residential and commercial buildings. While many of these are visibly intended for a more affluent clientele, they do include rooming tenements (Lupala 2002, 97) (Figure 2.4).[3]

In Chapter 7 I explain Nairobi's tenement typology which, alongside the actors and their decision-making practices in the market, is the most compel-

Figure 2.4: Redevelopment of Kariakoo, Dar es Salaam (Tanzania) with multi-story rental investment

Source: Author's photograph (2008)

ling reason for the use of the term 'tenement'. It can be argued that with the current mushrooming of not only tenement buildings but whole 'tenement districts' in Nairobi (see Figure 7.5 and Table 7.1), the term 'tenement city' could aptly apply here, as it did to Berlin or Glasgow in an earlier time (Huchzermeyer 2007). While there is no conclusive information on the number of households residing in Nairobi's multi-story tenements, my calculations based on the aerial photograph tenement count suggest that these tenements account for over a quarter of the 84.7 per cent of Nairobi's households that, according to the Central Bureau of Statistics (2004), rent or lease their accommodation.

Actors in the tenement market

Not only the density and physical imprint of Nairobi's tenement districts bear similarity to 'tenement cities' of the north. There are parallels also in the tenement market and the various actors involved in shaping the tenement environment, in particular the landlords and agents, through their decision-making within the market. Day (1999, 6) refers to 'nineteenth-century styles of tenement operation', many aspects of which apply to the tenement market of present-day Nairobi. As if speaking of Nairobi, Day (1999, 55–56) expands:

> Neglect and evasion of the law were not merely common practices; they were *essential strategies* for marginal property managers trying to make

a living... A central management principle, neglect – the avoidance of routine maintenance and health and safety precautions – offered a complex set of opportunities and hazards... [Tenement managers] lacked the economic leeway to alter significantly their business methods or, in any way, remedy the ills of urban tenements. (emphasis in the original)

Furthermore, according to Morgan and Daunton (1983, 282), '[h]ousing was... a major area of capital formation in any industrial society'. While there are no economic data on tenement investment in present-day Nairobi, and rental income is also not captured by economic statistics, all indications are that tenements make up a substantial percentage of total capital investment – indeed a major capital formation, but in a society that cannot be described as industrial. In Glasgow, 19th century tenement ownership was linked to the 'pattern of life-cycle related investment for small businessmen' (Morgan and Daunton 1983, 267). Once these businesspeople had paid the interest as well as debts on their business, funds would become 'available for investment outside the business' (*ibid.*). In terms of a Marxist analysis, this involves investing the surplus from a primary or productive circuit of capital in a secondary circuit which includes investment in the built environment (Harvey 1985b, 64). The preference in Glasgow was for local and secure outlets, so that the investment could 'provide an income for retirement and subsequently for widows and unmarried daughters. House property fitted these requirements better than most other outlets for investment' (Morgan and Daunton 1983, 267). This resulted in 'a close connection between ownership of a few tenements and the petty bourgeoisie' (*ibid.*). In Nairobi, I found similar ownership patterns. I also found that the perception of tenements as a secure investment for future purposes, including retirement, is influencing private decision-making. Therefore it is all the more important that we understand how the security of this investment was eventually undermined in the tenement markets of the early 20th century. I return to this question below.

Various publications provide detailed insights into tenement landlords and their decision-making (Morgan and Daunton 1983; Dennis 1995; Day 1999), which I did not find in the literature on Berlin (Forsell (2006) makes the same observation, and provides some analysis for Berlin and Stockholm). But even in the literature on Anglophone cities, there is a limited examination of the real role of landlords, since much of the literature celebrates 'the resistance of pioneer rent strikes' and merely portrays landlords as 'slumlords' or landlords benefitting from slum conditions (Dennis 1995, 306). The interest in tenant resistance is justified. In Glasgow, the 1915 rent strike resulted in the passing of a 'Rents and Mortgage Interest Restriction Act' in the same year (Castells 1983, 27). Up until that time, 'any attempt by the state to interfere with the market forces had been successfully opposed' (*ibid.*). From 1918 to 1920, New York was shaken by rent strikes, eventually leading to greater state involvement in regulating aspects of the relationship between landlords and tenants (Day 1999). Day (1999, 6) articulates the importance of

> [the] tenant movement that not only spelled the end to nineteenth century styles of tenement operation but also closed out the first era of landlord organisations in New York as they gradually lost their relevance in a new political environment shaped by federally sponsored rent control.

Day's own contribution (1999) was to examine the events leading up to, as well as during, this contestation from the side of the landlords. His detailed archival study, though not denying the dismal housing conditions produced, gives New York's tenement landlords their rightful place 'central to the city-building process' (Day 1999, 1). He contrasts the strong, though not necessarily good, role played by landlords with the relatively weak intervention by the reformers:

> Left with the task of housing *everyone* who could not afford to buy their own homes, urban landlords routinely undermined the grand schemes of urban reform and transformed so-called 'model' homes and communities into scornful tributes to the reformers' faltering commitment. (*ibid.*, emphasis in the original)

The maintenance of landlord legitimacy over a period of at least 70 years from the mid-19th century to the 1920s requires more explanation. This period was certainly marked by 'unrelenting demand for cheap rental' (*ibid.*, 16), which underpinned the success of the 'speculative builders', despite the poor quality of their designs and workmanship (*ibid.*). As in other late 19th century tenement cities, 'the sudden demand for housing which accompanied industrialization and population growth… was met almost entirely by privately rented dwellings' (Horsey 1990, 2).

In New York City, 'the political and financial interests… insulated the largely invisible owners of the tenements from responsibility for the conditions of their properties' (Homberger 1994, 110).[4] Day (1999, 58) expands on this, again almost as if speaking about the practices I later describe for present-day Nairobi:

> In critical ways, New York City's corrupt political structure greatly favoured landlords in the nineteenth century. Tenement owners found important allies in ward politicians and city officials who were indifferent to the need for better housing. Between 1844 and 1866, for example, corrupt officials staffed the City Inspector's department with incompetents who obtained their jobs through political patronage… These same officials and inspectors consistently threw their support to whichever political machine was in power; they misappropriated funds, and special interests employed some inspectors to lobby *against* housing reform… (emphasis in the original)

Furthermore, 'honest administrators of the law worried about the influence of local landlords and property owners' (*ibid.*, 59), a situation that seems to have direct parallels with Nairobi's administration where, despite a visible anti-corruption drive since 2003, practices have failed to change substantially.

Day's detailed case study of New York shows that landlord mobilization emerged only once a coalition of forces began to seriously challenge the corruptly propped up legitimacy of tenement investment and management, a situation that has not as yet arisen in Nairobi. Day devotes a chapter to 'the political emergence of landlord lobbying organizations as the growing discontent of tenants in the Lower East Side finally drove landlords into action. Assisted by landlord leaders and a larger public sympathetic to the landlords' rights, these nascent tenant movements were crushed' (*ibid.*, 5–6). However, middle class sympathy gradually swung to the side of the tenants, whose mobilization was 'co-opted into a middle-class reform agenda' (*ibid.*, 6). Legislation, civil courts, depression and 'resurgent tenant movement' contributed through a coalition of interests to the final abandonment of 'nineteenth-century styles of tenement operation' (*ibid.*).

An economic explanation for the decline of the tenement in 20th century Glasgow is offered by Morgan and Daunton (1983, 280): 'Rents were determined… by the trends in interest rates, local taxation, the number of vacant properties and the level of real wages.' Changes in these 'economic variables' in the first two decades of the 20th century led to 'erosion in the profitability of house property. The level of vacancies increased, at the same time as the outgoings in local taxation and interest payments rose.' This undermined the economic standing of landlords and their 'factors' or rental agents (*ibid.*).

However, tenement landlords of the 19th and early 20th century, as in Nairobi today, had sources of income other than rent. In Canada and the US, '[r]elatively few property owners were "full-time" landlords. Many had other business interests as shopkeepers, small manufacturers, lawyers or doctors, which took priority over their role as house owner' (Dennis 1995, 307). For Glasgow, Morgan and Daunton (1983, 267) quote a 1904 statement from the president of the Association of Factors (or rental agents) in which he states that

> you get them all sorts… A tradesman who had been thrifty and well-doing and has saved a little can go in for a single tenement or two; but it is not an exceptional thing at all that they should be owned by a better class of owners as well.

Like the *Glasgow Municipal Commission on the Housing of the Poor, 1904*, which presented this evidence from the factor, I found that rental agents in Nairobi were invaluable sources of information on tenement landlordism in that city. Landlords themselves largely evaded being identified and interviewed.

In 19th and early 20th century Glasgow, the factor played an important role in ensuring profitability for the landlord. The factor's role, much like that of the rental agent in Nairobi today, was fivefold: 'to find and select tenants' and let the units; 'to socialise tenants to the communal responsibilities demanded of them by tenement life'; to maintain the private communal components of the property; to collect the rents and manage defaults; and lastly, bookkeeping as well as valuation, in order to advise clients on investments (Morgan and Daunton 1983, 275).

In Glasgow, many factors also owned considerable property themselves, while others were builders. The lines between landlords, factors and builders were therefore blurred. Morgan and Daunton (1983, 269) suggest that 'factors should, perhaps, be considered alongside builders as forming the largest single interest group amongst landlords'. They add that, around 1900, almost 60 per cent of Glasgow's tenements were owned by private individuals, the other ownership categories being trusts, house factors, companies and public bodies (*ibid.*, 266). However, 'the emergence of a massive local authority presence' around 1900 eroded this dominance by the private landlord (*ibid.*, 281). While an equivalent version of Glasgow's factors or Nairobi's rental agents (whom I describe in Chapter 8) will have likewise played a role in Berlin's tenement market, the tenement literature tells us even less about them than about the landlords and investors whom these agents would have been serving in 19th century Berlin.

Unlike the practice in Glasgow or in present-day Nairobi, in New York landlords did not engage the services of agents. Instead, they leased their tenements to 'landlord entrepreneurs' or to 'former tenants willing to take risks' (Day 1999, 15), and who in turn 'underlet' the units. These lessees were in a vulnerable position. They often lived in the property themselves. 'With an exceedingly narrow profit margin and lacking the needed resources to make repairs, building leaseholders developed the reputation for being the worst landlords in the city' (Day 1999, 49). For the lessors or building owners, 'the leasing of... buildings proved particularly lucrative', while this 'business' approach allowed them to distance 'themselves from the grimy, dilapidated, overcrowded structures' (*ibid.*, 50). Within this system, tenants 'had little recourse in the courts if they were injured because of the landlord's neglect', and equally little protection from eviction (*ibid.*, 21). Referring to common law at the time, Day expands:

> The laws allowed some minor exceptions. The landlord was responsible, to some degree, for the common areas of the property such as staircases, hallways, entranceways, and the sidewalks that everyone used and yet were still in the possession of the landlord. However, even here, not until 1898... did a court actually hold a landlord liable. (*ibid.*, 21)

Tenement hazards, planning and regulation

The introduction of regulation in a previously self-regulated market is a relevant theme for this book, because most of Nairobi's tenements transgress official regulations. Nevertheless, they are governed by some form of self-regulation.

Tenants' decisions and landlords' perceptions thereof limit excesses in an unregulated rental market. New York's tenement market is particularly interesting, as it was initially unregulated. Building standards for New York were introduced in 1866, followed in 1867 by the Tenement House Act, though this was largely ineffective (Day 1999, 25). For instance, it mandated the provision of fire escapes, but allowed for wooden ladders to serve this purpose (*ibid.*, 27). More than a decade later, the new Tenement House Act of 1879 tightened tenement regulations, although this did not improve conditions directly (*ibid.*, 26). Building height remained unregulated for a further six years. It was technology and the market, and not regulation, that determined the height restriction of five to six stories in New York. In Manhattan, units on the higher floors were let at lower rentals, because of the excessive number of steps that needed to be climbed (Montgomery 2003). Additional floors, in the absence of elevators, would be difficult to let, particularly in a context of competition for tenants. With direct parallels to the practices I found in Nairobi's tenements, Day (1999, 46–47) describes this competition:

> While the fresh appearance of a new apartment was often inducement enough for many tenants, many builders frequently canvassed the surrounding neighbourhood to lure the tenants of other landlords into breaking their existing leases to move to new accommodations... At times, builders found themselves competing with other builders to fill their houses.

The invention of the elevator and of new structural and building materials, including the steel frame, revolutionized building construction. This enabled a new response to be made to the extremely high ground rents: from the late 1870s, taller buildings began to appear in Manhattan, whose uses included upper class residence (Montgomery 2003, 499). Montgomery (2003, 501) argues that given the chance, entrepreneurs would eventually have filtered the benefits of these technologies, and indeed the benefits of taller buildings, down to the lower classes of tenants. However, lobby groups representing prominent interests raised concerns about fire risk as well as the shadows cast by tall buildings. In 1885, the authorities introduced a residential building height restriction. They permitted tenements to reach 22 m on narrow streets and 25.4 m on wider streets (five to six stories), although a further act in 1897 liberalized these regulations. The height restriction unwittingly benefited those tall buildings that had been constructed before its introduction. It also benefited commercial and hotel developers, to whom the restriction did not apply, thus creating undue competition for residential investors. This perpetuated the compact tenement typology with its inadequate conditions well into the next century (Montgomery 2003).

A similar height restriction of 22 m was introduced in ancient Rome in AD64 (*ibid.*, 503). In 1913, the *New York Times* provided details of the Roman *insula* or tenement for a readership which must have consisted largely of tenement dwellers:

> In comparison with modern tenements [meaning those in New York at the time], those of Rome were excessively high. Martial alludes to a poor man, his neighbour, who had to mount 200 steps to reach his garret. That garret must have been perched nearly 100 feet [32 m] above the level of the street. Emperor Augustus, to make less frequent the occurrence of disasters, limited the height of new houses that opened upon the streets to about 68 feet [22 m]. (*New York Times* 1913)

In our estimation based on the mapping of tenements in Nairobi, an eight-story rooming tenement in Huruma is around 22 m high (see Figures 8.5–8.7 in Chapter 8). In present-day Nairobi floor intervals are presumably lower than in the 19th century tenements of New York, which at a similar height had fewer floors.

From the 1820s on, preceding and in parallel with regulation and legislation for New York's tenements, reformers attempted to improve tenement design through leading by example. According to Day (1999, 22), 'housing advocates tried to combine moral suasion, education, and mild regulatory measures to motivate landlords to voluntarily improve their tenements'. The reformers considered model tenements 'ideal projects for this kind of instruction' (*ibid.*). While these 'became important testing grounds for structural innovations… they failed to significantly improve living conditions in the slums' (*ibid.*). Built in 1850, the six back-to-back buildings (six stories each) that made up the model tenement Gotham Court failed to secure sufficient returns. Once sold by the philanthropists to private investors who doubled the occupation, Gotham Court became one of 'New York's most notorious tenements' and in 1895 it was finally demolished (*ibid.*, 24). Similarly, model houses had limited impact on the 19th century tenement market of Edinburgh (Robinson 2005, 115).

Landlord-tenant relations in New York's tenements remained unregulated throughout the 19th century and landlords could not be held to account. The relevant laws 'either did not exist, or they were weak, unenforced, and largely ignored by landlords, inspectors, and the courts alike' (Day 1999, 21). The reform movement in New York focused its efforts on improving tenement design, while ignoring 'the legal and social dynamics of the landlord-tenant relationship' (*ibid.*, 28). This was underpinned by a 'philosophical orientation' that 'viewed property rights as sacrosanct'. It was combined with a paternalist attitude to tenants and 'a fear of working-class differences and social unrest' (*ibid.*, 29). Day's conclusion is that '[i]n essence, tenants faced a property owner's city' (*ibid.*).

This perpetuated, for well over half a century, hugely hazardous living conditions for the majority of city dwellers. Health and safety risks were a component of daily life in 19th and early 20th century tenements. Overcrowding, damp due to inadequate ventilation, and inadequate provision of sanitation made it difficult for the individual tenant to isolate him- or herself from the spread of disease (Homberger 1994, 110). The risk of fire was ever present in New York's tenements, which builders inadvertently designed in such a way that a fire could easily spread from the lowest to the highest floor (Montgomery 2003, 503). Even in the dumbbell design that predominated after 1879, the fire risk was not resolved (Day 1999, 26). The steep wrought-iron staircases, sometimes ornate, that still disfigure (or adorn) New York's tenement façades are an indication of the extent to which authorities patched up inadequate conditions through *post facto* enforcement of subsequent building regulations. In contrast, as early as 1853 the Prussian state introduced and enforced fire regulations to be taken into account in the design of Berlin's tenements (which have no external fire escapes). This very effectively shaped the tenement typology. As already mentioned, in Nairobi's rooming tenements, overcrowding of individual units is not as excessive as it was in the 19th century tenements of the west. While health conditions are better than in the wattle-and-daub 'slums' that exist alongside these tenements, the excessive building height of many rooming tenements causes safety hazards, particularly for children exposed to inadequate railings on access balconies and around air wells or voids. While a structural investigation would have to confirm this, the inadequacy of railings seems to pose a greater risk to occupants than the outbreak of fire in a Nairobi tenement. I was surprised to find that among my interviewees there was no one with knowledge of any incidents of fire in Nairobi's tenement districts. Two factors that might account for a lower fire risk here than in the tenements of the 19th century west may be the availability, albeit intermittent, of electricity for lighting, and the much lower need for winter heating.

New York's tenements remained unregulated until 1864, when a Metropolitan Board of Health was established by law and had the 'powers to inspect housing and improve sanitation' (Homberger 1994, 110). The new Tenement House Act introduced in 1879 has already been mentioned, as it determined the dominance of the dumbbell tenement type. Legislation in the following two decades further improved tenement standards. However, the continued demand for shelter at a very low cost and the financial and political interests of the tenement owners undermined the implementation of any real improvements (Homberger 1994, 110).

The legitimacy of tenement markets

Reflecting on the extent to which tenements shaped the city of Edinburgh, Robinson (2005, 104) asks:

> Whatever we call them, an intriguing question is why people should want to live this way at all. Stacking one household above another is not a natural way of living, even now; and, in the more distant past, flat life was inconvenient, if not actually life-threatening through fire and collapse. There had to be powerful reasons to live in flats and for the practice to persist.

For the majority of tenement dwellers, life in tenements was, of course, not a matter of consumer choice. The reason for this way of life lay elsewhere. In this brief discussion of how the largely inadequate tenement markets of the 19th and early 20th century were legitimized, I make a distinction between a normative or prescriptive meaning of legitimacy (or 'normative justification') on the one hand, and a descriptive meaning which asks 'why people accept a social order in reality', on the other (Steffek 2003, 253).[5] I begin my discussion with the descriptive approach, which is linked to Max Weber's conceptualization of legitimacy as 'a social fact' (*ibid.*), by asking what allowed the tenement market to flourish largely unchallenged over many decades. I then turn to key arguments in the critical urban discourse on the normative justification or legitimization of the tenement market.

To some extent, it was the more adequate forms of tenements provided for the middle class that legitimized rental units in multi-story blocks as acceptable accommodation. Robinson (2005, 108) refers to the elegance and respectability of middle class flat living in Scotland already in the late 18th century, and 'an outlook generally tolerant of flats'. A 'Committee of the Working Classes of Edinburgh' in 1858 justified the tenement form of housing as 'the Scottish system of building', as well as being a traditional way of living – 'a Scotchman is quite wedded to his flats' (*ibid.*, 115). As Steffek (2003, 255) explains, '[m]ythological or identity explanations of legitimacy argue that certain persons are viewed as entitled to act on behalf of others, or to impose rules on them, because of a common history, ethnic origin or destiny'. One can argue that this applies, as in Scotland, to tenements in Nairobi; later in this book I provide insight into the middle class tenement district Umoja Inner Core which may play a legitimizing role similar to that ascribed to the middle class tenements of Scotland. However, the construction of tenement legitimacy through appeals to identity or tradition was weaker in cities such as New York and Berlin, where a large proportion of the arriving migrants were from other countries (or regions) and cultures. Apartment life became fashionable for Berlin's 'learned middle class' only in the 1880s (Treue 1969, 38). Though in part driven by financial pressures, the upper economic class led this trend.

The acceptability of the Scottish tenement was also underpinned by 'a legal and institutional framework capable of dealing with the complexities of tenement life' (Robinson 2005, 108). In Berlin too, the legal/regulatory framework reinforced tenement legitimacy, whereas in New York City, as mentioned above, tenement construction remained unregulated by law up to the mid-1860s. By that time, 'the first systematic sanitary survey of New York' had recorded 15 000 tenement buildings, all of which were unregulated (Homberger 1994, 110). Investors and landlord entrepreneurs largely transgressed the regulation once it was enacted. Instead, New York's tenements derived their legitimacy pragmatically, by offering a solution to the 19th century 'housing crisis' (*ibid.*). The landlords 'built the homes for the nation's growing industrial workforce' (Day 1999, 1). However, 'they managed those homes in ways that, in many cities, created some of the most haunting and lasting images of urban life – images that challenged generations of social reformers and mocked prevailing views of economic opportunity' (*ibid.*). As is evident from the review above, the fraught political legitimacy of landlords and the corruptly sustained justification for their investments perpetuated this situation for several decades, rendering reform efforts ineffective, although these eventually triumphed over the legitimacy of landlord practices. Discussing the question of compliance versus legitimacy, Steffek (2003, 255) suggests that an illegal action is legitimate as long as it is not challenged – 'legitimacy beliefs can exist in the absence of compliance'. This may be a step towards explaining the dominant tenement market in Nairobi, which evidently does not derive its legitimacy from the law.

The interaction between descriptive and prescriptive legitimacy is relevant, as it forms the basis for challenges, whether from those living the tenement experience or from expert reformers. The history of tenements suggests that when a normative discourse or raised awareness of the lack of normative/prescriptive legitimacy undermines tenement legitimacy as a social fact, challenges may materialize through reforms in urban planning practice.

One may argue that a further source of descriptive legitimacy of the tenement market lies in the widespread acceptance of a liberal economic logic, namely that landlords' competitive efforts at providing housing should be fairly rewarded by profit. This is to some extent the case in Nairobi, where capitalism enjoys extensive legitimacy within urban society. Harvey (1974) presents a normative challenge to such legitimacy, disagreeing with the neoclassical economic discourse that would seek to justify or prescriptively/normatively legitimize a tenement market or large-scale private rental housing for low-income households. Noting that '[t]he history of the rental concept is strewn with arguments for and against the legitimacy of the transfer or payment that rent represents', he goes on to criticize the neoclassical justification of rent as 'a coordinating device for the efficient production of value' within a (legitimizing) doctrine of 'social harmony through competition' (*ibid.*, 240). He explains how 'the urbanization process... multiplied the opportunities for realizing rent' (*ibid.*); and, applying Marx's concept of 'class-monopoly rents', he describes a situation that, he argues, prevailed in the nineteenth century (but clearly also applies in present-day Nairobi), where landlords behaved 'in accordance with a well-defined class interest', namely to realize 'a positive return above some arbitrary level' (*ibid.*, 241). Much of the capital of this class existed (as one can assume for Nairobi) 'in the form of housing' (*ibid.*, 242). Tenants in turn comprised a class through their shared lack of any 'alternative[s] but to seek accommodation in the low-income rental market; they [were] trapped within a particular housing sub-market' (*ibid.*, 241).

Therefore Harvey devalues the liberal economic explanation for (and justification of) rent as 'rate of return on capital investment', arguing instead that the realization of rent 'depends upon the ability of one class-interest group to exercise its power over another class-interest group and thereby to assure for itself a certain minimum rate of return' (*ibid.*, 242). In terms of this explanation, in certain circumstances neglect of maintenance and general deterioration into slum conditions form part of the class monopoly behavior that ensures rents 'above some arbitrary level'. Though not stated by Harvey, this class monopoly behavior may also explain the widespread transgression of official regulations and the self-regulation according to a certain unwritten standard by a loosely defined class of tenement landlords in Nairobi. However, the reality in the late 19th and early 20th century tenement market (as in that of Nairobi today) that landlordism tended (or tends) not to be the main and only source of income or identity of tenement owners is not addressed by Harvey's explanation, in which he explicitly applies 'the concept of *subjective* class which describes the consciousness which different groups have of their position within a social structure' (*ibid.*, 251, emphasis in the original).

It is important to note that critical urban discourse does not only provide arguments that question the justification of 19th century tenements, particularly when compared to other forms of housing or urban spatial arrangements designed to replace them. Lefebvre (1974/1991), for instance, a neo-Marxist whose writings coincided with the early publications of Harvey, is at pains to highlight the benefits of historical urban spatial complexity, compared to the 'authoritarian and brutal spatial practice' of urban redevelopment that led to its destruction: 'what is involved in all cases is the effective application of the analytic spirit in and through dispersion, division and segregation' (1974/1991, 308). If applied to Berlin, this 'brutal spatial practice' would refer to the destruction of tenement districts and their inherent spatial qualities. Lefebvre does not mention tenements explicitly. He merely refers to the 'shattered historical space of Paris', adding that '[t]he critics have perhaps paid insufficient attention… to the quality of the space Haussmann thus mortally wounded, a space characterized by the high and rare qualitative complexity afforded by its *double* network of streets and passageways' (*ibid.*, 312, emphasis in the original). He speaks of the destruction of 'the space of traditional residential buildings, where bourgeois lived on the lower floors, and workers and servants in the garrets' (*ibid.*, 316). This fits the description of the '*immeuble de rapport*' (multi-story building for profit) or '*maison mixte*' (mixed house), the prototypical Paris tenement, which spread across that city at the beginning of the 19th century (Barbey 1984, 52). It suggests that Lefebvre ascribes a certain quality to the tenement districts of Paris, and thereby provides some justification for this type of housing market.

Later in this book I examine what underlies the production of tenements in Nairobi, what underlies the city's contemporary tenement market, and how it is experienced by its tenants. This allows me to explore, in my conclusion, the relevance and dilemmas of arguments of urban spatial quality in this context. An important question is whether either Lefebvre or Harvey's position provides a sufficient basis on which to challenge or protect present-day tenement production and management in Nairobi. Berlin's history provides no easy answers to this. As I will show in Chapters 3, 4 and 5, the quality of Berlin's tenement environment that society began to revalue in the 1980s has since come to serve the short-term interest of extractive capital, with consequences that those initially rediscovering and articulating these qualities did not intend.

Themes and principles underpinning the comparison of Berlin and Nairobi

Tenement markets, where they have flourished across time and space, have two things in common: physical uniformity and a tendency to dominate housing supply. Unless entire tenement districts are demolished, tenement markets have a lasting effect on urban form. Urban space that is shaped by a tenement market is characterized on the one hand by problematic excesses of building height, density and unfavorable layouts, all the result of the maximum exploitation of space. On the other hand are urban qualities and complexities that result from this exploitation of space which in turn determine the articulation of streets and hierarchies of access.

A management approach that incorporates neglect of maintenance and transgression or evasion of laws and regulations characterizes the operation of a tenement market. Political impunity makes this operational approach, largely implemented by rental agents, possible. In some tenement markets, or in certain stages of tenement markets, perceptions of what is tolerable rather than what is permissible limit excesses in height, overcrowding, fire risk and neglect of other aspects of safety. Unrelenting demand for low income accommodation and the interests and connections of tenement owners undermine the introduction, enforcement or tightening of regulation that would limit excesses. Yet tenant activism, economic decline or, in the case of Berlin, enforced regulation have eventually undermined tenement markets after decades of unchallenged existence and expansion.

However, it must be asked what lends tenement markets their legitimacy within a society over many decades of unchallenged existence and expansion. Not all tenement markets derive their legitimacy from the law. Where transgression is unchallenged, it may be derived from social and traditional acceptability, as well as pragmatism in the face of overwhelming demand. A separate question, which has relevance for Nairobi today, is whether tenement markets are justified. Put differently, should they be challenged? Critical analysis that exposes the domination of a more-or-less definable class of landlords, through class monopoly behavior, over a powerless class of tenants has challenged a classical economic justification for tenement markets that is based on the assumption of an inherently fair return on investment. However, critical urban discourse has also highlighted the existence of value in the spatial quality produced through tenement markets. This requires us to engage not only with the barely tolerable excesses in today's tenement markets, but also with the positive qualities of the lived experience. My analysis of Berlin which follows takes this approach. My intention is to carry a more nuanced understanding of tenement markets and their challenges, derived from this analysis, into the next part of the book which deals with tenements in Nairobi.

Endnotes

1 Engels' book was one of many describing living conditions in England at the time, and according to Henderson and Chaloner (1958, xxii), it has remained in print due to its value as 'a brilliant political tract' rather than its historical accuracy. However, Clark and Foster (2006) point to its particular contribution in explaining how production and its forces influenced the living conditions of workers and the environment.

2 The 1998 *Encyclopedia of Housing* (Van Vliet 1998) has no entry on 'tenement'. A brief entry on 'Tenement House Law of 1867' (Birch 1998, 585) does not describe or explain the meaning of the term 'tenement'.

3 Lupala (2002, 106) provides the floor plan of a five-story rooming establishment with shops on the ground floor.

4 This is in contrast to what Daunton (1983, 3) refers to as the 'marginal position of the private landlord in British society and political formation'.

5 In a discussion of the legitimization of contemporary international governance, Steffek (2003) provides a useful review of different approaches to the concept of legitimacy.

Chapter 3

Growth and speculation in 19th century Berlin

The forces that shaped the construction of tenements in Berlin shifted, intensified, faded and re-surfaced as the city evolved across the 19th century. While the predominance of working class rental housing emerged in Berlin in the early 19th century, spurred by the industrial revolution and dramatic population increase, the refinement into the particular tenement development associated with Berlin occurred only in the second half of the century. Tenement construction then escalated in scale, continuing into the first two decades of the 20th century (this trajectory is summarized in Figure 3.6 towards the end of this chapter). The distinct form of tenement development that was sustained in Berlin over at least 60 years was a product of the twin processes of regulation and speculation. The political, economic and demographic shifts that marked the 19th century, and a governance system in which property owners enjoyed an elevated citizenship status and therefore had leverage over decision-making, determined a convergence of interests in physical planning, regulation and speculation. A rigorous bureaucracy in turn allowed regulation (and physical planning) to effectively shape the city. The resulting product was living conditions that were inadequate at the time, but were coupled with urban qualities which have endured for over a century. They have retained a universal appeal up to the present.

Early investigations into the poor living conditions in these tenement environments sparked debates on whether to justify or challenge this form of housing development. The dominant position in these debates eventually undermined the legitimacy of tenements as a form of housing. This dominant discourse, and the much later re-legitimization of tenements, produced contrasting accounts of the evolution of Berlin's tenements before and during the first half of the 19th century. Some of the historic tenement literature must therefore be read with circumspection, particularly as regards its claims about the influence of the military in shaping Berlin's tenements. Nevertheless, it is an undisputed fact that, throughout much of Berlin's history, the city's rulers were excessively preoccupied with military affairs and warfare. Berlin's domination by armed forces was accompanied by nationalist sentiment. As electoral democracy emerged, nationalism as a political force and its extreme form, fascism, contested both communism and the more liberal social democratic movement, thwarting a short-lived but influential period of idealistic modernism which sought an alternative to working class tenements in the city. Since the second half of the19th century, political contestations have closely informed debates and action regarding the future of Berlin's tenements.[1]

Conflicting narratives on the origin of tenements in Berlin's historical development

Berlin has its beginnings around 1230, when Germans colonized Eastern Europe. Two separate settlements, Berlin and Coelln, developed into trading towns on opposite banks of the river Spree. They were unified in 1432 into Berlin-Coelln and in 1470 became the seat of Electoral Prince (Kurfürst) Frederick II of Brandenburg. After substantial destruction in the Thirty Year War (1618–1648), the Great Elector Frederick William fortified the city, a project which also occasioned the preparation of the earliest cartographic map of Berlin (1652). He developed a formidable army, and under him the Prussian state grew to prominence and Berlin became a garrison town, a feature that dominated the city for three centuries. From 1701, it served as the capital of the Prussian Kingdom ruled by the Hohenzollern dynasty. Berlin was the residence of two successive Prussian kings obsessed with the military, Frederick William I (who ruled from 1713 to 1740 and was known as the 'Soldiers' King') and Frederick II (1740–1786, known as 'Frederick the Great'), each of whom extended the boundaries of Prussia. In the late 1730s, King Frederick William responded to the city's growth by removing its fortifications and constructing a new customs wall for a city of 90 000 inhabitants (Brockhaus 1968; Senator für Stadtentwicklung und Umweltschutz 1986, 10).

At the advent of the 19th century, people in or dependent on the military made up 14–20 per cent of Berlin's population (Senator für Stadtentwicklung und Umweltschutz 1986; Richie 1998). Historian Alexandra Richie (1998, 890) quotes a Scottish visitor to Berlin in 1789 who observed

> …soldiers parading and officers hurrying backwards and forwards. The town looked more like the cantonment of a great army, than the capital of a kingdom in the time of profound peace.

The 'military genius' Emperor Napoleon Bonaparte defeated the strong Prussian military under King Frederick William III (1797–1840) in 1806. This was followed by a seven-year French occupation of Berlin (Richie 1998, 89), with unsuccessful attempts at liberating Prussia from French domination coming from within

Berlin society (Presse- und Informationsamt Berlin 1993), and sparking a reign of repression, terror and increasing control (Richie 1998, 97).[2] Having defeated Napoleon, the Russians liberated Berlin from French rule in 1813. However, the Prussian king's subsequent lack of desire for change towards democratization disappointed liberal nationalist reformers in Berlin. Napoleon's defeat ushered in a 'dull, sentimental bourgeois culture' later referred to as 'Biedermeier', lasting up to the bourgeois revolution in 1848 (*ibid.*, 116).

Two seminal works explore the history of Berlin's tenements, which overlaps with the 'Biedermeier' period. The first, by Hegemann, was published in 1930; the second, a three-volume series by Geist and Kürvers, in the 1980s (1980, 1984, 1989). I contextualize these texts later in the book, and show that in themselves they are representations of how the historical discourse of the 20th century shifted together with the official treatment of the tenement stock. At this point, it is relevant to review their diverging accounts of the origin of tenements in Berlin.

In the 1920s, Werner Hegemann passionately wrote over 400 pages under the title *Berlin of Stone: The History of the Biggest Tenement City in the World* [*Das steinerne Berlin: Die Geschichte der größten Mietskasernenstadt der Welt*]. His work appeared as a book in 1930. I translate the German word '*Mietskaserne*' as 'tenement', but a literal translation would be 'rental barrack'. In Hegemann's 1930 account, the concept of a *Mietskaserne* in Berlin stems from the late 18th century, when the state provided rental barracks for soldiers and their families (Hegemann 1930, 163). Hegemann holds that in this way not only soldiers but 'equally the Berlin family were systematically drilled into a barracked way of living' (*ibid.*, 164). After describing the living conditions and restrictions imposed on the soldiers and their families, Hegemann proceeds to argue that King Frederick II 'similarly introduced barracking, a disgusting remedy for the housing need, for the accommodation of the Berlin public' (*ibid.*, 165).[3] Hegemann links this form of housing to the restrictions on urban expansion at the time, and the associated increase in urban land prices and pressure for vertical development. His emotive explanation is that

> ...ordinary people had to imitate what their much-praised king had demonstrated... The goal of becoming the greatest concentration of rental barracks in the world was, therefore, conceived for the city of Berlin by its 'greatest' king. (*ibid.*, 167)

In the 1980s, architects Geist and Kürvers presented an alternative and more accurate account of the origins of tenements in Berlin, in which the military plays less of a role. They published three extensive archive-based volumes titled *Das Berliner Mietshaus (1740–1862)*, *(1862–1945)*, and *(1945–1989)* (*ibid.* 1980, 1984, 1989). The German word '*Mietshaus*' translates simply into 'rental house'. Geist and Kürvers' choice of this term rather than 'rental barrack' stems from their archival searches, through which they traced the typological history of Berlin's tenements back not to military barracks but to private rental houses, so-called 'family houses', constructed as early as 1735 (Geist and Kürvers 1980). The most notorious of these family houses are the 'Von Wülknitzschen Familienhäuser' built from 1822 to 1824 in the Gartenstrasse outside Berlin's Hamburg Gate, in the present-day district of Mitte. Accommodating over 2 500 people, these houses certainly made up the largest single-room or rooming establishment in Berlin's history. The infamous Meyer's Hof of the late 19th century (see Figure 4.3 in Chapter 4) in the district of Wedding, commonly dubbed Berlin's largest rental barrack, housed 'only' in the order of 1 200 people (Ott 1989, 140).

The *Von Wülknitzschen Familienhäuser* consisted of a long central corridor with rooms on either side (Figure 3.1). Geist and Kürvers (1980, 41) explain that those designing these buildings might have drawn on the example not only of military barracks, as is commonly misunderstood (e.g. Forsell 2006, 162) but of the nearby and well known '*Invalidenhaus*' built in the mid-18th century – a hospital serving injured returnees of Prussia's wars who were incapable of working. It was the first building in Berlin with a long central corridor, and served also as an example in the subsequent design of barracks (Geist and Kürvers 1980, 84). The only direct and evidence-based link Geist and Kürvers provide between military barracks and rental housing at that time is that vacant military barracks temporarily housed the poor, and for that period were referred to as *Familienhäuser* along with those built specifically for this purpose (*ibid.*, 84–85).

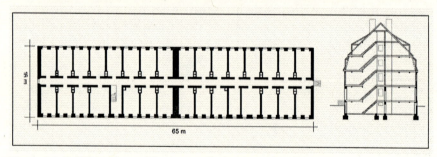

Figure 3.1: Building plans of the *Von Wülknitzschen Familienhäuser*

Source: Redrawn from Geist and Kürvers (1980, 104)

After several submissions and alterations, the authorities approved the building plans for the *Von Wülknitzschen Familienhäuser*. The largest building on the site had 30 rooms per floor, and five floors (including a '*souterrain*' or basement), making up a total of 151 rooms. A further 56 unlit and therefore officially uninhabitable cubby-holes were tucked into the roof pitch. With five additional smaller buildings, also with single-room accommodation, Von Wülknitz privately accommodated over 2 500 poor people. The landlord's interest lay primarily in the rent he was extracting and not in the value of his property. He catered for the city's poorest and had to deal with frequent rental arrears, threats of epidemics and unrest triggered by distress. Commentators at the time asked to what extent the Poor Authority, rather than private landlords, ought to be responsible for the residential needs of these households. With increasing regulation by the authorities, the introduction of a rental tax and competition from other landlords, profitability for such rooming establishments declined. In 1831 Von Wülknitz took out a mortgage on this property and skipped the country for Paris. His creditors lost most of their money, selling the family houses at a very low price to one Wiesecke who, facing a cholera threat in addition to the same challenges as Von Wülknitz, repeated his exit strategy. Wiesecke's successor resolved to impose stricter rules on the tenants and work more closely with the Poor Authority, seeking social support for his tenants in his own interest (Geist and Kürvers 1980).

Factually then, the emergence of Berlin's tenements in the 19th century can be linked to the military only on indirect grounds. In fact, hardly any barracks had been provided for the large number of soldiers and this contributed to the private rental housing demand (Senator für Stadtentwicklung und Umweltschutz 1986, 12). The royalty prioritized spending revenue on warfare rather than on urban development (Ott 1989), while reparation money from successful wars periodically flushed the economy with capital, triggering short-lived economic booms with irresponsible urban land speculation (Richie 1998). The 'barrack' typology of rooms leading off a central corridor did not become the dominant tenement form in Berlin. When Berliners coined the term 'rental barrack' or '*Mietskaserne*' during the tenement boom in the 1860s (Geist and Kürvers 1984, 220), tenements had no visible similarity to barracks, as the architect Theodor Goecke pointed out in 1891 (*ibid.*). The polemical expression captured public condemnation of the sheer scale, conditions and overcrowding in private tenements. In 1907, economist Rudolf Eberstadt defended the relevance of the term 'rental barrack' for all the tenement typologies in Berlin, arguing that it reflected the submission of the individual to an overarching purpose, namely speculation, not military concerns (*ibid.*, 219).

While 'barracking' for the purpose of capital extraction was already present in the *Von Wülknitzschen Familienhäuser* in the 1920s, the segregated concentration of poor people in this uniform offering of rooming did not come to characterize any part of Berlin. A far more compact and socially mixed tenement typology emerged, with larger units and shops in street-facing buildings and small, often unevenly sized, working class units in the backyards. Geist and Kürvers (1980, 149) point to a lesson from the early experience of large rooming tenements which was articulated at the time: there was a political risk for the ruling order in spatially concentrating poor people, as this created preconditions for spontaneous resistance for which the military and police were not prepared. This political concern about the spatial distribution of poverty is relevant to my later discussion on the few arguments that were put forward in favor of the tenement typology of the second half of the 19th century, which was to some extent mixed-income.

Berlin's rise as an industrial city: the emergence of class consciousness and socialist demands (1830s and 1840s)

Economic changes in both rural and urban areas fuelled intense migration to Berlin in the 19th century. Agricultural reform transformed rural economies, as did the emergence of mass production with the Industrial Revolution. The latter led to the 'breakdown of the medieval guild system' that had regulated craftsmanship (Richie 1998, 158). Linked to this was the breakdown of cottage industries and consequent loss of small-town livelihoods. In addition, famines in the 1840s led to the mass exodus from eastern regions to Berlin (Richie 1998).

The onset of industrialization in Berlin, which occurred later than in contemporary West European cities, marked the urban economy. In the 1830s Berlin rose to become one of the most important industrial cities in Europe. From 1819 to 1847 the number of factories in the city grew from 102 to 634, an increase of over 500 per cent (Pölking 1989a). The first railway came into operation in 1838, and the first three-story tenements with backyards appeared within the extension of the city walls at this time (*ibid.*, 76). In its early phase of mechanization, industry still relied very heavily on people (Wietog 1981, 116). Thus it attracted a large population, which in turn was the precondition for further industrial growth (Wietog 1981).

Around 1800, Berlin's population was insignificant when compared to the leading metropolitan centers of Europe (Bodenschatz 1987, 53).[4] However, the first half of the 19th century saw a transformation 'from provincial residence and garrison town of the Prussian kings to a bourgeois-capitalist trade and industrial metropolis' (*ibid.*). A population increase from 173 000 in 1800 (Senator für Stadtentwicklung und Umweltschutz 1986, 12) to almost 420 000 by 1850 (Wietog 1981), more than doubling in half a century, marked this period. By 1840 Berlin's population had surpassed that of Amsterdam, and it was the fourth-largest European city after London, Paris and Vienna (Bodenschatz 1987, 53). The annual population growth rate for this period hovered between one and three per cent (Table 3.1). Political unrest in Berlin around the time of the 1848 bourgeois revolution accounted for the drop to one per cent for the years 1847–1849.

Table 3.1: Berlin's population growth in the first half of the 19th century

Year	Period	Population	Annual population growth rate
1800		173 000	
	1816–1830		Average 1.6%
	1830–1846		Average 3.0%
	1847–1849		Average 1.0%
1850		420 000	

Source: Based on Wietog (1981)

Throughout Germany, industrialization and the emergence of an industrial society changed the dominant way of living, from families occupying individual houses to the renting of apartments in multi-story buildings or tenements. However, tenement construction could not always keep pace with the rapid population growth in the industrial cities. This resulted periodically in dramatic housing shortages (Häußermann and Siebel 1996, 81). 'Slum' conditions developed in the still partly medieval center of Berlin (Pölking 1989a, 76). A particular housing shortage noted for the year 1848 (Wietog 1981) is linked to the disruptions caused by the bourgeois revolution. A brief review of class stratification at the time helps to contextualize the course of events of that year.

By the mid-19th century, 15 000 residents of Berlin still belonged to the military. Many young men were drawn to Berlin by career opportunities presented by the army; for some, this was a step towards prospects beyond the military. Werner von Siemens, migrating to Berlin in 1834 from a modest farming background to be trained as an officer in the Artillery and Engineering School, became an inventor and industrialist and was awarded Prussian nobility in 1988 (Von Siemens 1986). But most migrants to Berlin did not surmount class barriers in this manner. Many instead found themselves pushed down the social ladder. Alongside the ruling 'landowning aristocracy' (Engels 1887/1935, 72) of the mid-19th century, a propertied middle class was being shaped (Richie 1998, 150). Two trends marked this bourgeois class formation. On the one hand there were those, largely privileged by existing capital, that prospered from new industries and growing trade (Pölking 1989a). The 'entrepreneurial Jewish population' played an important role in expanding 'banking, manufacturing and trade' (Richie 1998, 151). This rising class aspired to close association with royalty (Weiglin 1942). On the other hand, some 27 000 artisans still counted themselves part of the middle class, but competition from industries led to their gradual descent into the proletariat (Pölking 1989a). Socialists observed and criticized these tendencies. Among them was Friedrich Engels (Marx and Engels 1848/1964, 15), who himself chose to reject the middle class standing of his family (his father was 'a prosperous cotton manufacturer' in the Rhineland (Henderson and Chaloner 1958, xxvii)). As a young man, Friedrich Engels too was attracted to the military in Berlin. He arrived in 1841 and served as 'a volunteer in the Prussian Guard Artillery' for one year (*ibid.*), using this opportunity to attend lectures at the University of Berlin and engage in critical debate (Clark and Foster 2006).

Table 3.2 shows the various employment categories within the working class or 'proletariat' of Berlin in the mid-19th century. Considering the household members that each worker supported, the combined numbers of workers in each category of the table indicate that the working class made up the majority of Berlin's population of 420 000 at the time. The weavers constituted the lowest paid and most miserable section of the working class (Pölking 1989a), and to a large extent, they were the occupants of the rooming accommodation in the

Von Wülknitzschen Familienhäuser, which were demolished only in 1881.[5] Beggars, too, found accommodation in the *Von Wülknitzschen Familienhäuser* (Geist and Kürvers 1980). As begging was a criminal offence, the police regularly incarcerated beggars in Berlin's workhouses (*ibid.*). In 1839 alone, the police arrested 1 000 beggars (Pölking 1989a).

Table 3.2: Employee numbers in various categories of the working class in Berlin, around 1850

Employment category	Approximate number of people
Factory workers	20 000
Day laborers, railway workers and those doing earthworks	17 000
Messengers	22 000
Business assistants and apprentices	20 000–25 000
Other laborers	10 000
Weavers	7 000
Total	**100 000**

Source: Based on Pölking (1989a)

Some 2 000 students also lived in Berlin at the time (Pölking 1989a). Among these, from 1836 to 1841, was the then unknown Karl Marx, studying towards his doctorate in philosophy at the University of Berlin.[6] As a student, Marx was not yet interested in the political agency of the working class. In the 1840s, the organization or emancipatory intellectual development of the working class was also not a given. Jackson (1957, 14–15) describes the situation:

> The old police régime was continued in Prussia, with press-censorship and denial of civil liberties... The rural population was cowed and the industrial workman seemed satisfied in his misery, happy enough in the hope that he might end his days in no worse a state than he had begun them.

During his sojourn in Berlin, Marx was much inspired by the German philosopher Hegel and his followers (Richie 1998, 156). Under the 'old police regime' of the 1840s, the University of Berlin fell 'more and more under the control of a reactionary government alarmed at the dangerous thoughts of the Young Hegelians' (Jackson 1957, 44). Marx therefore chose to submit his doctoral thesis to the University of Jena and not Berlin (*ibid.*).

The nationalist sentiment that had emerged in Berlin during the French occupation at the beginning of the 19th century continued over the following decades. The Revolution in Paris in 1848 (Richie 1998), which the Prussian bourgeoisie set out to replicate, fuelled this nationalism across Germany. The middle class or bourgeoisie led the March 1848 battle in Berlin against the Prussian military. However, the working class suffered most of the losses in this encounter (Pölking 1989b). In Paris, the king fled and a French republic was declared. In Berlin, the king (Frederick William IV, who had succeeded Frederick William III in 1840 and ruled until 1861) soon conceded to pressure from the bourgeoisie and promised to democratize his regime. The revolution was celebrated as both successful and civilized (Richie 1998, 127). But the success was as short-lived as the king's promise of democratization. A few months after the revolution, military control returned to Berlin (*ibid.*). The 'cowardly' bourgeoisie, to use Engels' later description (1887/1935, 72), retreated, while socialist demands around working conditions began to emanate from the working class (Pölking 1989b). The first red flag was raised in Berlin in the same year, when military repression confronted a proletarian uprising, the 'October uprising of the engine attackers' (*ibid.*, 75). However, the first working class political groupings were formed only in the 1860s (Richie 1998, 171). Berlin continued to be shaped almost exclusively by capitalist interests.

Liberalism, warfare, speculation and depression (1850s to late 1880s)

Against the backdrop of failed democratization after the 1848 Revolution, Berlin's population doubled in a matter of 25 years from 420 000 people in 1850 to 824 500 in 1871 (and more than doubled in the next 25 years). By 1858 annual population growth rates had returned to two per cent, but subsequently rose to six per cent (Wietog 1981) (see Table 3.3). Within these urban growth rates, cityward migration far outstripped 'natural' growth by births. The years 1861 and 1871 stand out, with the highest migration figures – 53 771 and 49 986 people respectively (*ibid.*, 118). An urban boundary expansion in 1861 and the formation of the German imperial capital in 1871 explain these numbers. The worst years of unmet housing demand were 1856/7 and 1870/1 (*ibid.*, 125). Figures for the year 1868 (based on Treue 1969, 37), when population growth far outstripped growth in number of residential units produced, exemplify the undersupply of housing. Commentators at the time placed the blame for this on the speculative processes involved in tenement production (Wietog 1981, 125). Again in 1871, the mismatch between demand and supply was extreme. An average occupation rate of 5 people per housing unit, and an immigration to Berlin of around 50 000 people in that year, created a demand of 10 000 units against only around 4 500 new units built. More than half of those moving to the city in 1871 could not claim a housing unit (*ibid.*, 121).

Table 3.3: Berlin's population growth in the second half of the 19th century

Year	Period	Population	Annual population growth rate
1850		420 000	
1858			2%
1861			11%
	1863–1867		Average 4.2% (growth in housing units 6.3%)
1868			4.6% (growth in housing units 2.4%)
1871		824 500	
1880		1.1 million	6%
1890		1.53 million	

Source: Drawn from Treue (1969, 37); Wietog (1981); Leyden (1995, 86)

Shantytowns or 'tent cities... bloated with desperate people hoping to get work' appeared periodically outside Berlin's gates, particularly in the period of housing need around 1870/1 (Richie 1998, 160). Approximately 700 people or 163 families occupied an open field outside the city at Cottbusser Gate (Wischermann 1997) in what was referred to as the '*Barackenstadt*', essentially a shantytown.[7] Others camped in the open outside the Landsberger and Stralauer Gates. These squatters' greatest fear was to be classified as welfare cases. Authorities deemed that such people could not be integrated into society and therefore forced them into poorhouses, workhouses, asylums or institutions in which families were divided (*ibid.*, 338).

Evictions and demolitions were the order of the day, even though the occupants of the shacks or shanties were required to pay a lease to the City authorities (Wietog 1981). Police repression marked these shantytowns as much as it marks informal settlements in many countries today (see for example COHRE 2008). According to Richie (1998, 165), '[t]he authorities had little sympathy for the destitute families and were remarkably brutal when breaking up their settlements'. The media, too, were unsympathetic, labeling the squatters as adventurist. The political left, in turn, took issue with the police repression, highlighting the willingness of these households to pay rents, if only wages would permit this and adequate space was available (Wischermann 1997, 338). Police attempts to demolish the shantytowns around Cottbusser Gate and Blumenstrasse in 1871 triggered a violent street battle in which over 150 squatters were injured (Richie 1998, 165). A year later, insurrectionists in a similar situation again raised a red flag (an evictee's red handkerchief). Similar protest action in many other cities, including Paris, preceded these events (Treue 1969, 37). It was an expression of mass anger (*ibid.*), with no direct socialist involvement (Richie 1998, 165).

The state responded to the population expansion of the mid-19th century by introducing the 1853 Building Ordinance, primarily concerned with fire safety, though health measures were also included. Fire regulations included height restrictions in relation to street width, so that in the event of collapse of a building as a result of fire, the façade on the opposite side of the street would not be affected (Rodenstein 1988, 110). The state revised the Building Ordinance several times. The context of these amendments in the 1870s and 1880s was that 'the propertied middle-class was the foremost representative of national legislation at the expense of other social classes' (Forsell 2006, 193). The 1871 amendment reduced the curing requirements before occupation of new buildings, whereas that of 1887 mandated larger backyard dimensions. An amendment in 1897 increased the floor interval or distance from floor to ceiling. The Building Ordinance of 1925 prohibited apartments in backyard buildings. This finally halted the already declining construction of the dominant tenement type (Goerke 1969, 55; Geist and Kürvers 1984, 231, 240)

Until 1918, the end of the '*Kaiserreich*' and the advent of urban self-governance, officials appointed by the Prussian state planned and regulated Berlin. In this period,

> [p]olice presidents became powerful figures and were given jurisdiction over many other aspects of city life, such as the fire department and street cleaning, the construction of public baths and sewer and water systems and the granting of building permits. (Richie 1998, 133)

The 'building police' was 'a department of the Berlin police presidium which answered to the Prussian Interior Ministry', itself 'under the influence of the king' (Bernet 2004, 402). Thus the police president was responsible for the Building Ordinance (Häußermann and Siebel 1996) as well as for the 1862 Building Plan. In the next two chapters I set out the process that led to the plan, relevant content of the plan as well as debates that were waged on some aspects of it.

In regard to the broader historical background, it is relevant at this point to highlight the fact that capitalist interests significantly altered the 1862 plan (initially prepared by master builder James Hobrecht) before it was approved. The 'process of privatised production of the city result[ed] in a dominant or ruling block of interests' which influenced city production and in turn benefited from it (Bodenschatz 1987, 53). 'Private land speculators, banks, individual speculators, developers and building owners/landlords organise[d] and use[d] urban growth' (*ibid.*, 53–54). The 'old aristocracy, the modern bourgeoisie and parts of the petty bourgeoisie' were all involved in these activities. Urban landowners dominated local government politics in Berlin and its surrounds through a restricted suffrage which politically privileged those owning land (*ibid.*, 54).

The 1862 plan guided the urban expansion which the state had made possible in 1861 by increasing the city area by approximately 60 per cent to include present-day Wedding, Gesundbrunnen, Moabit and the northern parts of Tempelhof and Schöneberg (Figure 3.2). This resulted in a total city area of 70 km², only increased again in 1920 to form Greater Berlin, which incorporated the palace and affluent residential area of Charlottenburg (Materna 1997, 120). The reluctance to increase the urban boundary and allow for urban expansion or sprawl brought about higher densities than in other European cities. Furthermore, there was a correlation between high residential densities in Berlin and the late lifting of restrictions on the alienation of farmland for the establishment of urban areas in the districts surrounding Berlin (Leyden 1933/1995, 85).

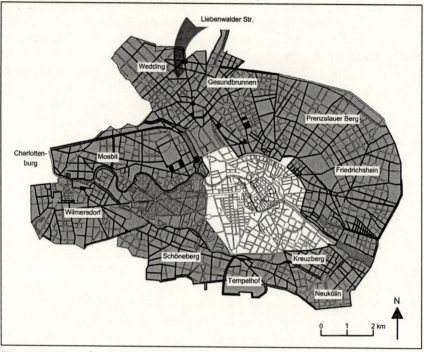

Figure 3.2: Map of Berlin, with its extensions of 1861 and street layout as per the 1862 Building Plan, broadly covering the tenement districts

Source: Based on Geist and Küvers (1984, 144)

However, building regulations, land subdivision and intense private land speculation also contributed to the dense development.[8] Together they informed Berlin's dominant form of rental housing: large tenement properties with buildings containing one- or two-roomed flats hidden in deep backyards behind decorated street-facing buildings that contained respectable multi-roomed apartments (Figure 3.3). While poorer tenants lived in multiple backyard buildings, they shared streets and urban amenities with their better-off counterparts from the street-fronting buildings. I return later to disputes about the extent and benefits of socio-spatial mixing in this context. Whether beneficial or not, this typology shaped a particular culture and way of life (romanticized, some would argue) that was widely associated with Berlin and enjoyed relative legitimacy, allowing its perpetuation up to WWI.

Not only the Building Plan marked the year 1862. After the death of King Frederick William IV, his successor (William I), who had already been ruling as regent since 1858 due to the king's illness, appointed Otto von Bismarck as prime minister ('*Kanzler*') of Prussia in 1862. Under Bismarck's leadership, Berlin was redeveloped as a political and economic metropole, with an expanding population (Geist and Kürvers 1980, 506). Bismarck also introduced an aggressive foreign policy with the aim of creating a German Empire (*Reich*) (Ott 1989). This saw wars in 1864 against Denmark and in 1866 against Austria and its allies Bavaria, Saxony and Hanover, all of which increased Prussia's dominance. In 1867 Berlin was made capital of the North German Federation (*Bund*) (Müller and Schmook 1991). While Bismarck's wars and those waged earlier by the royalty did not affect Berlin directly, the military expenditure consumed important resources that needed to be spent on urban expansion (Ott 1989). The first significant housing-related unrest in Berlin's tenement districts occurred at the beginning of Bismarck's tenure in 1863 (Bodenschatz 1987, 55), when protesters barricaded the streets, and in 1872 street skirmishes lasted several days (Rodenstein 1988, 106–107; Wischermann 1997).

Figure 3.3: Typical Berlin tenement street

Source: Author's photograph (2005)

In a fascinating turn of events, planning, speculation and financial crisis in Paris had a direct impact on the property cycle in Berlin. Harvey (2008, 26), in his (or rather Marxists') trademark reference to the history of Paris, explains that a financial crisis in France in 1868 had resulted from an over-extension of the 'speculative financial system and credit structures', which its civic planner Haussmann had set up as a 'proto-Keynesian system... Haussmann was dismissed; Napoleon III in desperation went to war against Bismarck's Germany and lost'. The reparation money from France spurred land speculation in Berlin.

Amid this war, which culminated in Germany's victory in 1871, Bismarck announced the unification of Germany and founding of the German Empire (*Reich*) (Senator für Stadtentwicklung und Umweltschutz 1986, 12). Bismarck rose to the position of Imperial Chancellor (Presse- und Informationsamt Berlin 1993) and Berlin received the status of capital of the German Empire (Müller and

Schmook 1991). This brought about 'a population explosion as well as rapid growth in business and industry' (Presse- und Informationsamt Berlin 1993, 4). Referring to the reparation money from the war against France, Engels (1887/1935, 7), in his preface to the second German edition of *The Housing Question*, describes this period as follows:

> ...the blessing of the French milliards [billions] was pouring over Germany: public debts were paid off, fortresses and [military] barracks built, stocks of weapons and war material reviewed; the available capital no less than the volume of money in circulation was suddenly enormously increased, and all this just at a time when Germany was entering the world arena not only as a 'united empire', but also as a great industrial country. These milliards gave the new large-scale industry powerful impetus, and above all they were responsible for the short period of prosperity, so rich in illusions, which followed on the war, and for the great crash which came immediately afterwards in 1873–74.

The paying off of state debt freed private capital. As a result,

> [i]ndustry boomed, the population skyrocketed and a frenzy of luxury and materialism marked the glorious age of the *Gründerzeit* [period of the founders]... a term which alluded not only to the Empire, but also to the sheer number of new companies created at the time. (Richie 1998, 201)

Engels (1887/1935, 74) debates whether the new imperial state would play any role in resolving 'the housing question'. He asks:

> Has even a single taler [the currency at the time] of all these milliards been used to provide shelter for those Berlin working class families which have been thrown onto the streets? On the contrary. As autumn approached, the state even caused to be pulled down those few miserable huts which had served the workers and their families as a temporary shelter during the summer.

Instead of investing the 'French milliards' (five billion francs (Richie 1998, 200)) in much needed housing for Berlin's proletariat, the state settled its debt, thus freeing capital and directly affecting the tenement market. The rapid development of land and building speculation created favorable investment opportunities (Ott 1989). Forty building banks and many similar 'joint stock' companies ('*Bauaktiengesellschaften*') emerged, in the first instance supporting the buying and selling of land or building sites rather than the construction of tenements. Land prices escalated with every transaction. The square-meter price increased from 0.12 marks at agricultural value in 1861 to 80–200 marks in 1889 (Ott 1989).

An ominous fault-line re-emerged in German society with the stock market crash. While religious prejudice against Jewish citizens had been present in Berlin, as in most other cities across Europe, anti-Semitism swelled as the crash came to be blamed on Jewish bankers and the largely Jewish liberal press. This tendency had parallels in a growing romantic nationalism (Richie 1998, 244). At the same time, radical workers' politics emerged and expanded. The nature or trajectory of the workers' movement explains both the scathing approach that Friedrich Engels took in the *Housing Question*, which he wrote shortly before the stock market crash (I return to Engels' arguments in Chapter 5 as they address the housing debate in Berlin and other German cities at the time), and the shifting position of the social democrats whose party eventually facilitated an end to tenement construction.

In the 1850s, a middle class concern for workers' wellbeing had emerged. This 'naive but well-meaning' approach saw the ideal worker as 'the ambitious man who wanted to pull himself into the middle class' (Richie 1998, 170–171). It 'rejected the idea of universal male suffrage', arguing that 'workers should not participate directly in politics until they had become educated' (*ibid.*, 171). Workers resented this, yet the 'first groups... by and for workers' formed only in the 1860s (*ibid.*). Prussian rulers ignored or repressed these groups, despite their initially moderate stance of seeking only integration into the existing system. State repression contributed to their radicalization.

In 1863, under the leadership of the somewhat contradictory Ferdinand Lassalle, the General German Workers' Association (*Allgemeiner Deutscher Arbeiterverein* – ADAV), a workers' party, was formed. Lassalle had become an enemy of Marx but friend of Bismarck, with whom he shared not only a 'dislike of bourgeois liberals' (Jackson 1957, 146). At one point, Lassalle believed the state could be used to serve both their interests. Unlike Marx, Lassalle campaigned for universal suffrage and workers' representation in Parliament (*ibid.*) – integration rather than revolution. The formation of the workers' party was a 'turning point in the history of Germany' (Richie 1998, 174). It also earned Lassalle the jealousy of Marx (Jackson 1957, 147). Lassalle's early death (as the result of a duel) in the following year changed the political course of the working class and destined them 'to follow the powerful Marxists who were putting pressure on them from the south' (Richie 1998, 174). In 1869 a rival Social Democratic Workers' Party (*Sozialdemokratische Arbeiterpartei* – SDAP) was formed in Eisenach under the leadership of August Bebel and Wilhelm Liebknecht, with ties to the international Marxist movement. This gave the Marxists 'a foothold in Germany' (*ibid.*, 175). The 'Eisenach Party' 'became the largest and best organized [workers' party] in Europe and began to exert an extraordinary political, economic, social and cultural hold on the working class' in Berlin (*ibid.*). The 'rootlessness of the workers in Berlin' explained this in part. Most workers 'were immigrants who were not integrated culturally or socially into the community or the Church, which left them more open to socialist ideals' (*ibid.*).

At this point, during the 1872 housing shortage which coincided with massive speculation, and when Marx's ideas already had a strong following in Berlin, his intellectual partner Friedrich Engels participated in the debate on 'The Housing Question' in Germany. Engels refuted the reform ideas that bourgeois socialists published at the time (Engels 1887/1935, 8; the text was written in 1872). In his text, in which he acknowledges Marx's collaboration, Engels (*ibid.*, 72) states that the 'rapidly increasing proletariat [in Berlin]... is intellectually highly developed and... becoming more and more organised every day'. In those years, Marx was directly involved in attempts to build a 'working class party in Germany', with the 'first task... to destroy the Lassallian influence' (Jackson 1957, 170).

In 1875, the ADAV and the SDAP merged to form the Socialist Labour Party (*Sozialistische Arbeiterpartei* – SAP). In 1891 it was renamed the Social Democratic Party of Germany (*Sozialdemokratische Partei Deutschlands* – SPD). I will return to the trajectory of this party as it later became the political bearer of an anti-tenement reform agenda. The earlier SAP was radicalized further in the late 1870s as a result of state repression. In 1883 it participated in Berlin's municipal elections, securing five seats (Richie 1998, 175). Over the following decades the party grew more moderate, with radical groupings eventually splitting away during WWI.

Unprecedented tenement construction marked 'imperial Berlin', from the decades following 1871 up to 1920 – Berlin's 'founding years' (*Gründerjahre*) (*ibid.*, 188). However, investment in tenement construction resumed only slowly after the 'great' stock market crash of 1873/4, which 'saw the destruction of economic liberalism' (*ibid.*, 201). It was followed by a period of quiet progress in tenement development into the surrounding areas of Berlin, coupled with a complete standstill of speculation, low land prices and a general economic depression that lasted until 1887 (Treue 1969, 46; Bodenschatz 1987, 55). In this period, Bismarck 'enhanced his comprehensive system of social security reforms' (Richie 1998, 201). These included worker's compensation, health insurance and retirement and disability benefits through mandatory contributions from the employers, employees and the state (Liedtke 2006). Bismarck's aim was twofold: on the one hand to achieve efficiency in the economy (which required workers' wellbeing), and on the other to reduce the appeal of the more radical alternatives that were being called for by the socialists (*ibid.*). The latter objective also drove the amendment of the Building Ordinance in 1887 to halve the permitted number of occupants per building, and double the minimum courtyard or backyard dimensions (Treue 1969, 38).

In any text covering both 20th century Nairobi and 19th century Berlin, an account of this period in Berlin's history would be incomplete without mentioning the now infamous Berlin Conference that took place from November 1884 to February 1885, which Bismarck had offered to host at his official residence in Berlin (Hochschild 2002, 84). The proceedings of the conference provide an indirect background for Nairobi's tenement boom today, through the long-running theme of dispossession and land grabbing; it is at this point in history that I pick up Nairobi's historical trajectory in Chapter 6. By 1884, Germany had 'entered the colonial scene'. Bismarck, having gradually discarded his belief in free trade, suddenly sensed a need to favor the interests of 'commercial ports and manufacturing' (Freund 1984, 95–96). The Berlin conference was a diplomatic gathering in which European rulers, greedy for land and power, clarified some of their conflicting claims to the African continent.[9] Hochschild (2002, 86) makes the clarifying point that '[c]ontrary to myth, the Berlin Conference did not partition Africa; the spoils were too large, and it would take many more treaties to divide them all'. However, Britain was represented at the Berlin Conference. Its interests in present-day Kenya and Uganda began in that period, initially through the Imperial British East Africa Company. The political status of Kenya changed from British protectorate to colony in 1920, assuming its name from Mount Kenya. As a country, Kenya's history began with the colonial land grab, and urban and rural land has remained a resource for illegal pilfering ever since (Klopp 2000, 15; Otiso 2002, 258).

A new era of land speculation in Imperial Berlin (1888–1918), and beyond

Weakened by the 1873 crash, Bismarck's liberal influence further declined with the crowning of the new 'foolish young Kaiser' (Emperor) William II in 1888 (Richie 1998, 202). He abdicated only in 1918, after losing WWI. The crowning of Kaiser William marked 'the beginning of the end for imperial Berlin' (*ibid.*). Kaiser William earned Berlin the reputation of having 'the most arrogant, militaristic, expansionist tendencies'; Berlin became 'the centre of an ever larger military machine' (*ibid.*, 203). He disagreed with Chancellor Bismarck, whom he defeated in 1890 by accepting his repeated threat of resignation. Bismarck died seven years later (*ibid.*, 253–254). Kaiser William's foreign policy 'became ever more inept and inflammatory' (*ibid.*, 254) and included Germany's colonial expansion. The years 1903 and 1912 saw unrest over food shortages in Berlin, and Kaiser William eventually 'pushed his people to the brink of world war' (*ibid.*, 203) in 1914.

In this new era of speculation, which continued undisrupted into the 20th century, tenement construction continued both for the middle and the working class, but increasingly on the urban periphery and with escalating land prices (Bodenschatz 1987, 55). The built environment of the city is evidence of just how lucrative land speculation and tenement investment became once more, though the latter involved more risk. 'Berlin's propertied middle class was becoming rich beyond its wildest dreams' (Richie 1998, 207). The aspirations of the new rich, who still sought association with royalty, marked the residential architecture of that period. In areas such as Charlottenburg, entire districts were developed solely for the moneyed classes. Here tenement apartments catered to the aristocratic taste of the tenant clientele. Large rooms had high and ornate ceilings. Generous street-facing bay windows, or balconies and façades resembling those of the royal palaces of the time, ensured the presentation of this image to the public. In mixed or predominantly working class neighborhoods such as Wedding, the street-facing buildings of even 'the most sordid tenements' were equally monumental in their façades, and displayed palatial elements within the apartments (*ibid.*, 209).

The dramatic population growth during this period (Table 3.4) saw the city's population reach almost 2.1 million at the onset of WWI (Leyden 1933/1995, 86), and occurred concurrently with intense tenement construction. Developers also catered for an increasing suburban taste on the part of the middle class. Before WWI, suburban development on Berlin's periphery (beyond the municipal boundary) consumed as much land as the entire area taken up by tenement construction in the 'Wilhelmine' period (Bodenschatz 2008). A much ignored fact of Berlin's urban development history is that developers at this time also pioneered attractive high density expansions for the middle class, in competition with the suburban offering (*ibid.*). While the official population reached 1.8 million around 1900, a further 1 million lived outside the official city boundary until 1920, when 880 km^2 of land was incorporated into Greater Berlin ('*Groß Berlin*') (Materna 1997, 120, 124). This consolidated 'eight towns, 59 rural communities and 27 farming estates' into 'the largest industrial city on the continent' (Presse- und Informationsamt Berlin 1993, 7). The total population figure for Berlin after the boundary extension was 3.7 million (Senator für Stadtentwicklung und Umweltschutz 1986, 12).

Table 3.4: Berlin's population growth from the late 19th century to 1920

Year	Period	Population	Annual population growth rate
1890		1,53 million	
	1890–1999		Approximate average 1.75%
1900		1.8 million	
	1900–1910		Average 0.86%
1905			2.68%
1910		2 million	
	1909–1919		Average –0.7%
1919		1.93 million	
1920		3.7 million (after boundary extension)	

Source: Compiled from Leyden (1933/1995, 86) and data from the Amt für Statistik Berlin-Brandenburg

Support for social democracy grew in the lead-up to WWI. In 1912, 'the socialists [in this case social democrats] won the majority of the votes in the city and more seats... than any other party in Germany' (Richie 1998, 260). Kaiser William, with his Chancellor von Bülow (Bismarck's successor), undertook to undermine this political grouping, and this in turn undermined his own credibility (*ibid.*). Despite their radical beginnings, the Social Democrats were now moderate, striving for 'gradual social change within a democratic framework instead of for revolution' – a revolutionary grouping was only to form during WWI (*ibid.*, 293).

The urban reform debate intensified in the pre-WWI years, articulating a position that rejected the tenement reality. Experts from a number of disciplines expressed a scathing criticism of Berlin's tenements from planning, social and aesthetic-architectural perspectives (Bodenschatz 1987, 57). Planners located the cause of the tenement evil in the 1862 Building Plan and the speculative process and profit-seeking tenement management that ensued. They could envisage only a complete alternative, either an idealized single-family suburban development on the urban periphery or a block-perimeter development in which the state was to play a stronger role, including that of subsidization. Those with social concerns focused on overcrowding, the perceived social delinquency this encouraged, and the political threat of radicalization and revolution. With no regard for the suggestions that tenants might have had, their solution was one of tenant education and control. Architects in turn criticized the fact that they themselves had no role to play in guiding the aesthetics of this form of housing production, in which one tenement design became the template for the next. Like the planners, they too could envisage only a complete alternative, one entirely guided by their superior aesthetic sensibilities (*ibid.*, 68). The moderation of the Social Democrats at this time was entangled with the urban reform debate. As a result, they became the political bearers of the anti-tenement agenda of bourgeois urban reform (*ibid.*, 80).

Despite the political differences that existed before WWI, Germans united 'under one banner for the first time in history' at the prospect of war, all believing in an inevitable victory in WWI (Richie 1998, 265). While the social democratic left hoped that war would speed up 'the creation of a democratic Germany', industrialists saw the demand for industrial production boosted, and the military recognized an opportunity to maintain a 'hold on power' (*ibid.*, 265–266). All these hopes were dashed with Germany's defeat in WWI, the early signals of which had been withheld (Richie 1998). Before this defeat, however, 'a small splinter group… abandoned the Social Democratic Party' and formed the Bolshevist movement Spartacus in 1916, under the leadership of Rosa Luxemburg and Karl Liebknecht (*ibid.*, 239).[10] A number of street demonstrations in the following two years expressed workers' discontent with the war and those benefiting from it (*ibid.*, 294).

In 1918 Kaiser William, refusing to join the frontline in the last battles of WWI, disappointed his conservative followers. He abdicated (soon fleeing to Holland), ending centuries of the Prussian/German monarchy. Directly after the end of the war, the Social Democrats staged the 'November Revolution' in the streets of Berlin. Liebknecht unsuccessfully contested this, calling for 'a republic modeled on Soviet Russia' (*ibid.*, 300). The Social Democrats formed a government, and in 1919 convened their National Assembly in the town of Weimar, hence the later name 'Weimar Republic'. It was soon clear that the Social Democrats would sideline socialist demands, leaving the socio-economic structure unchanged. Intense contestation ensued between left and right, radicals on both sides recruiting demoralized and desperate returnees from WWI. Germany's defeat produced deep divisions (Richie 1998), while 'Prussia's backward military tradition' was preserved. Assisted by the creation of a hidden (illegal) military force (the *Schwarze Reichswehr*), the military dealt with threats from the 'revolutionary Spartacus Union' (Hall 1998, 245). In January 1919, these forces brutally crushed a Spartacist uprising and murdered its leaders Karl Liebknecht and Rosa Luxemburg. In the previous month (December 1918), an influenza epidemic had reaped several thousand victims in Berlin (*ibid.*, 309). Representations of post-war Berlin in the arts were 'ever more terrible' (*ibid.*, 313). Urban historian Peter Hall (1999, 270) quotes a description of cities by German author and playwright Bertolt Brecht during the time of his 'early work in Berlin': 'beneath them there are sewers, within them there is nothing, and above them there is smoke...'

Inflation had begun during WWI, lasting into the early 1920s and reaching hyper-inflation in 1923. An 'American-inspired Dawes Plan' that included lowering Germany's reparation payments helped stabilize the economy and move it into yet another boom period (Richie 1998, 329). However, economic growth did not translate into the production of further tenements of the dense typologies known thus far – the 1925 Building Ordinance prohibited their construction (Geist and Kürvers 1984, 334). Yet thousands of tenants remained in the existing tenements, where rent control, introduced in the 1920s, led to disinvestment and decay. 'In the course of the 1920s, the catastrophic living conditions hardly improved' (Lefèvre 1990, 238). Increasingly, working class tenants organized against this situation, while landlords tried to blame the conditions on the behavior of tenants (*ibid.*).

The existing tenements were contrasted with a new typology of block perimeter development with large inner-block open spaces (Figure 3.4) dominating residential development up to WWII. In a society ascending out

Figure 3.4: Block perimeter type housing in Treptow (view from the large internal space) as permitted under the 1925 building regulations

Source: Author's photograph (2005)

of the dark post-WWI years, this new housing typology perhaps most vividly symbolized its rejection of Berlin's tenements. Hegemann captures this in his much exaggerated 1930 polemic *Berlin of Stone*. With the onset of economic growth from 1923, a 'change in mood' swept through Berlin and 'was reflected in all forms of art', opening 'the door for the very best of twentieth-century culture' (Richie 1998, 333). While confined to the arts and largely bypassing the general public (Richie 1998), in architecture it saw the flourishing of the Bauhaus School, initiated by the architect Walter Gropius. In the 'heady days of modernist fantasy', architects of this school – Bruno Taut, Hans Scharoun, Martin Wagner and Walter Gropius – carried out commissions for new housing estates on Berlin's urban edge (*ibid.*, 336). These were developed by non-profit 'public service building corporations' (Wiedenhoeft 1985, 175) affiliated to trade unions and in which trade unions played an important role (Mengin 2007, 14). They were justified by the realization that the market could not effectively produce workers' housing (Wiedenhoeft 1985, 173). Between '1924 and 1930 a total of 135 000 dwelling units were built in Berlin using public funds' (*ibid.*, 174).[11] Close on half a million people were housed in a period of seven years (*ibid.*). Built for the ideal nuclear family rather than an identified social group (Mengin 2007, 12), the vast majority took the form of small units in walk-ups of four to five stories (Wiedenhoeft 1985, 174). Architects and planners strove for a low-density city; in effect their orientation was anti-urban. Their ideal was low-rise row housing according to the English model, but financial constraints necessitated the use of more compact models (*ibid.*, 177). Production fluctuated widely, resulting in periodic unemployment in the construction industry and negatively affecting affordability or rents. Poor conditions persisted in much of the existing tenement stock, which made up Berlin's 'Wilhelmine ring' or 'belt', the expanded area of imperial Berlin that had come into being since 1871 under the two successive Williams (I and II) (Elkins 1988, 164). In 1931, this stock still housed 'more than 43 000 families... in badly decayed pre-war buildings, and approximately 40 000 families... in unsuitable attics or basements' (Wiedenhoeft 1985, 175). In addition, 11 000 families still lived in 'barracks and other temporary quarters' (*ibid.*).

With only a shallow enlightenment of the general public during the much mythologized 'golden twenties' (Richie 1998), and in the context of a world recession starting in 1930 (following the Wall Street crash of October 1929 (Hall 1998, 274)), right-wing National Socialists were able to capitalize on continuing fault-lines among Germans. According to Hall (1998, 245), 'society itself remained in upheaval throughout the Weimar period'; this was indeed 'one of the most complex and tragic periods of Berlin history' (Richie 1998, 358). Nationalist authoritarians, with increasing support from within Berlin's universities, challenged the modernist avant-garde as well as the Weimar Republic. In the context of massive unemployment facing graduates in the early 1930s, the nationalists won over the student movement (*ibid.*, 397).

In working class tenement districts such as Wedding, the recession brought about unemployment, hunger, rent distress and eviction threats. This contributed to the radicalization of the population of these districts. The National Socialists, who sought to expand their own support in these areas, violently contested German Communist Party (*Kommunistische Partei Deutschlands* – KPD) support among the working class. Tenant activism through house committees, which had emerged in this context, resulted in localized rent strikes. However, unlike those in Glasgow or New York, these actions met an abrupt end in the ascent to power of the National Socialists, when repression against tenant committees became ever more ruthless (Lefèvre 1990, 239, 241).

Voted into power in 1933, Hitler immediately abused this power by declaring a dictatorship, then leading Germany into the 1939–1945 WWII. The ambitions of his regime were reflected in planning for Berlin – which was driven by the vision of creating the world's greatest or most impressive city. Hitler's 'sycophantic architect Albert Speer worked to create plans for a new city called Germania [in place of Berlin] which was to house 8 million people' (Richie 1998, 470). Hitler's method of control over the population was through the faked delivery of economic recovery: job creation through infrastructure development was financed simply by printing more money. Optimism and hope in turn led to private investment. But Hitler accompanied this with the overarching aim of laying 'the foundation for war' (*ibid.*, 435). 'By the end of the 1930s, Berlin was the largest and most powerful industrial centre in Europe and the biggest single armaments producer on the continent' (*ibid.*, 436).

Contradictions abounded. Nationalist-traditionalist or romantic and anti-modernist 'rhetoric was maintained only when it did not interfere with industrial output' which relied on 'practical modernism' (*ibid.*, 437, 439). Critical of the modernist housing of the 1920s, the Nazi regime idealized a housing typology of small elementary units with steep pitched roofs on the urban outskirts (Wiedenhoeft 1985, 179). The Bauhaus School, which had moved to Berlin before 1933, faced closure by the Nazi regime, 'but many of the items produced under the Nazis clearly owed more to [Bauhaus' founding architect] Gropius than they did to anything else' (Richie 1998, 460). City architecture, including housing, was to become the 'propagandistic instruments of fascist mass manipulation' (Schäche 1989, 132). The gigantic axes and monumental spaces that were envisaged for the city were planned to take up entire districts. If implemented, 'thousands of dwellings would have had to be demolished' (*ibid.*, 134). The plan was to line boulevards with monotonous five-story 'barrack-like housing construction', very little of which was realized (*ibid.*).[12]

Through a 'dual strategy of terror and bribery', the Nazi regime crushed working class organization, whether trade unions or political parties, and proceeded to control 'every aspect of workers' lives' (Richie, 437). Social Democrats, too, faced severe repression (*ibid.*, 539). At the same time, the higher ranks exploited every opportunity for self-enrichment, also through 'the forced sale of Jewish-owned property' which formed part of the sinister and tragic strategy of Jewish extermination (*ibid.*, 444). The prime minister could seize magnificent estates 'and hand them out at will' (*ibid.*, 443). Eventually, '[t]he rot from the top began to work its way through the entire system of government' (*ibid.*, 445). Hitler expanded the public sector, allowing it to bloat with unqualified people receiving their positions through loyalty and nepotism. 'The Prusso-German bureaucracy, hitherto famous for its incorruptibility, was inundated with new employees who had no respect for its previous good name' (*ibid.*).

Berlin's population never reached 8 million under Nazi rule, but it increased into WWII, rising to an unprecedented 4.2 million in 1942 and peaking at 4.47 million in 1943, the highest population ever reached in the city (except for the temporary mass influx of refugees following the war). The destruction and casualties of the following two years substantially dented Berlin's population figures (the city faced attack only towards the end of the war). By 1945, at the close of WWII, its population had dropped to 2.8 million. The war had destroyed 35 per cent of its housing stock, predominantly tenements, and severely damaged a further 35 per cent (Wiedenhoeft 1985, 180). A total of more than 600 000 homes were lost (Presse- und Informationsamt Berlin 1993, 9).

What followed for the surviving population of Berlin under the 'soviet "liberators"' is described as having 'depths reached only by the Nazis before them. For two months, Berlin was completely surrounded, cut off from the rest of the world and at the mercy of rapacious victors... violence did not cease with victory' (Richie 1998, 607). The arrival of up to 20 000 refugees a day from the east exacerbated hunger in Berlin (*ibid.*, 635). People were rounded up on the streets to join the Soviet crews tasked with dismantling the city – first clearing rubble, then dismantling the factories for reassembly in the Soviet Union (*ibid.*, 613). 'Stalin had no interest in sharing Berlin or Germany with the west, nor did he share the western vision of the eventual creation of a democratic, capitalist German state' (*ibid.*, 630). Although the partitioning of Berlin by the winning allies was already being discussed in 1943 when Germany's defeat was certain, Stalin disagreed in 1948 when the division was implemented. In June of that year, he blockaded West Berlin, a crisis that marked the beginning of the Cold War. The Americans responded with an airlift of western goods into the city. The division of Berlin into separate sectors was cemented into East and West Berlin later in 1948 through two separate municipal administrations – one for the USSR, the other for the French, British and American sectors (Niggl 1989, 57).

Immediately after the war, modern architects and planners, including the French Le Corbusier, developed visions for a modern Berlin (Bodenschatz 1990). 'Le Corbusier wanted to flatten the entire city centre and replace it with gigantic rectangular skyscrapers' (Richie 1998, 705). The architect Hans Scharoun suggested in 1946 that the WWII bombing of Berlin had had the positive effect of loosening or de-densifying the tenement cityscape and that this needed to be continued through systematic planning. In the visions of architects of the time, housing estates were to flourish on the rubble of the tenements (Bodenschatz 1990, 22). Exactly like the modern town planners who were put to the task of designing the colonial city of Nairobi at that very time, Berlin's modern planners (with reference to American practice) envisaged a new city structured into neighborhood cells of 4 000 people each (Geist and Küvers 1989, 285). To their disappointment, tenements were instead given the most urgently needed repairs and made habitable once again. Only in the 1950s did redevelopment programs and initiatives such as the International Building Exhibition give West Berlin's planners the opportunity to demonstrate alternatives to the tenement city (Bodenschatz 1990). They prepared visions for the whole of Berlin; town planning across the different sectors of the city converged. The first neighborhood unit to be implemented was in the Friedrichshain district in the Soviet sector (Geist and Küvers 1989, 305). The 'socialist housing complex' (*sozialistischer Wohnkomplex*) superseded this model at a much larger scale. The Soviets developed the first such complex in 1958 along the renamed Stalinallee in the eastern city centre. They began to apply the newly developed prefabricated slab construction method (*Plattenbau*) (*ibid.*).

In the meantime, recovery and repair of the built environment, including the tenement stock, was slow. Refugees continued to seek entry into the west through Berlin, the refugee crisis reaching 'epidemic proportions in 1958' (Richie 1998, 713). The unexpected sealing off of West Berlin by the Soviets in August 1961 and construction of the Berlin Wall put an abrupt end to this migration, and resulted in separate and distinct trajectories for West and East Berlin.

In East Berlin the state drove a policy of 'de-commercialization of urban development and housing construction' under which it nationalized land ownership (Häußermann and Kapphan 2000, 59). It took '[l]arge sections of housing stock into public ownership' and subjected housing 'to state planning and control', while keeping the rents low (Reimann 1997, 301). The totalitarian socialist state also subscribed to architectural modernism, which Soviet architects developed. Their ideas were very similar to those of the French architect Le Corbusier. They envisaged 'new cities in the open countryside, in which everyone would live in gigantic collective apartment blocks' (Hall 1990, 211). As a symbol of state socialism, the state began rolling out a new form of rental housing, the monotonous, industrially produced tower block-type mass housing.

Only a decade later, at the beginning of the 1970s, did a shift in Soviet policy under Brezhnev lead to tentative cooperation with West Germany (*ibid.*, 730). At this time, the socialist ruling party also committed itself to improving living conditions. It pledged the construction of 500 000 housing units in 5 years, undertook to build 20 000 of these in Berlin, and promised 'to solve the housing question as a social problem by 1990' (Geist and Kürvers 1989, 529). In this conception, the historic tenements had no role to play in solving the housing problem. The East German state planned to replace them with modern tower block-type housing stock (Bernet 2004, 416). In 1989, with one year left to reach the target, the state disintegrated. Inasmuch as solving the housing problem meant eradication of old tenements, the target was nowhere near being met. In 1988, only one-third of the population of East Berlin could be housed in the new modernist mass housing estates (Häußermann and Kapphan 2000, 68).

Nevertheless, in 1978, the World Bank admitted that the East German state had achieved 'a higher standard of living than Britain' (Richie 1998, 748). This was through a combination of social policies, including industrial mass production of housing, and access to consumer goods (*ibid.*). A Communal Housing Administration provided for basic tenant-initiated maintenance of the old tenement stock (Liebmann 2002). However, despite advancing living conditions, the totalitarian system relied on repression. By the mid-1980s, it was evident that the centralized system 'was not working' (*ibid.*, 753). Gorbachev's reforms from 1985 onward 'unwittingly unleashed a demand for profound change which he had not foreseen' (*ibid.*, 769). The East German state resisted change until its sudden collapse in 1989. East Berlin's historic tenements made up part of the stage set for this collapse. The old tenement district Prenzlauer Berg in East Berlin had attracted a small scene of 'alternative' squatters, 'dissidents and other outcasts who were not awarded housing or who were not comfortable in other parts of the city' (Levine 2004, 92). In Prenzlauer Berg, 'the old ramshackle flat' of one of the dissident leaders 'became a focal point for reformers' (Richie 1998, 831). Demonstrations in this district in 1989, though paralleled across East German cities, 'helped lead to the fall of the Wall' (Levine 2004, 92).

In West Berlin city authorities had demolished damaged housing stock since the mid-1950s. In 1961, they carried through the first demolition of habitable and until recently inhabited tenement stock for the sake of de-densification and renewal (Geist and Küvers 1998, 530). Two years later, they proclaimed large urban renewal areas. 'Renewal' was an ambitious approach, meaning complete demolition and redevelopment. The Wedding Brunnenstrasse Renewal Area was the largest renewal program in Germany, and indeed probably in Europe (Bodenschatz 1990). 'At this time, there was no protest from affected people. The urban renewal programme appeared to enjoy comprehensive cultural legitimacy' (*ibid.*, 23). However, this was to change. The construction of the Berlin Wall in 1961 was perceived in West Berlin as a betrayal by the Americans, who had not sufficiently defended the city. A political anti-American counter-culture began to shape the city, in stark contrast to America's perception of itself as Berlin's savior during the 1948 airlift. With the emergence of a radical left student movement, conflict simmered in West Berlin's universities and broke into the streets in the late 1960s (Richie 1998). The formation of the Red Army Faction saw the militarization of Berlin's radicals, with violence and murders peaking in 1977. The West German state curbed the career prospects of those with proven involvement in anti-constitutional radicalism. Students themselves became discontented with the constant disruptions that had led to decreasing standards at Berlin's universities. In the late 1970s and into the 1980s, the counter-culture engaged more actively with the built environment. '[E]ver more young people became squatters', particularly in Berlin's former working class districts (*ibid.*, 784). The housing shortage which necessitated squatting resulted only in part from the destruction of buildings during WWII and the city's spatial confinement because of the wall (which separated West Berlin not only from East Berlin but also from its hinterland).[13] Tenement buildings were also made derelict as a result of economic policy. 'Immense tax write-offs encouraged speculators to buy old buildings and allow them to deteriorate; they would then have to be ripped down and replaced with expensive apartment or office blocks... Berlin activists began to identify derelict buildings and moved in as squatters' (*ibid.*, 785). The years 1980 and 1981 were marked by tenement occupations or 'squats', and violent street protest (Häußermann and Kapphan 2000, 76). By 1981, squatters occupied over 150 buildings in Berlin (Richie 1998, 785). As a strategy to pacify the protesters, the authorities replaced the policy of tenement demolition with one of 'cautious urban renewal'. This made public funds available for the upgrading of the existing tenement stock without disrupting resident communities (Bodenschatz 1987, 15).

By 1985, Berlin's combined population had recovered to just over 3 million, with West Berlin at 1.86 million and East Berlin at 1.2 million (Senator für Stadtentwicklung und Umweltschutz 1986, 12). Immediately following unification, when I spent two years out of South Africa working in a landscape architecture office in Berlin, the city experienced a massive under-supply of housing. This forced me into a variety of short-term sub-lets, mostly illegal, in different tenement districts of the city. However, Berlin's population has since decreased, also shifting to the low density housing estates that mushroomed in Berlin's post-unification hinterland (landscape architects were tasked with mitigating their environmental externalities). Vacancies in former East Berlin's industrially produced tower blocks impacted negatively on the housing market, compelling the city authorities to invest heavily in their implosion or partial demolition. When I accompanied my class of postgraduate housing students from Johannesburg on an invitation to the Technical University of Berlin in 2007, this mass reduction of modern housing stock was the most disturbing impression with which the students returned to consider the African housing deficit.

A number of processes and policies triggered large-scale gentrification in post-unification Berlin. One was a comprehensive restitution program which redressed the property injustices of the Nazi regime and expropriations by the East German state (Häußermann and Kapphan 2000, 180).[14] Up to the mid-1990s, this process inhibited investment. However, it has since unleashed levels of investment that were not anticipated (Häußermann and Kapphan 2000, 182). Most former owners or heirs sold the properties after these were returned to them. In cases of unclaimed Jewish property, the Jewish Claims Conference did likewise, using the proceeds to capitalize a fund for victims of Jewish persecution (*ibid.*). The restitution process did not recreate the former ownership structure (*ibid.*, 183). Instead, a 'professional structure of real estate ownership made up of real estate companies, bond assets [*Fondsvermögen*] and depreciation companies [*Abschreibungsgesellschaften*] established itself' (*ibid.*). Exploitative professional companies upgraded and modernized the tenement properties and sold the individual units under sectional title (*ibid.*).

Once the site of the East German counter-culture, the tenement district Prenzlauer Berg with its good location became trendy after reunification, rendering it 'ripe for gentrification' (Levine 2004, 92). In the 1990s, it became 'Europe's largest renewal area' (Holm 2006, 12). The municipality's aim was to achieve as much as possible, as quickly as possible and with as little public funds as possible. It relied heavily on private capital, which in turn led to increased living costs and inevitable displacements (*ibid.*, 14).

Elsewhere too, Berlin's historic tenement stock increased in popularity (Figure 3.5). Its real estate value, which hinges on convenience, charm and ability to be adapted to new lifestyles and demands, has guaranteed historic tenements a future in Berlin. However, despite East German initiatives to repair and upgrade them, after the fall of the Berlin Wall many pre-1925 tenement units in East Berlin still shared communal toilets, were poorly insulated and lacked central heating. A 'considerable need for... improvement' of Berlin's existing tenement stock

Figure 3.5: Berlin's convenient and much sought-after tenement environment today

Source: Author's photograph, Kreuzberg (2005)

as well as a 'public sector budgetary crisis' resulted in the introduction of tax incentives for those 'buying and investing in old houses' (Reimann 1997, 312). Therefore, at the dawn of the new millennium, the dilemma posed by past state neglect of the tenement stock in part paved the way for the new chain of private capitalization, as speculative interests were deliberately harnessed to the upgrading of the old tenement stock. The result is further gentrification and class stratification. Market interest in the old tenement stock is underpinned by its desirable urban quality, a characteristic that defies out-and-out condemnation of this housing form.

Figure 3.6: Schematic diagram of Berlin's history

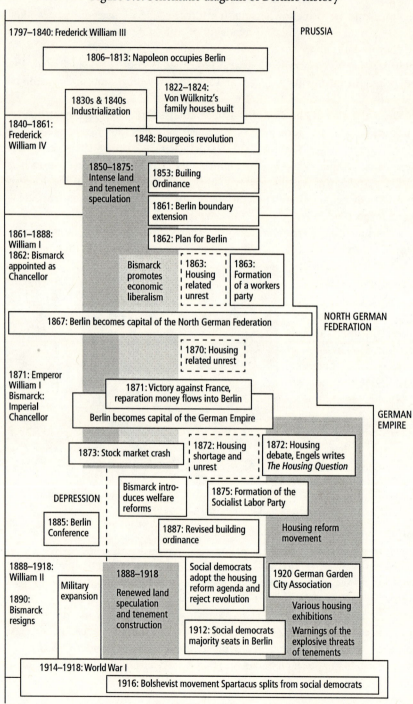

Figure 3.6: Schematic diagram of Berlin's history (continued)

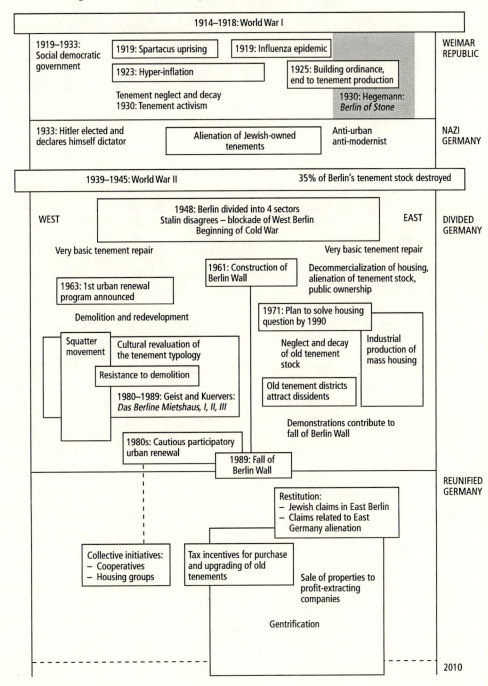

1914–1918: World War I

| | | WEIMAR REPUBLIC |

1919–1933: Social democratic government

1919: Spartacus uprising

1919: Influenza epidemic

1923: Hyper-inflation

1925: Building ordinance, end to tenement production

Tenement neglect and decay
1930: Tenement activism

1930: Hegemann: *Berlin of Stone*

1933: Hitler elected and declares himself dictator

Alienation of Jewish-owned tenements

Anti-urban anti-modernist

NAZI GERMANY

1939–1945: World War II — 35% of Berlin's tenement stock destroyed

WEST — 1948: Berlin divided into 4 sectors / Stalin disagrees – blockade of West Berlin / Beginning of Cold War — EAST — DIVIDED GERMANY

Very basic tenement repair — Very basic tenement repair

1961: Construction of Berlin Wall

Decommercialization of housing, alienation of tenement stock, public ownership

1963: 1st urban renewal program announced

Demolition and redevelopment

1971: Plan to solve housing question by 1990

Squatter movement — Cultural revaluation of the tenement typology

Neglect and decay of old tenement stock

Industrial production of mass housing

Resistance to demolition

Old tenement districts attract dissidents

1980–1989: Geist and Kuervers: *Das Berline Mietshaus, I, II, III*

Demonstrations contribute to fall of Berlin Wall

1980s: Cautious participatory urban renewal

1989: Fall of Berlin Wall

REUNIFIED GERMANY

Restitution:
– Jewish claims in East Berlin
– Claims related to East Germany alienation

Collective initiatives:
– Cooperatives
– Housing groups

Tax incentives for purchase and upgrading of old tenements

Sale of properties to profit-extracting companies

Gentrification

2010

The same quality motivates resistance to market displacement. In the context of a global shift in planning towards community participation, a few collective initiatives of private individuals in Berlin (Häußermann and Kapphan 2000, 183) have managed to insert themselves (with some state support) into this aggressive and state-incentivized market. A range of 'housing groups' pool capital, supplemented by special subsidies, in order to collectively acquire, upgrade and then either individually own tenement units or manage and inhabit a renovated tenement as a cooperative (Heyden 2007; Lafond 2007). While labeled, from my perspective unfairly, as a further dimension of gentrification (Holm 2009), these small-scale initiatives defend existing residents' rights to the historical tenement neighborhoods and their inherent qualities. Their impact, however, remains minimal.

What needs to be highlighted as perhaps the biggest structural change in the tenement market since its inception is the dominant real estate trend of selling off former rental units under sectional title. Even if individual units are purchased as small investments and once more rented to others, as is often the case, this cements an end to Berlin's tenement as a rented house, with one individual owner. Developers have valued the spatial quality of the commercial streets with cafés, pubs, stores and neighborhood services facing onto wide pavements, as well as the public transport convenience that is made possible by the density of the tenement development. Reaped by a new chain of extractive, speculative interests, these qualities are marketed to a new class of uncritical and 'hip' young professionals.

Endnotes

1 Where I quote directly from German literature in this and the following two chapters, the translation is my own.

2 In this context, a new culture of patriotic romanticism emerged in what was previously 'the centre of Prussian enlightenment' (Richie 1998, 97). Ominous claims 'to German cultural superiority, and, later racial purity as well' were made at the time (*ibid.*, 98).

3 Hall (1990, 32) uncritically adopts this explanation in his brief coverage of 19th century Berlin in *Cities of Tomorrow*.

4 In 1800, Berlin had a population of 173 000, compared to Amsterdam with 217 000, Paris with 581 000 and London with 1 117 000 people (Hall 1997). Vienna's population was approximately 232 000 (Hall 1998).

5 German playwright Gerhard Hauptmann's famous 1892 play *Die Weber* (*The Weavers*), set during an 1844 workers' revolt in Silesia (the *Schlesische Weberaufstand*), depicts the extreme plight of this class (Hauptmann 1892/1963). The play was banned in the 1890s (Richie 1998, 187).

6 Now called the Humboldt University in Berlin.

7 '*Baracke*', similar to the Portuguese/Brazilian term *baracão*, means shack or hut, not to be confused with the English word 'barrack'.

8   Hegemann (1930, 43) argues that land speculation in Berlin was fuelled by the abandonment of land taxes and their replacement with taxes on goods. He suggests that in English cities, where there was neither absolutism nor abandonment of land taxes, this intense land speculation (which contributed to high land prices and therefore dense development) did not arise.

9   The controversial British explorer Henry Morton Stanley and a crudely inaccurate map of Africa guided the conference. Stanley was the only participant who had actually set foot on the continent. His explorations had 'ignited the great African land rush' (Hochschild, 2002, 86), which was 'well under way... by the time of the Berlin Conference' (Freund 1984, 96).

10   The movement was '[n]amed after the leader of a Roman slave rebellion' (Richie 1998, 293).

11   Public funds assisted in the construction of two million dwelling units in the Weimar Republic from 1919 to 1932 (Mengin 2007, 11).

12   An example of urban housing construction under the Nazi regime can be seen along Grazer Damm near Innsbrucker Platz (Schäche 1989, 134).

13   West Berlin was an island of about 450 km², surrounded by a wall of 164 km (Niggl 1989, 62–63).

14   East Berlin had been 'the centre of the German Jewish community' (Reimann 1997, 303).

Chapter 4

Planning, speculation and the creation of Berlin's tenement typology

Berlin's urban planning in the second half of the 19th century is widely associated with the name 'Hobrecht'. A 'master builder' by profession (an occupation that was closer to that of an engineer than a planner), James Hobrecht was accidentally drawn into Berlin's planning initiative. His approach to the 1862 Plan for Berlin was cautious, taking account of existing conditions including the scarcity of urban land. Hobrecht consciously avoided the wasteful dimensions and demolitions that his slightly earlier contemporary, civic planner 'Baron' Haussmann, destined for Paris. Under Napoleon III (initially French president following the revolution in 1848, then emperor from 1852 to 1870), Haussmann's visionary but ruthless planning for Paris was implemented in the 1850s and 1860s. It drove 'a network of straight and broad roads through a crowded and ancient city, remorselessly demolishing everything which stood in their way' (Girouard 1985, 286). Friedrich Engels (1887/1935, 75) slates Haussmann's displacement of the working class from centrally located quarters.

Haussmann's planning served Napoleon's interests in Paris, including that 'of making barricade fighting more difficult' (Engels 1887/1935, 74). By contrast, the planning authority in Berlin allowed Hobrecht's modest planning proposal (which Engels did not find it necessary to mention or criticize in *The Housing Question*) to be adjusted before its adoption, in order to better serve the interests of land speculators. Despite all the demolition and displacement Haussmann caused in Paris, he gained and regained a 'reputation as one of the greatest urbanists of all time' (Harvey 2008, 27). Hobrecht, instead, is commonly blamed for having created the largest and densest tenement city in Europe.

One characteristic of the plan adopted for Berlin in 1862 was the excessive size of the street blocks. In combination with other factors, this brought about high residential densities and a unique tenement typology. Plots were extremely deep and developed to saturation, with only the courtyards mandated by the 1853 and 1887 Building Ordinances left unbuilt on. While there are many fascinating aspects and features of the adopted plan and its implementation, I focus here in particular on relevant content relating to the large street blocks and deep plots, and the implementation (as well as adjustment) of the plan through the production of tenement districts.

Planning process in the context of liberalism and speculation: myth, perception and fact

An inner city plan for Berlin, the so-called 'Schmidt Plan', appeared between 1827 and 1830, just as the city began to assume its industrial status within Europe. Given the rapid changes that occurred over the next two decades, the authorities considered a revision of this plan in the early 1850s, but eventually decided that a new plan was required altogether (Bernet 2004, 402). This would expand the built-up area of Berlin extensively. The city extended its boundary in 1861, a year before adopting the new plan.

While planning for Berlin fell under the police president and his administration, it was not entirely centralized. A decree 'provided for the involvement of the municipal authorities in the planning process. Thus according to the Prussian City Code of 1853, a commission was established' in which the city council participated (*ibid.*). James Hobrecht, who at the time was working on a long-distance railway line, received a request to stand in for an ill master builder who, since 1852, had been working on the revision of the Schmidt Plan. The police president then proposed Hobrecht as leader of the 'Commission to Prepare the Building Plans for Berlin's Surrounds' (Geist and Kürvers 1980, 485). With confirmation of the position in April 1859, Hobrecht was instructed to link the design for the plan to a drainage system for the city (*ibid.*).

Geist and Kürvers (1980) provide extensive archival detail of the lead-up to the final plan. With Hobrecht's common sense approach to planning, surveying work began immediately so that the plan could be based on a detailed capturing of existing buildings, paths and streets. Hobrecht divided the area to be covered by the plan into 14 sections, developed the design and explanatory text for each and submitted his drafts individually as they reached completion. The commission considered the plan section by section. By mid-1860, when Hobrecht had submitted his design and explanation for various sections, the Minister of Trade sent him on an almost three-month journey with a small team, including an engineer. Their task was to study the existing drainage systems in the cities of Hamburg, Paris, London and other English cities. Hobrecht used this opportunity to also make observations on street and building planning in these cities.

In 1861, after returning from these travels, Hobrecht included his observations on street planning in the explanatory texts of remaining sections of the Building Plan. These observations, which reflected common sense, went well beyond drainage systems. While he acknowledged the attraction of front gardens in side streets, he pointed out that investors who were merely held to a building line would not be inclined to actually plant front gardens. He also considered that front gardens would hinder small-scale commercial activity, where buildings have shops on their ground floors (Geist and Kürvers 1980, 503). He therefore suggested that not all side streets needed the additional width for front gardens. Hobrecht further considered it unlikely that side streets would need to be widened in future to allow for increased traffic. Referring to examples from London, he proposed greening the centre of streets, while some streets could have front gardens only on one side. He questioned the principle he had observed in Paris, whereby the beauty of streets was assumed to depend only upon their width. For Hobrecht, the residential house or apartment building should not require monumental treatment (as in the wide streets of Paris). Instead, its continued or combined mass should please the eye (*ibid.*).

During Hobrecht's travels, the submitted plans were sent via the police department to the magistrate and a group of delegates from the city representatives (councilors), constituted for the assessment of the proposed Building Plan. The councilors in turn informed landowners or speculators who would be affected by various proposals in the plans. After Hobrecht's return, the entire year of 1861 was spent in negotiation over the dimensions of streets, street blocks and public open spaces. Participants in these negotiations were 'landowners, the magistrate and city representatives on the one side and the Police Department with Hobrecht, on the other side' (Geist and Kürvers 1980, 491).

Landowners of large plots objected to streets crossing their land, arguing that these proposed roads were superfluous and would result in unsuitably shaped property boundaries (*ibid.*, 492). The Planning Commission was of the view 'that living conditions would benefit from the large construction lots with interior planting, the construction of numerous squares, a climatically favourable design and, finally, ample street widths' (Bernet 2004, 408, citing Geist and Kürvers 1980, 150). They did not foresee the model that maximized usage of a deep plot through the construction of several backyard buildings behind one another (Geist and Kürvers 1980, 505). Agreements for each section of the plan were based on a compromise signed by all participants.

In the second half of 1861, a further commission on which the city and the state were jointly represented met several times to negotiate the final design, which was then incorporated into the Building Plan (*ibid.*, 492). In March 1862, the Ministry of Trade considered the Building Plan and requested further adjustments. Four months later, the Building Plan overcame its final hurdle, approval by the Prussian king (William I).[1] According to Geist and Kürvers' detailed account, the separate sections of the plan were then printed at a scale of 1:4 000 and made available commercially to any interested party (*ibid.*, 493).

The original instruction to Hobrecht was to plan for plot depths that would allow for a single backyard (Geist and Kürvers 1980), which was common for tenements across European cities (Girouard 1985, 338). However, a letter from the police department stated that

> lots were to be designed as generously as possible. This was to occur not only out of the consideration for the expected land needs of industry, but also for health reasons. Sufficient air and light should be guaranteed. (Bernet 2004, 408, citing Lubowitzki 1990, 74).

Through the negotiating process, plots ended up three to four times the original size but with no clarity on their future use. The private speculator had the discretion to decide on the internal access to these deep plots. Access did not have to consist of streets, and could instead be achieved through a series of inter-leading backyards. The latter benefitted the developer, who was under no obligation to make his land publicly accessible (Geist and Kürvers 1980). However, '[b]ecause of the lot size, [later] reformers held the plan responsible for the "inevitable" construction of the *Mietskasernen*' (Bernet 2004, 408, again citing Lubowitzki 1990). Indeed, many commentators blamed Hobrecht directly and the 1862 Plan assumed the name 'Hobrecht-Plan'. To this day, it is often referred to as the 'infamous *Hobrecht-Plan*' (Häußermann and Siebel 1996, 79). Hobrecht was neither responsible for the plan with its plot and street block sizes nor for the subsequent unfolding of the speculative processes that shaped the production of Berlin's tenement environment up to the 1920s.

Geist and Kürvers (1980) make several observations to refute the personal blame placed on Hobrecht for the density and squalor of 19th century Berlin. Firstly, the planning commission had hoped that generous block-perimeter buildings would avoid the dense und unhygienic development model of the inner city. However, the legal instrument for preventing dense and unsanitary housing did not exist (*ibid.*, 505). Secondly, only areas bordering on the city center saw implementation according to the approved 1862 Building Plan. Later infrastructure, such as the rail ring, impacted on the execution of large parts of the original plan (*ibid.*, 495). Thirdly, Hobrecht personally planned a sanitation system that drained the city's effluent into peripherally located sewerage plants rather than into the River Spree, as his contemporaries were suggesting. It took the state 10 years of negotiations to agree to the costs of Hobrecht's sanitation system (*ibid.*). This drastically improved living conditions throughout Berlin (*ibid.*, 497).

Geist and Kürvers (*ibid.*, 496) also point out that the influential and much cited 1930 book by Werner Hegemann (*Das steinerne Berlin* or *Berlin of Stone*) over-emphasized Hobrecht's role in the 1862 Plan, while its criticism of the 'Hobrecht-Plan' is based less on an analysis of the plan itself than on an incorrect and inadequately referenced adoption of early critiques of the plan. The historian Alexandra Richie (1998), whom I rely on extensively to piece together Berlin's 19th century history, cites Hegemann (1930) (which still remains in print) uncritically, also not questioning this condemnation. She describes the 1862 Building Plan as a quintessentially Prussian piece of work which was brilliant, meticulous, all-encompassing, and fundamentally flawed... [T]he combination of the relentless wave of people coupled with the demands for burgeoning industry for cheaply housed labourers encouraged [the police president] to make disastrous decisions [of approving rather than rejecting the plan] which turned the 'Athens on the Spree' into the biggest working-class slum on the continent. As the peasants huddled in their tent cities, huge barracks were built within the city walls which would soon house them like virtual prisoners. (Richie 1998, 161)

Richie continues: '[f]or his part Hobrecht wanted to create a vast number of high density residential districts between the old Customs Wall and the S-Bahn ring railway... Hobrecht's rental barracks are still grim' (*ibid.*, 162).

Present-day misrepresentations aside, it is useful to quote Bernet (2004, 403) on the reception of the plan at the time. In some ways, this directly extended the contestation that had informed the planning processes:

The plan was firmly rejected by both conservatives and liberals... In the eyes of many real estate speculators, the plan was an impediment and a first step towards an eventual restriction of free enterprise. By contrast, social reformers thought the plan's regulations did not go far enough.

Plan, regulation and the densest tenement typology in Europe

Like the 1862 Building Plan, the Building Ordinance of 1853 also resulted from discussions (in the 1840s) between the city authority and landowners (Geist and Kürvers 1980, 505). The Building Ordinance adopted in 1853 regulated the growing trend of developing tenements at the highest possible density. It determined the building line ('*Fluchtlinie*') and required that backyard buildings be accessed by a 2.5 m-wide entrance gate through the street-facing building to allow access to fire engines (Häußermann and Siebel 1996). Minimum backyard dimensions were 5.6 m × 5.6 m to allow a fire engine to turn (Rodenstein 1988, 110). The Ordinance determined the building height according to street width. In streets of a 15 m width the Ordinance permitted buildings to reach a height of 11.3 m. In wider streets, this could increase (Häußermann and Siebel 1996).

A revised Building Ordinance in 1887 reduced the maximum permitted number of occupants per property of 20 m × 56 m (the assumed standard plot size) from 325 to 167 people, and increased the minimum dimensions of backyards from 32 m² (5.6 m × 5.6 m) to 60 m² (Treue 1969, 38). However, the increased minimum backyard dimensions had little impact on the quality of tenements as by this time most tenements were being built with larger than minimum backyards (Berning et al. 1994, 3). The 1871 and 1897 Building Ordinances did not revise the backyard size.

The dense construction of backyard tenements for poor households was in part brought about less by the 1862 Building Plan than by the 1853 Building Ordinance, which (until 1887) allowed for a relatively small minimum backyard size (Wietog 1981, 128). The 1853 Building Ordinance formed the basis of the 1862 Building Plan for Berlin, which did not set out to challenge the regulations in the Ordinance. However, as neither the 1853 nor the 1887 Building Ordinance stipulated the number of successive courtyards or residential buildings per plot, the dimensions of street blocks and property boundaries became an important determinant of density. Only the new Building Ordinance of 1925 disallowed backyard buildings for independent residential units altogether. For the latter part of the 19th century, then, the intersection between plan and ordinance determined residential density and typology in Berlin: the 1862 Plan and the deviations from this plan permitted generous plot sizes, while the Building Ordinance set out courtyard and building height dimensions.

The 1862 Building Plan contains a street hierarchy of three levels: 56.4 m-wide ring roads; 33.84–45.12 m-wide connecting streets; and 18.8 m-wide side streets. The dimensions of street blocks were based on the old '*Luisenstadt*'. The Plan envisaged these blocks as having perimeter buildings with gardens or industrial usage in the block interior (Geist and Kürvers 1980, 501). While it intended street blocks to be 120–150 m × 75 m, in the urban expansion that followed they were three to four times this size, allowing for multiple backyard buildings on all properties (Häußermann and Siebel 1996, 79). Confirming this trend, Berning et al. (1994) provide examples of street block sizes of 200–400 m × 150–200 m (Figure 4.1). Based on Hobrecht's detailed survey, the plan took into account existing agricultural plot boundaries, existing rural paths and streets, as well as existing buildings (Geist

and Kürvers 1980, 501). As a result, the street layout, plot shapes and plot dimensions are often irregular (Figure 4.2). Developers' frustration and lack of innovation in the case of sharply angled plots is illustrated in Figure 1.6 at the end of Chapter 1. It shows a standard symmetrical tenement façade in the district of Wedding, Berlin. On the pointed side of the plot the façade is fake, with no rooms behind it. This is strikingly paralleled in a tenement in Kawangware,

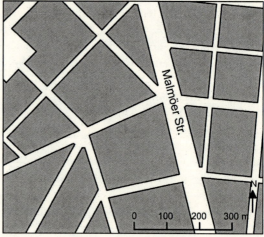

Figure 4.1: Section of the 1862 Plan for Berlin showing large street blocks

Source: Redrawn from Geist and Kürvers (1980, 489)

Nairobi, where investor decision-making in tenement design today has strong parallels with 19th century practice in Berlin.

Hegemann (1930), in his scathing and at times unsubstantiated or exaggerated attack on the 1862 Building Plan, criticizes the fact that the plan only provided for a higher order of streets and did not detail the residential side streets. While it is unclear whether his further legal explanation is factual, it does seem plausible: he argues that a

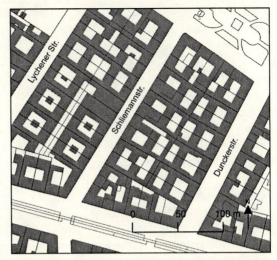

Figure 4.2: Example of dense tenement development on large plots

Source: Redrawn from Geist and Kürvers (1984, 233)

law to allow private land to be declared undevelopable or to be left unbuilt for the purposes of public road construction was passed only in 1875. Up to that date, the state had to alienate land (by purchase) from private owners for road construction. The state tried to appease landowners and induce them into the free alienation of their land, without much success – the 1850 Constitution had increased individual rights over property. Out of fiscal austerity, the state decided not to spend money on constructing residential side streets. Further, the municipality was not required to purchase this land, and the state had no means to oblige the municipality to do so. This allowed the landowners or developers to maximize density on the overly large plots (Hegemann 1930, 308), resulting in what Hegemann refers to as damaging urban densities through large, densely packed 'rental barracks'. Indulging in his trademark polemic, he passes judgment on the development of

> up to six poorly lit backyards… condemning four million future residents of Berlin to live in housing, worse than what the silliest devil or the most diligent secret councilor or land speculator could have conceived. (*ibid.*, 294).

Standard plot sizes of 20 m street-facing width and 56 m depth resulted from the so-called '*Hobrechtplan*' (Ott 1989, 138). However, Hegemann (1930, 302) mentions that plots of 20 m × 56 m existed before the 1862 Building Plan and suggests that the 1862 Plan allowed for even deeper properties. In reality, plot dimensions throughout Berlin's tenement districts varied considerably. Geist and Kürvers (1984, 264) provide building plans for tenements on a range of plot shapes and sizes, for instance 16.3 m × 40.4 m, 24 m × 52 m and 30.5 m × 28.6 m. Geist and Kürvers (*ibid.*, 233) also show how large parts of the Prenzlauer Berg district, developed only around 1890, had larger street blocks and plot dimensions than earlier districts, thus uniformly allowing for two courtyards on each property. Becker and Jacob (1992) in turn show how, around 1886, parts of the district of Moabit developed on plots of no more than 16.7 m × 37.5 m. By contrast, the atypical plot dimensions of the infamous Meyer's Hof, developed in 1873/4 with its six parallel tenement buildings (in

addition to an administrative section and bathhouse at the rear end of the property), was eight times this size, namely 39.8 m × 141.32 m (Geist and Kürvers 1984, 141) (Figure 4.3).

On the basis of deep plots, three tenement types (Figure 4.4) emerged at the intersection of the 1853 building regulations and the subdivisions under the 1862 Plan for Berlin (Geist and Kürvers 1980, 520). None are distinguishable from the street, as all three typologies share a uniform, usually symmetrical façade with the obligatory 2.5 m-wide entrance gate. Critics of Berlin's tenement typology described the generosity of the decorated façades as veils hiding the squalor that became evident only once one passed into the backyards (Berning et

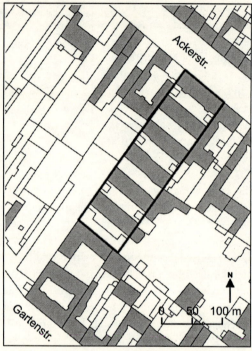

Figure 4.3: Plot layout of Meyer's Hof

Source: Redrawn from Geist and Kürvers (1984, 214)

al. 1994, viii). Geist and Kürvers' (1980, 520) three tenement types are as follows:

1. One or more courtyards surrounded by side and back buildings. On narrow plots the variation of this type is a building only on one side, the courtyard then facing either onto the courtyard next door, or less attractively onto the bare fire wall of the neighboring tenement.
2. Long narrow side buildings stretching from the street-facing building through to the back of the property. A narrow property has only one 'side wing'.
3. A series of parallel buildings stacked across the property. The plot dimensions determine the width and number of these buildings. This type, though not the most common, applies to No. 40 Liebenwalder Strasse in the district of Wedding, for which I later discuss the speculative development process. This tenement has three backyards defined by parallel buildings. At a much larger scale, the

infamous Meyer's Hof, with its six monotonous parallel backyard buildings, also exemplified this type. This tenement, though atypical, is documented in great detail in Geist and Kürvers' second volume (1984) and mentioned in most publications on Berlin's built environment history (Ott 1989, 140; Richie 1998, 163). In the late 19th and early 20th century debate about tenements, Meyer's Hof epitomized developer or landlord greed with little or no concern for living conditions, light or air.

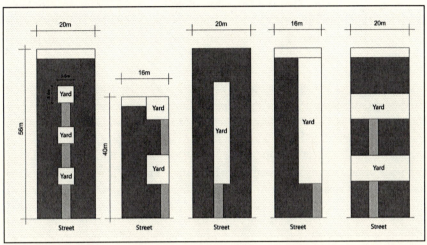

Figure 4.4: Layout of Geist and Kürvers' tenement typologies, from left to right: Type One (first two diagrams), Type Two (second two diagrams), Type Three (last diagram).

Source: Geist and Kürvers (1980, 234)

As is already evident from Hobrecht's concern for street-facing commercial activity on tenement ground floors, an understanding prevailed at the time that land uses should to some extent be mixed. Street-facing shops and light industrial activity in backyards formed an integral part of the tenement-scape and contributed to its functioning. This mixed use quality, which supports economic development, livelihoods and convenience, was to be lost through the dictum of land use separation in modern town planning from the beginning of the 20th century. Urbanists rediscovered and promoted the value of mixed use from the 1960s onward. Jane Jacobs, in her 1961 book *The Death and Life of Great American Cities*, calls for a recognition of the diversity of use sustained by high residential density. I return later in more detail to the kind of commercial activity that flourished in Berlin's tenement districts. Relatively little is known about the economics of this land use mix. Presumably the commercial rents benefited the landlords and stabilized landlord income, particularly in the later working class tenements where occupants periodically faced financial distress.

The particular typology that shaped Berlin's 'Wilhelmine ring', the fairly uniform tenement districts from 1871 onwards, is one of a property or built-up plot forming one component in a continuous building mass. It meets the street in a uniform frontage, one building distinguished from the next only by detailing on the façade. This lends Berlin a similar uniformity and public face to that described for Edinburgh (Robinson 2005, 122, 124). Once tenement development is complete, property boundaries and the perimeter walls of buildings are seldom visible. Buildings back and side onto one another, and gain light mainly from street-facing façades and internal courtyards. Images of the late 19th century, when entire districts had reached building saturation, give evidence of an extremely dense building mass covering large blocks and uniformly limiting public access to the well defined street and occasional urban square. The majority of urban space is built up, but is hidden behind decorative façades.

Bleak perimeter or fire walls – the windowless and unplastered backs and sides of street- and inward-facing buildings – characterized incomplete districts. Unfilled building gaps periodically marked Berlin: first during times of land speculation and construction of new districts throughout the late 19th and early 20th century, then after the destruction of buildings during WWII, and lastly as a result of post-war attempts at de-densification and redevelopment. Nowadays, the exposed window-less walls of an incomplete ensemble are the most unattractive aspect of Berlin's tenement districts, as are those of Nairobi (see Figure 1.3 in Chapter 1).

Hegemann (1930), in the title of his book, famously refers to Berlin as the biggest tenement city in the world. Present-day urban sociologists Häußermann and Siebel (1996) argue that the 1853 Building Ordinance and 1862 Plan invited the densest development ever in German cities. However, Berlin was 'the most densely settled city in Europe' only by the end of the 19th century (Treue 1969, 38). Tenement production on the large street blocks and deep plots in the Wilhelmine ring (seemingly unique to Berlin) brought about the city's excessive density that outstripped other German and European cities of the time. This often deviated from the 1862 Plan, and was already governed by the rules of the 1887 Building Ordinance, not those of 1853.

The 1875 population census recorded net densities of 800 people per hectare in small pockets within the pre-1861 boundary of the city (Leyden 1933/1995, 93). As new districts developed, the centre of the city became depopulated. The highest densities instead came to be concentrated in the Wilhelmine ring. By 1910, 1 010 people per hectare were recorded in Neukölln. In 1925, pockets with even higher densities were found in this belt: 1 324 people per hectare in a part of Moabit (Rostocker Strasse), 1 358 people per hectare in parts of Kreuzberg (Görlitzer Bahnhof), and 'even higher figures' in small localities (*ibid.*, 95).

While the Building Ordinance from 1853 onwards determined the maximum number of occupants per property (further reduced in 1887), Berlin did not have a housing office or authority with the role of inspecting occupation rates in tenements. The separate municipality of Charlottenburg pioneered the formation of a housing office in 1911. However, its role was purely to educate and control tenants, and not to discipline landlords who neglected the maintenance of their tenements (Bodenschatz 1987, 79).

Speculation and tenement construction

A tradition of debt long underpinned the construction of Berlin's built environment. King Frederick II ('Frederick the Great') introduced mortgage regulations already in the 18th century to promote the construction of a 'city' with multi-story housing (Hegemann 1930). This enabled long-term debt against urban land. Landowners made use of this facility to constantly bloat land prices. Debt generated by the purchase of land increased, with the result that by 1881, during the depression that followed the 1873 crash, the imperial Chancellor Bismarck remarked that the total debt on Berlin's tenements was higher than their collective value (*ibid.*, 169).

However, a switch in investment occurred in the second half of the 19th century. Up to the mid-1800s, landowners were usually the developers, and would also seek residence themselves in these same buildings. These landlords were the bourgeoisie (*Bürger*) of the city and identified with its political, social and physical developments. New investors that responded to opportunities for densification were '*Aktiengesellschaften*' (joint stock companies) headed by business people whose only concern was seeking fast and maximum returns. Thus the bourgeoisie as a class lost control over urban development. Minimally regulated, purely speculative interests took their place and generated ever increasing squalor (Häußermann and Siebel 1996, 80). In this context, the power to mediate the intense interest in rapid accumulation of profit against the social interest of adequate living standards lay in the hands of the land and building regulations (Häußermann and Siebel 1996). However, as I have mentioned above, these themselves resulted from a compromise that incorporated speculative interests.

Changes in Berlin's land market in the second half of the 19th century underpinned tenement production. These changes of course corresponded with liberal policy and the economic changes of that time. Intensive land speculation, with land prices suddenly multiplying ten- to 50-fold on the original agricultural value, peaked with the freeing of capital after the 1871 victory against France (Bodenschatz 1987, 55). With the expansion of the city according to the 1862 Building Plan, intense land speculation and subdivision took place in this period (Geist and Kürvers 1980, 520). Maximum rental income, anticipated through the densest possible development of a plot, determined the price of undeveloped building sites. The prices of the sites in turn determined the density at which they were developed (*ibid.*). Housing demand at the time spurred intense speculation, and 'in 1871–2 forty building societies were set up with capital of 194 million marks; in 1860, 9 878 sites had been developed; in 1870 this had reached 14 618' (Richie 1998, 162).

The 1873 crash preceded a period from 1875 of gradual expansion on Berlin's outskirts, along with a pause in land speculation. Starting in 1887, a new era of speculation continued undisrupted into the 20th century, characterized by the growth of tenements on the urban periphery and once again escalating land prices (Bodenschatz 1987, 55).

I have already mentioned that periodic undersupply of housing necessitated the creation of shantytowns on the edges of the city. The economic fluctuations in the second half of the 19th century also led to periodic oversupply of residential units. For many years after the building boom of 1871–73, Berlin had a significant number of vacant apartments, though primarily for the middle class (Treue 1969, 43). This oversupply explained why, up to 1900, rent increases did not outstrip increases in income, despite the introduction of amenities such as waterborne sewage with flushing toilets, piped gas supply and street lighting. According to Treue (1969, 47), 'the speculative building activity since 1871 had produced predominantly small units, whereas later, up to 1890, larger units dominated the supply'. This was followed by

> …construction activity in the north and east of the city producing exclusively small units in large numbers [as exemplified in Figure 4.5 and the discussion of No. 40 Liebenwalder Strasse below]. But at the same time, older tenements were making way for industrial expansion as well as more generally the commercial boom and formation of the city. (*ibid.*)

Thus the loss (through demolition) of older tenement stock paralleled the new supply of tenement units, enabling an overall modernization of apartments to take place in this period, with a significant increase in percentages of flats having toilets and baths. In this period, wages for construction workers also increased (*ibid.*), presumably raising the cost of tenement development, but also contributing to demand for better units.

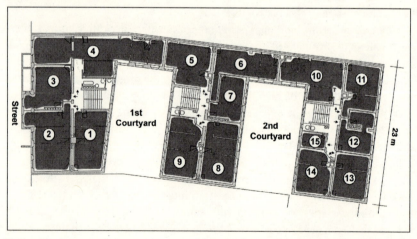

Figure 4.5: Layout of a tenement in Wedding built in 1905, with 15 small units on one floor

Source: Redrawn from Geist and Kürvers (1984, 272)

Furthermore, as residential rents rose towards the close of the 19th century, rents for commercial and light industrial space within the tenements increased at a higher rate (*ibid.* 46). As already mentioned, there seems to be no research on the role of mixed use (commercial, small industrial and residential) in ensuring profitability and resilience of this tenement model. Such insight would be particularly relevant for understanding and valorizing the (unauthorized) mixed use tenement model in Nairobi.

In Berlin, private developers built tenements with the sole purpose of selling the completed building immediately at a profit. Yet the uptake for completed tenement buildings with predominantly small units was slow. Investors considered the management and letting of these buildings problematic because of frequent rental arrears and evictions, high tenant turnover and rapid deterioration of buildings due to high occupancy rates (Rodenstein 1988, 107). In later chapters I will discuss similar perceptions of rooming tenements in Nairobi.

A chain of speculative interests characterized Berlin's tenement development: original landowners sold at gain; land speculating companies bought land and serviced it for development; traders of building sites benefitted from transactions; developers purchased serviced building sites and undertook construction; and banks and insurance companies participated in land speculating companies while also benefiting from mortgaging and other forms of credit that financed transactions in the chain. Ultimately, the economically weak and deeply indebted building owners/landlords passed their financial distress on to their tenants in the form of high rents (Treue 1969, 50; Bodenschatz 1987, 81; Rodenstein 1988, 112). This speculative chain and the resultant financial distress are illustrated in the tenement example that follows.

Speculation and risk: No. 40 Liebenwalder Strasse in the district of Wedding

The five-story tenement at No. 40 Liebenwalder Strasse in the predominantly working class district of Wedding was constructed from 1906 to 1910 in a process that had not significantly changed since the 1870s. Land and building speculation in this already urbanized area only emerged in the 1890s, with a rapid increase in land prices. I draw here on a case study by Lefèvre (1990, 230–233), but also visited this particular tenement in 2005 and heard from one of its residents about the very recent financial woes of the then owner, and implications for the occupants.

In 1890, the property consisted of a three-story street-facing building with side wing. A year later, the owner added a shed and stable in the yard. The surroundings displayed a 'suburban character' at the time. This changed dramatically towards the end of the 1890s when various industries located in the immediate vicinity, soon followed by the first tenements. The owner of No. 40 Liebenwalder Strasse, a well-to-do artisan, seized the opportunity and sold, as did the others in the street. Artisans made up the majority of landowners, alongside merchants ('*Kaufleute*'), people with an income from rents or interest on capital (*'Rentiers'*), and the Prussian Real Estate Joint Stock Bank (*Preußische Immobilien Aktien Bank*) which in the 1980s had already purchased a number of properties in the street.

Ownership changed twice, before a master bricklayer (*'Maurermeister'*) acquired No. 40 Liebenwalder Strasse. He planned a five-story tenement, submitted a building application and obtained approval in 1904. The plans consisted of one street-facing building with a representative façade with balconies and ornaments, and one parallel building behind it. The entire first floor above ground was a prototypical *'bel étage'*, a term derived from the French tenements, the so-called *'maisons mixtes'* or *'immeubles de rapport'*. In this case it was a generous apartment with bathroom, intended for the owner. To maximize on rental income and value, the remainder of the street-facing building and the parallel building behind it consisted of small one or two-roomed apartments with kitchen.

By-and-large, the small artisanal or construction businesses that erected the majority of tenement buildings up to WWI did not own much capital. To purchase properties and to construct tenements, they needed to take out several mortgages, at high interest rates. Inevitably, risk drove the owner of No. 40 Liebenwalder Strasse into bankruptcy. The same happened to two successive owners, although these managed to carry out the earthworks and initial construction respectively.

The owner who eventually succeeded in completing the building by 1908 did away with the *bel étage*, replacing it with two-roomed units plus kitchen, as in the floors above. He demolished the outbuildings a year later to make way for a further parallel building as well as a new outbuilding at the rear end of the property (Figure 4.6). Having maximized the usage of the property, this owner completed the construction work and sold the turnkey tenement to a merchant (*'Kaufmann'*) from a different city. In the late 1920s, a Jewish owner bequeathed the property to his daughter, a medical doctor. The Nazi regime forced her to sell the tenement in 1939. She, like most Jews who did not manage to flee the country, succumbed to the Nazi reign of terror and did not survive. Her heirs, scattered across the globe, received compensation in the early 1950s.

Before the war, the Nazi regime persecuted and murdered political opponents among tenants in this part of Wedding. From 1933 it increased control over tenants. This included new house regulations that forbade lingering at tenement entrances, in corridors, stairwells and entrances. During the war, particularly from 1943, tenants were often herded into basements to escape the bombings. In 1945, a bomb attack damaged one of the backyard buildings of No. 40 Liebenwalder Strasse, also rendering as many as 10 000 tenants homeless in that street and killing 24. The bombing destroyed water, gas and electricity supply, and even food was hard to come by. It took three years before poorly carried out repairs began for No. 40 Liebenwalder Strasse. In 1952 tenants lodged an official complaint about unrepaired war damage to the interior of the building.

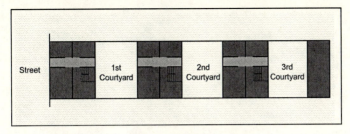

Figure 4.6: Layout of No. 40 Liebenwalder Strasse

Source: Redrawn from Lefèvre (1990, 230, 231)

Two decades later, the apartments of No. 40 Liebenwalder Strasse were finally modernized. The large-scale redevelopment that hit Wedding in the 1960s spared the immediate neighborhood from demolition. However, in expectation of mass redevelopment, landlords in Liebenwalder Strasse neglected maintenance and allowed their tenements to deteriorate (Lefèvre 1990, 244). Only in 1967 were units in No. 40 combined into larger apartments, bathrooms installed and, as had become fashionable, balconies removed from the façade. Yet the owner still sought to squeeze maximum rental income out of the tenement. In the same year, the building police barricaded a basement apartment in the second backyard building due to inadequate living conditions. A prohibition of use of a further basement apartment in this tenement was issued one year later (*ibid.*, 230).

During my visit to No. 40 Liebenwalder Strasse in August 2005, the tenement was once more undergoing renovation (Figure 4.7), and was only partly occupied. A tenant gave me access to the three successive courtyards through the 2.5 m gate in the street-facing building. The two parallel buildings in the backyard still exist, as does the single-story shed at the rear end. The tenant explained that renovations had been underway for 18 months. There were rumors that the landlord or building administrators had pocketed a renovation subsidy from the city government ('*Senat*'). This tenant was no longer paying rent.

The tenement next door also still consists of the original building volume: a five-story street-facing tenement (with ornate façade), a two-story side wing, a row of single-story garages (originally stables or small industrial spaces) in place of a second wing, and further garages along the rear end of the property. A local resident from a nearby tenement, who had parked his car in this yard, shared his opinion that 'these backyards are too dark'. He knew of two other tenements in the vicinity whose backyard buildings were demolished as recently as 1990. The conversation suggested a continued contestation over density and living conditions in this district. In my discussion of various aspects of living conditions in the next chapter, I return to the example of No. 40 Liebenwalder Strasse.

Figure 4.7: No. 40 Liebenwalder Strasse in 2005   Source: Author's photographs (2005)

Speculative interests accommodated: an initial comparison with present-day Nairobi

Nineteenth century planning for Berlin was not backed by the necessary legislation to stem the speculative excesses that produced the living conditions for which the 1862 Plan was commonly blamed. The minimalist building regulations of 1853 and subsequent amendments successfully shaped a tenement typology which, for instance, did not include the windowless rooms that are reported for New York's tenements up to the passing of the new Tenement House Act in 1879. Nevertheless, as I show in the following chapter, the living conditions in Berlin's tenements were dismal, though street space and activity provided some relief.

In Berlin, speculative interests had a strong influence on negotiations around planning and building regulation. These interests found their expression through committees of delegates who negotiated plans and regulations. In present-day Nairobi these same interests, protected by political patronage, range freely in transgression of planning schemes and building regulations, curbed only by a mechanism of self-regulation. A question that arises for Nairobi is whether a transfer of the speculative interests into an official decision-making process, without reducing the power of landlords, would result in any fundamental change. The larger challenge for Nairobi may lie in how to reduce the might (within the overall system of power relations) of those with capital interest vested in the built environment, without undermining the production of much needed housing.

The switch that happened in Berlin in the mid-19th century from land and tenement interests vested in the bourgeoisie to large, impersonal companies with the sole function of making large and rapid returns has not yet been witnessed in Nairobi. In Berlin, these far more anonymous interests drove excessive growth in land values, which in turn placed tight constraints on the profitability of anyone wishing to develop and manage tenements. They imposed near-intolerable conditions on tenants. Companies also made profits out of debt in this chain of extraction and exploitation. As I will show, this dilemma has taken on a new dimension in present-day Berlin, as the historic tenements enter another round of short-term capital extraction. An important preliminary conclusion in the case of Nairobi is that there is some consolation in the fact that its tenements are still largely owned by a loosely definable indigenous class of individual investors. Thanks to under-development of the banking sector and the unauthorized nature of tenement development in Nairobi, this form of housing is not undermined by massive debt, nor likely to be in the near future.

Planning for Berlin in the late 1850s and early 1860s did not anticipate the switch that was occurring in the land and tenement investment pattern. Planning was primarily concerned with spatially guiding what was already familiar. Unlike Haussmann's planning for Paris, Berlin's 1962 Plan neither anticipated new players, nor did it introduce any substantially new dimensions. The plan embraced and catered for mixed use, both with street-facing shops on tenement ground floors (leading onto generous pavements) and with the possibility of industrial activities in the large block interiors. Civic design was minimal, but emphasized the appeal of a street defined by a continued building mass, while also articulating a minimum concern for air and light. Only much later, after their neglect by the modern town planning paradigm, were the qualities of continuous urban form and mixed use given value again through a new orthodoxy in urban design. However, this was never again fully reconciled with urban planning. Today, physical planning, particularly as practiced in sub-Saharan Africa, instead over-emphasizes light and air in a complete inversion of tenement typology. The birth of this physical planning paradigm, which went hand-in-hand with the promotion of homeownership, had a strong influence on late 19th and early 20th century discourse on tenements in Berlin. As I will show in later chapters, in Nairobi, while this form of spatial planning remains on the books, it is rejected by actors across the board, and instead a market of densely developed tenements is facilitated. Berlin's cautious spatial planning approach of the mid-19th century can provide compelling pointers for a city like Nairobi.

Endnotes

1   Bismarck was only appointed as prime minister later that year, therefore had no influence over this decision.

Chapter 5

The contested legitimacy of tenements in Berlin

Land speculation and debt financing underlying Berlin's tenement development served the interests of large companies. The trajectory of a tenement in Liebenwalder Strasse described in the previous chapter illustrates the fact that this housing market, which to a large extent enjoyed legally derived legitimacy, was precarious and often detrimental to the small players who took the risk of constructing and managing the individual tenement properties. In response to both an overwhelming low income demand for housing and the tight economics of the tenement market, developers amassed units in unsuitable ways, while those managing the tenements tolerated and even encouraged unhealthy rates and patterns of occupation. As in many European cities at the time, Berlin's tenement market, despite its inadequacies, was capable of meeting a rapidly growing working class housing demand, thus servicing the larger industrial needs for reproduction of labor.

However, health conditions, concerns about the lack of light and air for the individual units, and fears that the dense tenement typology might radicalize the working class led to calls for reform and attempts at alternative housing. The housing reform debates eventually triumphed over the more radical revolutionary, but ultimately weak, position of the left, which largely avoided the topic of how best to house the masses but did provide arguments in defense of (or for the utility of) the existing tenement housing. Though inconsistent, radical threads in the debate led to the rediscovery of the quality of urban space in tenement districts by the 1980s, and helped revalue Berlin's historical tenements, while in present-day Berlin these benefits serve a new round of speculative interests.

Living conditions in the tenement city

Analyses of living conditions in late 19th and early 20th century Berlin inevitably focus primarily on the working class and the units it occupied. Here tenants experienced the worst deprivations. With the introduction of engineering services in the second half of the 19th century, the authorities alleviated some hardships across the city; however, economic and demographic trends, arguably coupled with landlord complicity and state complacency, undermined these gains, pushing desperate households into extreme overcrowding and other unhealthy housing solutions. Nonetheless, a discussion of living conditions in Berlin's tenements would be incomplete without also touching on middle class apartments. These too were far from adequate, and helped trigger a housing debate within the bourgeoisie. Localized interaction between the classes in the street or tenement neighborhood, in which small-scale commercial activity played an important role, was a further topic of bourgeois discussion, though not exhausted in the late 19th century debates.

Technological improvements

A significant improvement in living conditions reached Berlin's tenements in the 1870s and 1880s in the form of better sanitation, and to some extent healthier lighting. The 1860s saw the introduction of paraffin, which by the 1880s was widely used for lighting in Berlin. The gas mantle ('*Glühstrumpf*') was invented in 1884. Thomas Edison's precursor to the light bulb ('*Kohlenfadenlampe*') followed soon, and in 1898 Auer von Welsbach invented the conventional electric bulb ('*Metallfadenlampe*'). However, these all remained expensive alternatives to the paraffin lamp, which stayed in use up to 1900, always with the risk of causing fire. (Goerke 1969, 57)

I have already mentioned James Hobrecht's work in the 1860s on a sewerage system for Berlin, and the state's delay in its implementation. Only in 1874, much later than in Munich or Hamburg, did the state construct a sewerage canalization and treatment system for Berlin, basing it on the English waterborne sanitation model. This improved the city's living conditions considerably over the next ten years (Rodenstein 1988, 86). Up to the turn of the century, developers incorporated waterborne toilets mainly into middle class housing, whereas sanitation for the working class remained a bucket system (Goerke 1969, 63). Nevertheless, the provision of water pipes and sewers from the 1870s onwards reduced the incidence of epidemics across Berlin (Wietog 1981, 135).

Undersupply and inadequacy of housing

The better-off benefitted most from the engineering improvements, yet not even they were finding adequate housing in the tenement market (Rodenstein 1988, 107). 'The self-regulation of housing supply by demand, as per liberalist ideals, did not materialise' (*ibid.*). This clearly indicated to the middle class that 'profit-oriented land use' could not be reconciled with the visions of liberal market ideology (*ibid.*). This led to debates about housing supply. Engels (1887/1935, 21–22) commented at the time: '*[T]his* housing shortage gets talked of so much because it does not limit itself to the working class but has affected the petty bourgeoisie also' (emphasis in the original). I return to these debates later in this chapter. Here it is worth observing that whereas acceptable middle class tenement life had assisted in legitimizing the Scottish tenement (Robinson 2005), it was unacceptable middle class tenement conditions that undermined the legitimacy of this housing form in Berlin and helped trigger a housing discourse that ultimately halted this form of housing investment.

The German tenement literature uses several indicators of housing need. Besides street homelessness and periodic emergence of shantytowns, there is analysis of overcrowding, including subletting of bed spaces and the occupation of units unfit for human habitation in terms of public health. These were either the cold and damp basement units (also poorly insulated units in roofs (Rodenstein 1988, 106)) or apartments in newly constructed 'wet' buildings. Regarding damp basement units, similar concerns over basement living were reported for New York's notorious 19th century tenements (Day 1999, 49).[1] But there were also health concerns with other tenement units. Berlin's tenement typology, with buildings backing onto one another as side wings or at the rear end of properties, resulted in many units having windows only to one side, not allowing for cross ventilation. In addition, small courtyard or backyard spaces provided inadequate light and air, especially on the lower floors (Rodenstein 1988, 106).

Thus even apartment units for the middle class were often not laid out adequately. Engels (quoted in Geist and Kürvers 1984, 273–274), in a letter composed in 1883 during a visit to a communist colleague's evidently middle class apartment in Berlin, describes

> an apartment with rooms so terribly obstructed that I was appalled. Here in Berlin one has invented the 'Berlin room' with hardly a hint of a window, and in this the Berliners pass the majority of their time. To the front are dining room (the parlor, only used on special occasions) and the salon (even more posh and less frequently used), then the 'Berlin' dive, behind it the dark corridor and a few bedrooms *donnant sur la cour* [looking onto the yard] and a kitchen. Uncomfortable, terribly long, really typical of Berlin (that is of bourgeois Berlin): presentation and even gloss to the outside, darkness, discomfort and poor order on the inside; the palace front only as a façade, and for living only discomfort. Anyway, that is my impression thus far; let's hope it improves. (my translation)

While these conditions were disturbing, they bear no relation to the squalor in the small, over-occupied working class units, which Engels seems never to have described in detail, though suggesting knowledge of them in *The Housing Question* (1887/1935, 21, 33). He does not comment specifically on Berlin's residential density. The primary purpose of *The Housing Question* is to refute the bourgeois housing reformers' proposal of homeownership for the working class.

Working class tenement units in Berlin were one-roomed, one-roomed with kitchen, or two-roomed with kitchen. These made up 75 per cent of tenement units in the city in the decade from 1861 to 1871 (Wietog 1981, 132). Of all units at the time, half had only one room that could be heated, and these units in turn were occupied by half of Berlin's population, which consequently suffered exposure to severe cold and therefore health risks in winter.

Overcrowding and subletting

High levels of occupation in Berlin's working class units (alongside the high unit density of the typology) no doubt co-determined the high residential densities of the city's tenement districts. In the 1860s and 1870s, the authorities defined over-crowding as one- or two-roomed units (with kitchen) occupied by more than five or ten people respectively (Wietog 1981, 132). By present-day standards, the acceptable level of occupation was already alarmingly high. In 1861 and 1871, the years of particular housing shortage, 15 per cent and 13 per cent of tenement units respectively displayed overcrowding according to the criteria of the time, with lower percentages in the years between (Wietog 1981, 133). When measured by population and not by unit, 23 per cent of Berlin's population lived in overcrowded conditions in 1861 and 1862, 17 per cent in 1867, rising again to 20 per cent in 1871. The overcrowded units were predominantly one-roomed (with kitchen) (*ibid.*).

Despite continued production of tenements, the overcrowding does not seem to have abated by the turn of the century. Though possibly exaggerating, Hege-mann (1930, 20) observes that around 1900 half of Berlin's official population lived in flats that had an occupation rate of three to thirteen people per habitable room. Statisticians at this time recorded 3 400 one-roomed units (without kitchen) (*ibid.*).

One form that overcrowding took was the subletting of bed spaces. In 1871, eight per cent of Berlin's population comprised individuals renting space in tenants' flats or rooms (Wietog 1981). They were the so-called '*Schlafleute*' (*ibid.*, 136) or '*Schlafgänger*' (Häußermann and Siebel 1996, 83); their equivalent in the tenements of New York and Glasgow were referred to as 'lodgers' (Day 1999, 17; Robinson 2005, 114). In the same year, 1871, over half of households in Berlin that made bed space available on this basis, did so to more than one person. Shift work in factories enabled families to rent one bed in shifts to two individuals (Ott 1989, 139). Recent arrivals from rural areas, job seekers, whose only other option was the much dreaded asylums for the homeless, also resorted to renting bed space from tenant households (*ibid.*). It is not clear whether households took in lodgers out of compassionate response to their need or because the additional income was needed (Wietog 1981, 136). From 1880 to 1910, despite a significant increase in the worker population, subletting or lodging declined (Treue 1969, 46). Neverthe-less, lodging and the anecdotal rather than statistically reported abuse of minors of tenant households by lodgers became the 'spectacular and most important link in the chain that made up the entire social criticism against the tenement' (Boden-schatz 1987, 64).

Rent, leases and lack of legal protection

The intense usage of urban land that Berlin's planning and regulation enabled encouraged land speculation and land price hikes. In part, this contributed to rent distress (Rodenstein 1988, 107). Low income households tended to pay up to a third of their income in rent, whereas better-off households paid between one-fifth and one-tenth (*ibid.*). In Wedding in 1910, landlords charged an annual rent of 266 marks on average for newly constructed one-roomed units with kitchen and 403 marks for equivalent two-roomed units with kitchen (Lefèvre 1990, 233). At this time, workers earned an annual income of around 1 000 marks and skilled workers 1 500 marks. The little income these households did not spend on rent, they needed for food.

The state, in the form of the Weimar Republic, introduced legal protection against lease cancellation, along with rent control, only after WWI (*ibid.*, 238). Up to this time, as soon as rents were in arrears, landlords could cancel rental agreements. This contributed to high tenant mobility, particularly among low income earners. Tenancy seldom exceeded one year (*ibid.*). Inability to pay rents periodically led to evictions and street homelessness (a legal offence since 1843). During Easter 1872, 'there were so many people on the street that the city officials were forced to build a temporary shelter in Moabit' (Richie 1998, 165). As already mentioned, street homelessness periodically led to skirmishes.

Occupation of basements and uncured buildings

The occupation of damp basement units constituted as much of a health risk as the prevalence of overcrowding. According to the 1853 Building Ordinance, basement units were habitable provided their floor was one foot above the highest reach of the ground water table, their ceiling three feet (approximately 1 m) above street level, and damp-proofing was applied (Geist and Kürvers 1980, 521). The 1887 Building Ordinance instituted a minimum floor interval (or distance from floor to ceiling) of 2.5 m, applicable also to basements. The 1897 Ordinance raised this to 2.7 m. While the floor intervals above ground already complied with these dimensions, these regulations increased the height of basement (and roof) tenements subsequently built (Geist and Kürvers 1984, 240). Between 1861 and 1871, the percentage of Berlin's population occupying basement units rose from 9.4 per cent to 10.8 per cent. In this period, however, the average occupation rate of these units dropped marginally from 5 to 4.5 (Wietog 1981, 134).

As tenement construction increased, so did opportunities for desperate households to live in freshly completed but uncured buildings. Referred to as '*Trockenwohner*' (drying occupants), they 'occupied rooms in building sites while the fresh plaster dried' (Richie 1998, 163). The authorities did not officially sanction these units for letting, precisely because they deemed them unhealthy for occupation. The people to whom developers made these units available (usually at the beginning of winter) did not have the luxury of having their health considered (Ott 1989, 139). In return for rent-free occupation, these households with sparse belongings had to heat the bare rooms so that by the end of winter the units were dry and ready for rent-paying occupants (*ibid.*, 140). The practice of *Trockenwohnen* persisted despite the 1853 Building Code's requirement that buildings only be occupied nine months after completion (Goerke 1969, 55; Geist and Kürvers 1980, 521). This regulation was considered harsh, and the subsequent Building Ordinance of 1871 instead simply required a second inspection and written approval after completion (Goerke 1969, 55). With the practice of 'Trockenwohnen' and basement living alike, health problems arose from a combination of damp, overcrowding, inadequate heating and, in the case of basements, lack of natural light.

Community, street life and commercial activities

Under these conditions, the incidence of tuberculosis, infant mortality and rickets was high. Cartoonist Heinrich Zille's drawings of the time often depict visibly unwell children (Figure 5.1). Working class families had little resilience to illness or loss of employment. As soon as the rent was in arrears, the landlord would cancel the lease and the household would seek cheaper (usually less healthy) quarters. Tenant mobility in turn undermined community cohesion. However, households moved mainly within the neighborhood or 'around the corner', which underlines the importance of the public everyday culture of the street. The neighborhood lent stronger identity than the individual tenement or unit that was inhabited only for a short period (Von Saldern 1997, 202–203).

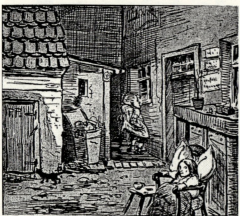

Figure 5.1: Children's illness is pervasive in Zille's depictions of backyard life

Source: Reinoß (1988, 28, 45)

With extremely cramped indoor conditions, life in Berlin's tenements inevitably spilled into courtyards or backyards and onto streets. Living conditions literally forced people into the outdoors (Becker and Jacob 1992, 32). Streets in the Wedding district are described as places of sojourn and meeting (Figure 5.2), and where something was happening every moment (Lefèvre 1990, 236). As in present-day rooming districts of Nairobi, early in the morning masses of people on their way to work moved through the streets of Wedding such as Liebenwalder Strasse (*ibid*.).

Figure 5.2: Zille's depiction of a typical gathering of working class women at a tenement entrance

Source: Reinoß (1988, 129)

Heinrich Zille depicted street scenes of the tenement district of Berlin in which he himself grew up in the late 1860s and the 1870s. As a child, he had discovered 'satirical etchings' of the 18th century English artist Hogarth in a local magazine and had compared the scenes with his own life (Reinoß 1988, 9). From his tenth year he lived in Berlin. His first home in the city consisted of a basement unit in present-day Friedrichshain. His family collected its meals from the local soup kitchen, common in Berlin's tenement districts (Reinoß 1988). One was located at No. 53 Liebenwalder Strasse in Wedding (Lefèvre 1990). Before school, Zille was out in the streets delivering bread rolls and milk, and later newspapers. After school, he would sell his mother's needlework to local shops. Only in his mid-thirties was he able to move his family to a modest apartment in a palatial middle class tenement in Charlottenburg (Reinoß 1988).

Zille's depictions of working class life in Berlin's tenement districts have drawn criticism. Some suggest that 'despite realism in word and picture', Zille's 'humorous backyard romanticism' could 'fake no less than that of Ludwig Richter' (the classical 19th century German romantic painter and etcher) (Treue 1969, 40). However, others argue that Zille's drawings are misunderstood as idyllic (Bodenschatz 1987, 57). I find that Zille's sketches of Berlin are a compelling representation of various aspects of working class life, with its tenement backdrop. For instance, he drew the tenement units, backyards and streets teeming with children (Figures 5.3 and 5.4). In 1894, an observer in Wedding counted 218 children playing in a street expanse of 12 tenements (Becker and Jacob 1992, 33).

Zille's street scenes depict predominantly working class families, though with satirical stabs at bourgeois snobbery (Figure 5.5; note the posture of the presumably middle class shop attendant in the doorway), suggesting some proximity between the classes. The extent and benefit of social mixing in Berlin's tenements is contested, as I show below. In actual fact, it was the petty bourgeoisie and not the bourgeoisie itself that shared tenement districts with the working class (Häußermann and Kapphan 2000). Officialdom and small business people made up a part

of the predominantly working class neighborhood of Moabit (Becker and Jacob 1992, 28). Here, '[d]espite the social differences, the living together alongside one another of the different social groups was characteristic, and the businesspeople with their shops played a binding role' (*ibid.*). Shops primarily served the social function of communication between women, whereas the many local pubs fulfilled this function for men. The local cinema constituted the only other form of entertainment or relaxation (*ibid.*). Liebenwalder Strasse in Wedding also had its so-called 'slipper cinema' at No. 26 (Lefèvre 1990, 237).[2]

Figure 5.3: Zille's portrayal of street life teeming with children

Source: Reinoß (1988, 33)

Figure 5.4: Zille's illustration of children playing in backyards

Source: Reinoß (1988, 38, 48, 62)

Virtually every tenement included commerce on the ground floor of the street-fronting building. In a part of Moabit, the list of shops – grocer, greengrocer, bakery, butcher, barber and specialized shops for milk or cigars (Becker and Jacob 1992, 28) – was much the same as those in Liebenwalder Strasse in Wedding (Lefèvre 1990,

236). However, this more uniformly working class and light industrial street also displayed washing and ironing services, cobbling and hardware, which are similarly present among the commercial activities in Nairobi's rooming district Huruma (see Table 8.1 in Chapter 8). Both parts of Moabit and Wedding were frequented by street traders, including those offering the all-important supply of coal and wood for heating (Lefèvre 1990; Becker and Jacob 1992). Zille depicts the indignation of an illegal potato trader at being ticketed by a local policeman. Behind her there is a vacant property and the windowless side and rear walls of five-story tenements (see Figure 5.6). Around her,

Figure 5.5: Zille's depiction of working class children commenting on the display in a middle class shop.

Source: Reinoß (1988, 167)

as if in solidarity, a group of equally incensed women and children are waiting to be served. The following description of Moabit in the 1920s and 1930s would have applied likewise in the late 19th century: 'Although daily life was marked by unemployment, need for money and overcrowded living conditions, the tightly knit communal living of people was almost a necessary form of self-help and solidarity' (Becker and Jacob 1992, 31). Community was defined both in the tenement or 'house' and in the neighborhood (referred to as a 'Kiez').

Commercial activity in the tenement-dominated street blocks was not restricted to the streets. Light industries were frequently located in the backyards. The deep

Figure 5.6: Zille's depiction of street life and ticketing of a street trader; bare fire walls of tenements dominate the background

Source: Reinoß (1988, 308)

plots of Liebenwalder Strasse in Wedding were home to many small factories, shielded from sight by street-facing tenement buildings (Lefèvre 1990, 233). In the late 19th and early 20th century, craftwork and machinery often made backyards noisy places. By contrast, present-day tenement units facing onto mostly landscaped backyards are sought-after because they are shielded from the noise of motorized traffic.

Debates and misconceptions about socio-spatial class integration in Berlin's tenement neighborhoods

What is evident is that the social integration of rich and poor was localized, and not typical of the entire tenement city of Berlin. Particularly the later tenement development, extending into the first two decades of the 20th century, took a clearly segregated form. Large, predominantly working class districts that included industrial concerns located in the north, east and south-east of the city (Moabit, Wedding, Prenzlauer Berg, Friedrichshain and Neukölln), and districts of middle class apartment houses and villas in the west and south-west (Charlottenburg and Wilmersdorf). Given this large-scale segregation, the social integration at the micro level within the individual tenement properties and neighborhoods which I describe above was relatively insignificant (Bodenschatz 1987, 55). Nevertheless, there was a localized 'social mixing' within the larger segregated structure of the city (Häußermann and Kapphan 2000, 35).

Discussion on social mixing in the literature on Berlin hinges on a much quoted statement by James Hobrecht, mostly taken out of context, on the social integration he observed in Berlin's tenement districts. As already mentioned, Hobrecht, having completed drafts of the Berlin Building Plan in 1861, had travelled to England to study the sewerage system. In the following years he remained vocal in the public discourse on planning and housing in Berlin. Before participating in a debate on the Building Plan in the Architecture and Engineering Association in 1870 (see Geist and Kürvers 1984, 158), he published a document titled *About Public Health and the Creation of a Central Department for Public Health in the State*, in 1868. Geist and Kürvers (1980, 513, 516) reproduce two pages of this document, in which Hobrecht reflects on Berlin's residential development. Though labeled in the literature as 'naive' (see Häußermann and Kapphan, 2000, 34), I find that Hobrecht's statement presents a pragmatic engagement with segregation, identity and fear.

Hobrecht highlighted the Berlin way of living in tenement neighborhoods that included flats for a range of income groups in one property. Rent for the generous first floor (or *bel étage*) apartment in the street-facing building was more than double that of the still generous apartments above it, five times that of the units in the backyard buildings and ten times that of the usually damp basement dwellings. Hobrecht contrasted this with the high level of income segregation in the English towns he had visited, where the well-off inhabited villas in completely separate districts from the working class. His observation was that working class children in Berlin benefitted from the neighborly charity of richer families due to the mixed nature of the living environment. Better-off adults and their children had no choice but to share pavements and entrances into their tenements with members of poorer families (Geist and Kürvers 1980, 513).

Hobrecht wrote about the 'cozy relationship' ('*gemütliche Beziehung*') in this built form between people of similar nature but different economic positions. He explicitly suggested that it would be more suitable for the state to adopt integration ('*Durchdringung*') than segregation or exclusion ('*Abschließung*'). In similar fashion to the legitimization of the Scottish tenement mentioned by Robinson (2005, 115), Hobrecht linked this 'togetherness' to 'the spiritual meaning of the German people' (Geist and Kürvers 1980, 513), which he argued was also expressed in culture and art. Again he contrasted this with the English working class district, which only the police visited, and the 'sensationalist poet' who would write a gruesome story that might produce tears from a young middle class 'lady'. At the most this would induce her into one short visit to a working class district, merely reinforcing her disgust and fear of the poor and resulting in a donation to a charitable commission, but no personal engagement with the lives of the poor (*ibid.*, 513, 516).

While praising the mixed nature of Berlin's tenements, Hobrecht condemned the maximization of densities. As an early and rather pragmatic reformer, he proposed an improvement to the mixed living environments – 'more air and more light' ('*mehr Luft und mehr Licht*') – as later promoted far more simplistically by the modernist architects of the 1920s in their attack on tenements and their promotion of segregation in various forms. Hobrecht suggested doing away with basement flats, and called for backyards that were four times the size of those permitted under the building regulations. He pleaded with the public health authorities for support (Geist and Kürvers 1980, 516).

In their brief comment on Hobrecht's passage, Geist and Kürvers (*ibid.*) express their concern that the literature frequently quotes a part of it (on the benefits of integration) incompletely, and presents it incorrectly as a justification by Hobrecht for '*his*' tenement plan. While Geist and Kürvers' three volumes have become often-cited seminal texts on Berlin's tenements, they, like Hobrecht's original passage, are seldom read in detail. Thus, many subsequent publications cite Geist and Kürvers (1980), yet misrepresent Hobrecht's involvement in the 1862 Building Plan and his text on socio-spatial integration. Examples are Häußermann and Siebel (1996, 79), Richie (1998, 162) and Häußermann and Kapphan (2000, 33–34), who quote an extract of the famous Hobrecht passage claiming or implying that Hobrecht wrote it at the time of planning to justify '*his*' large street blocks and dense tenement development. In a similar vein, Barbey (1984, 31) belittles Hobrecht's 'enthusiastic but idealistic vision about the possibility of [different classes] living together'. Barbey (*ibid.*) describes Hobrecht as having assumed 'alongside the roles of technician and city councilor, that of moral custodian of public interest... [and] proclaimer of social peace'.

Given Hobrecht's reference to segregated British towns as the antithesis of the class integration in Berlin, it is of course ironic that Heinrich Zille recognized much of his own life in the etchings of the British artist Hogarth. But Hogarth had lived and painted a century earlier. It was probably not evidence of cross-class integration that Zille found in Hogarth's drawings, but merely the impoverished urban working class conditions. One may safely assume that Hobrecht, having visited England himself, at least provides a first-hand comparison. In studying the English sanitation system he must have spent time in the segregated row housing or terraced cottage districts in which the waterborne sewers had been installed. While later tenement districts in Berlin had less cross-class mixing, density and commercial activity certainly shaped these neighborhood communities in a way that was not possible in the dormitory row housing districts that English developers constructed for the working class. In English towns and cities, the much lower density and the terracing of individual houses did not lend itself to the lining of streets with shop fronts.

Hobrecht's voice in support of integration appears as a lone position in the urban discourse in Berlin at the time. Barbey (1984) suggests that there were philanthropic proponents of similar mixing of classes in the tenements of Paris, where the '*maison mixte*' consisted of wealthy families living in the '*bel étage*', and above them in the same building several floors of working class families. Barbey argues that this proximity of living led merely to tolerance, acceptance and silence on behalf of the rich in regard to the conditions of their impoverished neighbors, and *vice versa*. Tensions emerged and this model of housing was questioned, increasing the chasm between the rich and the poor sharing one roof. In a similar argument, Häußermann and Kapphan (2000, 34) suggest that Hobrecht did not anticipate later 'intensification and sharpening of the contrasts in interest' between the classes in Berlin's tenements. This, they argue, rendered 'his ideals of social mixing and "cozy togetherness" trash' (*ibid.*). However, it must be acknowledged that the growing contrast in interests between the classes, or the radicalization of the working class, was in large part the result of state repression of working class organization which had initially sought integration. While such integration implied primarily an economic assimilation into the middle class, a spatial integration would have formed part of this ideal. As I explain in the next section, the bourgeois reformers perceived a threat in the radicalizing working class and, as a consequence, for their part sought spatial segregation.

Reform versus revolution: the legitimacy of Berlin's tenements in the late 19th century

The increasingly evident socio-political component of industrialization resulted in middle class concern for workers' housing, alongside concern for their political status, franchise, working conditions and hygiene, and their right to industrial action and wages (Treue 1969, 48). The middle class debate on Berlin's tenements, and more broadly on working class housing in Prussia and later Germany, can be grouped into four thematic strands, though with overlaps: philanthropic activity and model cooperative housing; surveys on workers' health; anarchist-motivated promotion of homeownership; and a radical Marxist position discarding all of the above.

One could argue that the cultural devaluing of the tenement began with private philanthropic engagement, which was 'a typical bourgeois behavior' in 19th century Germany (Adam 2007, 71). From the mid-19th century onward, housing constituted an important aspect of philanthropic activity (*ibid.*), with the express intention of providing an alternative to tenement housing rather than improving conditions in existing tenements. Philanthropy had a clear limitation in Berlin, however. It differed from that in cities without royal residences and where royalty was not represented, and which therefore had a greater independence of vision (*ibid.*, 53). In imperial Berlin, as in Dresden, the monarchy oversaw but also directly participated in and influenced the network of philanthropic social organizations up to the time of WWI. In this way, the monarchy had a significant say in such activity (*ibid.*). The Prince of Prussia (William) was the patron ('*Protektor*') of the Berlin Communal Building Association (*Berliner gemeinnützige Baugesellschaft*), which groupings of the middle class had founded in 1848 (Treue 1969, 48). The association's objective was merely to contribute to the 'satisfactory conciliation' between the propertied class and those not owning property (*ibid.*), with no attempt to address the underlying situation. 'Healthy, comfortable and cheap housing' was to be constructed for working class families (*ibid.*). The association envisaged these dwellings, unlike the tenements, to be buildings of eight to twelve units, spread across different parts of town. By 1857, it had produced 24 buildings with a total of only 222 units.

Along with housing produced by building cooperatives (*Baugenossenschaften*), that of the Berlin Communal Building Association from the mid-19th century had little or no impact on the housing market. In 1865, the Congress of German Economists (*Kongress deutscher Volkswirte*) and the Central Association in Prussia for the Wellbeing of the Working Classes (*Zentralverein in Preußen für das Wohl der arbeitenden Klassen*) still had faith in the building cooperatives (Treue 1969, 49). Yet it became evident that their role was minimal. These organizations, with their 'model units', were unable to compete and provide less dense housing at more affordable rents than the conventional tenements in a financially viable way (Berning et al. 1994, 3). The funders withdrew and such organizations collapsed (*ibid.*). Alternative housing, including a less dense block perimeter typology, became more successful only at the turn of the century, and from 1925 was sanctioned by the new Building Ordinance.

It must be noted that within the socialist movement, the idea of mutualism and anarchism (as opposed to Marx's collectivism or communism) reached Berlin from its birthplace in France only around 1865, via the Russian anarchist Bakunin. This was also the time of the death of the 'father' of anarchism, the Frenchman

Pierre-Joseph Proudhon (Jackson 1957, 157).[3] While Bakunin respected Marx, he judged him to be authoritarian, whereas, in Bakunin's view, Proudhon better 'understood the idea of freedom' (ibid., 159). Tension between Marx and Proudhon's positions within socialist thought at the time is evident in Engels' merciless attack on the anarchist followers of Proudhon in *The Housing Question*, where he implies (as I show below) that they had promoted the idea of cooperative housing construction without fundamentally challenging the *status quo*.

In the 1890s, several organizations tried to address in particular the health conditions in Berlin's working class housing. Treue (1969, 50) lists the Association for Social Politics (*Verein für Sozialpolitik*), the German Association for Healthcare (*Deutsche Verein für Gesundheitspflege*) and the Centre for Organizations Concerned with Workers' Wellbeing (*Zentralstelle für Arbeiterwohlfahrteinrichtungen*). Many publications on housing appeared in the field of public health, not only for Berlin but also for other German cities (*ibid.*).

In 1892, Berlin's first cholera case was officially recorded. In the same year, in the wake of a cholera threat, the social democrats created the Workers' Health Commission ('*Arbeitersanitätskommission*'– ASK). In accordance with the SPD's revolutionary stance at the time, the commission was aware of the limits of its effectiveness within capitalist society. It acknowledged that the obstacles to real 'social hygiene' lay in the bourgeoisie, and that its ideals could only be met in a socialist society (Rüdiger 1985, 94). ASK's main demands were in relation to public health institutions. In 1893 it undertook a detailed survey of housing conditions, including occupation rates. Through that process it encouraged workers to make use of the existing hospitals. It published its findings widely. Though focused primarily on health, the commission, when disbanded in 1903, had contributed to a better understanding of working class housing conditions in Berlin (*ibid.*, 103).

In the political realm, the rejection of tenements was an agenda item for the political opposition (Bodenschatz 1987), including the socialist political formation within the middle class. Engels (1887/1935) reviewed and critiqued this thinking in *The Housing Question*, in which he addressed divergence of thought within the broad socialist grouping. He differentiated the position or doctrine of his intellectual collaborator Karl Marx (to which he himself ascribed – Engels is often referred to as the 'first Marxist' (Clark and Foster 2006)) from that of other socialist thinkers, which he identified as deeply flawed. Marx foresaw a social revolution occurring only through working class emancipation that would lead to the working class seizing control of the means of production. Engels contrasted this with the position of those that he labeled as followers of Proudhon, who foresaw a social revolution occurring through the abolition of landed property and the replacement of rental tenancy for the working class with homeownership, to be purchased in installments.[4] Proudhon's much referred to early work was titled *What is Property?* To this, he answered 'property is theft', which 'became the most famous revolutionary phrase of the nineteenth century' (Jackson 1957, 29). Crowder (1991, 85) clarifies that Proudhon did 'not attack all ownership but only that... which is characteristic of the bourgeois system'. Proudhon rejected 'interest on loans and income from rents' (*ibid.*). He viewed ownership rights to goods as legitimate, if these were 'produced by the work of the owner or necessary for that work' (*ibid.*). Referring to the Proudhonist influence among the German housing reformers, and associating it with the promotion of homeownership, Engels (1887/1935, 10) argued that 'bourgeois and petty-bourgeois socialism is strongly represented' by 'professional socialists and philanthropists' who 'wish to turn the workers into owners of their dwellings'. With reference to Marx and Engels' *Communist Manifesto*, Engels (*ibid.*, 46) associated this position of 'the bourgeois socialist' with the desire to redress 'social grievances in order to secure the continued existence of bourgeois society'.

The intense housing shortage of 1872, not limited to Berlin but also affecting other cities in Germany, led to a proliferation of media articles on 'the housing question' (*ibid.*, 8). Outraged at some of the positions presented, Engels had complained to the press and was invited to respond. His response in Parts I and III of *The Housing Question* was addressed in particular to housing reformer A. Mühlberger's media articles, and in Part II to Emil Sax's 1869 book *The Housing Conditions of the Working Class and their Reform* (*ibid.*, 44). Both rejected rental tenancy and promoted homeownership for the working class. Richie (1998, 909) misrepresents Engels when she refers to his 'fierce, and rather unfair, attack on housing policy in Prussia'. Far from this, Engels (1887/1935, 31) fiercely attacked those that sought the 'abolition of rented dwellings' and hence the direct relevance of his arguments for my discussion on the legitimacy of the tenement market. Engels' text was banned in imperial Germany, but as mentioned in his 1887 'Preface to the Second German Edition', this only increased sales (*ibid.*, 8), suggesting significant interest in his argument.

Engels (*ibid.*, 49) associated Mühlberger's position with the bourgeois philanthropic initiatives I have discussed above. He responded in particular to philanthropic visions of social harmony between the classes, dismissing the institutions that aimed at achieving this harmony:

> The gospel of harmony between labour and capital has been preached now for almost fifty years, and bourgeois philanthropy has expended large sums of money to prove this harmony of interests by building model institutions, and... we are today exactly where we were fifty years ago.

Engels (*ibid.*, 40–41) also responded to cooperative housing initiatives, as well as to surveys of housing conditions, as measures promoted by those he perhaps unfairly identifies as Proudhon's followers:

> Deprived of the pompous and solemn phraseology of their author, [Mühlberger's conclusions] mean nothing more than that, in order to facilitate the business of redemption of rented dwellings, what is desirable is: 1. Exact statistics on the subject; 2. A good sanitary inspection force;

and 3. Co-operatives of building workers to undertake the building of new houses. All of these things are certainly very fine and good, but, despite all the clothing of quack phrases, they by no means cast 'complete light' into the obscurity of Proudhonist mental confusion.

Further, Engels engaged with a particular idea among the bourgeois reformers, namely of workers' housing colonies linked to factories, but where workers would invest in their own units. Philanthropists had already implemented this in the English countryside. Engels argued that

> [i]n England whole villages have grown up in this way, and some of them have later developed into towns. The workers, however, instead of being thankful to the philanthropic capitalists, have always raised very considerable objections to this 'cottage system'. Not only are they compelled to pay monopoly prices for these houses because the factory owner has no competitors, but immediately a strike breaks out they are homeless, because the factory owner throws them out of his houses without any more ado and thus renders any resistance difficult. (*ibid.*, 56)

Engels did not apply Marx's concept of 'monopoly rent' which Harvey (1974, 241) used in his discussion of rental housing a century later. Bodenschatz (1987, 80) identifies a gap in Marx's writings, in which 'one finds only fragments on the theme of "production and reproduction of the city", on the role of urban infrastructure and of urban land rent'. In Bodenschatz's analysis, Engels was also 'not able to fill this gap' and therefore 'the road was ideologically open for the adoption of the thesis of bourgeois reform' (*ibid.*). The propagation of this void (and its plugging with modern utopian ideas) was characteristic of Marxist urban thinking into the 1970s. Souza (2003, 192) writes that

> [s]temming in part from the typical anti-'reformist' viewpoint of Marxism (that is everything which contributes to social improvements outside the framework of a proper revolution can just contribute to the stabilisation of the *status quo* and is therefore 'conservative'), and partially from a purely academic mode of conceptualisation, scholars influenced by this approach were able to criticise eloquently, but refused offering alternative proposals *hic et nunc*.

Nevertheless, Engels did provide three arguments that in his view legitimized tenement housing and that are therefore relevant to mention here. They all relate to his primary criticism of the capitalist mode of production and of class exploitation in industry, the housing shortage being a mere 'secondary evil'.

Firstly, Engels argued that the tenement economy is based on demand and supply, in a context of competition:

> [W]e are dealing here with a quite ordinary commodity transaction between two citizens, and this transaction proceeds according to the economic laws which govern the sale of commodities in general and in particular the sale of the commodity, land property. (Engels 1887/1935, 25)

Landlords were not cheating workers more than they were cheating any other customers in the tenement market, whereas employers singled out and exploited workers in the labor market, denying them the real value of their labor. The problem therefore did not lie primarily in the form of housing but in the labor market (*ibid.*, 22).

Secondly, the tenement market allowed for worker mobility, necessitated by periodic strike action, unemployment or change of employment. With industrialization, '[t]he possession of house and garden was now of much less advantage than the possession of complete freedom of movement' facilitated by rental housing (*ibid.*, 13–14). Here Engels used the hypothetical case of a worker, 'Peter', who was required to purchase his dwelling in installments rather than pay rent. Peter lost his economic stake when insecurity in the workplace necessitated mobility (*ibid.*, 33). Engels found that his bourgeois socialist opponents did not address this reality.

Thirdly then, and for Engels of greatest significance, was the argument that tenement housing, which freed the worker from being bound to property, fostered the 'intellectual emancipation' of the working class, which Engels saw as an essential precondition for a revolution in which workers would take control of production.

> It is precisely modern large-scale industry, which has turned the worker, formerly chained to the land, into a completely propertyless proletarian, liberated from all traditional fetters and *free as a bird*; it is precisely this economic revolution which has created the sole conditions under which the exploitation of the working class in its final form, in the capitalist mode of production, can be overthrown. (*ibid.*, 28, emphasis in the original)

There are two aspects of Engels' argument that would have caused intense discomfort to the late 19th and early 20th century bourgeoisie. This, in addition to the void that Bodenschatz (1987) identifies, no doubt influenced the bourgeois social democrats' decision to reject their revolutionary agenda. The first was Engels' point that the emancipation of workers is enabled through tenement, or more precisely rented, housing, all towards the end of a workers' revolution that would fundamentally change the economic structures and in the event dismantle the bourgeoisie. The second was that Engels' only suggestion for a solution to the housing question lay in the direct redistribution and equalization of housing conditions through the revolution. While mentioning 'the expropriation of the present owners' and 'quartering in their houses the homeless or those workers excessively overcrowded in their former houses' (*ibid.*, 36), Engels consciously refrained from suggesting any detail in terms of tenure form, typology or mode of housing production:

> I am satisfied if I can prove that the production of our modern society is sufficient to provide all its members with enough to eat, and that there are houses enough in existence to provide the working masses for the time being with roomy and healthy living accommodation. To speculate as to how a future society would organise the distribution of food and dwellings leads directly to *utopia*. (*ibid.*, 101, emphasis in the original)

Engels does suggest that the state has a role to play, but provides no hint as to what this role ought to be. Concerning the question of whether the state, within a continuum of capitalist social relations, could resolve the housing shortage, he argues that '[i]t is perfectly clear that the existing state is neither able nor willing to do anything to remedy the housing difficulty' (*ibid.*, 71). Indeed, it was not until the 1920s, in the social democratic Weimar Republic (Engels would have referred to this as a 'bourgeois state'), that state subsidization of a new model of working class housing was introduced. However, as with many subsequent state-funded housing solutions across the capitalist world, it missed its target group (see Häußermann and Kapphan 2000, 48, 50) and went only some way towards 'solving the housing question'. As I showed above, it was the socialist East German state that undertook, a century after Engels' statements, to 'solve the housing question' in less than twenty years (and eradicate tenements). It, too, did not succeed entirely.

Engels' ideas on the housing question (and those of Karl Marx to which his text was aligned) increasingly found followers in Berlin.[5] By the 1870s, Berlin had become the 'new centre of the European working-class movement' (*ibid.*, 153). Thus Engels inserted his ideas on the housing question into a context of radicalization, but also of bourgeois fear of radicalization. An important distinction needs to be made here. Whereas for Engels the freedom and mobility of rented housing provided the basis for revolutionary emancipation, the bourgeois reformers believed it was the inhumane living conditions associated with this form of housing that led directly to radicalization. Bodenschatz (1987, 80) observes that the dark tenement backyard symbolized this threat among middle class reformers. They perceived the building type, and not only the poverty, ill health and overcrowding, as a threat. However, more so than freedom and mobility, and poor living conditions, in Berlin it was state repression that led the early working class political movement to abandon its demands for integration and instead embrace a revolutionary Marxist agenda.

Engels' writing was not addressed to the detail of the tenement situation in Berlin in particular, and the intellectual left that he represented did not provide any deeper analysis or guidance for the once-revolutionary social democratic movement. Non-utopianism, as promoted by Engels, is today a difficult notion for those seeking to address urban ills. Pinder (2005, 17) explains that Engels used the term 'utopia' to mean a reactionary response to a given reality, and adds that neo-Marxists have since reconceptualized 'utopianism as an "anticipatory consciousness" and a "principle of hope"' (*ibid.*), arguing that 'drawing on alternatives remains indispensable in enabling critique of human geography' (*ibid.*, 265).

An important political shift hinged on the urban and housing reform debate in the early 20th century. The much hated 'bearer of the social revolution – social democracy – adopt[ed] important agenda items of housing reform'; this signified its renunciation of 'the concept of a social revolution' (Bodenschatz 1987, 80). The social democrats became a 'potent political bearer' of the 'cultural devaluing of the tenement'. This was a precondition, unchallenged for six decades after WWI, for a strategy of destruction and redevelopment of the tenement city (*ibid.*).

The main objective of those opposing tenements was to prevent revolutionary radicalization of the working class by stabilizing the new urban society. Their aim was 'integration', rather than the further alienation of the city-ward migrants (Häußermann and Siebel 1996, 81). Ironically, these reformers believed that this required an end to the conditions of high mobility and mixed living present in the tenements (*ibid.*). The bourgeois view ignored Hobrecht's pragmatic argument for integration and for improved tenements. Instead it promoted a utopia of segregated homeownership. Ott (1989) argues that the bourgeois demand for housing reform was less one for better conditions for the working class, than for the isolation or segregation of the bourgeoisie from the working class, along the lines of the English cottage system.

Shifts in the approach to urban history and in the treatment of Berlin's tenements beyond the 19th century

Informed by the rejection of tenements and the advent of utopian modernist town planning, the new form of housing promoted for Berlin was uniform and functionally segregated. As captured in a sketch by the expressionist and architect Bruno Taut (Figure 5.7), originally published in his 1920 book *The Dissolving of Cities*, modernist architects and town planners discarded the dense and socially mixed tenements in their totality and promoted light, air and sun in a complete break in urban form, unlike the improved tenements that the pragmatist Hobrecht had suggested. Taut and his fellow utopian architects were informed by 'radical and often anarchist politics' (Pinder 2005, 60). Taut's ideas were influenced by those of the anarchist-communist and anti-authoritarian Kropotkin, as well as by Ebenezer Howard and the Garden City Movement, which actively sought and tested a new typology and tenure form for the working class. The German Garden City Association (*Deutsche Gartenstadt-Gesellschaft*) was founded in 1902, basing itself on Ebenezer Howard's writings and early projects in England (Berning et al. 1994, 4).[6] Howard, too, acknowledged the influence of Kropotkin in his own work (Pinder 2005, 38).

Figure 5.7: Cartoon by architect Bruno Taut promoting destruction of the tenement and its replacement with an idealized suburban model

Source: Taut (1920); Wiedenhoeft (1985, 14)

An architectural exhibition in 1905 focused on model working class housing and examples of simple houses (Treue 1969, 50). Furthermore, leading urban reformer Eberstadt promoted alternatives to the tenement in his 1909 *Handbook of Housing and the Housing Question* (*Handbuch des Wohnungswesens und der Wohnungs-frage*) (Bodenschatz 1987, 57). Not surprisingly, Werner Hegemann himself was a strong voice among the expert reformers of the early 20th century. Bernet (2004, 411) describes him as 'Germany's most international city planner' (at the time) who

> spoke out vehemently for a reformed urbanism and socially oriented administration… As the general secretary of the Berlin Urban Planning Exhibition of 1910 and as a participant in numerous reform-oriented projects and organisations, Hegemann also possessed a practical influence which was taken even further with his successful book *Das Steinerne Berlin* [*Berlin of Stone*]. Already in 1911 he had summarized his basic criticism and by 1930 he had expanded it into an unparalleled diatribe.

The town planning or urban design exhibition in 1910 displayed the entries of a competition for Greater Berlin. It brought together criticism of and alternatives to Berlin's tenement development and presented this to the broad public. In this sense, it was the most important pre-WWI event in devaluing this form of housing (Bodenschatz 1987, 58). In line with the positions presented at the 1910 exhibition, and in good bourgeois tradition, Hegemann argued a year later that the explosive danger posed by the city population was nowhere more acute than in the 'milieu' created by Berlin's housing conditions. Hegemann exaggerated, portraying the 'slum' as the norm. In his view, the entire city was a 'slum'. In calling for the eradication of slums, he was envisioning a redevelopment of the whole of Berlin (*ibid.*, 64, 66).

I have already introduced two seminal works on Berlin's tenements, Hegemann (1930) and Geist and Kürvers (1980, 1984, 1989). The contrast between these extensive texts highlights a close relationship between the urban policy discourse and the approach to urban history at any given time. It also demonstrates how the urban history discourse in turn shapes the way historical urban spaces are valued, devalued and revalued, thus shaping urban policy. The particularities of the two texts reflect the changing legitimacy of tenements as an inherited typology over the course of the twentieth century.

Hegemann (1930) captures early 20th century sentiment. His narrative is shaped by its time – it is a strong condemnation of the tenement era, referring to the 'ideal' modernist housing developments to this end. It was only under the social democratic Weimar Republic in the 1920s, and more so once the new Building Ordinance was adopted in 1925, that the ideas of housing reformers found fertile ground. By the time of Hegemann's (1930) publication, Berlin had thrown off 'the Prussian imperial mantle, becoming the capital of modernism' (Richie 1998, 325). New housing estates such as Bruno Taut and Martin Wagner's famous 'Horseshoe Settlement' (see Figure 5.8) were providing an antithesis to the tenement, not only spatially but also in their construction and management by cooperative building organizations (Wiedenhoeft 1985).

Figure 5.8: Bruno Taut's Hufeisensiedlung
Source: Author's photograph (2007)

However, by the early 1930s, subsequent to the publication of Hegemann's work, economic uncertainty and a complex bureaucracy had halted the ideal modernist-socialist housing construction (Wiedenhoeft 1985). The National Socialist (Nazi) regime that took control in 1933, with its contradictory anti-urban, anti-modernist attitude, was critical of Hegemann and immediately banned all his writings (Bernet 2004, 412). Nevertheless, it intended to gradually remove Berlin's tenements. Incorporating one aspect of bourgeois fear, the regime perceived tenements as a breeding ground for Marxists (Bodenschatz 1990, 22). The anti-Semitic program of the Nazi state impacted on Berlin's tenements through the already mentioned alienation of Jewish-owned properties. As I will show below, this had implications for Berlin's tenement market in the 1990s. Yet the greatest impact of Nazi ideology on Berlin's tenement-scape was WWII, with the massive destruction and damage of Berlin's housing stock (Wiedenhoeft 1985). Although Ladd (2005) cautions that 'it was not (and is not) so clear what was and wasn't a Nazi legacy', one can argue that, perversely, the seemingly anti-modernist Nazi regime paved the way for large-scale housing modernization. This was perhaps not only through the damage inflicted by the war. The Nazi banning of Hegemann's work may well have legitimized the text in the post-WWII period. Bernet (2004, 412) notes that '[i]n the post-war period respect for Hegemann was as strong as ever and served as a theoretical justification for the defenders of large-scale demolitions in Wilhelmine residential districts, seen as slums and relics of a vanished era'.

Such plans were delayed. When West Berlin's authorities introduced large-scale urban renewal in 1963, this enjoyed legitimacy. A decade later, however, extensive political opposition to the urban renewal policy had emerged. A 'cultural re-evaluation' of the tenement districts accompanied this opposition (*ibid.*). In 1976, the Secretary General of the European Council expressed heritage concerns: 'The Berlin of Stone [the phrase coined by Hegemann in 1930] is as much the product and cause of social ills as it is the bearer of qualities, which we're beginning to rediscover today' (Kahn Achermann, quoted in Bodenschatz 1990, 24). In addition, as already mentioned, the 'grave crisis in the urban renewal policy in the context of the squatting movement' led to the ultimate abandonment of the cost-intensive renewal program (Bodenschatz 1987, 15).

But the left was not only squatting and protesting. Berlin's tenements provided the space for 'experiments with new residential arrangements such as communes or single-person flats' (Bernet 2004, 415). Furthermore, '[l]eftists believed that the neighbourhoods of *Mietskasernen* might nurture anti-authoritarian countercultures in West Berlin' (*ibid.*). This seems to have arisen more from an identification with bourgeois determinism (the assumption that building conditions, including dark backyards, would in themselves nurture a particular political orientation), than the more complex (though also not conclusive) Marxist idea that the mobility afforded by rental housing allowed for working class emancipation. Indeed, Sennett (1974, 252) warns that the Marxist 'slogan that material conditions determine consciousness is, and has been, easily vulgarised'. He adds that '[a]t best, Marx [and by implication Engels] meant by it that every new material situation in society forces a reformulation of belief only because the work informing those beliefs has altered' (*ibid.*). West Berlin's movement of young leftist students in the 1980s to a large extent stemmed from bourgeois rather than working class backgrounds. Struggling with their own legitimacy, they perhaps naively sought to identify with working class consciousness through their occupation of working class housing.

In this context, 50 years after Hegemann's *Berlin of Stone*, the second seminal text appeared on the topic of Berlin's tenements – Geist and Kürvers' three volumes (1980, 1984, 1989). These could not be greater opposites to Hegemann's text. Geist and Kürvers did not subject their three books to a narrative. Instead, they reproduced building plans and original texts of the time, be they official reports, media statements or personal positions. Geist and Kürvers' own factual descriptions accompany some of these reproductions, though mostly the reader is required to peruse pages of historical text. This largely unsynthesized collection or reproduction of historical documents is an invaluable resource, though not easy to read. As the second and clearly more important seminal piece on Berlin's tenements, it is frequently cited by the subsequent tenement literature; but this literature, which is itself sparse, utilizes its actual content poorly.

The Iron Curtain isolated the changing interpretations and the rediscovery of tenements in West Berlin from thinking in the Communist East of the city. Under state socialism, tenements did not regain their legitimacy. The East German state complemented its obsession with monotonous mass housing at the time with the view that Berlin's tenement districts represented 'capitalism *par excellence.* The government planned to eradicate them' (Bernet 2004, 416). The dominant narrative is that, with a diehard (but unrealized) vision of complete demolition of historic tenements and their replacement with modern housing stock, old tenement neighborhoods were largely left to decay (Kristen 1990; Häußermann and Kapphan 2000, 68). Richie (1998, 756) observes from her own experience in the late 1980s that

> the back streets of East Berlin contained scenes of decay difficult to find in even the poorest and most neglected areas of West Berlin. In these areas a flat cost only 5 per cent of a family's income but young couples had to wait for years before they could move into one.

As already mentioned, East Berlin's historic tenements, in particular in Prenzlauer Berg, attracted political dissidents and others rejecting or excluded from the modernist tower block housing (Richie 1998; Levine 2004). However, a fascinating book titled *Berliner Mietshaus* (Liebmann 1982/2002) provides a very different and compelling window onto ordinary East German tenement life in Prenzlauer Berg. Written by an East German, its narrative is based on interviews with tenants in four Prenzlauer Berg tenements in 1979 and 1980. It includes evidence of people's efforts to improve their flats and buildings, the agendas of the House-Community Leadership (*Hausgemeinschaftsleitung*) and their dealings with the Communal Housing Administration (*Kommunale Wohnungsverwaltung*). The latter bore the costs and supplied materials, but relied on tenants themselves to carry out the improvements, whether painting walls, replacing windows or installing showers (Liebmann 2002, 10, 125, 156). A remarkable shift from conditions in Wilhelmine Berlin is the permanence of tenants' occupation. Among Liebmann's interviewees there are women who had lived their entire life in one tenement. It is particularly the lives of elderly women, for whom the tenement was a home, that Liebmann celebrates in her text. When she endeavored to make the manuscript available to a wider audience after the fall of the Wall, West German publishers responded to the innocence of this approach with reluctance (Liebmann 2002).

Since the unification of East and West, gentrification, segregation and socio-spatial change have shaped the narrative on Berlin's tenements (Reimann 1997; Kemper 1998; Häußermann and Kapphan 2000; Levine 2004; Holm 2006). It revisits Berlin's history from this perspective, but with (partly uncritical) reference to the earlier seminal texts. Its focus and contribution is on understanding the very recent past.

The need to avoid a destructive discourse: initial warnings for present-day Nairobi

As accommodation was a precondition for labor's ability to work, Berlin's tenement market derived the same pragmatic legitimacy as those of New York and Glasgow discussed earlier. Berlin's tenements also enjoyed legitimacy throughout the 19th century because of their legal compliance with building regulations. However, a combination of bourgeois discomfort and fear and working class distress, unrest and radicalization undermined the legitimacy of this form of housing in the eyes of the middle class. Firstly, the experience of dark and poorly ventilated tenement conditions for the middle and lower middle class seemed to lead to the conclusion that even an improved working class tenement would not be acceptable. Reformers were preoccupied with conceptualizing and piloting complete alternatives rather than considering improvements to the existing tenement stock, which remained largely untouched and continued to play an important role in housing the masses. Reformers also rejected rental as a form of tenure, and instead promoted cooperatives and home ownership. All along, they gave little thought to how existing tenements could be converted into a more acceptable tenure form. Secondly, working class health sparked concern among the middle class less about the suffering of the working class than about the threat of epidemics spreading to the middle class. Modernization of water and sanitation systems reduced these threats, but did little to address the ill health that was conditioned by overcrowding and occupation of technically (though not always legally) uninhabitable units – a result of both meager wages and periodic undersupply of housing. Wages and working conditions, however, did improve over the course of the late 19th and early 20th century, in part in response to a third bourgeois concern, namely that of working class rebellion, radicalization and revolution. When working class tenement residents, especially those evicted due to rent distress, protested against their experience, the bourgeoisie and the state interpreted this less as a call to improve conditions than as a threat to political stability.

Within the reform debates, minority voices put forward arguments in favor of Berlin's tenements and called for their improvement. The mainstream reform movement discarded these attempts to justify or normatively legitimize Berlin's tenements with reference to the quality of the streets and social mixing. The arguments in favor of tenements also found no political bearer or agent among Berlin's political formations. In the divided East and West Berlin the opposing regimes implemented the reformers' ideas in different ways, but in both cases at a vast scale and with dramatic loss of street quality. In West Berlin, the renewal program of the 1960s began to lose legitimacy in the 1970s. In East Berlin, the entire totalitarian regime, along with its resolution to solve the housing question through the complete eradication of the old tenements and their replacement with industrially produced mass housing, lost its legitimacy in the late 1980s. In both cases, anti-authoritarian movements from within the old and decaying tenement districts were instrumental in deconstructing the legitimacy of the large-scale development programs.

In the 19th and early 20th century, tenement ownership was widespread among at least sections of the middle class. As already mentioned, the literature tells us little about this and does not explain why these individual stakes in the tenement market did not result in the defense of the tenement as a form of middle class investment against the reformers' later ideas of renewal through complete demolition. Perhaps it was landlord mobilization that led the reformers initially to refrain from suggesting intervention in the existing tenement market, and to promote instead the construction of model alternatives on vacant land (most of which, as in 19th century New York, did not succeed). Only much later, once the SPD adopted the anti-tenement agenda, did reformers begin envisaging the demolition and redevelopment of the existing tenement stock. The question of how existing tenements could be improved was long neglected. While the 1925 Building Ordinance paved the way for developments according to a new typology, the existing stock in large parts of the city continued to house tenants in much the same conditions as before 1925. This lasted at least a further 40 years in West Berlin (modernization of the tenement at No. 40 Liebenwalder Strasse was carried out only in 1967, earlier improvements having been discouraged by the expectation but delay of large-scale urban redevelopment) and in East Berlin for at least a further 60 years up to the fall of the Berlin Wall in 1989, although piecemeal modernization was possible with tenant contributions through the Communal Housing Administration. The collapse of the East German state was not followed by immediate tenement renovation in former East Berlin. The need for modernization of the old tenement stock led to the unified German government's decision to introduce tax incentives for private investors willing to purchase and upgrade old tenements. However, it inadequately anticipated and mitigated the consequences of gentrification, displacement and segregation caused by the release of modernized units into a sectional title homeownership market. Adapted to the demands of a new generation of end-users and speculators, the historical tenement stock remains of relevance to key interests in the city and therefore has a renewed future in Berlin, although the tenement as single-owned building with multiple rental units is losing ground.

Marxist-socialist thinking had only a perverted impact on the history spanned by this chapter. The totalitarianism of the USSR and the East German state was founded on a twisting and stretching of Marxist thought (Jackson 1957, 181). Similarly then, Marxist thought on tenements or housing more broadly, as expressed in Engels' *The Housing Question*, only found perverted expression. It would be hard to claim that 'solving the housing problem' through demolition of tenements and monotonous mass production of modernist blocks was an expression of the working class emancipation envisaged by Marx and Engels. In its combination with totalitarian control over society, this form of housing actively suppressed emancipation. Those unwilling to conform to the state's prescriptions chose to live in the less controlled historical tenement stock, no matter how decayed. Their intellectual emancipation (though not determined by the housing typology) helped undermine the authoritarian system from that base. At the core, however, is the problem that Marxism, like other strands of thinking at the time, had avoided proper engagement with the tenement and wider urban reality. Providing no alternative but the revolution, and no alternative beyond a revolution, Marxists helped pave the way for soulless modernist architecture and planning to become the orthodoxy across east and west.

It is from the debates that were waged and the mistakes that were perpetrated in the tormented history of Berlin's tenements that lessons must be drawn for present-day Nairobi. I carry these into the following chapters. In the first instance, tenant mobilization and articulation of suggestions for improvements should be encouraged, not repressed or politically abused. However, politics do play an important role. For any improvement to materialize for tenants in Nairobi's tenement market, a powerful coalition of interests or a 'potent political bearer' will be needed. In the absence of any debate on the future of Nairobi's tenements, as I show in Chapter 8, there is a real danger that modernist ideas of demolition/eradication and mass redevelopment may find political ground. Since the 1980s, Berlin has had political bearers of an approach based on collective and participatory tenement upgrading. However, in the current climate of urban competitiveness, governments more often become the agents of massive foreign capital investment in the built environment on prime land, even if already inhabited, and involving heavily contested plans for mass forced removal and demolition of a kind one would shiver to see unfolding in Nairobi's tenement districts.

The qualities inherent in the tenement districts of Nairobi need to be valued. However, these values should not be traded or handed to local or foreign investors whose interventions would ultimately displace the current tenants. Local and foreign urban researchers' lack of interest in Nairobi's tenements today is reflective of a larger situation and sentiment, with which I engage in the following chapters. However, Berlin's history also suggests that, if carried out and actually read and debated, studies of Nairobi's tenements could influence the course of events. By constructing arguments of normative/prescriptive legitimacy or de-legitimacy, they can actively build or destroy descriptive legitimacy or legitimacy as experienced. In my analysis, Berlin's history suggests that any engagement with Nairobi's tenements should begin with an understanding of the tenement reality, including its economy, its investors and its inhabitants, and work with these to reduce the excesses of this market. Pinder (2005, 262) argues, with reference to Lefebvre and the recent writings of Harvey, that there is a place for utopianism in addressing the 'sclerosis' in urban planning, but this need not be a spatial utopia. In Nairobi there is above all a need to acknowledge, accept and work with the existing spatial reality. In the absence of any acknowledgement of the tenement reality, it would be irresponsible to encourage a Kenyan urban discourse that considers and promotes utopian spatial alternatives. Towards the end of the book, I return to this discussion, emphasizing the relevance of a utopia of process rather than that of spatial form.

Endnotes

1   Engels (1845/1958, 65) mentions 'damp, dirty cellar dwellings' underneath the 'cottages' of Manchester's New Town.

2   'Slipper cinema' referred to a neighborhood establishment that people did not feel compelled to dress up for. It is not to be confused with the more recent use of this term as a television in a home.

3   Crowder (1991, 39) argues that the English writer William Godwin, who lived more than half a century earlier (1758–1836) was the 'pioneer of systematic modern anarchist theory'. Though not referring to the term 'anarchism', Godwin already articulated the central anarchist ideal of a 'stateless society characterized by freedom' (*ibid.*, 4). Proudhon (1809–1865) wrote 'in apparent ignorance of Godwin's genuinely anarchist message', therefore representing 'a new start for the tradition' (*ibid.*, 74).

4   Proudhon had already been critiqued by Marx in the *Grundrisse*, fifteen years earlier (Ritzer 1996, 624). According to Jackson (1957, 64), an opportunity was lost when Marx and Proudhon decided not to collaborate, after meeting in Paris in 1844. 'The two main streams of socialist thought which might, had they flowed together, have led to the emancipation of the working-class, henceforth diverged' (*ibid.*).

5   Richie (1998, 153–187) dedicates a whole chapter to 'The Rise of Red Berlin'.

6   An earlier (1896) publication in Germany by Theodor Fritsch had presented very similar ideas to those of Ebenezer Howard, but had not attained prominence (Wiedenhoeft 1985, 10).

Chapter 6

Growth and enrichment:
20th century Nairobi

The construction of multi-story tenements in Nairobi from the 1980s onward is the result of a steady and as yet undisrupted process. It has its origins in structures and practices that had entrenched themselves in the colonial city. Early dispossessions, together with urban exclusion, meant that informal or unauthorized settlements formed part of Nairobi from its outset, as did early forms of private rental accommodation which provided some legitimacy for later tenement development. Other enduring phenomena that have their origin in the colonial period include the establishment of a middle class and an elite from which a cast of capitalist and autocratic leaders were to emerge.

The first such leader, Jomo Kenyatta, recognized by the west for his pro-capitalist stance, navigated several political crises by means of repression and ruled up to his death, allowing his family and cronies to amass dizzying levels of wealth, much of which was vested in land. In the absence of serious efforts at redistribution, Kenyatta called on the middle class and impoverished masses alike to create wealth for themselves. In the housing market, poor targeting of subsidized projects allowed the entrepreneurial middle class to edge its way into large-scale tenement construction, often on land intended to benefit the poor. Kenyatta's successor, Daniel arap Moi, though more autocratic and ambivalent in his rule, provided continuity. While publicly condemning corruption, his regime condoned massive grabbing of public urban land for private development at the same time as it was navigating donor withdrawal. Corruption permeated all levels of government and enabled the multi-story tenement market to flourish. Vigilantism emerged as a new force that was to help thwart popular optimism about the prospects for meaningful democratization in the post-Moi era. As a ruthless and extractive force, it has provided the first dampener to growth in Nairobi's tenement market.

The periodization of Nairobi's history (summarized in Figure 6.2 in Chapter 6) serves as a political, economic and demographic backdrop to Nairobi's early (colonial) physical planning, its wide-scale transgression from the 1980s, and the emergence and operation of the tenement market. It also provides the larger context of tenement living conditions, and of the weak urban and housing discourse which neither undermined nor underpins the legitimacy enjoyed by the tenement market today.

Colonial control, urban class differentiation and early forms of private rental housing (1880s–1963)

The city of Nairobi emerged out of a process of commercial and colonial invasion, land alienation and exclusion. In 1888, Britain granted the Imperial British East Africa Company rights to activities in the territory that would become Kenya. The company's first interests were in establishing the Kenya Uganda railway (1896–1902). Because of the financial difficulties it experienced, the British government soon assumed control (Miller 1984, 9). In 1895, it declared both Kenya and Uganda British protectorates (*ibid.*, 9). According to Freund (1984, 97–98), colonial territories emerged at the time: 'In 1890 Germany recognized a northern border for its new East Africa colony which acknowledged a British sphere of control in what became Kenya and Uganda.' Nine years later, the Kenya Uganda Railway established its headquarters in the area where the city of Nairobi was to emerge, and one year later the first Nairobi Municipal Community regulations appeared (Obudho 1997, 297).

The railway became operational in 1903 (Aseka 1990). Between 1902 and 1908, activities along the rail route involved massive land alienation, including in the fertile Kikuyu-inhabited southern Kiambu area close to where Nairobi was being established (Soja 1968, 17). This occasioned the first rush of European settlers (*ibid.*). Only in 1919, immediately after WWI, did the British governor agree to the establishment of the Nairobi Municipal Council, intending it to cater for the needs of the Europeans who were increasingly demanding a say in the city's affairs (Hake 1977, 41). While this coincided with an extension of the urban boundary, the emerging town did not welcome African urbanization. In the following year, in which Britain also made Kenya its colony (Aseka 1990), a Native Pass Law was enacted, followed by a Vagrancy Ordinance two years later. These measures prohibited those not formally employed from residing in Nairobi. However, the size of the area seemed to hamper their implementation (Nevanlinna 1996, 129).

Colonial rural policy drove city-ward migration in this period. Fertile land continued to be alienated from indigenous rural communities, who were consigned to overcrowded 'reserves' on land with little agricultural potential. Private ownership and property rights replaced communal tenure. The imposition of taxes forced Kenyan peasants into a system of wage labor on European farms (Otiso 2002, 258).

It was primarily impoverished and displaced Kikuyus, from both Kikuyuland and the Rift Valley (a Kalenjin tribal area into which Kikuyus had been displaced), who 'poured' into the early 'slums' or 'villages' of Nairobi (Meredith 2006, 84). The 'villages' or African hut settlements of Pangani, Masikini, Kaburini and Mji wa Mombasa sprang up 'to the north and northeast of the town centre' and in Kileleshwa to the west (Nevanlinna 1996, 136). With the exception of Pangani, 'Muslim Swahili headmen' controlled each of these settlements (White 1990, 45). The military administration established the 'village' of Kibera in 1912 'for Sudanese soldiers' (*ibid.*, 46); this settlement, outside of the then town boundary, was never demolished. Those constructing housing in these settlements enjoyed usufruct rights (*ibid.*, 146).

Landlordism in Nairobi emerged in parallel among its segregated communities. For 'European and Indian families', it was 'the express lift to the top income brackets' (Hake 1977, 41). By the early 1920s, building plans had been submitted proposing as many as 280 tenancies to the acre (*ibid.*). In the Indian 'bazaar area, most of the plots in the early years had been bought by a handful of wealthy Indian businessmen', who constructed buildings with shops and accommodation for letting (Nevanlinna 1996, 108). Given the demand, these were extremely lucrative, with up to '100 per cent yearly return on the original investment' (*ibid.*, 109). However, in 1902, the remedy for 'another outbreak of plague' was 'to burn down the infected parts of town, essentially the Indian bazaar' (*ibid.*, 105). At the time, and reflecting the discourse of urban reformers in Berlin and elsewhere in Europe, city officials thought that the proximity of the buildings in the Indian bazaar 'neutralized the natural advantages of air and light' (*ibid.*, quoting a source from 1907). They moved the bazaar to the south and there 'single storey buildings' with 'shops at the front and at the rear living quarters for families and a host of lodgers and sub-lessees' developed (Halliman and Morgan 1967, 104). Commentators described conditions at the time as acutely overcrowded and 'little better than those that had given rise to the plague a few years earlier' (*ibid.*).[1]

In Nairobi's African settlements, a 'property-owning petty bourgeoisie' consisting of male and female investors emerged at the same time (White 1990, 45). These early entrepreneurs constructed

> four- to eight-room huts in which they lived, renting out the remaining rooms. The monies from which they built urban property had been earned primarily from the sale of services – whether gun bearing or prostitution – to the Europeans, Indians, and Africans who hunted, traded, and worked in the protectorate, and the sale of agricultural produce to settlers and African labourers alike. (*ibid.*, 45–46)

In Pangani, an Englishman had built the first 'lodging house' around 1899. 'By 1913, the Pangani "hotels" were famous' (Hirst 1994, 62). However, the ideology of 'sanitary segregation' had taken root and 'rules for native location' began to be drawn up (White 1990, 46). While 'medical arguments' legitimized plans to demolish African settlements, 'property values and political pressure', including demands from the 'Indian community to survey those areas for their own residential use... provided the motivation' for the removals. By 1920, the authorities had planned and developed the first African 'location', Pumwani, within the municipal boundary on land it had leased from the government (Nevanlinna 1996, 137). It consisted of latrines and communal ablutions, roads and individual plots 'for the construction of temporary structures' (ibid., 138), in essence a site-and-service scheme (Etherton 1971, 7). The name Pumwani, meaning 'resting place', was given to the scheme by the people that were relocated there (White 1990, 48). Planners based Pumwani 'on South African models' at the time (ibid.). They envisaged a maximum of 15 family members per stand, with no subletting. Pumwani was to replace all unauthorized villages and to 'contain all the Africans of Nairobi... into the foreseeable future' (ibid.), and thus to 'provide for greater administrative control over the African population (Stren 1978, 189). In 1923, the Municipal Council, through its Medical Department (White 1990, 67), demolished Kaburini, Mombasa and Masikini villages (Bujra 1973, 13). However, 'Pumwani grew only slowly', and the remaining unauthorized villages continued to play an important role in African urban cultural and political life (Nevanlinna 1996, 137). Although subletting was not envisaged officially, Pumwani and the other African settlements provided opportunities for 'women from societies in which they could not own property' to build houses and rent out rooms 'at extremely profitable rates' (White 1990, 119). Many of these women were '*malayas*', the Swahili term for prostitutes. This occupation gave women financial independence and enabled investment in rental stock (ibid.).

The world recession around 1930 impacted on labor demand in Nairobi, and saw a reduction in the African population up to 1936. As a result, African housing was less overcrowded in the years from 1931 to 1934. However, African landlords did not reduce their rents. Where pressed by lack of income, several tenants would share a room to make up the rent. Landlords were also willing to rent out sleeping space in passages to those not able to afford room rent. The profit-oriented stance of the private landlords drove many financially distressed people into 'squatting' elsewhere in the city, where landlordism also emerged (White 1990, 80–82). White (ibid., 211) mentions 'absentee landlords', though not detailing the emergence of this extended form of accumulation. However, she explains that the accumulation-driven practice of the African landlords 'served the state in ideological and practical ways; the high rents... sent more men into their rural homes or into urban homelessness than the pass laws did, and gave the state its self-righteous tone in condemning landlords' (ibid., 131). It was common to portray

landlords and tenants as completely antagonistic... In the invention of the colonial state, landlords were tired, old, dependent on official goodwill and tolerance; in reality, African landlords were dynamic, committed, with close ties to their tenants and communities. Until the 1930s the imaginary landlords of official rhetoric and the real landlords of African settlement rarely met: policy was constructed for the former and routinely subverted by the latter. Private landlords built, owned, and supervised African housing in Nairobi. (White 1990, 131, 145)

By 1938, when the authorities demolished Pangani, the idea of municipal housing had superseded the site-and-service concept of Pumwani. The municipality had built the first municipal housing estate, Kariakor ('the ex-Carrier Corps settlement' (Bujra 1973, 15)) or Quarry Road Estate, in 1929, initially with dormitories which were soon converted into rooms (Nevanlinna 1996, 139). With the removals from Pangani, the municipality relocated many households to Shauri Moyo (Pumwani Extension) (Figure 7.2 in Chapter 7), where '155 blocks' had been constructed, 'each containing 6 rooms with one communal kitchen in each block and 20 other blocks with four rooms with communal kitchen,' and a total of '11 shared abultion blocks' (Shihembetsa 1991, 234–235). Policy towards landlords shifted in the Shauri Moyo scheme. Here, the municipality made private landlords do the work of the state (White 1990, 146). 'The former landlords were allowed to select their tenants, set the rents [in most of the houses], collect and keep them, for 4/ a month plot-holding fee' (*ibid.*, 138). However, these landlords were barred from passing their rights on to their children (*ibid.*). The formal 'rooming' provided in Shauri Moyo reflected 'contradictions' in 'the Kenya government's African urban policy' (Stren 1978, 196). In its determination 'to keep wages low', the government caused dissent and 'strike action', which it sought in turn to quell through segregated public housing rather than by improving wages (*ibid.*). In 1942, a committee was appointed to investigate 'the African housing situation in Nairobi' and a year later 'a new housing ordinance' was enacted 'to set up a Central Housing Board and a special fund to make loans to local authorities' (*ibid.*, 199).

In the mid-1940s, Kikuyus made up half of Nairobi's population, with 'a growing tide of desperate, impoverished vagrants' in addition to 'ex-servicemen returning from the war' (WWII) (Meredith 2006, 84). Discontent and crime rose with poverty, unemployment, 'poor housing, low wages, inflation and homelessness' (*ibid.*). By this time, a contrast between wealth and deprivation had firmly emerged. This was also when 'Nairobi began to assume its "urban" character due to the erection in local stone of many larger buildings' (Halliman and Morgan 1967, 104). In the years after WWII, Nairobi's population 'doubled in size' (*ibid.*) (see Tables 6.1 and 6.2). As a result of its WWII losses, Britain changed its colonial policy from one of mere extraction to one that encouraged British industry 'to invest in manufacturing in the colonies' (JAM 1982, 7). 'International capital, large banks and trading companies moved into Nairobi', transforming 'the city into a regional financial, marketing and manufacturing centre for Eastern Africa' (*ibid.*).

It was at this point that an interdisciplinary team of three South African 'experts' (an architect, a sociologist and an engineer – an innovative combination at the time (Hirst 1994)) were called upon to draw up the 1948 Master Plan for Nairobi to which I will return in more detail. The planning team observed that large parts of Nairobi (in this case not its 'slums' or 'villages') had developed out of 'an erroneous respect for the sanctity of private rights of property, including the right to do wrong' (Halliman and Morgan 1967, 104, quoting from the Master Plan). This became an enduring approach to property rights in the city. It is generally believed that the South African consultants planned Nairobi on the one hand 'to create a model' of the British Garden City, and on the other hand 'to create an essentially European city in the African setting' (see Kurtz 1998, 77). However, the planners were in fact critical of the Garden City approach, promoting instead the neighborhood unit which they deemed appropriate to the social needs of rural Africans moving into the city (Nevanlinna 1996, 171).

Table 6.1: Nairobi's pre-independence population growth

Year	Period	Population	Annual population growth rate
1928		29 864	
	1936–1948		Average 7.6%
1948		118 579	
	1948–1962		Average 5.9%
1962		266 795	

Source: Based on Obudho (1997)

Table 6.2: Differentiation of Nairobi's early population growth up to 1944 and in 1962

Year	European	Asiatic	African
1906	559	3 582	7 371
1926	2 665	9 199	18 000
1936	5 600	16 000	28 000
1944	10 400	34 300	64 200
1962	21 476	87 454	157 865

Source: Compiled from White, Silberman and Anderson (1948, 43); Obudho (1997, 301)

Linked to the policy of attracting foreign capital was the active creation of an African middle class which could mediate the needs of foreign capitalists 'and consume their commodities' (JAM 1982, 7). Already in 1920, there were intentions to give preference to 'educated Africans' over 'Asiatics' in the allocation of 'all minor government and other posts' (Nevanlinna 1996, 139). After WWII, the active creation of the African middle class inevitably led to demands for political participation (JAM 1982, 8). In 1944, the first African (educated in Oxford) was 'appointed to the colonial governing body' and through him 'demands grew perceptibly for broader African representation' (Miller 1984, 21). At first, this sparked fears of communist radicalism (JAM 1982, 8), not only due to the international political constellation, but also because of the emergence of a national resistance movement.

Resentment had arisen among ordinary Kikuyus in 'heavily populated' rural reserves where the colonial government's 'conservation measures' and 'restrictions on African production of lucrative cash crops like coffee', as well as the accumulation of 'ever more land' by 'senior tribal figures' combined with the concerns of those displaced from their tribal land into the Rift Valley (Meredith 2006, 83). The Kikuyu tribal land was close to Nairobi, therefore the Kikuyu 'felt the impact of colonial rule more fully than most others' (*ibid.*, 81). When Jomo Kenyatta, who was to become Kenya's first post-independence president, returned to colonially ruled Kenya in 1946 'the first stirrings of rebellion amongst [his tribe] the Kikuyu had already begun' (*ibid.*, 81).[2] Kenyatta never fully identified with the 'resistance campaign' of Kikuyus, which from 1948 began to be referred to as Mau Mau (*ibid.*). For Kenyatta and the emerging Kikuyu elite, there were strategic advantages to reap in not being associated with this radical mobilization. According to Ed Soja's analysis published in the late 1960s, 'the unique geographical situation of Kikuyuland with respect to Nairobi and the major European farming areas was the necessary spark which kindled… other ingredients and thrust the Kikuyu into the modernizing vanguard' (Soja 1968, 25). Thus, 'a favourable combination of factors enabled the Kikuyu to dominate the history and geography of modernization' (*ibid.*, 24). Though not uncontested, this applied well beyond the early years of independence, when Soja was conducting this research.

However, Soja's 1968 study did not provide the full picture. In his 1979 'radical reappraisal' of 'the geography of modernization', Soja acknowledged 'the increasing gap between rich and poor classes' and the processes of underdevelopment (Soja 1979, 34). Indeed, the modernization, wealth creation and political advancement were the privilege of the traditional Kikuyu elite and emerging middle class, including 'the African agents of the colonial state, merchants, artisans, wealthy commodity producers and elements of traditional ruling classes' (Berman 1992, 197). Colonialism, and with it urbanization, shaped an African class formation that 'inherited patterns of inequality already present in precolonial institutions' (*ibid.*, 198). It also shaped contradictory consciousness of class. 'Structural wealth and poverty were known but little understood' (Lonsdale 1992b, 462). 'Sorcery was a more common explanation of injustice than the inequality of state power', and '[t]he proverbial truth [recently perpetuated by the proliferation of prosperity churches in Nairobi] that wealth proved virtue and poverty delinquence' were believed by most (*ibid.*). With this consciousness, which 'failed to wrestle with the deepest contradictions of capitalism and the state', a Kikuyu nationalism emerged and sought solidarity (*ibid*.). Nevertheless, 'a politically oriented general workers' union... appeared for a time to herald the birth of class-based politics', with general strikes in Nairobi in 1950 (Freund 1984, 218).

According to Ferudi (1989, 141), '[a]lthough Mau Mau was primarily Kikuyu, it was not a tribalist movement. The emergence of Mau Mau was restricted to certain sections of Kikuyu society.' Furthermore, 'the trans-ethnicity of daily survival brought Mau Mau many willing non-Kikuyu allies' (Lonsdale 1992b, 464). Officially, Mau Mau was interpreted as being 'savagely tribal rather than justifiably national' (Lonsdale 1992a, 285). Marxist analysts publishing anonymously in the Journal of African Marxists (JAM) note that the interpretation that Mau Mau (or the Kenyan Land Freedom Army, as the movement referred to itself) was 'the manifestation of purely Kikuyu frustration' played 'into the hands of the colonial rulers and their African successors with a stake in dividing the country on "tribal lines"' (JAM 1982, 10). They argue that Mau Mau 'aimed at nation-wide independence', something neither the colonialists nor Kenyatta liked to acknowledge (*ibid*.). The Mau Mau became a 'virtually forbidden' topic in Kenyatta's newly independent Kenya (Meredith 2006, 268). However, 'Mau Mau failed to develop a distinct political programme and an ideology' (Ferudi 1989, 142). Its nationalism remained a 'diffuse and ill defined' principle, and '[t]he aim of most activists was winning access to land' (*ibid*.)

Two distinct groupings among the Kikuyu did not identify with the increasingly violent discontent of the displaced and impoverished, expressed through the Mau Mau insurgency. They were 'the old Kikuyu establishment – chiefs, headmen and landowners – and the aspiring middle class – businessmen, traders, civil servants and government teachers' (Meredith 2006, 85). In a bid 'to enforce complete unity among the Kikuyu people', Mau Mau leaders turned against Kikuyus who opposed them, thus 'horrifying the Kikuyu and whites alike' (*ibid*., 86). The state chose to interpret this as 'a Kikuyu civil war'; it declared an Emergency 'after the assassination of Chief Waruhiu, not the murder of a few settlers' (White 1990, 204). Kenyatta was falsely accused of masterminding Mau Mau and was imprisoned for seven years; he was released only in 1961 (Meredith 2006). The authors of JAM challenge the dominant narrative, adding that 'finding himself on the Mau Mau death list... [Kenyatta's] detention was in fact a form of protective custody' (JAM 1982, 23). It coincided with a State of Emergency imposed from 1952 to 1960, during which, in the JAM authors' words, 'a puffed-up African middle class' was created, 'a group of nascent grabbers and looters whose prosperity grew out of treachery to our people... They could be trusted to make "independence" safe for the continued operations of international capital' (*ibid*., 11).

During the State of Emergency, one official interpretation of the Mau Mau activism (also used to explain Berlin's working class movement in the 1860s) was that 'slum conditions' had provided a 'breeding ground' for 'subversive activities'

(Stren 1972, 75). As a result, tough measures were instituted to gain control over the unplanned urban 'villages' (*ibid.*). From 1952, African settlements in Nairobi were regularly cordoned off and searched and 'vagrancy regulations and employment laws' were used to expel Kikuyus suspected of Mau Mau involvement, 'in an effort to re-establish government control and to displace Mau Mau organisers' (Anderson 2003, 160). Once repatriated, 'they were forbidden to leave [the reserves] without a pass' (Leo 1984, 59). The repatriation efforts culminated in the three-week Operation Anvil in 1954 – 'a decisive move... to isolate the Mau Mau bands in the forested mountains of Nyandarwa and Kirinyaga' (Anderson 2003, 160). Police and military troops searched Nairobi, detained 27 000 Merus, Embus and Kikuyus and expelled a further 20 000 (Leo 1984, 59, 60). 'The radical wing of the labour movement was also squashed' (Freund 1984, 219). Military control over Nairobi's African settlements continued after Operation Anvil. British troops, which were involved with the police in the operation, were withdrawn only in 1956, 'after the capture and execution of Dedan Kimathi, leader of the best armed forest faction' (White 1990, 205).

In the late 1950s, wages increased but employment shrank (and with it, the then unrecognized phenomenon of African self-employment grew), whereas existing African housing became increasingly overcrowded (White 1990). Squatter settlements, in which people built their own huts or houses, expanded exponentially until the early 1960s. The bulldozed Mathare settlement 'was once again inhabited in 1958, bulldozed, and a thriving village again by 1962' (*ibid.*, 215). In Nairobi, Luhya and Luo migrants had difficulties finding 'accommodation in the municipal estates' in the late 1950s and increasingly 'moved to Kibera, where a decade later, they outnumbered Nubian [Sudanese] landlords two to one' (*ibid.*, 216).

From these pre-independence days, Kenyan politics (and later wealth) came to be dominated over long periods by a handful of individuals (and dynasties), contesting power with one another while avoiding commitment to a constitutional democracy. In 1957, 'the first African elections... brought eight elected Africans into legislative council; they included... a minority Kalenjin leader, Daniel arap Moi' (Meredith 2006, 87), who was to become vice-president for 11 years of Kenyatta's 15-year rule, and the second president of independent Kenya for 24 years. In 1958, 14 seats were made available, and two Luo leaders, Tom Mboya and Oginga Odinga, were elected 'and offered ministerial posts', though they refused the offer in the absence of more significant African representation (Miller 1984). Both were to become influential in post-independence politics. In 1962, Charles Rubia became the city's first African mayor (Lee-Smith 1989, 279). Initially aided by 'various European mentors', he too 'became one of the country's wealthiest and most powerful Africans (Werlin 1966, 181, 182).

In 1960 (before Kenyatta's release) Britain, in the hope that Kenyan nationalism might distract the indigenous leaders from communism, announced its intention to grant Kenya independence. At the same time, the Kenya African National Union (KANU) was formed as a national party with a manifesto promising to advance 'the good of the country as a whole and not merely the interests of a few' (quoted in JAM 1982, 17). Its line on housing was directed at those living in 'slums': 'before citizen E has 20 rooms to protect him from rain, citizen A must have shelter' (*ibid.*). Ironically, the housing market of the following decades took on excesses that no Kenyan would have dreamed of in the mid-1960s. By the early 1980s, just as the unauthorized high-rise tenement market began to dominate the residential landscape, the authors of JAM (1982, 17) asked '[w]hich Kenyan can read the *Manifesto* today without a bitter laugh?' However, before independence the bitter laugh was already in the hearts of the 'rural and urban proletariat who had formed the bulk of the Mau Mau' (Owino 1999, 460, 461, with reference to Ogot and Ochieng 1995). They were sidelined in the land redistribution or 'settlement schemes' of the colonial state in the years leading up to independence. These schemes rewarded loyalists or collaborators, granting the largest and most fertile portions to 'leading collaborators' (Ferudi 1989, 199). In the state's view, it needed these collaborators 'to oversee the transition into independence' (*ibid.*). The purpose of 'colonial reform' was also to create a capitalist society, 'to mobilize transitionals, once and for all, out of their lingering communal solidarities and into the individually responsible, class-divided electorate of multiracial self-government' (Lonsdale 1992a, 285). Former supporters of Mau Mau became resentful and hostile as 'Kikuyu loyalists' were rapidly promoted 'into local civil service positions' and granted land (*ibid.*, 200). Pressure from the landless Kikuyus 'against the loyalists was sufficiently effective to lead to the postponement of "landing the gentry" until after independence' (*ibid.*).

A call to private wealth creation and silencing of alternative voices: the Kenyatta 'royalty' (1963–1978)

Beyond what had already been established under colonialism, enduring structures that were to dominate Kenyan society and shape the housing market in Nairobi emerged in the first post-independence years. With a highly centralized and personalized pattern of governance from the outset, the personal preferences, ideas and convictions of the first president, Jomo Kenyatta, shaped Kenyan society. The combination of a particular form of entrepreneurialism, political patronage, a self-serving civil service and the silencing of demands for alternatives formed the basis of the early stages of a largely unauthorized tenement market in Nairobi. Hegemann's now discredited narrative (1930, 167) that 'the biggest concentration of rental barracks in the world was... designed for Berlin by its "greatest" king' (Prussian King Frederick II) may hold more truth for Kenya's so-called 'King' Kenyatta, although as I show below, his role in shaping the housing market was indirect and not with any particular urban vision in mind.

Independence in December 1963 briefly tolerated a multi-party system with two main parties, KANU led by the newly elected president (initially prime minister) Jomo Kenyatta, with Oginga Odinga (father of the current prime minister, Raila Odinga) as vice-president, and the Kenya African Democratic Union (KADU) 'led by Ronald Ngala, Daniel arap Moi, and others' (Miller 1984, 28). However, already in 1964, KADU was dissolved, 'its leaders incorporated by KANU' and multi-partyism 'implicitly abandoned in favour of a strongly "presidential" single party system' (*ibid.*, 73). Within KANU, Vice-President Oginga Odinga 'assumed leadership of the ideological left', colliding with the increasingly 'anticommunist stands' of the president, who took steps to reduce Odinga's powers (*ibid.*, 35). 'The Odinga-led dissenters disagreed with Kenyatta over the centralizing elitism they saw developing... and what they perceived as Kenyatta's autocratic control of the economy' (*ibid.*, 35–36). Odinga responded to increasing hostility from within the party by resigning from KANU and the government, and forming 'an opposition party, the Kenya People's Union (KPU)' (*ibid.*, 36). In 1968 'Odinga was implicated in receiving communist funds with the intent to cause national unrest' (*ibid.*). The KPU's leaders were arrested and the party 'driven from the political scene by sheer presidential power' (*ibid.*).

Kenyatta's rule is described as 'authoritarian' (Kjaer 2004, 402) and Kenyatta himself as 'ruthless in dealing with any challenge to his authority' (Meredith 2006, 266). With Kenya operating as 'a de facto single-party system', KANU became a dormant party, activated only in times of crisis and for elections (Miller 1984, 41). Kenyatta's family was known as 'the royal family' (Meredith 2006, 267), suggesting some parallels with the system of rule in Prussia, and in imperial Germany. 'The President was literally above the workings of the law' (JAM 1982, 27). This also applied to his family. Corrupt activities enriched his daughter (also Nairobi's mayor) and made Kenyatta's young Kenyan wife 'one of the richest individuals in the country' (Meredith 2006, 267).

Newly independent Kenya saw an unprecedented rate of migration into its capital Nairobi (Kurtz 1998, 79), with the city's highest annual population growth rates recorded in the first six years of independence (see Table 6.3). In 1963, before the democratic elections and 'to facilitate independence', the colonial government extended the urban boundary to its current delineation (see Figure 6.1) (Nevanlinna 1996, 204), including the airport to the east, Nairobi National Park to the south, Dagoretti to the west and Karura Forest to the north. This created new opportunities for landlordism: in 'Dagoretti, long the most densely populated area in Kiambu', the owners of land 'almost at once... built mud and then timber huts as rental properties' (White 1990, 216). The average annual growth rate of 9.8 per cent from 1963 to 1969 outstripped the highest growth rates recorded for Berlin (with the exception of the 11 per cent growth in 1861 as a result of Berlin's boundary extension). The ethnic composition of Nairobi in 1969 was 47 per cent Kikuyu, 16 per cent Luhya, 15 per cent Luo and 5 per cent Kamba (Kanyinga 2006, 363).

Table 6.3: Nairobi's population growth during the Kenyatta era

Year	Period	Population	Annual population growth rate
1963		350 000	
	1962–1969		Average 9.8%
1969		509 286	
	1969–1979		Average 5.1%
1979		827 775	

Source: Based on Obudho (1997)

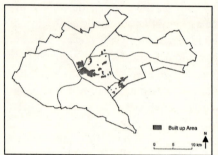 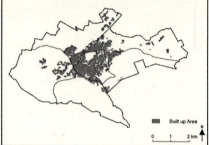

Figure 6.1: Map of Nairobi's boundary established in 1963, and the built-up area in 1976 (*left*) and 2000 (*right*)

Source: Based on Mundia and Aniya (2006, 104)

Note: Low density suburbs are not indicated as part of the built up area.

Since independence, Nairobi's municipal government has been in conflict with the central state. In an early study of post-independence local government in Nairobi, Werlin (1966, 182) observed that '[t]he Minister for Local Government feels that he must run the city – an attitude at complete variance with that of the British and former Kenyan ministers'. The minister in turn justified his control through the lack of competence or experience of council members. Mayor Rubia at the time found this attitude imperial (*ibid.*, 183). 'To complicate matters, all the chief officers, at the beginning of the new regime, were European holdovers from the colonial period, many of them capable people but not sympathetic with African problems and aspirations' and unwilling to transfer skills (*ibid.*, 194). Central government was 'in no better position than the City Council to run the affairs of Nairobi' (*ibid.*, 197). The lack of intergovernmental cooperation that Werlin identified has remained a characteristic of the city's governance.

One of the independent state's first housing projects was the demolition of Kariakor, 'its replacement by New Kariakor, an estate for middle class income earners', and the development of Kariobangi as a site-and-service area beyond Mathare (Bujra 1973, 17), which had already been conceptualized in 1954 (Loeckx

1989). During Kenyatta's rule, housing projects and plans received 'a great deal of national publicity' (Stren 1972, 81). The primary purpose of such projects was to portray the country's aspirations towards modernity, and this continues to determine public housing and 'slum' interventions in present-day Nairobi. The National Housing Corporation (NHC) was created in 1967 (after recommendations by a United Nations (UN) mission on housing), replacing the Central Housing Board (Stren 1972, 87; Stren 1978, 219). The NHC's mandate was 'the large scale production of low-cost housing', and for this purpose it received generous allocations from Treasury (Stren 1978, 219). The NHC's public housing was built to a high standard and at high cost; therefore only a small percentage of those on the waiting list were able to afford the rent (*ibid.*, 222), the others having to resort to private rental, or accessing public stock through the unauthorized 'room-by-room' subletting which soon prevailed (*ibid.*, 223). The strong bias towards middle class public housing production is explained in part by the influence of councilors, who

> were by and large an upwardly mobile group who shared the middle-class consumption aspirations of Nairobi's elite, and benefited politically from allocating council housing mainly to other members of this elite. (Temple and Temple 1980, 238)

Relatively generous public resources flowed into public housing and infrastructure in Nairobi in comparison to other Kenyan cities and towns, in part because 'Nairobi was home to a disproportionate number of senior politicians, African corporation executives and top-level bureaucrats' (Stren 1978, 229). Alongside 'middle-level civil servants', many of these became 'heavily involved in urban land and business' (*ibid.*). Their influence was exacerbated by the absence of effective ways in which the poorer population could participate in the formulation and implementation of policy (Temple and Temple 1980, 242).

The NHC (formally located under the Ministry of Housing) complemented two other 'governmental organisations' with the 'primary responsibility for responding to Nairobi's housing need', the 'Housing Finance Company of Kenya, Limited', and the Nairobi City Council' (*ibid.*, 229). However, the City Council carried the 'primary responsibility for low cost housing', borrowing 'from the NHC' in addition to 'issuing stock on the local market and negotiating loans with international agencies' (*ibid.*, 230).

Foreign donors funded planning and implementation of various housing projects in Nairobi's low income east, always with some disagreement over the standards of the development, and ultimately with results that neither government nor donors had anticipated. The World Bank's first urban project in the country, Urban I, included 6 000 site-and-service plots in Dandora, on the eastern outskirts of the city (MacInnes 1987, 45). High-level decision-makers in government delayed the project's approval by a year over concerns that serviced sites did not align to the country's modern aspirations. Indeed, 'housing standards' remained 'a sensitive political issue' in a country whose leaders sought distance from colonial practice without confronting questions of affordability (Temple and Temple 1980, 235). The World Bank's Urban II project included the Mathare North site-and-service scheme in the early 1980s (MacInnes 1987, 45). In the course of the 1980s, both Urban I and Urban II projects were to develop with unauthorized multi-story tenements for low income households, densifying further in the 1990s and beyond. In the mid-1970s, the Nairobi City Council and its consultants planned a large low income estate, Umoja (meaning 'unity'), to the east of Outer Ring Road. Umoja I, completed in 1976, was funded by the United States Agency for International Development (USAID) (Obudho 1997, 319). Large parts of Umoja, in particular Umoja Inner Core (one of my case studies in the following chapters), were to develop (largely in transgression of planning regulations) into a middle class tenement district.

While Nairobi City Council, with the help of donors, created new opportunities for urban dwelling, which private landlords later multiplied through vertical densification, it is argued that city-ward migration of poor households was discouraged by making city life 'as unattractive as possible' (Kurtz 1998, 82). Most poor households had to resort to unplanned settlements. 'Tiny shacks proliferated on empty land throughout the city', although '[o]ver time, the use of permanent building materials and the development of rooms for rent [within these 'slums'] became widespread' (Obudho 1997, 316). Already in 1970, one-third of Nairobi's population was living in unauthorized settlements (Nevanlinna 1996, 214).[3] Particularly from 1966 to 1960, the post-independence government adopted a 'policy of slum clearance' (Leys 1975, 179). This did not meet with resistance, in part because of the repression Kenyatta's government exercised under its 1966 Preservation of Public Security Act (*ibid.*).

While discouraging the poor from finding an urban foothold for themselves in the city's informal settlements, Kenyatta promoted an entrepreneurial spirit among Kenyans, which also underpins the tenement market. A sessional paper in 1965 introduced the idea of 'African socialism', embracing nation building and developmentalism. It was initially debated but came to be 'viewed as an effort by the KANU government to silence the radical voice within KANU's ranks' (Gona 2003, 46). 'Kenyatta's pragmatism and entrepreneurial approach' soon replaced the real idea of African socialism (Miller 1984, 37). Indeed, Kenyatta's economic policies contrasted with 'the socialist programmes fashionable in Africa' in the 1970s (Meredith 2006, 265). Although he had visited the Soviet Union, and studied in 1932 'at Moscow's special revolutionary institute for colonial candidates', Kenyatta 'adhered to capitalist policies, encouraging both indigenous private enterprise and foreign investment' (*ibid.*, 81, 265). Setting in place an ethic that seems to have shaped most spheres of Kenyan society, including the urban housing market, Kenyatta 'often aggressively encouraged his new electorates in the 1960s to learn how to build wealth for themselves and for their communities' (Edozie 2008, 59). Miller (1984, 37) points to a direct consequence for the civil service, which Kenyatta had expanded and rewarded with status and salaries in return for loyalty: 'Taking their cue from the top leadership, civil servants engaged increasingly in outside business interests.' The early single-story tenement investment (Etherton 1971, 8), seemed to be among these. In 1972 the Ndegwa Commission 'allowed Kenyan civil servants to engage in business', thus 'providing a big loophole for corruption' (Anyang' Nyong'o, 2007, 80).

The encouragement of entrepreneurial initiative also manifested itself in thriving open-air and unauthorized trade and light industry; they were originally referred to as 'clusters', but in 1972 the International Labor Organization (ILO) applied 'the concept of the informal sector' to them (King 1996, xiv).[4] Sixteen years later, national policy embraced the concept and provided (and sporadically reversed) support (King 1996). The informal sector would also shape the urban housing market (*ibid.*, 50).

In the 1970s and 1980s it was generally recognized that there was relatively little state intervention in Kenya and that the economy was successful (Kanyinga 1995, 70). Nairobi 'reflected Kenya's growing prosperity', the city flourishing 'as an international business and conference centre, its skyline constantly changing with the construction of new hotels and office blocks' (Meredith 2006, 265). Kenyatta had also encouraged Kenyans to 'pool their resources' in order to purchase land (Musyoka 2006, 239). In the 'local development sphere… voluntary development initiatives, such as *harambee* (literally, pulling together) were considered to occupy an almost uniquely autonomous and therefore significant role' (Kanyinga 1995, 70). In 1972, the ILO had drawn parallels between *harambee* and the thriving 'informal sector' (King 1996, 11).

However, these presumed positives overshadowed a 'state of crisis' in Nairobi, where urban population growth by far outstripped the infrastructure, social services and housing (Kurtz 1998, 79). A 1973 Metropolitan Growth Strategy for Nairobi, with UN involvement (Nairobi Urban Study Group 1973a, 1973b), remained unimplemented 'due to lack of political will' (Gatabaki-Kamau and Karirah-Gitau 2004, 160).

Many of the city's unauthorized settlements were concentrated along Mathare River (which flows into Gitathuru River in Mathare Valley), to the north-west of the city center (Etherton 1971, 5; Nevanlinna 1996, 214), an area which was later to accommodate the city's densest pockets of tenements. Informal settlements or 'villages' had emerged in Mathare Valley since the 1920s and had survived various 'clean-up' operations before and after independence (Nevanlinna 1996). 'Double standards' applied across Nairobi's unauthorized settlements: some having been demolished, others granted protection (Gatabaki-Kamau and Karirah-Gitau 2004, 163). Already in 1971, there was 'a growing trend' in Mathare Valley as well as in Dagoretti (a Kikuyu customary area or former reserve just within Nairobi's eastern boundary) 'towards the construction of single-room [and single-story] tenements by land owners' (Etherton 1971, 8). Although Mathare Valley had 'enjoyed the protection of the first Kenyan President' since 1963 (Gatabaki-Kamau and Karirah-Gitau 2004, 163), the squatter households had sought to protect themselves further by forming cooperative organizations to purchase the land parcels they occupied. By 1969, cooperative companies had begun to buy private land in Mathare Valley and developed company housing between the various villages (Etherton 1971). Rich and influential outside partners joined the companies. Rather than serving the interests of the original squatters, they transformed these companies into vehicles for speculation through the construction of rental housing (*ibid.*). In the next chapter, I discuss in more detail the complex weaving together of politics and landlordism which Chege (1981) unpacks for both Mathare Valley and Dagoretti.

Poorly administered site-and-service schemes such as Kariobangi also attracted tenement development. Though developed 'for former squatters', by the mid-1970s Kariobangi functioned 'as a housing area for newly-arrived migrants, with absentee landlord-investors collecting rents' (Nevanlinna 1996, 215). Already in the early 1970s there was 'considerable dismay over the growth of "landlordism" in the Kariobangi scheme' (Harris 1972, 39). However, the landlordism 'contributed to some easing of the housing shortage' (*ibid.*, 48), and this in turn lent it pragmatic legitimacy. Landlordism also enjoyed political sanction. In Pumwani, where in the early 1970s half the landlords were non-resident and the average house had 12.9 rooms, the landlords had organized themselves in 'an association of Pumwani landlords... a branch of... the Kenya Landlords' Association', which however was banned in 1972 (Bujra 1973, 29, 79, 84). Pumwani's landlords exerted pressure on the City Council, while also enjoying sympathy from planners (*ibid.*, 19). A municipal survey in 1965 in preparation for the redevelopment of Pumwani argued that the landlords had legitimate expectations of influencing the scheme, and recommended that this be taken into account (*ibid.*, 19, citing Mbogua 1965).

Planners officially incorporated the idea of income generation through small-scale landlordism into subsequent site-and-service schemes of the 1970s, funded through the World Bank's Urban I project (Shihembetsa 1989). These schemes expected low income allottees to pay off their partly subsidized loans by constructing and renting out rooms on their predominantly 7 m × 21 m lots. The plot dimensions allowed for two rows of rooms with a corridor in the middle – a layout that unintentionally lent itself to vertical duplication or multi-story development. Many original allottees lacked the resources to construct even a room for themselves while paying rent elsewhere (*ibid.*). A stronger economic class recognized the potential for rental investment, bought up the plots and developed rooms, initially single-story. It later realized the potential for second, third and up to seventh floors in the 1980s and beyond (Huchzermeyer 2007).

At this point, a link must be made between the practice of cooperatives/companies (as well as the tolerance of unauthorized and officially unintended forms of commercialization of housing through absentee landlordism) and the political economy of the time. The call to pool resources directly encouraged and legitimized land buying groups, cooperatives and companies. It is acknowledged that they 'played crucial economic-cum-political roles in facilitating access to land by ordinary Kenyans' (Gatabaki-Kamau and Karirah-Gitau 2004, 165). While the principles of cooperatives and self-help had already been part of the pre-colonial societies in the region (Musyoka 2006, 239), after independence the flexibility of the share-holding system allowed access to farm land for the poor, while also providing space for democratic decision-making in which the state would not interfere (*ibid.*).[5] However, in the Nairobi setting there is little evidence that the poor were benefitting other than through the production of a commodity which they were offered to rent. In Zimmerman, as in Mathare Valley, poor squatters had invaded under-utilized land, and under threat of eviction had formed housing or land buying companies in a bid to secure a hold on the land (Gatabaki-Kamau and Karirah-Gitau 2004). Speculative interests unfolded, and while a small number of individual squatters benefited, the residential population as a whole converted into tenants. Zimmerman was transformed into a middle class tenement area (*ibid.*).

While the economically advantaged benefited from urban land buying company developments which were independent of the state, 'national development initiatives' served the political and private interests of the elite. The president and his private and public 'inner circle', an ethnically defined 'elite clique', were 'key patrons in local and national development initiatives' (Kanyinga 1995, 73). The inner circle was 'therefore strategically placed to obtain key public resources by which [it] improved [its] own social standing and Kenyatta's political stature' (*ibid.*). Local elites' closeness to the 'inner circle' became critical in the retention of influence at the local level, as this was the only way they could capture development resources from the centre. This entrenched 'patron-client networks', with 'control by the centre through selective distribution of benefits to the grassroots' (*ibid.*, 74).

Despite '[h]igh economic and political expectations' during the struggle for independence, the new Kenyan government 'took over intact the apparatus of the colonial state including the centralised civil service and the highly coercive provincial administration network' (Kanyinga 1995, 72). Members of parliament and elected councilors had limited powers in relation to the appointed 'sub-chiefs, chiefs, District Officers (DOs), District Commissioners (DCs) and Provincial Commissioners (PCs)' (*ibid.*).[6] The latter quickly came to compete with elected officials in patronage over local self-help initiatives and institutions (*ibid.*). Similarly, initial land and land tenure reforms did not benefit 'most of the urban poor and rural squatters created by colonial policies... Instead, the programmes largely benefited the African *petite bourgeoisie* that had formed and prospered under colonialism', and which 'inherited the state apparatus at independence' (Otiso 2002, 258).

Independent Kenya took over a coffee-producing but oil-dependent economy, which therefore benefited from booms in the coffee industry (1975–8 and 1986), but also suffered from oil crises (1973–4 and 1979) and droughts (Bigsten 1993). However, the worst crisis related to the struggle in the leadership level immediately below the president, those 'orbiting' him – to use JAM's (1982, 140) expression – in expectation of 'lucrative priorities in the new economic order' (Miller 1984, 44). In ruthlessly crushing its opponents, the regime also ensured that potential political bearers or agents of social democratic reforms, or even just the enforcement of existing laws and regulations (for instance those intended to govern the housing market), could not gain ground. One prominent victim was Tom Mboya, whose 'power lay in his early trade union contacts' (*ibid.*, 45). Mboya was able to bridge 'national factions' and weave 'alliances between otherwise competing groups'. However, as a Luo he was 'an outsider in Kikuyu subethnic politics' (*ibid.*). His assassination in 1969 triggered riots and violence in Nairobi and the main Luo city, Kisumu (*ibid.*).

A further high-level assassination and resulting political crisis followed in 1975. Kenyan politics in the early 1970s had what could be seen as the equivalent of the controversial pro-poor Ferdinand Lassalle, who had led the first workers' party in Berlin in the early 1860s. Lassalle's early death (not by assassination) had made way for Marxist mobilization among Berlin's working class. In Kenya, the socialist J.M. Kariuki, who had once been detained by the colonial authorities in the Mau Mau era, 'emerged as a champion of the poor and landless, with a popular following that came close to rivalling Kenyatta's own' (Meredith 2006, 267). Kariuki had ambitions to succeed Kenyatta as president, and was known for 'sharp business practices'. Nevertheless, 'he possessed an unerring popular touch and he skilfully exploited the groundswell of discontent that was building up over the greed and corruption clearly evident at the top of Kenyan society' (*ibid.*). Kariuki fiercely criticized the elite and its corrupt practices, and despite the virtual ban on this topic, he publically recalled both the ambitions and the sacrifices of the Mau Mau rebellion and the unresolved questions over land (*ibid.*, 268). Calling for a comprehensive overhaul of the system, he 'presented a clear threat… to the ruling elite'. In 1975 he was removed from the political scene in a murder in which 'Kenyatta's inner circle' was later implicated (*ibid.*).

Unlike Berlin in the 1860s, there was no Marxist movement equivalent to that which captured Lassalle's political space and led to the formation of the initially radical SPD (later the bearer of the anti-tenement agenda) in Germany. Although Kariuki's assassination was met with student and spontaneous riots in many urban areas, for three years after his death the regime silenced all dissidents (Miller 1984, 52).

Inasmuch as a comparison is possible, another explanation for the divergence of Berlin and Nairobi's trajectories following Lassalle and Kariuki, respectively, lies in the different class formations in the two cities. While urban classes existed in Kenya, they differed from those of 19th century Europe and America (JAM 1982, 39, 60). The main distinctions lay in the Kenyan urban migrants' continued ties with rural land and therefore only 'transient' affiliation with urban culture (Leys 1975, 181), their education that led to increased expectations of 'non-manual employment' and 'upward mobility' into the bourgeoisie, and the technology in industry which was no longer labor-intensive (JAM 1982, 60). Even though they were not absorbed into industry, but 'canalised predominantly into intermediary activities as self-employed craftsmen, petty traders, and into a variety of illegal means of earning their livelihood' (Chege 1981, 76), the existing system of individualized wealth creation had already shaped their intellectual emancipation. Towards the end of Kenyatta's rule, the dense tenement districts that would provide working class mobility and flexibility were only beginning to emerge in Nairobi. Even once these outstripped the densities of 19th century tenement districts in Europe, they would not serve the emancipatory function that Engels foresaw for Germany's industrial era tenements (Engels 1887/1935).

A more compelling parallel with late 19th century Berlin was the lack of independent thinking regarding urban reform. Royal patronage had marked philanthropic activity in Berlin; and in the absence of a Marxist urban agenda beyond or alongside a revolution, the once revolutionary SPD had become the political bearer of a bourgeois reform agenda. In Kenya up to today, alternative political voices have been hastily silenced. Political challenges are tolerated (reluctantly) only from within the politically established Kenyan elite. However, Kenya's lack of independence in defining a reform agenda is also a result of the involvement of international donors, aid organizations and consultants, a theme to which I will return when I discuss the Kenyan urban discourse and its treatment of tenements.

The mushrooming of tenements with the spread of corruption and defiance of planning under Moi's rule (1978–2002)

Not unlike the Prussian kings, Kenyatta ruled up to his death in 1978, when his vice-president Daniel arap Moi, took the reins. This set the course for the intensification of processes already entrenched under Kenyatta's rule. Moi's government is often referred to as the 'Nyayo regime'. Nyayo ('footsteps' in Kiswahili) referred to Moi's undertaking to ensure the continuity of Kenyatta's approach – Kenyans were 'not to expect a revolution' (Ogot 1995, 192). As a national slogan based on Moi's personal philosophy, 'Nyayo' stood for 'continuity, love, peace and stability' (*ibid.*, 193). Initally, Moi expressed this through 'political tolerance and reconciliation' (*ibid.*). However, 'nyayoism' soon took on 'ideological functions', marking 'a further entrenchment of the political monolithism which had been introduced under Kenyatta' (*ibid.*, 193, 194). Moi's regime ultimately weakened local government, reduced civil and political rights, increased repression, intensified the already existing practice of allocating land to political loyalists, and expanded corruption and lawlessness. The thriving informal sector received its first support in the Moi era. However, the state and the urban vigilantism that emerged in the democratic deficit of Moi's governance later harassed those making a living within this sector.

Two years prior to Kenyatta's death and in anticipation thereof, his 'inner court' had attempted to 'change the constitutional provisions on succession' to avoid a Moi presidency (Kanyinga 1995, 75). But Kenyatta shelved these, in order 'to avoid further divisions and possible disenchantment from other ethno-regional groups' (*ibid.*). Moi, once ascended into the presidency, relied on a different clique (which included current president Mwai Kibaki), each member representing a strategic ethnic-regional base (*ibid.*, 76). Moi also sought support from 'the numerically strong Luo and Luya ethnic groups' that had hitherto been excluded from the benefits of independence, 'in order to expand his power base' (Gibbon 1995, 10; Kanyinga 1995, 76). Moi, '[a]ware that Kikuyu domination and corruption caused super-hatred of them by these ethnic groups... also enunciated a plan to end corruption... Moi gradually established hegemony by playing off one ethnic group against another' (Kanyinga 1995, 76–77).

Commentators label Moi as even 'more autocratic' than his predecessor Kenyatta, 'repressing competition and even encouraging ethnic tension' (Kjaer 2004, 402). Moi's presidency has therefore been referred to as 'imperial' (Mueller 2008, 188). In the fashion of many emperors, 'Moi also sought to raise his populist stature by showing that he was "caring" and "loving" for the poor and destitute' (Gona 2003, 155). This explains the recognition he gave to the informal sector. In 1985 the cabinet had discussed its role in the context of macro-economic changes (King 1996, 13). Later that year, the president visited Kamukunji in Nairobi, where a 'cluster' of metal workers were recycling drums and sheets into useful utensils. '[I]n a highly symbolic act he promised sheds to shade these "hot sun" (*jua kali*) workers from the weather' (King 1996, 1). Several further presidential visits, encouragement of *jua kali* workers 'to form groups as a way of qualifying for assistance', a policy paper in 1986 and a development plan in 1989 all entrenched the uniquely Kenyan concept and term '*jua kali*' (*ibid.*, 13). This was significant, given that in the late 1980s, only 12.6 per cent of the labor force (which had 'no clear vanguardist union' (Gona 2003, 252)) was in formal employment, a figure that dropped to 10.9 per cent by 2000 (Bigsten and Durevall 2006, 467). As a result of the pro-informal sector policy, in the 1980s 'urban planners began to set aside land' for the *jua kali* sector, established 'three open air markets in Nairobi' and provided *jua kali* sheds (Muraya 2006, 132), although licensing was not fully resolved (*ibid.*, 131).

Along with his competitors, Moi had ambitions of ruling through a 'one-party dictatorship' (Meredith 2006, 382). In 1982, he entrenched a one-party system by law. A failed coup attempt in the same year, involving the military, led to efforts by the president to 'redistribute many of the advantages hitherto enjoyed by the Kikuyu', thus changing 'the geography of regime legitimacy and illegitimacy' (Gibbon 1995, 10). To those calling for reinstatement of a multi-party system, Moi responded that 'they were intent on re-establishing Kikuyu hegemony; he insisted that a multi-party system would divide Kenya along tribal lines' (Meredith 2006, 401). The dissatisfaction then intensely expressed by the Kikuyu 'contributed to new measures taken in the late 1980s... to restrict political freedoms' (Gibbon 1995, 10). These included condoning harassment, torture and the surveillance of public places against opponents, limiting the judges' and auditor general's autonomy, and most controversially, abandoning 'the secret ballot in primary elections, replacing it with a "queuing" system', and reducing parliament's function to that of 'a rubber stamp' (Meredith 2006, 384).[7] Already in 1983, the state had responded to corrupt practices (among other factors) in Nairobi City Council through 'the dismissal of its councillors and many officers, and the replacement of the council by an appointed City Commission' (Lee-Smith 1989, 285). This reinforced the already 'existing controlling role of central government' (*ibid.*).

Curtailing of civil and political liberties in turn undermined the 'international political legitimacy' hitherto enjoyed by the Kenyan state, and led to foreign aid being withheld (Gibbon 1995, 10, 11). Kenya at the time relied on foreign donors for 'nearly 30 per cent of government expenditure' (Meredith 2006, 403). The international perception of exemplary economic success had faded, with evidence of the politicization of and state patronage over local development (Gibbon 1995, 11). It also became evident in this period that individuals were amassing 'considerable landholdings' (Meredith 2006, 266). Of concern to the World Bank was the fact that Kenya had not honored the conditions of its structural adjustment loans, the first of which was granted in 1980 (Gibbon 1995, 11). So-called 'political banks' proliferated, issuing frequently non-performing loans to 'political figures', leading to cyclical 'liquidity crises' and 'bail-outs by the Central Bank of Kenya' (*ibid.*, 13). With the fall of the Berlin Wall and the end of the Cold War, 'the Kenyan government's pro-western orientation' no longer shielded the country from 'public criticism over its failure to conform to donor-set norms and policies' (*ibid.*, 11, 13).

Moi's form of governance was paralleled by the creation of a massive 'business empire' for his family cronies (Meredith 2006, 384). The most enduring legacy of Moi's rule, however, was that corruption 'spread from the top' and 'became embedded in the system' (*ibid.*, 385). Corruption and greed among the elite became a ubiquitous theme in Kenyan novels (Kurtz 1998, 86). Moi's regime brutally murdered prominent opponents of corruption, whether within government or in the church. With the increase in corruption in the 1980s, Kenya 'experienced increasing decay in government services' (Ruteere and Pommerolle 2003, 595). A government 'deconcentration' rather than 'decentralisation', which eroded 'the power and status of local authorities', also hampered municipal service delivery (Gona 2003, 146). The state stripped municipal councilors of power and thereby provided new 'leverage to grant patronage' (*ibid.*). The boldness with which tenements mushroomed in many districts of Nairobi (in defiance of zoning and other regulations) during this period is explained in part by decline in the functioning of local government, the emergence of corrupt land allocation and corrupt authorization of construction, and continued urban growth and therefore housing demand (see Table 6.4).

Table 6.4: Nairobi's population growth during the Moi era

Year	Period	Population	Annual population growth rate
1979		827 775	
	1978–1989		Average 4.8%
1989		1 324 570	
	1989–1994		Average 5.0%
1999		2 143 254	
	1999–2002		Average 4.8%
2002		2 470 850	

Source: Based on Obudho (1997); K'Akumu and Olima (2007); Central Bureau of Statistics (2009)

In 1991, a pressure group, 'Forum for the Restoration of Democracy' (Ford), formed but was immediately banned (Meredith 2006). However, the extent of corruption put Moi under pressure from western donors. This, and state-induced Kikuyu-Kalenjin clashes in the Rift Valley Province, led Moi to capitulate and announce intentions to hold multi-party elections (Meredith 2006, 402, 403).[8] Ford re-emerged as two political parties contesting elections. Ford-Asili politically dominated the mainly Kikuyu Central Province, and Ford-Kenya politically dominated the 'Luo areas of Nyanza Province' (Weinreb, 2001, 446). Current prime minister Raila Odinga's father Oginga Odinga, 'who had served under both Kenyatta and [briefly] Moi', led Ford-Kenya (Meredith 2006, 403). With the non-Kalenjin displaced from Rift Valley Province before the elections, Moi's ruling KANU party controlled the now 'Kalenjin-dominated' province (Weinreb 2001, 446). Moi's victory in the 1992 multi-party election has been traced back to 'violence, intimidation, rigging, electoral malpractice and propaganda from state-owned radio and television' (Meredith 2006, 404). However, these elections also resulted in an enduring ethnic-regional political division; '[t]hese general distributions were repeated in 1997' (Weinreb 2001, 446). What also marked both the 1992 and the 1997 elections was 'politically mobilized inter-ethnic violence' (Anderson 2002, 533), a theme that has persisted to date, complicated by the advent of vigilantism later during Moi's rule. Nevertheless, the political opening in 1992 allowed 'independent political movements' to challenge 'the hegemony of the state in various ways', particularly as opposition parties gained a majority in parliamentary seats for Nairobi and other large urban areas (Halfani 1997, 132).

The decade starting in 1990 extended the economic decline of the 1980s. 'During the 1990s, Moi seemed to concentrate more on staying in power than on improving the economy' (Kjaer 2004, 403), and in a multi-party system, remaining in power required strategic maneuvering. To extend his patronage, Moi was 'reluctant to reduce public spending and curb inflation' and unwilling to undertake structural reform (*ibid.*, 402). In 1993, Moi agreed to a Civil Service Reform Program, but limited this largely to workshops and seminars (*ibid.*, 403).

In 1997, following the Goldenberg 'mega-scandal (Anyang' Nyang'o 2007, 79) which involved embezzlement of export subsidies, Moi, under pressure from the International Monetary Fund (IMF), set up the Kenya Anti-Corruption Authority, which was to investigate corruption among officialdom (Kjaer 2004, 404). However, parliament blocked this initiative, 'resisting '"good governance" reforms, though with the argument that the reforms were not far-reaching enough' (*ibid.*). By 1999 Moi, still in desperate need of donor funds, had agreed to tackle corruption in the public sector, appointing a new team which included 'conservationist Dr Richard Leaky as head of the civil service' (*ibid.*, 403). However, Moi found Leaky's approach 'too radical' and replaced him two years later. Moi supported reform only to the extent that it did not shake up 'the existing system' or hurt 'influential interests' (*ibid.*). At the city level, this explained the impunity with which the state handled illegal 'slum' and tenement investment. Thus Nairobi of the 1990s was 'a city without any pretence to planned amenities and where corruption and outright incompetence abounded' (Katumanga 2005, 510).

In this period, 'aspects of Kenya's political economy were dominated by the bourgeoisie, working in collaboration with agents of external interests'; thus there was a lack of independent agency even of the middle class (Owino 1999, 460). Furthermore, Kenya's 'rulers remain[ed] disinclined to change the country's political economy because it allow[ed] them to acquire (often dishonestly) unrestricted amounts of land, wealth and political power' (Otiso 2002, 258). The decline in foreign aid to Kenya in the 1990s had 'substantially reduced the amount of public funds available for pilferage', requiring public functionaries to 'seek other means of accumulating private wealth or maintaining political power' (*ibid.*, 259). Due to 'the ease with which they can be disposed of, urban public lands [had] come to be a handy means for this purpose' (*ibid.*). The strategy of rewarding political supporters with land or depriving opponents of the same intensified after the reintroduction of multi-party politics (*ibid.*, 260). The grabbing of public sites was 'a particularly dramatic display of corruption for most Kenyans' and did not remain unchallenged (Klopp 2000, 8). With political odds as they stood, there were 'ever more violent struggles around "land grabbing" with important long term consequences, for both the security of property rights and the prospect for democracy in Kenya' (*ibid.*).

In 1997, the Kenyan National Council of non-governmental organizations (NGOs) launched Operation Firimbi as a project to oppose land grabbing. Through an awareness campaign, it encouraged the registering of complaints. A 'boldness' towards land grabbing became evident at this time, as did bold resistance (*ibid.*, 9). Klopp (*ibid.*, 10–13) uses the case of the Westlands Market in 1994 to illustrate this point (markets are typically located on high value real estate). Not unlike the repressive treatment and subsequent radicalization of Berlin's fledgling working class movement in the early 1860s, organized resistance to the grabbing of the Westlands Market land was met with brutal state repression, leading to radicalization and an increasing resort to violence. This included the training of street children to fight the police hired by the former Nairobi city commissioner who was grabbing the land (*ibid.*) – the Kenyan police force is considered a 'key agent of crime' and has 'never enjoyed a high degree of popular legitimacy' (Ruteere and Pommerolle 2003, 588). At this time, commentators also raised concern over a 'growing culture of political violence' (Anderson 2002, 533). I return below to its links with the growing urban vigilantism in this period.

Klopp's (2000, 13–15) other case study of public land grabbing is of the 1998 illegal allocation of more than half of Karura Forest (hitherto public land) in the north of Nairobi to private developers. In this case the resistance, led by prominent environmentalist (and 2004 recipient of the Nobel Peace Prize) Dr Wangari Maathai, involved the middle class, university students, the National Council of Churches and the Architectural Association of Kenya. Here too, resistance was met with violence, which in this case led to 'widescale riots' in Nairobi (*ibid.*, 14). Moi, in typical fashion, 'blamed the violence on "hatred and tribalism"' (*ibid.*, citing the *Daily Nation* 1999). In 2000, private 'construction on what was once national forest' was well underway (*ibid.*, 14).

It is in this troubled era that multi-story tenements found their niche in the urban economy and in urban space. They mushroomed alike on donor-funded site-and-service schemes such as Mathare North, Dandora and parts of Umoja (Omenya 2006; Huchzermeyer 2007), on land purchased and initially developed by land buying companies in areas such as low income Huruma (Mathare Valley) and middle income Zimmerman (Gatabaki-Kamau and Karirah Gitau 2004), and on land grabbed and, if contested, fought over by hired urban gangs (see Katumanga 2005; Mueller 2008; Obala forthcoming). In parallel with tenement development, Nairobi's low-rise 'slums' continued to expand, though in areas such as Mathare Valley they were gradually 'demolished and redeveloped as permanent high-rise buildings' (Otiso 2002, 261). As I show later, it is 'slums' that have drawn the attention of donors, and the NGOs and academic consultants that they fund. The unauthorized development of multi-story rooming remains largely ignored. It is not surprising, then, that statistical data do not differentiate between the 'slum' and multi-story tenement markets. It is impossible to say how many people have lived in Nairobi's multi-story tenements at any particular time. While not providing any insight into the actual scale of the tenement market, the Central Bureau of Statistics shows that towards the end of Moi's rule, of the 84.7 per cent of the city's households who were tenants (Central Bureau of Statistics 2004) 70.7 per cent were renting from private companies and individuals, the remainder renting primarily from the public sector (Central Bureau of Statistics 2002); 66.6 per cent of households in Nairobi were occupying single rooms (*ibid.*) and 64.4 per cent sharing a toilet with another household (Central Bureau of Statistics 2004).[9]

A prominent and sinister feature of Kenyan society which was also to shape the tenement environment emerged towards the end of the Moi era. Already in 1987, a religious-cultural movement had formed among the Kikuyus, initially providing an alternative to the material values of many Pentecostal church groups. From this, a splinter group called Mungiki emerged 'before 1990', and unsuccessfully aspired to 'contest seats in the 1992 elections' (Anderson 2002, 534). The movement attracted support from Kikuyus displaced from the Rift Valley at the time of the 1992 and 1997 elections, and 'has become firmly embedded among the urban poor of Nairobi's slum estates' (*ibid*.). The food price hikes, redundancies, declining real wages and deterioration in the public education system in the 1990s, resulting from structural adjustment programs imposed by the international financial institutions, 'created near revolutionary conditions and spawned atomisation and subjectivism in Kenya' (Katumanga 2005, 508). School dropouts migrated to Nairobi, constituting 'a disaffected youth' (*ibid*.), thousands of whom 'drifted into gangs, militant formations under the labels such as *Talibans, Bagdad boys, Jeshi la Mzee* (the elders' battalion), *Jeshi la Embakasi* (the Embakasi battalion) and *Mungiki*... [deriving] its name from *muingi* (meaning masses in Kikuyu)' (*ibid*., 512).[10] Therefore, 'Mungiki speaks for the poor and dispossessed but with a distinctively Gikuyu voice', displaying a 'materialist, instrumentalist and ethnocentric character', which is paralleled by 'local Kenyan politics' and has left non-Gikuyu 'deeply suspicious' (Anderson 2002, 534–536). By the mid-1990s, Mungiki and other vigilante groups had taken control of sectors of the informal economy, for instance extracting protection money from the urban *matatu* (kombi-bus) industry (Katumanga 2005, 506). Mungiki 'also engaged in other business activities, including demanding payments from *jua kali* car repair men' (Mueller 2008, 192).

Katumanga (2005, 517) defines a role for Mungiki and its rival gangs in what he terms the 'bandit economy', which 'the regime literally sustained' in 'parallel to the weak formal economy'. Mueller (2008, 192) adds that it was in the 'milieu of decay that urban gangs began to appear as significant actors', from 'the mid-1990s onward' operating 'almost as a shadow state in some of Nairobi's slums'. Initially 'offering security, protection, and services in Nairobi's slums and the working class [tenement] housing estates that had been largely abandoned by the state... its main import soon became that of a well-armed violent gang' (*ibid*.). It 'evolved into a classic capitalist operation... a gang for hire' (*ibid*., 193).

By 2001, 'Mungiki's entanglement with urban vigilantism' had become apparent (Anderson 2002, 538). During rent protests in Nairobi's 'slums' in that year, it was believed that vigilantes fighting on the side of landlords were supported by Mungiki. Anderson (*ibid*., 540) carefully adds that '[a]lthough there is no direct evidence of government or KANU backing for Mungiki there has been considerable press speculation about the likely political "sponsorship" of the movement'.

Accounts of Mungiki's alliances are as contradictory as the alliances themselves probably are. In the tenement context, Mungiki may be hired in support of landlord interests, while it may also align itself to the interests of Kikuyu tenants. One narrative portrays Mungiki as a 'youth movement' severely repressed by the police, yet having 'played a significant role in placing youth as a central issue on the agenda of the 2002 general elections' (Rasmussen 2010, 307, citing Kagwanja 2005). In this account, Mungiki empowers the youth through understanding of 'historical injustices' and 'cultural roots', and by providing 'an alternative for unemployed youth and school dropouts' in addition to 'a forum where youth can gain leadership and agency' (*ibid*, 307–308).

A less significant movement in this period that nevertheless needs mention is *Muungano wa Wanavijiji*. Originally a rights-based protest organization formed in 1996 (Otiso 2002, 262), by 2000 it had been deradicalized by development actors of the middle class into a federation of savings groups modeled on the approach promoted by the donor-funded NGO Slum/Shack Dwellers International (SDI), which refrains from confrontation with the state in favor of 'partnerships with government organisations' (Weru 2004, 48).[11] Belief at the time that there existed fertile ground for this approach stemmed from signs in the late 1990s of imminent reform. Demolitions had declined due to the Kenyan government's 'entry into a UN-HABITAT / government [slum] upgrading partnership' as well as the state's adoption of a Poverty Reduction Strategy Paper (*ibid.*, 47). This IMF-imposed strategy paper required the Kenyan government to collaborate with donors as well as with national and local stakeholders to map out economic and administrative reform (Kjaer 2004, 395). However, NGOs, their donors and the grassroots alike were to be disappointed by what they had read as signals of change.

Failed reform: continued growth of tenements, vigilantism and resistance to democratic reform in post-Moi Kenya (2003–2010)

The removal from power of Daniel arap Moi ushered in a period of hope and optimism. However, this was short-lived. Socio-political formations entrenched in the Moi era persisted (Wrong 2009), driving a deep crisis that now permeates every aspect of Kenyan society, bearing also on the tenement market and environment. With an ever greater and more urgent need for meaningful democratization, the new constellation also poses increasing challenges for such a process.

The fight against corruption was squarely on the agenda of the post-Moi regime. In the 2002 elections, Mwai Kibaki 'made electoral pledges to combat corruption', and once elected, 'declared himself personally in charge' of this objective (Kjaer 2004, 404). However, under his rule, the Kenya Anti-Corruption Commission (KACC) remained 'compromised by the high personal stakes of the political elites involved' (Edozie 2008, 61). Nevertheless, Kibaki's steps towards reform are considered 'much more far-reaching than his predecessor's and do not merely represent "within-system" reforms' (Kjaer 2004, 404). In 2004, Kibaki's government visibly tackled urban land corruption through the demolition of upmarket houses (as well as dwellings in 'slums') that land grabbers had constructed on public land (Warah 2004). However, Kibaki was balancing 'change with continuity', and already one year into his rule, 'his own cabinet ministers were accused of corruption' (Kjaer 2004, 405). The resulting cabinet reshuffle was again 'interpreted as a careful balancing act' between factions within his National Alliance Rainbow Coalition (NARC) (*ibid.*, 405). Kibaki certainly proved not to be the political bearer of far-reaching reform. Lacking a 'solid political base', he was preoccupied with 'balancing the many ethnic… and regional interests' within the fragile ruling coalition, which eventually split over his resistance to long-awaited constitutional reform (Kjaer 2004, 406). Raila Odinga, formerly an ally of Moi and Minister of Roads, Public Works and Housing in Kibaki's administration, became Kibaki's most important opponent, rallying support from the popular demand for a parliamentary system (*ibid.*).

Post-Moi corruption, exemplified by the massive Anglo-Finance Leasing scandal (beginning in 2002 and surfacing in the media in 2004), points to a 'distortion of the relationship between democracy, business and the economy' (Edozie 2008, 47). In this scandal, US$24 million of Kenyan public revenue (much of it donor funding, with public debt standing at 50 per cent of GDP) remained unaccounted for, though alleged to have funded the ruling NARC party and its elite.

In the same period a 'democratic crisis' emerged, beginning 'as a constitutional crisis', and leading to an 'inter-party faction within NARC' (*ibid.*, 51). NARC had campaigned in 2002 with a promise to develop a Constitutional Reform Bill that was to remove powers from the Office of the President and re-establish 'the role of a Prime Minister as the head of government, thereby empowering the legislature and establishing a people's representative democracy' (*ibid.*, 52). In the campaigning over a Constitutional Reform Referendum, which divided Kenyans over 'the structure of the executive and devolution of power' (Anyang' Nyong'o 2007, 123), the faction led by Raila Odinga formed the Orange Democratic Movement (ODM) which became a new political party. (My fieldwork in Nairobi took place at the time of campaigning for the Constitutional Reform Referendum in 2005).[12] The crisis had deepened with exposure in the media of the Anglo-Finance Leasing scandal. Kibaki's main opponent, Raila Odinga, predicted that this scandal would contribute to a 'chaotic and violent aftermath' of the 2007 national elections (*ibid.*, 59). The press in turn claimed that Odinga had conspired with the head of the KACC and concocted the scandal to weaken Kibaki and NARC's chances in the elections (*ibid.*, 60).

Cheeseman (2008, 180) warns that '[d]emocratic elections do not sit well with an authoritarian constitution', this explaining in part the violent aftermath of the December 2007 elections. In Mueller's (2008, 186) analysis, given the close running in these elections, a number of factors triggered a 'descent into a spiral of killing and destruction along ethnic lines and the consequent fracturing of the fragile idea of nation'. These factors were, firstly, that the monopoly that the state had enjoyed of being a 'legitimate force' had declined, resulting in a 'generalized level of violence' that was not always in the control of the state (*ibid.*). Although Kibaki had banned Mungiki in 2003, the gang continued its operations unchecked (*ibid.*, 193).[13] 'Ordinary citizens were constantly plagued by violence in their daily lives', and 'those in poor housing estates... experienced the worst of it' (*ibid.*, 194). Secondly, democratic institutions including the electoral commission were deliberately kept weak and continued to be overridden by the presidency. They were therefore unable 'to exercise the autonomy and checks and balances normally associated with democracy' (*ibid.*, 186). Thirdly, in a context where the presidency ruled, political parties – namely Kibaki's renamed Party of National Unity (PNU) and Raila Odinga's ODM – had a 'winner-take-all view of political power', did not have policy programs and 'were driven by ethnic clientelism' (*ibid.*). A further factor, of direct relevance to my study but not mentioned in the published literature, is revealed in the Waki Commission of Enquiry into the Post-Election Violence (Waki 2008). The election campaigns unwittingly exploited long ethnicized landlord-tenant tensions in Nairobi's 'slum' and multi-story rooming districts, which erupted into the epicenters of violence in Nairobi.

In an election outcome which 'EU and domestic observers' confirmed as having been 'manipulated', the PNU was declared the winner (Cheeseman 2008, 171). As Kibaki hastily arranged for himself to be sworn in, violence erupted in several parts of the country (*ibid.*, 166), its spread facilitated in some measure through the recent spread of mobile phones, which at the same time countered state control (*ibid.*, 169). In Nairobi, violence erupted in the 'slums' and low income tenement areas of Nairobi – 'Kibera, Mathare, Dandora, Kariobangi and Kawangware' (Waki 2008, 196). 'Citizens of various ethnic groups in different areas, who happened to be in the "wrong" place', faced unforgiving violence and in some cases death (Cheeseman 2008, 203).

The harrowing report of the Waki Commission includes a detailed analysis of the situation in Nairobi immediately before the general election. This includes mention of 'the void left by the absence of the state' in low income residential areas, which gangs, also 'available for hire by powerful political actors as instruments of intimidation against opponents', had come to fill (Waki 2008, 194). In the lead-up to the elections, the state was aware that 'some politicians had... enlisted the support of multiple gangs like Mungiki to intimidate opponents' (*ibid.*). In addition, 'ODM presidential aspirant Raila Odinga... had reportedly promised that an ODM government would regulate rents' (*ibid.*, 195). In Mathare, Kayole, Kibera, Kawangware, Dandora and Pipeline Estate (with the exception of Kibera and parts of Mathare, these are all multi-story tenement areas), Kikuyu landlords 'had issued eviction notices to Luo [and Luhya] tenants', fearing non-payment or worse from their tenants if the ODM were to win (*ibid.*). Before the elections, the National Security Intelligence Service warned the state that this 'was likely to foment ethnic tension'. The Waki Commission finds it unacceptable that the police did not prepare for this and provide safety in low income neighborhoods, given these predictions. The police force (which to the state's knowledge had planned a wage-related 'go slow' on election day) was largely deployed to prevent an ODM rally at the centrally located Uhuru Park, rather than to secure low income areas (*ibid.*, 200, 202). Itself divided along ethnic lines, the police force was 'just as brutal as the marauding gangs causing the violence' (*ibid.*, 204).

Three phases of violence were waged for over four weeks. They unfolded as predicted, delivering 111 bodies to the city's mortuary (though the commissioner of police deemed the fatality in Nairobi to be no more than 28) and many gunshot victims from Nairobi's low income tenement areas to the city's hospitals (*ibid.*, 203). During my return to the dense rooming district of Huruma in May 2008, Luo tenants' personal accounts corroborated the evidence in the Waki Commission report, which includes accounts of equally atrocious violence against and expulsion of Kikuyus by Luos. In Huruma, I was told that Luos from tenement areas with predominantly Kikuyu tenants, such as Dandora and Kayole, had left their belongings behind and braved the walk past several other warring tenement areas to Huruma (the middle class tenement districts remained calm) to seek refuge among enclaves dominated by their own ethnic group. Once in Huruma, they were summoned to fight at the barricades that ethnically divided the area. No leadership personalities were identifiable. Kikuyu caretakers and rent collectors had fled from the area after the killing of some caretakers in Mathare North, the densely developed tenement area across from the Gitathuru River, where tensions ran even deeper. In Huruma, eventually even women were called upon to join the stone-throwing and noise-making at the barricades, leaving only children in the shelter of the tenements. As the area was 'ringed by police', food supplies ran out (after the looting of most local shops). One supermarket had paid protection money and was guarded by 50 armed men. Only after two weeks of 'active no-joke' with the constant manning of ten barricaded points in Huruma, did the fighting finally cease. By that time, the tenants were surviving on water. However, once the lack of food and parents' inability to obtain basic remedies from pharmacies endangered the children in the tenements, 'people came together' and offered security so that shops could reopen (Tenants 1 and 5, interviews, May 28, 2008).

The rival political leaders signed a power-sharing deal two months after the elections (Edozie 2008, 64). By May 2008, ethnic tensions and lack of trust persisted in Huruma (as elsewhere in the country (Githongo 2010)). Things were still not 'business as usual' (Tenant 1, interview, May 28, 2008), a condition which the local media reported for other low income estates of Nairobi as much as a year later (Muiruri 2009a). As an ongoing trend, 'violence has pitted poor people against each other, divided them along ethnic/political lines and has eroded social networks and reinforced ethnic segregation', with 'internally displaced people' hosted by 'already stressed communities' (Klopp 2008, 309).

Figure 6.2: Schematic diagram of Nairobi's history

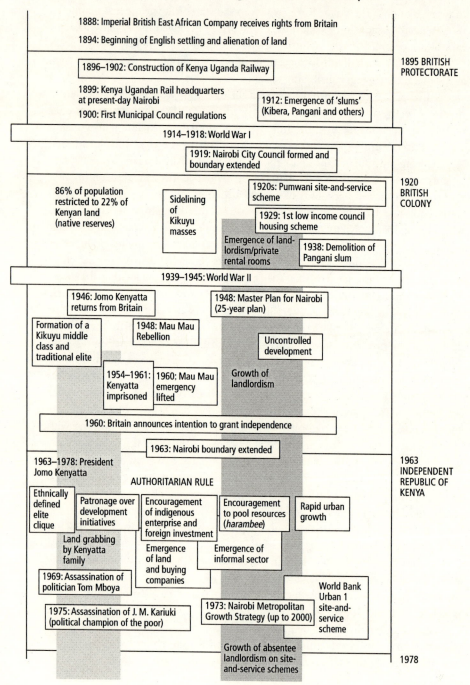

Figure 6.2: Schematic diagram of Nairobi's history (continued)

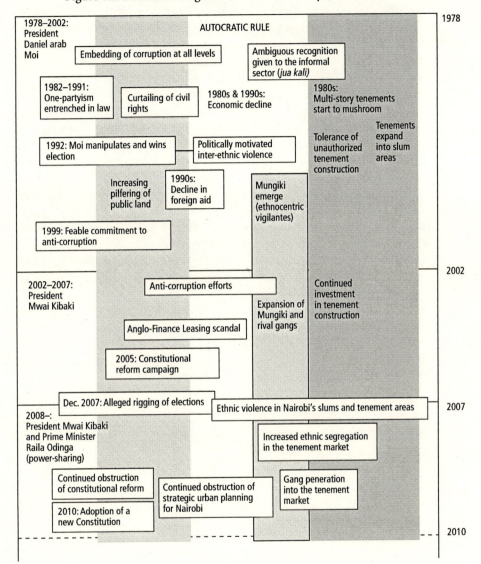

In May 2008, tenants were still withholding payment of rents in Mathare North, whereas in Humura they had allowed caretakers to return and had resumed payments. But an increased demand for accommodation had also impacted upon Huruma's tenement market. An increase in overcrowding translated into an added burden on the already stretched infrastructure. This was sustained well beyond the ebbing of violence. In April 2009, the press reported that 'the political and social crisis that drove Kenya into near ruin still persists' (*Daily Nation* 2009). Only after a further referendum in August 2010 was a new constitution adopted which finally curtailed the powers of the head of state, provided for the devolution of governance and introduced a bill of rights (Republic of Kenya 2010). It promised a basis for democratic reform.

For a study on Nairobi's tenements, an equally disturbing media report at the time of writing was that 'gang activities have spread into real estate and are distorting the actual market value of properties... The Mungiki, Taliban and Kamjesh gangs are the major threats to would be investors' (Muiruri 2009b). In tenement areas such as Kayole, Kariobangi and Dandora, developers complained that approval needed to be bought from gangs before a building could be constructed. Extending their influence in the tenement industry, gangs were also 'manning quarries within the region thus inflating the cost of procuring construction materials' (*ibid.*). With continuing urban growth (see Table 6.5), any decline in tenement production and inflation of building cost is likely to translate not only into increased overcrowding but also into tension due to competition for the available units.[14] An improvement in the situation for individual tenants seems nowhere in sight. Particularly the rooming districts are poised to display their worst conditions yet.

Table 6.5: Nairobi's population growth in the post-Moi era

Year	Period	Population	Annual population growth rate
2003		2 563 297	
	2003–2005		Average 3.6%
2005		2 751 860	
	2005–2008		Average 3.3%
2008		3 038 553	
2009		3 138 369	

Source: Based on population projections in Central Bureau of Statistics (2009);
Kenya National Bureau of Statistics (2010)

How Nairobi's tenement market survives the escalating extractive force of urban gangs is a study for the future. My exploration of the tenement market in the next chapter is based on fieldwork undertaken in 2005, with only a brief follow-up in 2008. It therefore mostly predates both the impact of the post-election violence of early 2008 and the growing penetration of gang activity into the operation of the tenement market.

Endnotes

1 There were suggestions at the time that Nairobi could be moved to a healthier, more suitable location, but it was deemed too late for this to be done (Halliman and Morgan 1967, 104).

2 Jomo Kenyatta spent the 1930s and the first half of the 1940s in London, studying anthropology, teaching and publishing (Meredith 2006, 81).

3 This figure has grown steadily. By 1983, 'it was estimated that 35 per cent of all urban households lived under slum conditions in informal settlements' (COHRE 2005, 23). In 1997, this had risen to 55 per cent (Nairobi Informal Settlements Coordination Committee 1997) and more recent estimates are 60 per cent (Syagga, Mithullah and Karirah-Gitau 2001). However, it remains unclear where the line is drawn between unauthorized tenement development and so-called 'slums' or informal settlements.

4 Keith Hart coined the initially unorthodox idea of an 'informal sector' in 1971 in relation to activities in Accra, Ghana, whereas its first wide application was to Kenya in 1971 and 1972 (King 1996, 7). At that time, Kenyan novelists explored the same phenomenon (Kurtz 1998, 80, 82).

5 JAM (1982, 57, 59) provides evidence of widespread practices of embezzlement among directors of agricultural cooperatives, also showing how *harambee* initiatives were used to enforce the collection of contributions which were not accounted for.

6 The provincial administration is an undemocratic colonial structure of government. It is directly answerable to the Minister in the Office of the President and the President. In Nairobi, its functions are in relation to security and health, as well as land allocation. It is able to overrule the Nairobi City Council (answerable to the Minister of Local Government) (A Omenya, personal communication, June 14, 2009). Devolution of governance in the 2010 Constitution has raised hopes that the provincial administration system may be replaced by elected officers, but this depends on the enactment of new legislation (L Obala, personal communication, September 3, 2010).

7 A queuing system was used for elections in ancient Rome.

8 According to Anyang' Nyong'o's (2007, 154, 155) analysis, donor pressure played an insignificant role compared to 'the struggle for democracy from below' in the return to 'multiparty politics'.

9 In the 1962 census, the number of households occupying single rooms stood at 70 per cent (Stren 1972, 83).

10 *Jeshi la Mzee* was formed by 'senior members of KANU' (Anderson 2002, 549). It is the best known of the so-called 'youth wingers' or 'private armies' that 'prominent Kenyan politicians maintain' (*ibid.*, 549, 551).

11 The SDI-affiliated NGO Pamoja Trust was formed to give support to *Muungano wa Wanavijiji*. As of mid-2010, under new directorship, Pamoja Trust models its approach less directly on that of SDI.

12 The word 'Orange' in the ODM originated from the electoral commission's choice of 'orange' and 'banana' on the ballot paper to visually represent 'no' and 'yes' respectively to a partly illiterate electorate. ODM as a party was formed out of the 'no' vote campaign.

13 In March 2009, the media reported a new resolve to 'eradicate the gang' (*East African Standard* 2009).

14 With a relatively low level of urbanization (20 per cent in 1999 (Ministry of Roads, Public Works and Housing 2003)), much city-ward migration is still to be expected.

Chapter 7

Defiance of the modern plan: the creation of Nairobi's tenement districts

Nairobi, like most cities with a British colonial (if not apartheid) history, is socio-spatially polarized. In terms of residential distribution, it has a very clearly defined impoverished east and an affluent west. The lower income wedge in the west, Dago-retti/Kawangware, is an exception. Here a Kikuyu tribal area reaches into the current urban boundary drawn up in 1963. Residential densities today are highest in well located areas in which low income households initially settled in an unplanned fashion. Among these, the densest areas are in Mathare Valley to the north and east of the city centre and parts of Dagoretti and Kawangware to the west. In Mathare Valley, informal occupiers became tenants as landlordism emerged, offering rooming accommodation. This expanded vertically in an ongoing densification that has not yet reached saturation. At the same time, continued horizontal expansion of the multi-story tenement development is gradually displacing the single-story 'slums', which re-emerge elsewhere on environmentally precarious land while also encroaching into formal residential areas (K'Akumu and Olima 2007, 96).[1]

For a city of its growth rate and size, the Kenyan government has done relatively little over the last fifty years to service and release land for housing in Nairobi. The scarcity of developable land has contributed to a demand for rental accommodation at ever higher densities. The few site-and-service schemes that the urban authorities developed with donor support from the 1970s onwards quickly attracted tenement investors who sought to maximize their rental income by adding additional (unauthorized) floors. While most new schemes were intended for low income residents, a clear distinction emerged between those areas in which landlords offered low income rooming and those in which they chose to offer self-contained lower middle to middle income apartments.

In this and the following chapter, I home in on two of Nairobi's tenement areas. One is the multi-story rooming district Huruma in Mathare Valley, which quite possibly has the highest residential densities in the city and even on the African continent. The other is the more recently developed middle class district Umoja Inner Core. Both are to the east of the city centre (Figures 7.1 and 7.2). In 2005, Andrew Kimani, Kevin Osodo and I schematically mapped the tenement density for a four- to five-hectare sample area in Huruma and Umoja Inner Core. Kevin Osodo and I returned in 2008 to record further densification. In both sample areas, we interviewed a small number of tenants in 2005 and again in 2008. For the middle income Umoja Inner Core these interviews were limited, as few tenant household members were at home during the day. In 2005 we also discussed both areas with municipal officials, rental agents and the few willing landlords we managed to identify as owning tenements in Huruma or Umoja Inner Core (I provide profiles for the landlord and agent interviews in Tables 8.2 and 8.3 in the following chapter).

The development of Nairobi's residential areas involves an extreme departure from the official plans and an equally extreme transgression of regulations. Yet an element of realism exists in the development control practiced by municipal officials – a willingness to accept the existing built form in recognition of qualities and contributions that are not acknowledged in the official planning and regulatory paradigm. However, this practice stops short of providing certainty for a tenement future. The development trajectories for Huruma and Umoja Inner Core, pieced together towards the end of this chapter, provide deeper insight into the densification in these areas. For Huruma in particular, my review of existing literature on the 1970s helped point also to the political means through which the interests of emerging tenement investors were accommodated, despite modern/anti-tenement town planning and regulation. But the literature provides no insight into the political dimension of Huruma's development beyond the 1970s, and none at all for the development of Umoja Inner Core, where it is likely that tenement investment, though less contested, also enjoys political patronage. For the 1980s and into the 1990s, 'the politics of urban governance' in Nairobi 'has not been adequately studied... as the restriction of free political discourse discouraged researchers from investigating the political realm' (Halfani 1997, 139). Even in 2005, we deemed it too difficult and sensitive to interview politicians on the topic of tenement investment.

The failure of modern planning for Nairobi

Every level of Nairobi's city-making process ignored or dismissed official plans at the city level. This is not unique to urban development in Kenya (Stren 1989, 60). UN-HABITAT (2009, 140) notes that 'the ability of planning systems in African cities to prevent or deal with widespread informal economic activity, land subdivision, housing construction and service delivery remains extremely limited, with the partial exception of South Africa'. Cited reasons are the inappropriateness of existing plans and regulations, limitations in skills and capacity among officials

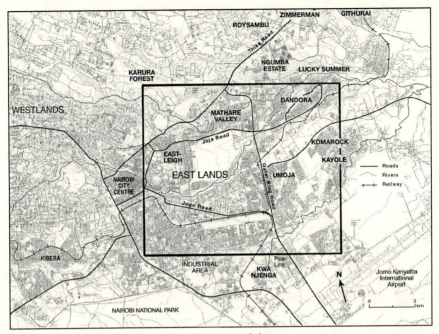

Figure 7.1: Map of Nairobi contextualizing Nairobi's east

Source: Based on 2002 GIS/cartography from Geomap

in both implementation and reform, the fragmentation of administrations, politicians' and bureaucracies' visions of modernity (*ibid.*) and a lack of 'authority and enforcement power for planning agencies' (Stren 1989, 60). In the 1980s, Okpala (1984, 75) explored this reality for Nigerian cities, in particular Ibadan, where over 60 per cent of developments did not seek building approval. He found frustrated attempts at enforcement, and the bending of rules 'to contain and satisfy personalities' (*ibid.*, 82).

In addition to these tendencies, in the offices of Nairobi's City Council I encountered a level of realism and pragmatism in facilitating dense multi-story tenement development. To a far greater extent than single-story 'slums' or unplanned informal settlements, this type of development embodies the antithesis of modern town planning, not only in building type (compact as opposed to suburban or tower block) and land use (mixed as opposed to segregated), but also in the formal street layout (permeable as opposed to cellular). In this sense, planning officials in Nairobi were not just ignoring the norms of modern town planning in favor of informality and corruption, but had replaced them with a parallel planning logic. This logic subscribes to a similar set of norms to that which governed city building in most of Europe's industrializing and rapidly growing cities before the advent of modern town planning. Their re-emergence in Nairobi is itself a strong critique of modern planning principles. In order to expose this contrast, it is necessary to first

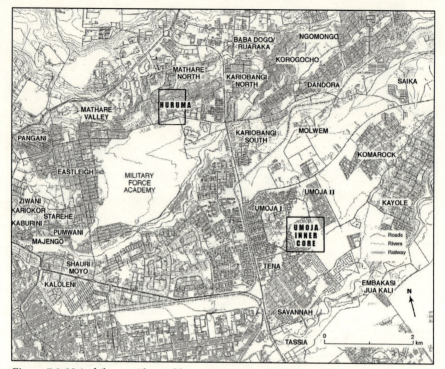

Figure 7.2: Nairobi's east: Physical layout in 2002 and location of the case study areas

Source: Based on 2002 GIS/cartography from Geomap

Note: Names to the west of Eastleigh are partly 'slum' and housing areas mentioned in Chapter Six, some of which do not exist today.

examine the premises of Nairobi's modern plans and the way they sought to order urban space, as these same premises remain influential in physical planning and road engineering practice today (UN-HABITAT 2009, 56). In Nairobi, any revival of their legitimacy among the city's decision-makers poses a threat to its dense, complex and convenient (though also largely inadequate) urban environment and the economic stakes invested in it.

A precursor to Nairobi's 1948 Master Plan was a zoning plan drawn up in 1926 (Obudho 1997, 327). However, following this exercise, 'little was done to curb land speculation, and development occurred in an uncontrolled manner' (Nairobi Urban Study Group 1973a, Section 43). In 1948, the *Nairobi Master Plan for a Colonial Capital* 'laid down the guidelines for the following twenty years' (*ibid.*). According to the analysis provided by the 1948 master planning team, a particular moment in the assumed evolution of Nairobi had been reached:

> [P]eople begin to think about the future in earnest. There is a plethora of new regulations. Government is by legislation. At the same time,

modernity breaks through in the physical realm in the form of multistorey buildings and corrugated iron huts are replaced and ferro-concrete makes its entry at petrol stations. Zoning arrangements are made and the foundation of municipal enterprise is laid. (White, Silberman and Anderson 1948, 5).

The 1948 Master Plan (and subsequently the 1973 *Nairobi Metropolitan Growth Strategy* (Nairobi Urban Study Group 1973a, 1973b)), in line with planning orthodoxy at the time, sought to order space through principles of modern suburban town planning. These were derived from an assumption that private motor vehicles would become the primary means of transport for every urban household. Modern planners and engineers sought maximum convenience for vehicular traffic, including its total separation from pedestrians, whom they confined to internalized 'neighbourhood units'. These arranged 'dwellings... around a central pedestrian open space' and kept 'vehicle access to a system of external cul-de-sacs' (Houghton-Evans 1978, 94). Neighborhood units were segregated from one another by large motorways in the 'superblock' system developed in the USA in the 1920s and 1930s (*ibid.*). In the USA, the development of the neighborhood unit (and superblock) 'responded to the high levels of automobile ownership by then already reached' (*ibid.*).[2] Low and extremely skewed distribution of car ownership in Nairobi seems to have gone unnoticed by the modernist experts, who embraced rigid street hierarchies and a minimum of street intersections (the inverse of a permeable gridiron layout), which were integral to the superblock system.

Neighborhood units 'owed much to the Garden City Movement' (*ibid.*), which according to Nairobi's 1948 master planning team 'wishes to preserve as much of the rural atmosphere as possible in an urban area by restricting densities, *decountenancing flat tenements* and excluding non-residential, non-conforming buildings' (White, Silberman and Anderson 1948, 45, my emphasis). With this somewhat simplistic appraisal, the team pointed to limitations of the garden city approach, arguing that 'it falls short of deliberate encouragement of planning for communal activities and of deepening the social bonds within the local community' (*ibid.*; see also Nevanlinna 1996, 171). This justified their preference for the 'neighborhood unit' (rather than a pure garden city approach) in the 1948 Master Plan.

The 1948 Master Plan did not prescribe or even suggest physical dimensions for neighborhood units. Each 'neighborhood' (Figure 7.3) was planned to consist of 1 000 units, with rows of 'detached houses and terraced houses surrounding a central green area with five nursery schools, two junior schools, three churches several shops and a community centre' (White, Silberman and Anderson 1948, 173). The planners criticized Nairobi's existing low density. Their analysis showed its highest density at the time as 12 houses per acre (30 dwelling units per hectare). However, while acknowledging that some 'might wish to live in flats' (*ibid.*, 45), they modeled the neighborhood unit at only one and two units per acre (two to five houses per hectare) for affluent areas and eight units per acre (20 houses per hectare) for lower income areas (Nevanlinna 1996, 172, 175). Somewhat ambiguously, the Master Plan foresaw a total of fifty neighborhood units 'readily adaptable to any density standards' (White, Silberman and Anderson 1948, 73). The post-1948 transformation of Nairobi's low income residential areas to over 1 500 units per hectare today, as I show in this and the following chapter, cannot possibly be what the Master Plan intended.

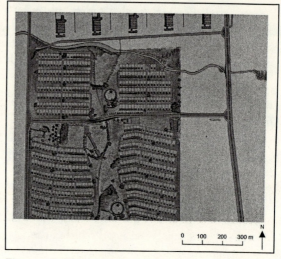

Figure 7.3: The 1948 Master Plan's model neighborhood unit

Source: White, Silberman and Anderson (1948, 72)

In accordance with 'modern practice' (Houghton-Evans 1978, 95) Nairobi's 1948 planners foresaw a total separation between different land uses and in the way different modes of mobility accessed the individual plot. Each residential stand was to be reached on one side (by car) through a *cul de sac* or street loop and on the other (on foot) through a park and pathway system connecting to a central spine of public facilities and open space (White, Silberman and Anderson 1948, 46; Nevanlinna 1996, 173). While concerned with pedestrian convenience within the neighborhood, the planners failed to take into account the inconvenience for pedestrians trying to cross from one neighborhood to another or needing to reach main roads for public transport.

To Nairobi's expert team, modern town planning was not only a paradigm that sought to accommodate an assumed already modernized technology and life-style (including dependence on the motor car), as was the case in the USA. The planners believed that 'translation of the values of tribal life into modern terms' would be 'most clearly realised in "Neighbourhood Planning"' (White, Silberman and Anderson 1948, 8) – indeed one of the 'key assumptions' of master planning (UN-HABITAT 2009, 50). The plan was not envisaged as a blueprint. Instead, it was to be 'flexible and able to adapt itself to changes' (White, Silberman and Anderson 1948, 76). Within this flexibility, the achievement of 'unity' required

> people outside of the public service, the ordinary people, [to] know what it is all about. The Plan must be communicated. It must be explained and

of tenements visibly under construction, is Kayole, 10–12 km from the city centre. The densest concentrations are in parts of Mathare Valley – immediately to the east of Pangani, at the western end of Huruma (the former Ngei II), and north of Gitathuru River Mathare 4A and Mathare North. All these are within a 7 km radius of the city centre. The 1973 Growth Strategy's projection to the year 2000 (Nairobi Urban Study Group 1973a) envisaged only low density residential development, stretching 27 km to the north-west of the city (Figure 7.6), well beyond Zimmerman, Githurai and the city boundary, therefore also proposing a boundary change. To the south-east, it projected residential cells up to the boundary, 17 km from the centre. To date, Nairobi's expansion has not even reached the Growth Strategy's projections for 1985!

While Nairobi's authorities implemented neither the boundary extension nor most of the spatial development proposed in the 1973 Growth Strategy, some of the Strategy's recommendations on housing found their way into practice. In part they reflected already existing practice that enjoyed pragmatic legitimacy. Perversely, they helped invert the modern spatial plan. The Strategy encouraged housing provision by 'private entrepreneurs' (Nairobi Urban Study Group 1973a,

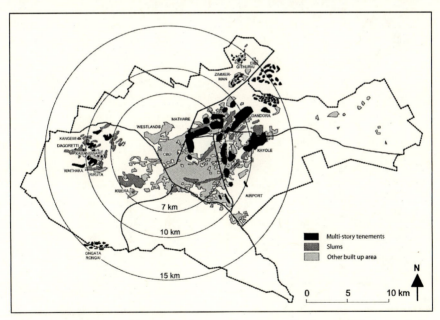

Figure 7.5: Nairobi's built-up area, slums and tenement districts, and their proximity to the city centre

Source: Author's own construction from various maps and aerial photographs, superimposed on a
base drawn from Mundia and Aniya (2006, 104), various maps and aerial photographs

Note: Low density suburbs are not shown.

Section 30). The World Bank had begun its involvement in financing and planning sites-and-services to minimum standards (rather than public housing) under its Urban I project for Kenya (*ibid.*, Section 105). The Growth Strategy aligned itself to this (*ibid.*, Section 142(h)(ii)), also suggesting 'prototype plans and layouts' in cases where 'co-operatives, private building companies and individuals' were 'undertaking to provide' low income housing (*ibid.*, (iii)). 'Multi-storeyed structures' were to be avoided, as the Growth Strategy deemed these 'incapable of enlargement' (*ibid.*, (v)). The Strategy recommended '[d]esigning homes for [temporary] subletting', as this increased 'the number of households provided with shelter' while adding to the assumed owner-occupier's income (*ibid.*, (vi)).

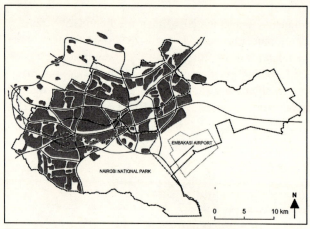

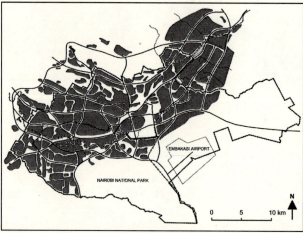

Figure 7.6: Spatial projection to the year 1985 and 2000 in the 1973 Nairobi Growth Strategy   Source: Based on Nairobi Urban Studies Group (1973a)

Table 7.1: The distribution of multi-story tenements across Nairobi

Broad region	Area	Sub-area	Multi-story tenements counted		
North-east	Along Thika Rd	Kawa West	570	1 695	4 861
		Githurai (outside city boundary)	232		
		Kawa South/Githurai	254		
		Zimmerman	417		
		Roysambu	113		
		Ngumba	109		
	Dandora and surrounds, east of Outer Ring Rd	Lucky Summer	89	1 490	
		Baba Dogo/Ruaraka	482		
		Korogocho Estate	113		
		Kariobangi North	40		
		Light Industries	272		
		Dandora	480		
		Saika	14		
	Mathare Valley, west of Outer Ring Rd	Mathare North	342	1 138	
		Mathare 4A	101		
		New Mathare	225		
		Huruma/Ngei	277		
		Other, north of Juja Rd	33		
		Directly east of Pangani	160		
	Older inner city areas: Eastleigh	Eastleigh	317	538	
		Eastleigh South	221		
South-east	East of Outer Ring Road, south of Juja Rd	Kariobangi South	261	3 648	3 985
		Kariobangi South / Molwem	32		
		East of Molwem	86		
		Umoja 1	180		
		Umoja 2	41		
		Umoja Inner Core	760		
		Tena Estate	240		
		Kayole	1 700		
		Savannah	128		
		Tassia	150		
		Embakasi Jua Kali	54		
		Other – bordering airport	16		
	Directly west of Outer Ring Rd	Pipeline	202	337	
		Kwa Njenga	135		

Broad region	Area	Sub-area	Multi-story tenements counted	
West	Vicinity of Riruta		548	1 820
	Vicinity of Kawangware		728	
	Waithaka		85	
	East of Kangemi		125	
	Kangemi		96	
	Ongata Rongai, west of Nairobi National Park		238	
TOTAL				10 666

Source: Based on 2009 photography

Note: Table 7.1 is based on a count of multi-story residential tenements recognizable by shape and shadow on 2009 aerial photograph imagery. It is an undercount for several reasons: a) It was difficult to distinguish between buildings directly adjacent to one another where not every building cast its own shadow; b) the imagery was unclear (and clouded) in Nairobi's west; c) tenement areas which developed on customary areas in Nairobi's west have a largely organic layout, tenement designs are not as uniform as in Nairobi's north-east, and building shadows are often concealed by trees. Using the total figure in Table 7.1 and an assumed average of 3 residential floors per building, 7 units per floor, therefore 21 units per building, and 1 household per unit, a conservative estimate is that 223 986 households live in multi-story tenements in Nairobi. This does not include single-story tenements in the same areas, with the same building layouts, and for which landlords may well be planning to add additional floors. At an estimated average of 3.3 people per unit, currently at least 739 154 people live in multi-story tenements in Nairobi.

This early step towards embracing and encouraging landlordism, which reflected the practical discourse at the time and led to site-and-service schemes designed for small-scale letting of rooms, was disconnected from the modernist paradigm of the suburban spatial plan. Perversely, it helped unleash an unstoppable process of rental speculation, to which Nairobi's authorities never adapted the overall city plan. This goes to the heart of the urban planning challenge for Nairobi today, as (international) physical planning orthodoxy becomes ever more irrelevant to the city's unfolding urban reality. This challenge also includes a context of widespread land grabbing or corrupt disposal of public land, as well as large-scale corruption with implications for both public revenue and flows of donor finance. The pilfering of public funds and public land helped render large-scale servicing of new tracts of land for low density development on Nairobi's urban fringes impossible, and may provide some explanation as to why the authorities never implemented the spatial structure of the 1948 Master Plan and the 1973 Growth Strategy. In those few cases where urban authorities subdivided new land for public/donor-financed housing estates (such as Umoja), they did not base street layouts on the Master Plan's neighborhood unit. Where remnants of this concept found their way onto the ground, residents and landlord investors subsequently inverted these. For instance Kariobangi Estate, implemented in the early post-independence years, was laid out in 'clusters' of 32 houses, a smaller version of a 'neighborhood unit' (Loeckx 1989). Already in 1976 urban researchers observed that with the rapid emergence of absentee landlordism, the Kariobangi 'squatter resettlement as initially planned never had much chance of success' (Weisner 1976, 78). A decade later, they documented how 'dwellers' (and landlords) modified this layout through a 'commercial front' consisting of kiosks, shops and bars 'along the main road', the use of the 'semi-public square… as garbage belt' if not 'transformed into private use', and '[b]reakthroughs' modifying 'the blind alleys into streets parallel to the main road' (Loeckx 1989, 67).

Huruma, seemingly laid out in the 1970s primarily by land buying companies seeking to maximize the number of their rental units, is structured in a permeable gridiron that is convenient to tenement investors and pedestrians alike (Figure 7.7) – no blind alleys have needed to be modified or broken through by frustrated users. An official of the Housing Development Department (HDD) of Nairobi City Council in Dandora confirmed that his department had formally drawn up the subdivision plans (Anonymous A, interview, October 27, 2005). Presumably this was a case of formalizing a spatial structure that to a large extent was already manifested on the ground.

The 1970s greenfield (or clean slate) planning for Umoja Estate incorporated the superblock approach with a rigid street hierarchy. Umoja I, II and Inner Core each form one or more isolated cells. Similar to Kariobangi, the layouts for Umoja I and II are in small clusters rather than neighborhood units. Consulting firms designed these subdivision plans (Anonymous A, interview, October 27, 2005).

Umoja's third phase, Inner Core, has no recognizable sign of neighborhood units or clusters. Nairobi City Council officials, not planning consultants, prepared the subdivision plan (*ibid.*). The individual plot access is an inconsistent variation on a gridiron street layout with only some *culs de sac* and looped streets, and no internal park and pathway system (Figure 7.8). Less pedestrian-friendly than the consistent gridiron layout of Huruma, it

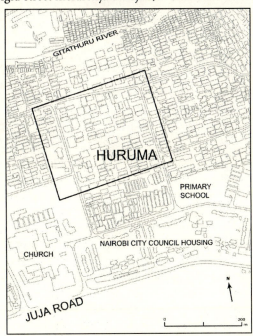

Figure 7.7: Huruma, showing the location of the sample area

Source: Based on aerial photography from February 2000, Geomap, Nairobi

is clearly aligned to the interests of tenement investors. The City Council's planners not only accommodated speculative interests in the original subdivision plan; upon demand, they subsequently subdivided some of the limited 'open space' for further tenement plots, as an Umoja landlord explained in relation to the site he was developing with a five-story tenement:

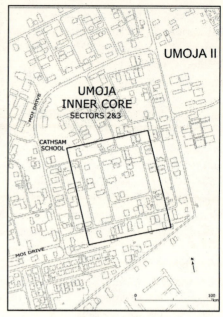

> The plot was for sale. I knew the owner, and he approached me. This plot, including the building next door, was supposed to be an open space. But the municipality had sold the land to the previous owner. The survey plan was changed from open space to residential. (Landlord 4, interview, October 18, 2005)

Figure 7.8: Umoja Inner Core, showing location of the sample area

Source: Based on aerial photography from February 2000, Geomap, Nairobi

Adding to the town planning confusion, the survey plan we obtained from the Nairobi City Council (perhaps not the latest version) showed the two adjacent plots divided in a different direction than what we found on the ground.

Beyond the transgression of subdivision layouts, Ochieng (2001, 1) discusses defiance of planning intentions on individual properties. He documents a 'severe form of densification and physical change' in the 1990s in Komarock, originally a 'mortgage-housing scheme... developed by the Kenya Building Society' with single-story row housing. Plot owners had inserted 'slender blocks' of up to five stories into the original design and in some cases left no trace of the original housing (*ibid.*). 'Kiosks' were introduced on the 'front facade' (*ibid.*, 7). This densification pattern is typical where developers originally constructed suburban, single residential or terraced housing such as Buru Buru and Umoja I (Figure 7.9). A Komarock plot owner interviewed in Ochieng's (2001, 8) study legitimized his investment by stating 'this is Nairobi', and 'we all need to raise funds'.

This reflects the logic that King (1996, 50) observed in the mid-1990s in his study on Nairobi's *jua kali*. Though not having investigated this aspect any further, King mentions a whole new city growing up... The character of the development seems very much that of an intimately mixed residential and micro-enterprise style. Here, the familiar distinctions between residential, commercial and industrial districts seem to have broken down and jua kali, mixed mode Nairobi seems to be spreading relentlessly acre by acre. (*ibid.*)

Referring to the owners of these buildings, King (*ibid.*) recognizes '[a] kind of middle-class self-help that finds expression in the phrase: "We're all jua kali these days!"' Omenya (2006) explores this form of middle class self-help, analyzing networks through which resources have flowed in the production of individual tenement buildings in Dandora and Kawangware. This includes the 'exploitative personal ties of relatively well-to-do individuals' (*ibid.*, 175), whose networks 'undermine both planning regulations and development control' and include particular forms of protection through links to the provincial administration (*ibid.*), which plays a strong role in political patronage.

Two tenement areas, Githurai and Komarock, have featured in popular Kenyan lyrics. Nyairo (2006) analyzes the songs *Wasee Githurai* and *4 in 1*, through which 'one captures the spatial and the social geography of these areas, and gains a better understanding of the people who inhabit these spaces, and of the pleasures and dreams that daily lubricate their existence' (*ibid.*, 88). In these songs, she finds 'actual parallels' to

Nairobi's own mimicry of global concepts of town planning and urban design. It is as if to say that Nairobi only pretends to be a modern enclave whereas in fact its character is derived more from the ethnic ingenuity that has collapsed all plans of a green city and made illegal densification of informal settlements the order of the city's development. (*ibid*)

Figure 7.9: Tenement development in a single residential area of Umoja I

Source: Author's photographs (2005)

I have already alluded to a seemingly collective consensus that modern urban planning, with its particular spatial order, had little relevance for Nairobi. This consensus recognizes homeownership, the tenure form attached to modern suburbia, primarily as a means for tenement investment. This is the case even in areas such as Umoja II (Figures 7.15 and 7.16 below), where planners have attempted to design away any opportunities for multi-story tenement construction by absentee landlords.

In 2005, when we conducted interviews in the Nairobi Municipal Council, city-wide planning was on the cards. The physical planning director informed us that

> we are thinking about metro- or future-planning for the next 30 years. We are wanting to get the World Bank involved with a City Development Strategy and growth strategy. This will be a policy document to guide and coordinate long-term investment and physical development. We are now developing a proposal on how to consult stakeholders for this plan... We are expecting this process to take about two years. (Anonymous B, interview, October 13, 2005).

In May 2008, he was no longer in office. Another senior official in the department expressed little hope for change, explaining that cabinet had 'made a U-turn' on the City Development Strategy. A 'Vision 2030' document had been prepared, but was only for the medium term and 'no more than a list of flagship projects'. The state had created a new Ministry of Nairobi Metropolitan Development, but this still lacked a legislative framework. The new ministry did not seem interested in long-term planning and the situation remained 'very fragmented'.[5] However, Nairobi City Council was in discussion with the French Development Agency as well as the Japan International Cooperation Agency regarding 'proposals for master plan studies' (Anonymous C, interview, May 26, 2008).

While I did not further investigate the political obstruction of overall planning for Nairobi, the unplanned development of Huruma, which I return to below, suggests how the interests vested in a continuation of the *status quo* counter the efforts of well intentioned officials. In the process, a dense and complex tenement city is constructed, with the total inversion of what Bruno Taut's pro-suburban and anti-tenement cartoon (Figure 5.7 in Chapter 5) envisaged for Berlin in the 1920s. Given that tenement markets made their exit from the international planning discourse in the 1920s (other than as 'immigrant enclaves', zones of decay or alternatively of gentrification (UN-HABITAT 2003b, 22)), it is unlikely that international town planning consultants would be in any position to engage with Nairobi's tenement reality.

Beyond Nairobi's modern spatial plans: traces of realism in regulating urban space

In 1979 the Kenyan state released a 'rationalisation strategy', focusing 'on structural development of the city' through 20 zones that 'introduced specific densities, plot coverage and land subdivision' (Okumu 2007, 17). Whereas Okumu (*ibid.*) criticizes this rationalization as it foresaw only the 'provision of alternative infrastructure' for unserviced areas (*ibid.*), the adoption of 'special density zones' was nevertheless a step towards accepting the actual shape and pattern which the city was taking. A development control official of the Nairobi City Council explained that this zoning increased the permitted ground coverage from 35 per cent to 50 per cent, extended the floor ratio to one and reduced the building line or setback to zero (Anonymous D, interview, October 5, 2005).[6] As I will show in more detail for Huruma, in many parts of Nairobi plots are covered 100 per cent with up to eight stories, amounting to a floor ratio of eight.

In 1980, a year after the rationalization, the urban authorities developed 'single issue plans' for water, sewerage and drainage, solid waste and transport (Okumu 2007, 17). This included a World Bank-financed plan to address acute shortages in Nairobi. The urban water authorities delayed implementation by four years, due to 'mismanagement, particularly in the award of contracts' (Lee-Smith 1989, 284). Okumu (2007, 17) further explains that 'with lack of resources and coordination, implementation of the various plans became difficult and led to the eventual collapse of development control and enforcement in the city'. At the HDD in Dandora, of which the first floor windows provide a view only of unauthorized multi-story tenements, an official confirmed this lack of coordination, suggesting (as is widely assumed) that this was also assisted by corruption:

> The Water and Sewer Company provides meters on plots that are grabbed. They should check that it is a legal plot. The owner has to fill in a lot number [when applying for a water meter]. The same applies to the Electricity Company. Many buildings ignore the way leave, therefore the seventh-floor balcony may be right next to a power line. Here there was probably *kitu kidogo* ['something small', meaning a bribe] given. (Anonymous A, interview, October 25, 2005)

At the time of our interviews in 2005, a visible anti-corruption initiative of the relatively new (though already embattled) Kibaki administration reminded everyone entering municipal offices of the widespread practice of *kitu kidogo* and its illegality (Figure 7.10). This eased reference to this practice during our interviews.

An engineer at the Nairobi Water and Sewerage Company explained the company's pragmatic approach to water supply: 'The company connects, as long as the landlord pays [irrespective of whether the building is approved]. About ten years ago, Nairobi City Council used to check authorization of the building before connecting water' (Anonymous E, interview, October 27, 2005). With unplanned densification as well as the unplanned development of entire housing estates such as Zimmerman and Githurai through land buying companies, a significant problem emerged with 'supply from the mains' (*ibid.*). Two other officials at the Eastleigh office of the company (dealing with regional commercial coordination and meter reading) added that water supply was also strained by lack of formal provision made for the activities of the vibrant *jua kali*. For instance, 'the car wash places on Outer Ring Road were wasting water, tapping straight from the mains', which caused 'a water

Figure 7.10: Anti-corruption suggestion box at the entrance to the Nairobi City Council

Source: Author's photograph (2005)

shortage problem in Huruma' (Anonymous Group I, interview, October 17, 2005). Throughout Nairobi, tenement investors had responded to water supply disruptions by providing underground storage tanks from which water was pumped into tanks on the roof. In the next chapter I show how water supply affects living conditions, particularly in Huruma's dense rooming market. In middle class Umoja Inner Core, the presence of water vendors (Figure 7.11) indicated an even graver water reticulation problem.

Figure 7.11: Water vendors in the sample area of Umoja Inner Core

Source: Author's photograph (2008)

The tenements right outside the office of the HDD in Dandora were not in the area of responsibility of the official we interviewed. He therefore felt at ease to discuss them: 'These buildings are happening all over... People were just willing to break the law everywhere... Richer people are able to construct bigger and to force the law... And the demand exists... Many get approval for three floors and then build more floors…' (Anonymous A, interview, October 25, 2005). Our interviews with landlords confirmed this ongoing trend. An Umoja landlord who had already built to the permitted three floors above ground, and was seemingly unaware of improved law enforcement, shared his intentions, justifying this in terms of the general practice in the area: 'I will try to do four floors when Council sleeps. Some people are even doing five floors' (Landlord 1, interview, November 1, 2005). A development control official explained that deviations from plan applied not only to additional floors, but also to plot coverage (Anonymous F, interview, November 2, 2005). Similarly, an urban planner in the Forward Planning Department explained that 'investors submit ground floor plans as residential, but then use them as commercial' (Anonymous G, interview, October 31, 2005).

Our interviewee at the Dandora HDD explained that the officials were only able to tackle those buildings for which they received complaints, as they lacked the capacity to 'go around finding illegal buildings' – not that they would have to go far, but where would they start? He further observed that whereas in Dandora 'the roads are respected… in Huruma people are even building on parking areas and roads – grabbing land' (Anonymous A, interview, October 25, 2005). Our fieldwork confirmed this. In our sample area in Huruma in 2005 a small open space was graced with a rusted sign stating: 'Warning: No grabbing. Not for Sale. This is a public place' (Figure 7.12). In 2008, this sign had disappeared. A tenant explained that the steel had probably been used for defense in the post-election violence in January of that year. As far we could distinguish on the ground, the land had not yet been grabbed. However, by June 2009, someone had constructed four stories of a new tenement (Tenant 1, interview, June 15, 2009). There remains little to suggest that the assurances of improved development control from an HDD official in Dandora in 2005 ('Now people are sensing there is a law. Prosecutions are taking place' (Anonymous A, interview, October 25, 2005)) could be sustained.

Figure 7.12: Attempts to protect a small public space in the sample area in Huruma

Source: Author's photograph (2005)

An urban planner in the Forward Planning Department of the Nairobi City Council alluded to an improvement in enforcement, but also a frustration of this process by the courts which seemed to continue siding with non-compliant landlords:

> ... enforcement is improving. Occupational certificates are being denied if buildings are not compliant. Hefty fines are given in the city court, e.g. Kshs 100 000 [US$1 444]. It used to be only Kshs 2 000 [US$29], which was no deterrent... [But] the court process is giving City Council a hard time... It can take up to six months before a court hearing takes place. (Anonymous G, interview, October 31, 2005)

In the case of new construction, landlords were using this delay to complete their buildings and place tenants in the units, even though an occupational certificate would not have been issued. 'Then it's a whole procedure to evict. The law is not clear on what happens once the building is occupied' (Anonymous G, interview, October 31, 2005). The other official whom we interviewed in Development Control explained that submission of plans, even if not approved and not approvable, would give the courts further reasons to delay hearings. Investors also assumed (seemingly with the problematic court system on their side) that if the council did not respond to a submission within one month, the plans had been approved. In reality, the plan approval still took the council five months (Anonymous F, interviews, November 2, 2005).

Lack of law enforcement interacted with investor decisions in various ways, also fuelling densification in Huruma. In the late 1990s, in the last years of Moi's reign, even vacant private land was not safe from grabbing. The Huruma landlord we interviewed (Landlord 1, interview, November 1, 2005) explained that the reason his family had decided to construct tenements in 1998 and 2000 on the two plots that their late father had purchased in the 1980s was that 'there was grabbing going on; we had to develop the plots to prevent someone from grabbing them'. While landlords had to protect themselves from the lack of enforcement by the municipality, they also exploited this. Referring to the collapse of development control in the late 1990s, the same Huruma landlord explained why both his buildings, with their five floors above ground, are above the permitted height: 'It used to be compulsory to submit plans to the City Council. But when I started building, it was chaotic. You submitted plans but you never heard from the Council' (Landlord 1, interview, November 1, 2005). It was probably not accidental that in these last, deeply corrupt years of Moi's administration, the HDD in Dandora, which has a role to play in plan approval, was closed. According to the HDD official, housing plans had been missing ever since, and this was hampering development control:

> There was a time when the HDD office was going to be scrapped. At the time, the layout plans were taken to the Director of City Planning, and some of them have not been given back. From 1997 to 2000, there was no HDD. (Anonymous A, interview, October 27, 2005)

Municipal officials, while sharing their frustration with the situation, also voiced pragmatism and an acceptance of the reality, along with an implicit assumption that the tenement densification trend would not be reversed. The official in the HDD noted: 'There is a high demand for single rooms, for this size of units. This won't end' (Anonymous A, interview, October 27, 2005). A town planner in the Forward Planning Department explained that 'the City Council accepts that this housing has developed out of pressure... Council is unable to keep up with the pace' (Anonymous H, interview, October 5, 2005). This realization seemed to lead to a reluctance to enforce unsympathetic regulations: 'The issue with Huruma is that if one were to insist on compliance, demolition would be required, and this would push people into the slums' (Anonymous F, interview, November 2, 2005). A development control official linked this tacit acceptance to the residential reality that officials faced in their private lives:

> Even officers in the Nairobi City Council live in high density [tenement] areas. We are very aware of these areas. Therefore it will not be possible to pull [the unauthorized tenements] down. Instead, one will have to improve the infrastructure. The City Council is also aware of the demand for housing. (Anonymous D, interview, October 5, 2005)

Officials also voiced interest in exploring forms of legalization: 'There is overwhelming demand in the market. Maybe planning needs to make available other development opportunities and relax the enforcement a little for the additional floor' (Anonymous G, interview, October 31, 2005). Officials equally applied this line to the transgression of the residential zoning, which did not permit shops on the ground floors of tenements. A development control official recognized the employment created through the unauthorized commercial space in tenement areas: 'Often there is illegal conversion from residential to commercial, because of the high unemployment. The City Council is not keen to enforce the laws there, because of the poverty' (Anonymous D, interview, October 5, 2005). His colleague in Forward Planning added, 'One might need a comprehensive study to see how the shops in the ground floors of residential buildings are working' (Anonymous G, interview, October 31, 2005).

While I did not come across initiatives that would legalize the residential and commercial mix in Nairobi, the revision of the city's housing standards has been on the agenda since the 1970s. The 'housing policy and programme recommendations' in the 1973 Growth Strategy annexure also called for the development of 'appropriate and realistic housing standards for each income group', failing which the lowest income groups would be driven 'into illegal and unauthorised housing not meeting any standards at all' (Nairobi Urban Study Group 1973b, Section 5.56). Politically, this recommendation has met with sustained resistance, even though in 1984 the media reported President Moi's support for 'an immediate amendment to the... colonial building by-laws' (Osiemo 1984). Nairobi's 'planning regulations, infrastructure standards, sanitation rules, densities and ratios, the building code and building materials standards' were 'inherited from the British colonial power' (Tuts 1996, 608). Amendments that the Kenyan government enacted after independence were all introduced within the first decade after colonial rule, therefore still 'heavily inspired by British regulations' and the standards remain 'rigid and prohibitively high' (*ibid.*, 609). In 1997, observers optimistically reported that '[a]t central government level, there is a consensus that the building regulations should be revised' (Obudho 1997, 318). At the time of writing, the revision of standards for Nairobi, like overall city planning, was still on the seemingly not-too-urgent government agenda. Their reappearance in the media in October 2009 (Aron 2009a; Owuor 2009) was accompanied by fears of 'empty talk... Over the past ten years ... nothing has happened' (Aron 2009b).

In effect, single-room occupation by an entire household remains unauthorized throughout Nairobi despite initiatives to have this legalized. In 1979 the World Bank commissioned a 'Housing By-law Study', with a final report submitted in 1980 (Yahya 1987). In 1992, over a decade later, a proposed 'Code 92' was developed, providing for single-story 'dormitory accommodation' with a minimum of 4 m² per person (if 'two tier bunks are provided', 3 m² per person with increased ceiling height), and a single-story 'multi-purpose room' with a minimum of 10.5 m² (The Interministerial Task Force n.d., reproducing 'Code 92' Special Scheduled Areas Building By-laws, By-law no. 216 and 227). In two of the three tenements we measured in the sample area of Huruma, the 'multi-purpose' rooms were smaller than 10.5 m² (see Figures 8.5–8.7 in Chapter 8)! It took three years for the proposed Code 92 to be gazetted; therefore its official name is 'Code 95' (Agevi, personal communication, October 24, 2005). However, it remains an 'adoptive' code, 'not mandatory for local authorities' (*ibid.*). Whereas the city of Nakuru adopted it for certain housing areas, this has not been the case for Nairobi (*ibid.*), where the widespread practice of rooming still enjoys no legitimacy from the law. This may be explained by the fact that Code 95 does not accommodate multi-story rooming, therefore would not in fact legalize most of the existing tenement stock in Nairobi. However, not even a 'Building Code Review Board' was set up (*ibid.*), as envisaged to ensure 'relevance and applicability' of 'all the planning and building By-laws' on an ongoing basis (The Interministerial Task Force n.d., 44). The Review Board would be the vehicle through which to develop appropriate standards for multi-story rooming (Agevi, personal communication, October 24, 2005). It would also be the body through which to explore legalizing the absence of lifts in tall tenements. As a development control official explained, 'according to the Building Code, what is permitted is four floors without a lift; this 1968 Code is outdated' (Anonymous F, interview, November 2, 2005).[7]

In the absence of a Building Code Review Board, the HDD in Dandora had taken steps to have certain rooming tenements legalized, by requesting Council to approve the appropriate 'type plans' or prototype building layouts and specifications.[8]

Two rooms [per household] were intended in the type plans. But people tend to live in one room if they're hard off... [We prepared a] type plan for a two-story house with ten rooms. Shower and WC [are] shared by five rooms on each floor. This plan has been submitted to Council for approval as a type plan... HDD has requested 70 per cent plot coverage, but I'm not sure Council will accept this. We're still awaiting approval. (Anonymous A, interview, October 27, 2005).

However, even if approved, the new type plan would not assist in legalizing the majority of Nairobi's tenements which are shaped by a process of self-regulation, though they do contain elements from early 'type plans' such as inter-leading doors between two rooms (see Figure 8.6 in Chapter 8), even though the demand is overwhelmingly for single rooms. In the next chapter I show how tenement investors' decisions regarding the building design are influenced by the existing market, from which they seek their inspiration and confidence to transgress regulations, but within which they also seek to compete for tenants. The limit of eight stories (though with exceptions) is regulated by what is considered acceptable to the rooming tenant.

The unplanned and unregulated development of Huruma

Of our two tenement case study areas, only Umoja Inner Core has its origin in urban planning. Huruma, the older of the two, was transformed 'from squatter village to multi-story tenement district' (Huchzermeyer 2007, 720), in a seemingly unplanned way and primarily to serve speculative interests. The extent of densification, and the electoral power this gave to the constituency, could leverage high-level political patronage. This obstructed both enforcement of planning regulations and the introduction of a new building code which seemingly did not go far enough in legalizing speculative tenement development in this constituency at the time. Umoja Inner Core provides an interesting contrast, as its planning consultants based the officially adopted proposal on a reflection of the unauthorized development trends in adjacent areas, though what actually materialized goes well beyond what the forward-looking planners envisaged.

The name 'Huruma' means 'Mercy'. It appears that the area assumed this name only in 1975, when authorities relocated households from former Kaburini (meaning 'Cemetery', a settlement on the north-eastern bank of the Nairobi River, directly east of the city centre). They had housed these households for five years on a site called 'Mji Wa Huruma' ('Home of Mercy') to the north of central Nairobi and from there had moved them to an NGO-inspired 'site-and-phased-in-service scheme' on state-owned land in south-eastern Mathare Valley (Hirst 1994, 147). This must have been to the east of our sample area (Figure 7.7), which the current topographic map refers to as 'Ngei II' (and Huruma).[9] In 1964, Ngei II was the former village that overlapped with our sample area in Huruma (Etherton 1971, 15).

In the late 1960s, small-scale landlords were already operating in these 'squatter' villages, with '[w]ell over half the adult population' recorded as tenants (*ibid.*, 36). The shift to speculation with large-scale landlordism began in 1969, when cooperative companies started buying private land in Mathare Valley. Company housing was initially developed between the various villages, then gradually displaced them (*ibid.*). With the annual rental income from each structure adding up to its construction cost, thus a return on investment above 50 per cent, company housing was 'one of the most attractive investments in Nairobi' (*ibid.*, 50). Company share prices had risen, even though the companies frequently increased the number of shares. Land values also rose in this period (Yahya 1990). However, the early 'village' occupants were sidelined: 'These companies were originally planned on a co-operative basis and attempted to include each head-of-household in the squatter village as a shareholder... [But] the original objectives were soon swept aside in a surge of speculative tenement building' (Etherton 1971, 10). Therefore, '[c]lass struggle between landlord and non-company squatter, i.e. the poorest of the Mathare poor... was a recurrent theme in Mathare politics' (Chege 1981, 79).

With 7 628 'room-units' built by housing companies in Mathare Valley, the population of this area doubled in the early 1970s (Etherton 1971), and again by 1979 (Chege 1981, 78). Whereas Mathare Valley had been a predominantly Kikuyu area, the new tenants were 'Luo, Luhya and Kamba... tending to congregate on ethnic lines in specific Mathare localities' (*ibid.*, 79).[10] By 2005, and as manifested in the post-election ethnic violence in early 2008, our sample area was partly Luo to the north and dominated by Kikuyu tenants to the south, towards Juja Road.

Researchers had already noted overcrowding and a lack of 'social amenities and public utilities' in the early 1970s (Etherton 1971, 12). Authorities planned a trunk sewer along the river at the time (*ibid.*). Given the housing demand and proximity to the city centre, Etherton (*ibid.*, 9) predicted a 'prosperous future' for Mathare Valley. Chege (1981) shows how this realization of prosperity for the predominantly Kikuyu landlords over the next decade depended on their navigation of politics. This was necessary in order to prevent attempts at enforcing regulations through demolition of the unauthorized rental development. The political patron of 'company and political leaders' in Mathare Valley and neighboring Kariobangi, Dr Munyua Waiyaki,

> intervened effectively to quash new building regulations which would have hurt property development in Kariobangi housing co-operatives... and stood consistently against demolition of Mathare Valley and against real estate development by international capital [from the World Bank or bilateral donors] via the City Council. His political fate therefore very closely identified with the fate of the Mathare community. (Chege 1981, 78–79).[11]

According to Etherton's (1971, 44–45, 47) study, in 1971 our sample area consisted of two parcels of undeveloped land, one portion housing some of the 'squatter' structures of the Ngei II 'village'. The company with the biggest land holding in Mathare Valley had recently purchased this portion. The other portion was of unidentified ownership at the time – neither state-owned, City Council-owned nor privately owned (*ibid*, 47). For the former portion, the land owning company had signed a purchase agreement. In total, it owned 9.92 hectares in Mathare Valley, with a further 4.86 hectares subsequently being purchased (seemingly the portion in our sample area). On its other land portions, the company had constructed 228 structures, with an average of 8 rooms each, resulting in a density of 597 units per hectare in its built-up areas, the highest density in Mathare Valley at the time (*ibid*.). An average of 4.4 people lived in each room. Rooms were constructed initially of timber and later of concrete blocks. The company had 500 members, 375 of whom lived in Mathare Valley. It offered the worst sanitation conditions among land buying company developments in the valley, with only two pit latrines and three water points for its total tenant clientele of 8 026 people. By 1971, the company had submitted plans for its portion in our sample area (Etherton 1971).

Beyond Etherton's (1971) detailed study on Mathare Valley, I found no documentation on the subsequent physical development in our sample area. The current layout as per 2000 aerial photography and our own mapping indicate a gridiron development pattern with long blocks that served to maximize the amount of developable land, similar to those Etherton shows for early company housing in 1971. As already mentioned, officials in the HDD in Dandora, and not a planning consultant, had prepared the subdivision plan for 'Huruma Ngei' (Anonymous A, interview, October 25, 2005). Again displaying lack of coordination, base plans used by the Nairobi Water and Sewerage Company in 2005 indicated the portion, which in 1971 was purchased by the land buying company, as undeveloped (no street and plot layout), yet the tenements with up to eight stories in this area are connected to the company's water reticulation system.

Chege's (1981) account of electoral politics in Mathare and Dagoretti shows that Mathare Valleys' development trajectory was determined politically and not by official programs. A 'genuine faction of indigenous capital accumulators' had its patron in the KANU loyalist Dr Waiyaki who was close to President Kenyatta, yet whose power was not uncontested (*ibid*., 78). In the run-up to the 1979 election in the Mathare constituency (subsequent to Kenyatta's death), Waiyaki's opponent Andrew Ngumba (who was the mayor at the time, having replaced Kenyatta's daughter in this position in 1977) threatened 'replacement of company and individual housing with middle class, City Council housing estates' (*ibid*., 81). However, 'threats of demolition unified the landlords and the Mathare crowd as was never the case before'. In response, Ngumba proceeded to 'buy' the constituency. The 'vast poor, floating population' welcomed the unprecedented flow of money (*ibid*.).

In 1978 there was talk in City Hall of demolishing part of Mathare Valley and putting up a £290 million World Bank 'low income housing' project. Slum demolition had begun on the eve of the election and was only stopped by Presidential intervention at the request of Waiyaki. (*ibid.*, 82)

According to a Huruma landlord (Landlord 1, interview, November 1, 2005), whose two tenement properties are immediately to the east of our sample area, the authorities allocated unserviced plots in this area in the late 1970s, and at the time 'it was just grass'. In his recollection this was a scheme of the Nairobi City Council on state-owned land, with the purchase of the plots through City Council loans. The original allottees received allocation letters. Title deeds were to follow once the loans were fully repaid. Some of the allottees could not afford to construct housing while servicing their loans and therefore sold the plots, which is how his father had acquired the two properties. Although Landlord 1 had paid off the seller's loans in 2003, at the time of the interview in 2005 he still held only allocation letters.

Our interviews with tenants and landlords of buildings in and near our sample study area gave some indication of the more recent history. One tenant, who grew up in a tenant household renting two rooms in Huruma in the late 1970s and early 1980s, does not recall any multi-story buildings in his childhood, other than the Huruma council housing scheme (Tenant 1, interview, October 25, 2005). Its modern structures float in wasteful open space (Figure 7.13), a typology that is very different from that of the private rental tenements. Apart from the direct threat the council housing scheme had posed to private tenement development in Huruma, the wasteful typology is unlikely to have inspired Huruma landlords to develop multi-story housing.

Figure 7.13: Huruma's multi-story council housing
Source: Author's photograph (2005)

Instead, as in the case of the Girhurai landlords who took 'their cue' from 'unauthorised housing' in neighboring Zimmerman (Gatabaki-Kamau and Karirah-Gitau 2004, 171), according to one Huruma landlord the inspiration to build high-rise tenements in Huruma came from what was visible across Gitathuru River, the Mathare North site-and-service scheme:

In the early 1980s, Huruma started going multi-story. It started with two to three floors. Then it standardized to five floors by 1985. That was when Mathare North just popped up. In Huruma people were building low-rise [three to five stories], but people bought plots in Mathare North and went high-rise [up to eight stories]. The owners in Huruma saw this and then decided to also go high-rise. (Landlord 1, interview, November 1, 2005)

The City Council developed the 1 497 plots of the Mathare North site-and-service scheme between 1980 and 1982, and housing construction started in 1985 (Shihembetsa 1991). Plot sizes measured 7 m × 21 m or 12 m × 19 m (Anonymous A, interview, October 27, 2005). The municipality encouraged 'low-rise' multi-story

development by issuing municipal type plans for single- up to four-story buildings, with five to eight rooms. As the original allottees lacked the resources to construct, others purchased the plots from them (Shihembetsa 1991) and developed them without adherence to the height restrictions. Their excesses were visible from Huruma, and were indeed inspiring (see Figure 7.14).

Figure 7.14: Mathare North as seen from Huruma

Source: Author's photograph (2005)

In the next chapter I detail the ongoing densification of the Huruma sample area and provide our measured drawings of three rooming tenements representative of the area (two have eight stories and one has six stories; none have lifts). Already in 1991, Shihembetsa (1991, 232) mentions densities in Mathare Valley of 1 600 to 2 600 people per hectare. Our calculation for the sample area in Huruma in 2005 was well beyond 5 000 people per hectare. By 2008, landlords had further densified the area. As can be expected, many aspects of the Huruma tenements violate building regulations. Huruma's zoning appears to fall under Residential Zone Seven of Mathare, which is designated as a 'special density area' (Anonymous D, interview, October 5, 2005) permitting a 50 per cent plot coverage and a plot ratio of one. Most buildings in the sample area display a plot coverage of 100 per cent. Commercial tenants occupy the ground floors, making for a vibrant and convenient urban environment, though unauthorized in the purely residential 'special density' zone.

The planned but unregulated development of Umoja Inner Core

A far more recent residential area than Huruma, Umoja Inner Core is the third and last of three sections of the 298 hectare Umoja Estate initiated in 1971 (Shihembetsa 1991, 233). The Development Plan for Umoja was completed by the Nairobi City Council in 1974. Umoja Estate is to the east of Outer Ring Road (outside the urban boundary of the 1948 Master Plan) in a previously undeveloped or green-field area. The 1973 Growth Strategy designates this area schematically as 'housing'. The 1974 Development Plan for Umoja shows Umoja I bordering onto Outer Ring Road, Umoja II furthest east and five sectors of Umoja Inner Core in the centre. A large wedge labeled 'public park' on the 1974 Development Plan has long since been converted into the residential Tena Estate. The 1974 plan proposed one-, two- and three-bedroom 'extendable semi-detached new houses' in Umoja I and II (Wanjohi Consulting Engineers et al. 1983, 2/1). Sectors One to Three of Umoja Inner Core (64 hectares) were envisaged as 'serviced plots', and Sectors Four and Five (23 hectares) as 'maisonettes and flats' (*ibid.*). As already mentioned, Umoja as a whole forms a superblock, surrounded by high-order roads and with only limited access into and between the various residential cells.

Development for Umoja I began as early as 1975. In the early 1980s, a USAID/Nairobi City Council-commissioned team of Kenyan consulting firms led by Wanjohi Consulting Engineers planned the development of Umoja II. This included an evaluation of the first phase of development at Umoja I. In their report, Wanjohi Consulting Engineers et al. (1983) noted that the 1974 Development Plan had under-catered for community facilities for the officially anticipated population of 60 000–70 000 people. At the average household size for Umoja of 4.4 people (as per the *1999 Population and Housing Census* (Central Bureau of Statistics 2001)), the anticipated gross density (including public facilities) for Umoja I had been 53 dwelling units and the net density (including only access roads) 76 dwelling units per hectare. This was substantially higher than the recommended densities for neighborhood units in the 1948 Master Plan.

However, most of Umoja developed at higher capacities than planned, with multi-story tenements replacing the original extendable units or inserted into their front- and backyards (see Figure 7.9). Already in 1991, Shihembetsa (1991, 234) noted that '[h]ighrise flats are being put up by the owners, against the zoning regulations'. In 2001, Ochieng (2001, 2) described Umoja I as a 'sprawling high density' scheme. In an attempt to prevent the densification from replicating itself in Umoja II, its planners (led by Wanjohi Consulting Engineers) developed a 'condominium' concept, with six one-room units extendable to a second ground floor room, arranged around a common courtyard with shared kitchen and ablution facilities (Figure 7.15). The municipality allocated sectional titles to those purchasing the units. However, even here, a change of hands has led to individual units extending vertically as narrow tenements (Figure 7.16). An owner-occupier of a two-roomed single-story unit whom we interviewed in 2005 justified her absentee neighbor's transgression, saying 'everyone needs money'. Arguing for the necessity of multi-story living by referring to the prevalence of crime, she added that if she were to extend vertically, she would move upstairs herself, as 'thieves climb over the wall' (Umoja II owner, interview, October 26, 2005).

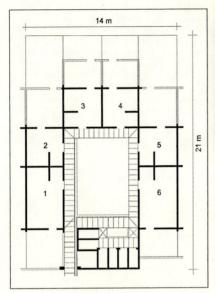

Figure 7.15 *(left)*: Layout of the condominium units designed for Umoja II
Source: Based on De Troyer (1991, 106)

Figure 7.16 *(above)*: Multi-story tenement development in defiance of the condominium concept in Umoja II
Source: Author's photograph (2008)

In the development of the third and final phase of Umoja, Inner Core, there appears to have been little concern with targeting the low income, whether in design or in plot allocation. In Sectors Two and Three, the location of our sample area (see Figure 7.8), there is no evidence of owner-occupation. All plots appear to be owned and developed by tenement investors. As flats were envisaged for Sectors Four and Five of Umoja Inner Core, the Nairobi City Council once again designed and made available type plans. These were for three-story blocks with 50 per cent plot coverage. An official of the HDD in Dandora explained that some of these official type plans were for three-bedroom units (Anonymous A, interview, October 25, 2005), therefore not intended for lower income tenants. An urban planner in Forward Planning at Nairobi City Council explained that many investors choose not to use the type plans, so as to accommodate more units. The Council approves their plans, provided they conform to the 50 per cent plot coverage and the applicable floor ratio (Anonymous G, interview, October 31, 2005). Though not originally intended for flats, Sectors One, Two and Three of Umoja Inner Core have all developed in the same fashion.

In Umoja Inner Core, many plots are still undeveloped, contributing to a relatively low overall density for Umoja Estate. In 1999 this stood at only 48 people per hectare (Central Bureau of Statistics 2001). However, as I show in the following chapter, our calculations of the sample area in Umoja Inner Core in 2005 resulted in a density of over 2 000 people per hectare, with further densification by 2008.

The official plans for Umoja Inner Core set aside specific pockets for commercial development. The official intention is a clear separation between commercial and residential land use (Anonymous G, interview, October 31, 2005). However, as with Huruma's tenements and in accordance with a general trend that municipal officials were aware of, most ground floors in our sample area have commercial tenants or residential tenants operating a 'tuck shop' from their street-facing room (Figure 7.17).

Figure 7.17: Commercial use of tenement ground floors in Umoja Inner Core

Source: Author's photograph (2008)

The two landlords we interviewed owning buildings in Umoja Inner Core (Landlords 3 and 4; see Table 8.2 in Chapter 8) gave further insights into the more recent development in the area. Landlord 3 owns two buildings in Sector One, the first constructed in 2000, the second a year later. By 2000, 'people had already started building in Umoja Inner Core' (Landlord 3, interview, November 3, 2005). He bought both his plots through the Nairobi City Council. As he 'happened to know someone in the City Council', he asked to be informed if this official 'knew someone who wanted to sell in Umoja Inner Core' (*ibid.*). The landlord held an allocation letter and had not received any information as to when title deeds would be processed. He constructed the earlier building with four stories, two two-bedroom and three one-bedroom units on each floor above ground level, and bedsitter units as well as a hairdressing salon and a small shop on the ground floor. He constructed his later building with only two stories, but his intention was to go up to six stories. As I have shown above, officials were well aware of such intentions. The landlord justified his high-rise vision with reference to existing seven-story buildings in Umoja Inner Core (Figure 7.18).

Figure 7.18: Seven-story middle class tenement in Umoja Inner Core

Source: Author's photograph (2008)

Landlord 4 (interview, October 18, 2005) was constructing his first tenement, which happened to be in our sample area in Umoja Inner Core. He had approval from Council for his five-story building. Like Landlord 3's buildings, his tenement was to have two two-bedroom and two one-bedroom units on each floor. He envisaged the ground floor as bedsitter units that could be converted into shops. By the time of my return visit in 2008, this attractive-looking tenement, in accordance with the tolerated trend in the area, included one floor more than had been approved and had commercial tenants on the ground floor.

The accommodation of speculative interests: transgression rather than reform

Nairobi's city-wide plans have had little influence on built environment decisions. Like the regulations, they were designed for a reality that is distant from what has unfolded in the city's residential areas over the last five decades. Transgressions occur at many levels. Proposed regulatory reform has taken small steps, but remains removed from the reality of multi-story and mixed use tenements, even in middle class areas. It is interesting that Nairobi City Council's in-house planners designed the street and plot layouts for Huruma and for Umoja Inner Core with little resemblance to the modernist ideas that planning consultants incorporated into housing estates they were tasked with laying out. In both its layout designs and its leniency towards building approval, the Nairobi City Council stands out as a key agent in the tenement development in these two areas. Today, individual officials are in the difficult position of operating in a dual system. Formal regulations make little sense in the face of an entrepreneurial process that is leading to large-scale production of much needed housing coupled with economic opportunities. Tenement development, despite its many transgressions, makes sense to many officials, even though those with formal town planning training were presumably schooled in the modernist spatial and regulatory paradigm.

The lack of development regulation in Nairobi has similarities to 19th century New York, where building inspection processes were deeply fraught. Up until the passing of the new Tenement House Law in 1879, tenements in New York were built, for instance, with rooms that had no windows. Officials tasked with building inspection were employed through political patronage, and landlords in turn had strong allies in politicians (Day 1999, 58). Although I am unable to provide direct evidence in Nairobi of the alliances between landlords and their patron politicians, and likewise between officials and politicians, the same constellation as documented for New York does seem to exist. This is particularly likely where investor transgression of plan and regulation, as well as the exchange of bribes, have been met with a tolerance that has endured despite the visible post-Moi anti-corruption initiative. In relation to Mathare Valley, I have mentioned political obstruction of regulatory reform and development programs that would have been harmful to tenement investment. In this context, a certain level of self-regulation has established itself, and is demonstrated to some extent through the investor decision-making onto which I provide a window in the following chapter.

In Berlin, tenements were a dominant and widely accepted form of housing already by 1862, when the relevant authorities finalized the city's plan – which to an extent accommodated speculative interests. An inadequate legal framework allowed for some departure from the plan to better serve these interests. However, the authorities enforced the key health and safety requirements (initially minimalist) in the Building Ordinance. Unlike the situation in Nairobi, in Berlin the regulations effectively contributed to shaping the tenement typology, though did little to improve the existing stock. Once substantially revised, they terminated tenement construction.

Berlin's tenement development unleashed a rigorous though biased reform debate, which ushered in the principles of modern town planning. These in turn informed Nairobi's colonial and post-colonial city plans. From its inception, and paralleled across European and North American cities, the modern town planning movement met with criticisms from urban researchers and theorists. However, these have had little impact on mainstream town planning and traffic engineering practice. The wholesale dismissal of Nairobi's Master Plan and Growth Strategy premises by every actor in the city for the past 60 years represents a far more powerful and effective criticism of modern urban planning (in this context) than that of the critical urbanists.[12] These critics from the north were and are seemingly unaware of Nairobi's multi-story tenement market (or of similar contemporary tenement investments elsewhere). In some cases, their writing predated its emergence. In their celebration of complex and disordered urban qualities *lost* through modern planning, these critical theorists have referred only to the western (tenement) past. In a post-peak oil era and one of global economic uncertainty, Nairobi's dense, unplanned urban form, despite its many inadequacies, uneasily offers qualities for a robust urban future. It is to these qualities, their inherent challenges and the silence about them in the policy discourse that I turn in the next chapter.

Endnotes

1   An exception to the unplanned redevelopment of older 'slums' is Kibera. Unlike the 'slums' in Mathare Valley, it is surrounded by planned middle class estates rather than unauthorized tenement development. In Kibera, the single-story 'slum' has endured to date, despite continued government and donor-funded attempts at planned redevelopment through multi-story apartments.

2   The concept was also embraced in Forshaw and Abercrombie's 1943 County of London Plan (Houghton-Evans 1978, 92, 94) and 1944 'Greater London Plan', to which the interdisciplinary South African planning team mentioned in Chapter 6 referred (White, Silberman and Anderson 1948, 46).

3   By 2009, an attractive curving footpath had been paved along with the much delayed resurfacing and widening of Mombasa Road, the main connector to the airport. However, few pedestrians use this route, unlike the routes providing access to dense tenement areas, such as the congested Outer Ring or Juja Roads.

4   Most notorious for adherence to modern physical planning are South Africa's cities (UN-HABITAT 2009, 55), where peri-urban sprawl continues through class-segregated home ownership schemes with freestanding units, assuming future car ownership by the cities' poorest residents despite deepening inequality.

5   This interview was conducted half a year before the official launch of *Nairobi Metro 2030: A World Class African Metropolis* (Ministry of Nairobi Metropolitan Development 2008) in December 2008. The document ignores the fragmented nature of planning. It simply states that the new Ministry of Nairobi Metropolitan Development 'is strictly assigned the role of policy formulation, planning and regulation' (*ibid.*, 105), without explaining how this will relate to local authority functions.

6   A floor ratio of one means the floor space of the building (which may be distributed across several stories, equals the plot size. A building line of zero allows a building to extend up to the street-facing plot boundary.

7   Berlin's historic five-story tenements, with much higher floor-to-ceiling intervals than in Nairobi and today often with added loft apartments in the roof, provide middle class accommodation still largely without lifts.

8   In October 2009, Aron (2009a) mentions a new report by a 'Building Review Harmonisation Committee', proposing 'the formation of [yet another] agency that will strip the corruption-riddled, under-staffed and inefficient local authorities of having the final word in approving and supervising any building construction activities'. The proposed 'Planning and Building Authority' is to be based in the Ministry of Housing (*ibid.*). Mentioned examples of 'faulty buildings' that would be addressed by the agency and 'new legislation', however, are all commercial, with no mention of the non-compliant tenement stock (*ibid.*).

9   Ngei II was presumably named after Paul Ngei, '[i]mprisoned with Kenyatta during the emergency' and the first minister to lead the newly created Ministry of Housing in 1966 (Stren 1972, 85).

10 Chege (1981) does not explain this ethnic spatial grouping. Bujra (1973, 44), though referring to social rather than spatial grouping, explains for early 1970s Pumwani that 'isolation... from their homeland, together with their politico-economic interests... tended to reinforce [in this case the Bajunis'] cohesiveness as a group', whereas the Kikuyus' proximity to their homeland immersed them in 'wider political trends' that in turn accentuated Kikuyu 'ethnic awareness'.

11 Munyua Waiyaki, a medical doctor, was foreign minister for the period 1974–1979 and member of parliament for 1963–1983 for the Mathare Valley constituency (then 'Nairobi North East). He then returned to his medical profession and later engaged in real estate dealing and livestock farming (Mugonyi and Kimani, 2007).

12 I have reviewed the arguments of David Harvey and Henri Lefebvre in Chapters 1 and 2, and those of Jane Jacobs in Chapter 5. In Chapter 9 I expand on this theme with reference to other critical urbanists such as Doreen Massey, Richard Sennett and Ash Amin.

Chapter 8

Quality, decisions and discourse: the uncontested legitimacy of tenements in Nairobi

Whether in official analyses for planning and policy or in descriptive depictions of the city, it goes largely unacknowledged that residential densities in Nairobi are extreme, yet have still to reach their peak. My in-depth interviews with tenants opened a window on the implications of increasing congestion, and on ways in which households are managing the adversities they experience in this environment. Challenges are more pronounced in crowded lower income Huruma than in Umoja Inner Core. Congestion interacts with factors such as strained infrastructure, crime, ethnic solidarity, community and street life. Undoubtedly there is a risk inherent in the choice of well located tenement living. But there are also tangible benefits that accompany this choice.

Similarly, in their decision-making tenement investors weigh off expected gains against possible insecurities. Our in-depth interviews with landlords, rental agents and an auctioneer cast light on the trends and individual choices that bring about high unit densities and particular typologies, as well as socio-spatial distinction or segregation. In Berlin, these characteristics of the tenement market shifted somewhat throughout the six or seven decades of tenement construction, with density and segregation increasing towards the end of the 19th century. They were central to an intensifying and ultimately destructive discourse or discussion on tenements. In Nairobi, there are structural limitations to a discourse on housing. It has largely skirted the topic of multi-story tenements, yet displays parallels with the strands of thought and action that I identified in relation to Berlin's tenements in the late 19th and early 20th century, notably the mostly unsuccessful philanthropic model housing and the suburban homeownership orientation of the bourgeois housing reform agenda.

Density and building typology

Available data on residential densities in Nairobi are calculated and presented by the Central Bureau of Statistics at a low resolution, therefore not capturing the extreme residential population densities that exist at localized level. Nevertheless, for the 70 hectare Huruma (including schools and spatially wasteful public housing) the *1999 Population and Housing Census* (Central Bureau of Statistics 2001) shows the highest residential density in Nairobi, namely 862 people per hectare. For the overall area of Umoja (460 hectares) it shows a density of 137 people per hectare. An official at the Central Bureau of Statistics explained that detailed housing statistics are collected through the municipality's issuing of occupational certificates (Mwando interview, November 2, 2005). However, a large proportion of tenements are unauthorized and not captured in that way. His colleague added that the consumption of cement is used as an indicator of the rate and volume at which 'modern' residential construction occurs (Mushiri interview, November 2, 2005), but this could not be spatialized.[1]

Our own mapping and calculation for a four hectare sample area in Huruma in 2005 (Figure 7.8 in Chapter 7 and Figure 8.1) reveal an average of 1 638 rooms or dwelling units per hectare (including road space). The photographs in Figure 8.2 give an indication of how this dwelling density is physically manifested. Each room is occupied by one household or shared by several adults. Applying the Central Bureau of Statistics (2001) average household size for Huruma of 3.2 people, this results in a density of 5 242 people per hectare, close to four times the density of Berlin's tenements at their peak around 1900. Figure 8.1 provides a breakdown of how this density is distributed across the sample area: 14.1 per cent of buildings had reached 8 stories (7 floors above ground), 25.4 per cent 7 stories and 13.6 per cent 6 stories; a significant potential for densification still remained, with 7.9 per cent of plots still vacant, 15.8 per cent only built with a ground floor or single story, and 22.1 per cent built to a height of 2–5 stories (the remaining 1.1 per cent had foundations only); 16.6 per cent appeared to be under construction (foundations or additional floors). A tenant in Ngima House, a tenement I describe below, observed that 'buildings grow every now and then. Behind us are two new buildings, in front of us are two new buildings. All came up in the last four years' (Tenant 3 interview, October 25, 2005). Another tenant observed 'they are building each and every day' (Tenant 4 interview, October 31, 2005).

On our return to the sample area in 2008, most tenements we had recorded as being under construction had not progressed. However, landlords had constructed a new six-story tenement on one of the vacant plots, started constructing two further tenements on previously vacant plots, expanded two formerly single-story tenements to five and eight stories (Figure 8.3), and added one floor to a two-story tenement. We estimated that landlords had added 162 additional rooms in the sample area since 2005. At the assumed occupancy rate of 3.2 people per room this made for 518 additional people, raising the estimated population per hectare to 5 371 (further densification had occurred by June 2009). As I explain below, the qualitative interviewing in 2005 had already suggested occupancy rates of more than 3.2 per room in many tenements, and in 2008 we were told that occupancy rates had increased across the area due to the ethnic displacements and refuge-seeking resulting from the post-election violence earlier that year.

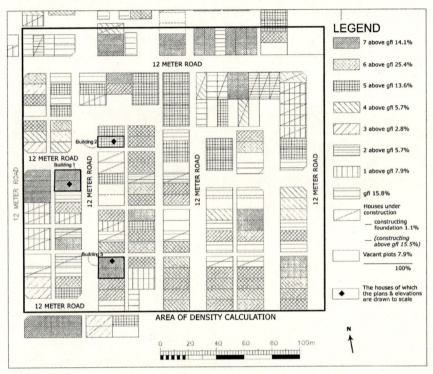

Figure 8.1: Density diagram of a sample area in Huruma

Source: Drawn by FNDA Architecture (K) Ltd, from own measurements (2005)

Figure 8.2: The extreme unit density in the sample area of Huruma, as viewed from the eighth story of various tenements

Source: Author's photographs (2005)

Figure 8.3: Two narrow tenements newly inserted into the already dense fabric of the sample area in Huruma

Source: Author's photographs (2008)

The building typology through which landlords achieve this density is, in its typical form, a lining up of rooms on either side of a central corridor. Stacked horizontally, this results in several rooms only deriving light and ventilation from the internal corridor (Figure 8.4). One room per floor is sacrificed for an internal stairway. One shared toilet and water source is provided on each floor and shared by at least nine households. Figure 8.5 presents our measurement of this prototype on a 7.5 m × 17 m plot, with 100 per cent plot coverage and six stories, therefore a floor ratio of six. We also measured two larger tenements in the sample area, seemingly occupying double plots (approximately 12 m × 19 m and 16 m × 22 m) (Figures 8.6 and 8.7).

Figure 8.4: Top floor of a five-story tenement in the sample area in Huruma, rooms deriving light only from the internal corridor

Source: Author's photograph (2008)

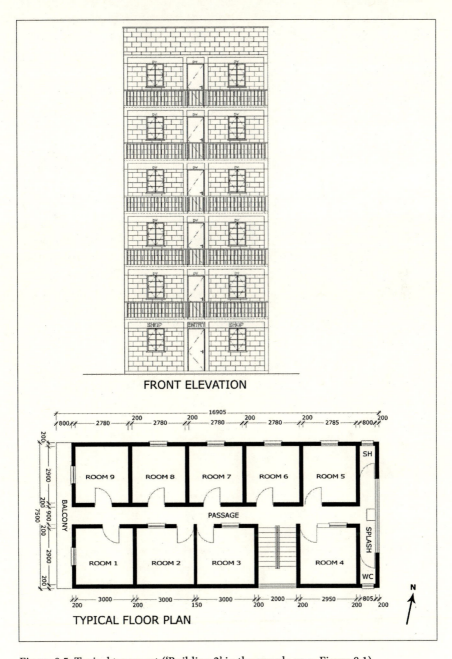

FRONT ELEVATION

TYPICAL FLOOR PLAN

Figure 8.5: Typical tenement ('Building 2' in the sample area, Figure 8.1)

Source: Drawn by FNDA Architecture (K) Ltd, Nairobi, from own measurements (2005)

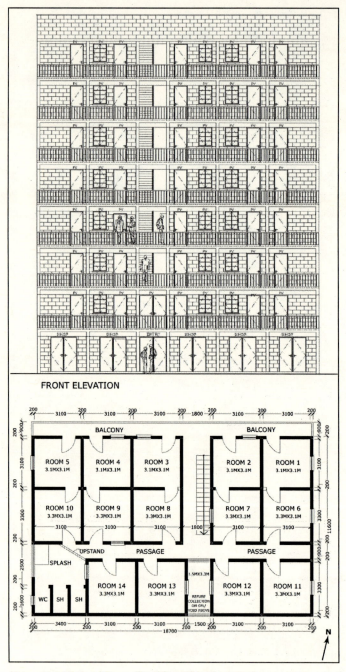

Figure 8.6: Ngima House ('Building 1' in the sample area, Figure 8.1)

Source: Drawn by FNDA Architecture (K) Ltd, Nairobi, from own measurements (2005)

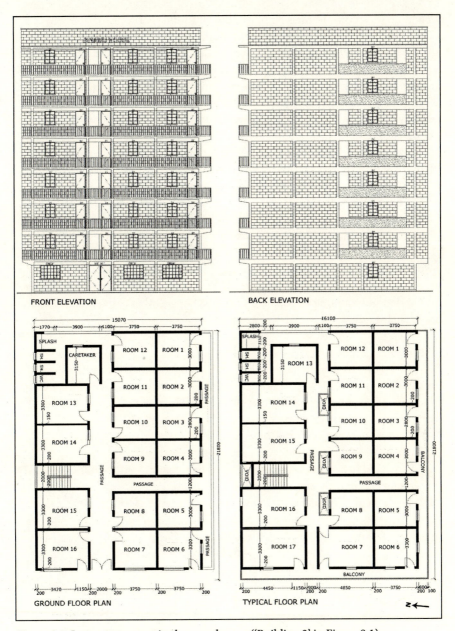

Figure 8.7: Largest tenement in the sample area ('Building 3' in Figure 8.1)

Source: Drawn by FNDA Architecture (K) Ltd, from own measurements (2005)

In addition to rooms leading off both sides of an internal corridor, these have an outside balcony that provides access to the additional row of rooms. This amounts to 14 and 17 rooms per floor respectively in these two tenements sharing toilet and wash space. Variations in this typology are in the orientation of the building to the street, the room size, and the location and dimensions of the staircase and air wells or voids. Ngima House (named after the agency managing the building), the tenement drawn in Figure 8.6, has interconnecting doors between two rooms, thus allowing for double room occupation. As mentioned, this was a feature in Code 95 (never adopted for Nairobi) for single-story rooming. With a total of eight stories, Ngima House displayed no other attempts to adhere to proposed or applicable building regulations, and most of the rooms were let individually.

A less common building type in Huruma is a courtyard house with an internal balcony providing access to a single square of rooms on each floor (Figure 8.17). Though predominantly a rooming district, the sample area also contained one (atypical) tenement, Juja Road House, with self-contained flats. In my discussion below on how tenants cope with Huruma's high density, I return to these various tenement types. An important feature of the tenement typologies is the possible conversion of ground floor rooms into small shops. Only the internalized courtyard typology does not lend itself to street-facing commercial use. Below I list and comment on the intensity of 'mixed mode' commercial activity that has taken root in Huruma.

Across the board, the tenement typology presents a public face towards the street, often an ornamented façade. The visible concrete frame which carries the stone walls is painted and sometimes patterned (Figure 8.8). These aesthetics and their meaning call for an entire research project of their own. Between 2005 and 2008, landlords had painted several tenements in our sample area afresh, in a bid to appease their tenants lured by the completion of new tenements in the area or 'to hike the rents' (Tenant 1 interview, June 15, 2009). However, the street-oriented tenement typology also marked the neighborhood in a less attractive way, through massive windowless side walls along plot boundaries. As illustrated by Heinrich Zille's 19th century cartoons, this was the case in Berlin wherever the tenement ensemble was incomplete. In Huruma, two factors intensify this feature. There is a greater variation in building height, but also seeming confusion over subdivision, with little clarity as to whether current open space is a vacant plot or is publicly owned and designated for public

Figure 8.8: Ornamentation on visible façades of rooming tenements in Huruma

Source: Author's photograph (2005)

use. If publicly owned, there is no certainty as to whether an official or politician will dispose of it corruptly for tenement construction in the future. A number of windowless walls faced directly onto publicly used space (Figure 8.9). If permitted to reach the self-regulated building height limit of eight stories across the board, fewer of these walls would be visible. However, the density in our sample area would increase by a further 73 per cent to 2 846 rooms per hectare or (assuming a constant rate of occupancy of 3.2 people per room) 9 107 people per hectare.

Within the rooming tenements there is a visible variation in quality across the units, relating to height, natural light, ventilation, security and possibilities for drying of laundry. Given degrees of income-mixing in Berlin's tenements, I was interested in whether the variation in rooms within Huruma's tenement market allowed varying affordability groups to live together. However, we were told that rents were largely uniform, because the advantages and disadvantages of rooms across one tenement were cancelled out. For the added security of higher floors, tenants had to climb more stairs, whereas the darker, unventilated rooms in the interior of the building had the advantage of being cooler on hot summer days. Only the commercial ground floor rents were higher.

Figure 8.9: Exposed windowless side walls due to varying building height or facing directly onto publicly used space

Source: Author's photographs (2005)

In Umoja Inner Core, our 4.8 hectare sample area (Figure 7.8 (Chapter 7) and Figure 8.10) consists of tenements with self-contained apartments catering for the middle class. Individual buildings combine bedsitter up to two-bedroom units, often with attractive balconies or other distinguishable features. Typologies vary, and we only measured the internal layout of one building (Figure 8.11). Across the range of typologies, we estimated an average of four units per floor. Our 2005 mapping of building heights in the sample area revealed an overall density of around 493 units per hectare. Figure 8.12 indicates how this unit density manifests itself. Applying the Central Bureau of Statistics (2001) average household size of 4.4 for Umoja, the sample area had a density of 2 169 people per hectare in 2005, also above the highest density recorded for Berlin. One building in the sample area reached 7 stories, 2 per cent reached 6 stories, 11.6 per cent reached 5 stories and 17 per cent reached 4 stories. Forty-four per cent of plots were still vacant and 22 per cent had 1–3 floors.

The Umoja Inner Core sample area displayed many opportunities for densification. In 2005, 16.6 per cent of properties were under construction. By 2008, owners had constructed up to four stories on nine previously undeveloped plots, had added one floor to three existing buildings, and three properties which in 2005 only displayed foundations had progressed, one reaching six stories. Landlord investors had increased the rental stock by a total of 18 tenement floors, adding an estimated 116 units or 510 people. They had increased the estimated density to 2 275 people per hectare. Eight previously undeveloped plots had foundations by 2008. The construction of foundations on vacant plots seems to be a means to stake a claim against those out to grab or reallocate properties, multiple plot allocation or sale being a frequent source of land conflict in Nairobi's site-and-service-turned-tenement areas (Obala forthcoming).

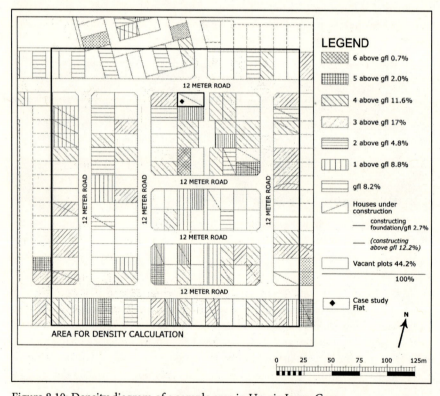

Figure 8.10: Density diagram of a sample area in Umoja Inner Core

Source: Drawn by FNDA Architecture (K) Ltd, from own measurements (2005)

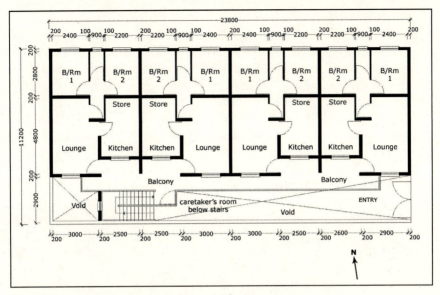

Figure 8.11: Umoja Inner Core tenement with six stories

Source: Drawn by FNDA Architecture (K) Ltd, from own measurements (2005)

Unlike Huruma, most owners of four- to six-story buildings (and one exception with seven stories) in Umoja Inner Core had completed their tenements with pitched roofs (see Figure 8.12). This signaled that they did not have intentions of adding additional floors. Further densification in the sample area will primarily be through construction on vacant sites and sites currently staked out with foundations only. If owners develop these remaining 47 plots to 4 stories, the density in the sample area will increase to 2 900 people per hectare.

Figure 8.12: The high unit density in the Umoja Inner Core sample area

Source: Author's photographs (2005)

What it means to live with density

In her seminal book *The Death and Life of Great American Cities*, Jane Jacobs (1961) cautioned of an alarmist approach to high densities of residential units. She argued that modern urban planners made the mistake of equating a high unit density with the negative attribute of overcrowding (or high occupation of individual units). 'Nothing gained by overcrowding!' was, for instance, the slogan that accompanied garden city planner Raymond Unwin's publicity tract, as pointed out with irony by both Jacobs (1961, 206) and Hall (1990, 66–75). Jacobs and many of her contemporary critics of modern town planning pointed to qualities of urban complexity and diversity that were made possible by 'the dense concentration of people' (Jacobs 1961, 205). What was more important than the number of people was the performance of the urban environment, and for Jacobs (*ibid.*, 209) diversity was an important urban performance criteria. By diversity she referred to the range of uses, including economic activities, that an area generates and supports.

What is needed then is a finer grain of qualitative understanding of life among the high unit densities. The diversity of commercial activities in the two sample areas, which I detail below, is nurtured by their residential density while also providing livelihoods and convenience to the growing population. However, in the perception of the small sample of tenants we interviewed in Huruma, there were other important indicators by which performance was declining with the increasing unit and population density. In the seeming absence of any municipal provisions made for the increasing population, many burdens were being shouldered by tenants' discipline and their pockets.

The equivalent information on living conditions in late 19th century Berlin, which I reviewed in Chapter 5, is not available for Nairobi's tenement areas. I therefore draw on a small window of insight provided by in-depth interviews and observations – primarily on life in Huruma, where the unit densities are more than triple those of Umoja Inner Core. The middle class nature of Umoja Inner Core also meant that in many households both husband and wife were working, leaving only a child minder (commonly referred to as a 'maid') at home during the day. In Huruma, households could not afford a 'maid', with the result that wives tended not to work and instead took care of the household and infants. As Huruma was the home of my research assistant Kevin Osodo, we could also access a group of young men who had grown up together in the area, and were partly self-employed. They shared broader insights about their rapidly changing neighborhood than the female tenants we interviewed, whose lives tended to be restricted to individual tenements.

Infrastructure and services

In Berlin, a gradual improvement in tenement living conditions was experienced in the second half of the 19th century due to technological advancements, including water supply and sewerage systems. For Huruma and Umoja Inner Core, to some extent the reverse is the case. Given that the areas were intended for a much lower level of development or unit density, water supply and sewers are increasingly over-burdened. As already mentioned, service delivery coordination in Nairobi is inadequate and tenement investors are forced to take water storage precautions. From the side of tenants, the poor supply requires discipline and consideration in sharing. It also imposes costs, since most of the problems are resolved informally by private enterprise or collectives. At the same time, the way services are dealt with in a tenement is one consideration that tenants weigh off when seeking the best deal in the tenement market.

In the rooming tenements, landlords or their agents include electricity and water consumption in the rent, as both the water and the electricity companies supply only one meter for the entire building. However, electricity supply varies from one tenement to another. Tenant 1 (his household consisting of husband, wife and two small children) informed us that some tenements were on a single electricity circuit, meaning that a switch tripping due to overconsumption would affect all rooms. However, in his tenement, Ngima House (which has a total of 112 rooms), the landlord had invested in a circuit breaker on each floor. Therefore when the electricity tripped, it affected only one floor and not the entire building. Tenant 1 added that 'when the power trips, we go to the caretaker. Sometimes he asks for a soda [meaning a small bribe] before reconnecting' (Tenant 1 interview, October 25, 2005). Tenant 3 (interview, October 25, 2005), also in Ngima House, explained that 'the voltage is not high enough for ironing. There is a kiosk down in the street, which does ironing using charcoal in an iron box. They charge Kshs 10 [US$0.14] per shirt.' Tenant 1's account was that the voltage was sufficient for only two people to iron simultaneously on one floor, adding that 'in the communal washing area, there is a place to indicate who is busy ironing. They [referring to his wife and other women on the floor] take turns, it works' (interview, October 25, 2005).

Beyond the disciplined sharing of electricity between the tenants on each floor, electricity was sometimes also rationed for the entire building. 'Then there is no power during the day except on weekends and public holidays. It is switched off at 9 am and switched back on at 5 pm' (*ibid.*). This further explained the need for an ironing kiosk in the street. Whether tripped or rationed, the electricity was off on the afternoon of our interviews, displaying how dark the internal corridor leading to the washing/latrine area was during the day. The walls were painted dark so as not to show up the heavy wear. A landlord owning two tenements in Huruma (Landlord 1 interview, November 1, 2005) explained that in his buildings 'the corridors are painted in brown and blue oil paint. I chose brown because of the dirt.'

In some buildings, landlords also rationed water from 9 am to 5 pm. According to Tenant 1, when looking for a room in the tenement market, prospective tenants enquire about the extent of rationing. He also knew of a tenement in the area that had no electricity or water. It was common knowledge that the landlord had failed to pay the bills, therefore the water and electricity companies had cut the supply. The building stood vacant for three years, but in 2005 it had been rented out 'to poorer people at about Kshs 1 000 [US$14.5]/room' (Tenant 1 interview, October 25, 2005). This was almost half the standard room rent in the area, but still double the rent in the unserviced single-story 'slums'. In May 2008 a tenant in the Huruma sample area mentioned that there had been no water in his building for the past three months. In his assessment, Huruma is 'slowly turning into a slum, no one is noticing' (Tenant 5 interview, May 28, 2008).

A landlord who owns two tenements in Huruma expressed his hope that the Nairobi Water and Sewerage Company would 'come up with a better solution' for water metering. Currently, 'one bill is high, the next is low, the next is an estimate, sometimes inflated. This means you can't predict your income. And if the bill is not paid, they cut off the water supply' (Landlord 1 interview, November 1, 2005). In the last three rows of Table 8.2, I compare the income and expenditure breakdown for a rooming tenement in Huruma with that of a self-contained apartment tenement in Umoja Inner Core. This indicates how the water and electricity consumption affects landlord profits. The same landlord explained that water supply was

> a big headache. I installed a huge tank on the roof, originally, with the construction of the building. There is a small tank at the bottom. I use an electric pump to pump the water up. The [municipal] water comes on at 11 pm. By 3 am there is no more water. There is just water for three hours.

In this context, it was in the interest of the landlords and the tenants not to waste water. The very basic communal sanitation facilities to some extent facilitated modest use of water. These shared facilities required discipline and organization on the part of the users. Women on the third floor of Ngima House organized the cleaning of the communal washing area among themselves (Tenant 5 interview, May 28, 2008). A tenant in Ngima House gave her description of the communal facilities:

> The 'bath' is only a room with a drain. It has no light. We have to take a candle with us... There is no shower. We have to take a bucket with us. First we have to boil the water. The latrine has no flush, we pour water with a bucket. It's a hole in the floor... The sewer has often blocked on this floor. It happens if someone puts something in the latrine that can't be flushed. We tenants then find someone to fix it, we have to pay. (Tenant 3 interview, October 25, 2005).

A sewerage problem was evident during our visits in 2005 and 2008, with an open sewer flowing downhill from the tenement area through the single-story 'slum' and into Gitathuru River (Figure 8.13). Tenant 1 explained that 'sewerage blocks periodically and comes out of one of the big manholes, particularly when it rains'. The Huruma landlord confirmed this, adding that water shortages were another cause of sewerage blockages (Landlord 1 interview, November 1, 2005). The Nairobi Water and Sewerage Company does not repair these. Instead, as Tenant 1 (interview, October 29, 2005) explained, 'there is a group of people that has formed a cartel. They do the sewerage unblocking. They advertise in the area.' The work of the sewerage group, like that of refuse collectors, is territorialized. But unlike refuse collection

Figure 8.13: Open sewer flowing out of the Huruma tenement area towards Gitathuru River

Source: Author's photograph (2005)

which is paid for by tenants, it was the landlords that were called upon to finance the unblocking of larger sewage spills. Landlord 1, as shown in Table 8.2, indicated this as a regular expense that affected his rental income – 'they charge about Kshs 300 [US$4.34] per trip'.

Refuse disposal is a growing challenge with the densification of Huruma. Refuse was visibly congesting open spaces within the sample area (Figure 8.13). On the return visit in 2008, the refuse problem seemed more pronounced (Figure 8.14), though I was told that the piles were awaiting removal by municipal trucks.

Figure 8.14: Refuse piled up in open spaces in Huruma

Source: Author's photographs (2008)

205

According to the 2003 Demographic and Health Survey, only 2.9 per cent of Nairobi's households benefit from regular refuse collection by government and a further 2.8 per cent from 'infrequent collection by government'. Paid private collection is used by 51.7 per cent, while 22 per cent dump in the street or on vacant land (Central Bureau of Statistics 2004). Huruma's tenement households fall into the last two categories. Some households resort to dumping, as payment to private refuse collection groups is voluntary. A refuse group chairman, who happened to be one of the tenants we interviewed in 2005 (Tenant 4 interview, October 31, 2005) explained this situation. His livelihood was a combination of 'garbage collection, community work, also doing some business'. A 'group of idle friends' had formed a group, named the 'Meta-Meta Youth Club' after the popular name for the sub-area they serviced with garbage collection. The group consisted of 21 young adult residents, including three women. It owned one wheel-cart which the members used to take the refuse to a collection point from where the municipality transported it to the Dandora dump, roughly 4 km to the east of Huruma. Meta-Meta was collecting garbage from some 20 tenements on Wednesdays and Saturdays, servicing a total of around 500 rooms, including shops and kiosks. It carried out street cleanups twice a month. It collected Kshs 30 (US$0.43) /door/month. The group members tried to make friends with their clients as they had no means of forcing them to pay.

The Meta-Meta group had competition from other garbage collection groups (One-Stone, Yard Post, Suya Suya and Stream Line). The chairman explained that Meta-Meta was not in dispute with any of these groups, but their presence did mean that Meta-Meta could not expand, unless new tenements were completed or additional floors added. The street clean-ups were also limited by the fact that they could not enter narrow lanes between tenements, into which people were dumping. The entrances of many of these lanes were blocked by shacks. Landlords were not taking responsibility for this problem (Tenant 4 interview, October 31, 2005).

Congestion, crime, community

Through the door-to-door garbage collection, the garbage group chairman had useful insight into the 500 or so households his group was servicing. While our visit to Ngima House gave the impression that most rooms were occupied by young couples with two small children at the most, in his own tenement he estimated an average of four adults per room. For the entire sample of rooms that his group serviced, his estimate was that half of the rooms were occupied by more than two adults, and in his understanding, the high occupancy rates were a result of the high rents. Couples often shared the room with an adult sibling. He also knew of rooms that were shared by several single people (Tenant 4 interview, October 31, 2005). In 2008, after the post-election violence which led to increased occupancy rates, estimates were higher. A local tenant youth whose occupation was 'area coordinator' for the Christian organization Mission of Hope, which undertook health work with many local households, estimated an average of six to seven occupants per room – 'the single room at night is not the same room of daytime' (Tenant 5 interview, May 28. 2008). Only four months since the post-election violence, it was not clear whether the ethnic convergence of people on this sub-area of Huruma was temporary.

Tenancy in Huruma was not only sought-after because of ethnic solidarity in the area. Tenants expressed the convenience of short walking distances to the *matatu* service on Juja Road as well as the clustered *jua kali* livelihood opportunities on this road. One tenant's husband made furniture 'near the bend in Juja Road'. As the household had no transport expenses, it could afford to rent a two-bedroom unit in the six-story Juja Road House (also referred to as 'Juja Court'), the only non-rooming building in our sample area. The household had moved into this newly completed tenement in 1998. Considering the option of renting in Umoja, they had found Huruma's offering attractive. The landlord of Juja Road House also owned the building next door. This was 'the oldest multi-story building in the area', built in the late 1980s (Tenant 2 interview, October 25, 2005). A narrow bridge from the sixth floor of Juja Road House to the tenement next door provided access to a drying space on the roof (Figure 8.15). This distinguished Juja Road House from most other tenements in our sample area, for which landlords only provided washing lines on narrow balconies. At the high unit and occupation densities, laundry hanging out to dry formed a daily dressing for all tenements with outside balconies (Figure 8.16).

In the less common tenement type with rooms arranged around an internal courtyard, washing lines are strung across the courtyard on every floor (Figure 8.17). The constant dripping of wet washing from higher floors makes the lower

Figure 8.15: (*left*) Juja Road House, further back and adjacent to the area's oldest multi-story tenement; (*right*) a narrow bridge crosses from Juja Road House to the washing area
Source: Author's photographs (2005)

rooms less attractive. Tenant 1 had lived in a seven-story courtyard tenement before moving to Ngima House. He confirmed that washing took 'days to dry' (Tenant 1 interview, October 29, 2005). Although this tenant's main criterion when looking for a better deal in Huruma's market was the rent, his wife appreciated that the outside balcony of Ngima House provided for quicker drying time. Upon reflection, he added that the courtyard arrangement made for a friendly community, as everyone knew one another across the central space. A different perspective came from Tenant 3 (interview, October 25, 2005) in Ngima House, who said that she preferred buildings with outside balconies because of their connection to the outside world: 'you have a view, you can see the street, you can see what is happening'. This tenant, like other women she had befriended on her floor, spent most of her time in Ngima House (and on its balcony – Figure 8.18). She could even do her grocery shopping at the general dealer on the ground floor (Figure 8.19 – in 2008 Ngima House and its shop fronts had received a fresh coat of paint). Only on weekends did she sometimes venture beyond the tenement, in the company of her husband.

Most tenants we interviewed expressed concern about security. They did not consider the lower floors in the tenements safe. Tenant 1 (interview, October 29, 2005) explained that 'when there is no electricity, the thugs climb up on the outside of the building. They step on each other's shoulders. That is why some flats don't have balconies on the first floor.' His household's room at the time was on the third floor of Ngima House. His preference would have been for a room on a

Figure 8.16: Daily drying of washing on outside balconies

Source: Author's photographs (2005)

higher floor because of security and privacy concerns. Between 2005 and 2008, Tenant 1 had found a larger room at the same rent, but in the more recently developed Kayole on Nairobi's eastern outskirts. On my second visit in 2008, Tenant 1 had returned with his household to the sample area of Huruma. He had not anticipated the ethnic expulsion from Kikuyu-dominated Kayole that Luos experienced immediately after the December 2007 election (Tenant 1 interview, May 25, 2008). In May 2008, his household occupied a room on the top floor of Steka House (managed by Steka Commercial Agency), one of the two newly constructed tenements in the sample area. The top floors of older tenements were not liked, as roofs were known to be damaged by those attaching their television aerials, but in a newly constructed tenement a room below the roof was acceptable. Nevertheless, by June 2009 the household had moved to a larger room, still within the case study area (Tenant 1 interview, June 15, 2009).

Figure 8.17: Washing strung across the courtyard on all seven stories of a courtyard tenement

Source: Author's photograph (2005)

Again expressing a security concern, Tenant 3's biggest reason for appreciating Ngima House, besides the outside balcony and the friends she had made among the tenants, was the guard: 'He lives in the building and walks around at night. The landlord pays him' (interview, October 25, 2005). The perception of Huruma as crime-ridden was not confined to its inhabitants. One of the rental agents we interviewed was cautious of doing business in Huruma for this very reason: 'You can send someone to look at a house and the guy gets beaten. This has happened… People in Huruma are tough, thugs stay there' (Agent 2 interview, October 17, 2005). Another agent explained that due to the

Figure 8.18: Women spend most of their time in the tenement and on the balcony

Source: Author's photograph (2005)

security risk of carrying cash in most tenement areas, tenants are asked to deposit the rent into the agent's bank account (Agent 3 interview, October 22, 2005). Tenant 1 (interview, October 25, 2005) confirmed this practice for the Huruma tenement (Ngima House, managed by Ngima Agency) in which he was renting in 2005. The perception of Huruma of two officials in the Nairobi Water and Sewerage Company was that 'those doing meter readings are mugged. It's a very hostile area' (Anonymous Group I interview, October 17, 2005).

The chairman of the refuse group (Tenant 4 interview, October 31, 2005) explained that with the increasing population in the Huruma sample area, 'you get congestion, and the crim-

Figure 8.19: The convenience of shopping facilities on the ground floor of Ngima House

Source: Author's photograph (2008)

inals can hide. You can't say who is who.' A small group or gang was operating in the area, stealing mobile phones at gunpoint from those walking to work in the mornings – one of the gang's members, with a wife and two children, was a former neighbor of Tenant 1. Both Tenant 1 and Tenant 4 had grown up in Huruma and knew some of the thieves: 'Often they are school dropouts... they get influenced by bad friends' (Tenant 4 interview, October 31, 2005). The refuse group had tried to offer security services, 'but this was too difficult. The community tended to blame us if something happened', so they had given up (*ibid.*). Tenant 2, who spent most of her time in Juja Road House with seemingly little connection to the outside world, was not aware of crime in the area. Her building was close to the single-story 'slum' area that bordered Gitathuru River. She observed that this 'slum' was gradually being replaced with multi-story tenements, adding to the congestion, which she worried about. Her other concern was that public spaces had been grabbed by tenement investors. Given these trends, she added, 'If you pass here in the evenings or on Sundays at 11 in the morning, or when people go to work, the streets are very full, like in town... In ten years' time, it will be very squeezed...'

The tenant from Juja Road House made these observations in 2005. As already mentioned, congestion had increased by 2008. Tenant 1 (interview, May 25, 2008) noted in 2008 that many 'middle class' households, who could afford to live in larger units elsewhere, had moved to the sample area of Huruma for safety from ethnic persecution. While congestion provided a niche for crime, the ethnic solidarity offered by this crowded community had attracted more congestion. Tenant 5 commented in 2008 that 'Huruma has lots of bad things, but it also has brotherhood, people are friendly'. Underlining the necessity for this solidarity, he added:

...since the skirmishes there is a status that [makes] you feel odd wherever you don't have your tribe around you... The biggest effect [of the skirmishes], though it's too early to say, is the lack of trust between the two tribes, even in the neighborhood... If you want to go shopping you think 'where is the Kikuyu shop?' if you're Kikuyu, and 'where is the Luo shop?' if you're Luo. (Tenant 5 interview, May 28, 2008)

The group that we interviewed in 2008 had been friends since school, and comprised Luos and Kikuyus. Together, they had started Furaha Academy in 2005, one of several private schools in the sample area (Figure 8.20). They first offered only an afternoon tutorial program for children. A friend from the US had donated some textbooks, and this encouraged them to start a school for children whose parents couldn't afford school fees. Teachers volunteered for two hours a week. In 2008, Furaha had 500 primary school children. This group of friends was also involved in *Mazingira Bora* (Swahili for 'Better Environment') (Figure 8.21), an initiative to address environmental challenges, among which garbage collection remained the primary focus. Reflecting on the ethnic clashes in 2008, one of the friends commented, 'Huruma is like home... we didn't think it could happen' (Tenant 6 interview, May 28, 2008).

Figure 8.20 *(above)*: Private schools in tenement ground floors shed neatly uniformed children into the streets

Source: Author's photographs (2008)

Figure 8.21 *(left)*: Meeting space of the environmental group *Mazingira Bora*, in the sample area in Huruma

Source: Author's photograph (2008)

Neighborhood and street life

Ground floor commercial activity in most of Huruma's tenements defines life in the relatively narrow streets (Figures 8.19, 8.20 and 8.22). None of the ground floor shops and wooden kiosks were vacant. By contrast, many shops and kiosks in Umoja Inner Core stood unused. Given the dormitory nature of the area, it was possible that some of these kiosks were in use only on weekends. Huruma's commercial activities displayed greater variety than those recorded in Umoja Inner Core, where the density was lower and consumption patterns or habits determined by higher incomes. Nevertheless, even Umoja Inner Core supported a range of services and retail outlets (see Figure 7.17 in Chapter 7 and Table 8.1). An attendant in a general store in our sample area (Shop attendant interview, October 31, 2005), who lived in neighboring Umoja 1 and walked to work, said her opening hours were 6.30 am to 7 pm. This was indicative of the rhythm of exit and entry into Umoja Inner Core by its working tenants. Responding to our observation that the shop seemed very quiet during the daytime, she commented that 'the clientele is improving'. Ongoing tenement construction in the area brought new clientele in the form of tenants and temporary construction workers. This was gradually building up economic opportunity in the area. In contrast, economic opportunity in Huruma was already optimized at many levels, from a fairly large tenement 'supermarket' down to small street traders. Cars could enter the Huruma sample area only with great difficulty due to erosion. Kiosks and stalls had encroached onto the street and capitalized on the high volume of passersby. The stalls underlined the pedestrian nature of the neighborhood (Figure 8.22). By May 2008, the municipality had begun resurfacing the roads and separating pavements from road space. While this had yet to penetrate into the internal multifunctional street system, it was evident that the road improvement would impact on the fine grain of economic activity. Nevertheless, the benefits of properly surfaced and drained road space could not be underestimated.

Figure 8.22: Ground floor shops, services and stalls on Huruma's streets

Source: Author's photographs (2008)

In the Huruma sample area, operators of *jua kali* manufacturing activities also appropriated street and open space. Their operations spanned primarily carpentry and welding of gates, burglar bars and metal doors, all of direct relevance to the tenement market (Figure 8.23). In Umoja Inner Core, *jua kali* operators tended to make use of vacant properties. They were therefore a less visible part of street activities than in Huruma.

Living with risks

In many ways, tenants' choice of living in our sample area in Huruma was a tradeoff. Convenience of location, economic opportunity and ethnic solidarity made up for a number of risks. I have already mentioned the fear of crime. In the buildings we visited, tenants kept health risks at bay through

Figure 8.23: *Jua kali* activities in the streets of the Huruma sample area

Source: Author's photograph (2005)

their collective discipline in cleaning the communal areas. However, without a doubt dumping, open sewers and lack of storm water drainage in streets and public spaces exposed the public, children in particular, to health risks. But the tenement clientele was privileged above that of the single-story wattle-and-daub 'slum' market, where landlords don't provide access to water and sanitation. One health risk that the Huruma sample area shared with the 'slums' was that emergency vehicles had difficulties entering the neighborhood: 'the ambulance doesn't come here' (Tenant 3 interview, October 25, 2005).

Building collapse was not a concern in people's minds. One rental agent held that 'not many buildings collapse or burn [down]' in Nairobi. For this reason, 'few landlords are insured... risk is not perceived to be high' (Agent 3 interview, October 22, 2005). Unrelated to the earthquake tremors of December 2005 and July 2007, in the unplanned middle income tenement area Zimmerman '[a] few of the multi-storey houses have recently started sinking into the waterlogged ground' (Gatabaki-Kamau and Karirah-Gitau 2004, 171). In October 2009, the media reported a building collapse in Kiambu, 15 km to the north of Nairobi, taking the lives of 16 construction workers (Aron 2009b). As an aside, one journalist also mentioned that 'one person died and several were injured when a house collapsed in Huruma Estate' (to the east of Huruma's Ngei II and the sample area) a few days before the Kiambu disaster (Owuor 2009). No further details were available from the media, but Tenant 1 (interview, February 9, 2010) confirmed that this three-story building was under construction and had collapsed in heavy winds. The victim was struck by the debris while sleeping inside a nearby tin structure.

Table 8.1: Commercial activities in the two sample areas

Commercial activities	Umoja Inner Core sample area	Huruma sample area
Ground floor shops	General store; grain/cereal store; butcher; hardware; milk bar/dairy products; chemist; carpentry	General dealer; supermarket; butchery; hardware; dairy produce (yogurt and milk); chemist; sodas/soft drinks; cell phone accessories; buckets and pots (cooking utensils); clothing/fashion
Vacant ground floor shops	3	None
Ground floor services	Salon; barber; shoe polish; pub; telephone	Salon/beauty therapy; barber; pub; tailoring; video lounge; internet; photo studio; medical services; preschool; primary school
Kiosks in wooden structures in front of shops	Fruit and vegetables; coal; kerosene	Fruit and vegetable; kerosene; 'cafe'; telephone (landline); battery charging; ironing
Vacant kiosks	4	None
Open air traders in streets	Water vending	Fruit and vegetables; cooked maize; fresh fish; live chicken
Open air services in streets	Washing car seats	Shoe repair
Jua kali (open air) manufacturing	Carpentry and upholstering; metalwork	Carpentry; metalwork

During our interviews in 2005 and 2008, no one we spoke to knew of buildings sinking or collapsing in Huruma. There were also no accounts of fires trapping tenants on upper floors. However, it is of concern that none of the tenements have fire escapes. In Berlin, developers had to build tenements to fire precautionary standards. In New York, steel fire escapes were fastened to the street-facing façades of tenements only once the authorities effectively enforced fire precautionary measures. In Huruma, people were more conscious of the risks posed by exposure to height than they were of a fire hazard. Tenants told of small children tragically falling to their deaths from the higher floors. Daily washing contributed to the rusting of railings, whether around air wells (Figure 8.24) or on narrow balconies. In one account, the affected family had blamed the landlord but had not taken legal action. In 2005, the mother of the diseased child still lived next to the air well into which her child had fallen (Tenant 4 interview, October 31, 2005). Tenant 4 explained:

In the neighboring buildings there were several cases... The children know the danger, but they still play. It happens with children below five years, they can't judge the danger. Most children are born in the area and know the danger, unlike children visiting from the rural areas.

With inadequate legal protection and empowerment of tenants, landlords were not held to account for structural negligence in their tenements. Related to this was

Figure 8.24: Air wells or voids in and between Huruma's tenements

Source: Author's photographs (2005)

the legally precarious nature of the rental agreement, which offered no protection against unfair eviction procedures. One of the rental agents explained that in low income areas such as Huruma, turnover was so high that it was not viable to use formal lease agreements. Instead, they used a letting memorandum (Agent 3 interview, October 22, 2005). One of the tenants in Ngima House had witnessed several evictions in her building:

> The tenants had accumulated rent arrears... They had probably lost their jobs... The eviction took place at 5 am. The landlord hired youths. They moved everything from the room onto the corridor and locked the room. No force was used. The tenants had been given notice, but they did not know when the youths would come... They moved to another building where the rent is lower (Tenant 3 interview, October 25, 2005).

This eviction practice was confirmed by two of the rental agents we interviewed (Agents 2 and 3, see Table 8.3). They knew of cases where auctioneers had carried out such evictions when they were unable to recover the arrears through the 'normal' procedure of attaching assets, because these economically distressed tenants did not own enough. Agent 3 (interview, October 22, 2005) explained that the auctioneer just throws the tenant out... The proprietor of the auctioneering firm can be a very decent man, but he hires thugs... They try to skip the legal channels, it's very rough. Thugs come very early in the morning. They just put the tenant and belongings on the street. Some tenants resist, but the tenant usually finds himself outnumbered.

One auctioneer (interview, November 1, 2005) who gave a reluctant interview further explained that the auctioneers' role is to recover revenue for the landlords, and not primarily to attach assets. They therefore follow various coercive steps to persuade the tenant to pay, before eventually attaching and auctioning off assets.

Tenants we interviewed expressed the view that rents were unfair, and that rental agents were harsh. One landlord, who was constructing his first tenement in Umoja Inner Core (his plan was to own 'as many [tenements] as possible'), decided not to engage the services of an agent. He was aware that 'agents harass the tenants... People opt for houses without agents' (Landlord 3 interview, November 3, 2005). One of the agents we interviewed admitted that even he 'would prefer to rent directly from a landlord [rather] than from an agent' (Agent 2 interview, October 17, 2005). In the Umoja Inner Core tenement market, where some units stood vacant, newly investing landlords were more concerned to attract tenants. In Huruma's context of high demand, tenants had less leverage. Agent 1 recalled a political move before the 2002 elections for tenants to pay only half of their rents. Politicians had started the rent boycott in Kibera in their efforts to campaign for votes. In Huruma, this did not succeed: 'Before the Huruma tenants could gang themselves up, the landlords or agents evicted them. The landlords ganged up to not give room to the difficult tenants. This killed the movement' (Agent 1 interview, November 1, 2005). Rents were again irresponsibly used as a political football in the December 2007 election, leading to Kikuyu landlords acting cohesively in cancelling Luo tenants' lease agreements (Waki 2008). This periodic action seemed to be the only form of landlord mobilization. Landlord 1, who owned two tenements in Huruma, said that he knew the landlords of the neighboring buildings, but 'there is no committee. We're all busy with different things' (interview, November 1, 2005).

After the 2008 post-election violence, which in part targeted landlords or their agents, Tenant 1 (interview, June 15, 2009) was of the view that landlords had become more cautious not to offend their tenants. On the other hand, the increased rental demand in the area suggested the continuation of a landlords' market. In my discussion in 2008 with the group of friends who had grown up in Huruma, we considered the possibility of community initiative to improve tenement conditions. In this context, Tenant 5 mentioned a further ground on which landlords would evict, namely if tenants were to take initiative in improving their building beyond emergency maintenance: 'The only thing that tenants could come together to do would be to address a health hazard, like unblocking a toilet or fixing a balcony.' It was also not viable for tenants to try to work with landlords for improved conditions. Firstly, they did not know the identity of their landlords. Secondly, 'landlords don't know one another, they are hard to lobby' as a collective (Tenant 5 interview, May 28, 2008).

Technically, Huruma's tenants have recourse to the rent tribunal created under the Rent Restriction Act (Government of Kenya 1982). It has discretionary powers in determining rents on a case-by-case basis and applies where rents are below Kshs 2 500 (US$36). In 2006, there were calls to raise the applicability of the Act to rents of up to Kshs 5 000 (US$69) (Huchzermeyer 2008). By 2008, room rents in Huruma had already risen to Kshs 2 500 (US$42), from Kshs 1 800–2 000 (US$26/29) in 2005 (Tenant 1 interview, May 28, 2008). However, even if the tribunal's applicability were to be extended, a number of limitations would remain. Joireman and Vanderpoel (2011), though referring specifically to experiences in Kibera, indicate that the tribunal takes up to five years to resolve a single dispute, fees are prohibitive, and both landlords and tenants perceive it as biased. Mwangi (1997) mentions that there have also been calls to decentralize the tribunal to municipal level.[2]

The creation of density and typology: decision-making in the tenement market

Landlords were not easily identified for the purposes of this research. Caretakers, mostly employed directly by landlords and living on the premises, had strict instructions not to divulge landlords' identities. The tenants we spoke to only had contact with rental agents, who did the advertising and received the rental payments. The auctioneer we interviewed predicted that it would be difficult to 'get hold of' landlords of rooming tenements – 'one will have to go through other landlords'. This was exactly how we had identified two of the landlords whom we managed to interview.[3] The three rental agents we interviewed (their profiles are provided in Table 8.3) were also not willing to disclose their clients' identities. They complained that it was difficult even for them to get hold of their clients – landlords did not like to be disturbed. Most landlords were business people, and tenements only a side investment (Table 8.2 presents the profiles of the four landlords we succeeded in interviewing). The rental agents confirmed that this was broadly representative of their tenement landlord client base, adding though that they also managed properties for landladies, either widows who had inherited tenements from their deceased husbands, or businesswomen in their own right. One owned a tall 'building' in Huruma as well as several tenements in two other areas. Though the agents did not know the other income sources of most of their clients, Agent 1 (interview, October 21, 2005) knew that this particular landlady's main business was an electrical shop. She had divulged this when recognizing a market for her wiring and electrical fittings in the tenement construction market. The agents implied that landladies were more likely to make use of a rental agent than their male counterparts. Agent 2 (interview, October 26, 2005) stressed that his female clients took a greater interest in their tenements, therefore he was more acquainted with them:

> They like to know who is not paying, why rent is not being paid, how the property is handled. They enquire whether any repair work is needed. They come in personally to collect their check... The men just collect their check from the receptionist.

The Huruma landlord we interviewed (Landlord 1 interview, November 1, 2005) in turn provided his experience of rental agents. During construction of his tenement, many agents had visited the site and offered their services. However, his lawyer had cautioned him, warning that some agents are dishonest and disappear with the rent. With the substantial total monthly income from the rent of one tenement (I provide two examples in the last rows of Table 8.2), this was a real temptation. This landlord had settled on the agent managing the neighboring tenement and had no complaints.

This same landlord also gave a useful account of his investment decisions. When planning to construct his tenements in Huruma, he had first visited other tenements in the immediate vicinity. His impression was that most rooms and internal corridors were very dark, that tenants would be exhausted from climbing more than five flights of stairs, and that the higher buildings might not be stable. He asked the engineer friend who drew the plans for his tenements to limit the height to six stories, and to provide an internal courtyard for light. The 13 m × 26 m plot (wider than most) allowed for this layout. He also requested that the two top floors be fitted with interconnecting doors between two rooms. His assumption was that households able to afford two-roomed units would prefer to live on separate floors from households living in one room. However, he added that many of the two-roomed units were in fact rented out as single rooms. Apart from this, he replicated the tenement design conventions already established in the area. On the whole, his decisions on the design of the building were a matter of balancing two concerns: competitiveness, that is, attracting tenants, if necessary from other buildings; and the maximization of his profits. When he constructed his second tenement in Huruma, he managed to adjust the layout so as to include more rooms per floor.

One of the Umoja Inner Core landlords, constructing his first tenement in 2005, gave a similar account. Through his construction business, he had already built tenements for other investors. Once he had acquired a plot of his own, he 'went around to look at other buildings, to find out what is easy to rent out' (Landlord 4 interview, October 18, 2005). He had noted that three-bedroom units were not popular in the area, and was confident that his particular design with a range of options from bedsitters up to two-bedroom units would do well. He also emphasized that appearance was important, and that private balconies were attractive to tenants. He further recognized a demand in the area for small commercial units on

Table 8.2: Tenement investment profile of the four landlords interviewed in 2005

	Landlord 1	Landlord 2	Landlord 3	Landlord 4
Place of interview	Downtown grain trading store	Downtown, long distance *matatu* station	Downtown, long distance *matatu* station	At construction site, UIC
Livelihood beyond tenement	Grain trade	*Matatu* owner	*Matatu* owner	Owns a construction company (previously lecturing).
Place of tenement investment and date of construction	Huruma × 2 (1998, 2000) Kariobangi × 2	Githurai × 1 (after 2000) (Huruma × 1, but sold it in 2000)	UIC × 2 (2000, 2001)	UIC × 1 (2005)
Plot acquisition	Inheritance. Father had bought from original allottee who was unable to pay off NCC loan.	Purchase	Purchased from NCC.	Purchased from an acquaintance, who bought from NCC (although it was planned 'open space').
Plot size	Huruma: 13m × 26m (× 2) Kariobangi: 6.5m × 26m	–	–	12m × 21m
Proof of plot ownership	Allocation letter (title deed outstanding)	–	Allocation letter (title deed outstanding)	Title deed
Construction finance	Resources pooled by the family	Huruma: loan from a cooperative From tenement sale in Huruma, plus retrenchment package from an insurance company	Business loan based on his *matatu* logbooks (24 per cent interest) Second tenement built with cash	Savings, plus loan from HFCK (18 per cent interest)

	Landlord 1	Landlord 2	Landlord 3	Landlord 4
Tenement type	Huruma: single rooms Kariobangi: bedsitters	Githurai: self-contained units, size not specified Huruma: single rooms	One- and two-bedroom, bedsitters on ground floor	One- and two-bedroom, bedsitters on ground floor
Number of stories	Huruma: both 6 stories Kariobangi: 4 stories	Githurai: 3 stories	4 stories 3 stories (planning to go to 6 stories)	5 stories
Gross monthly rental income/ tenement	Ø Kshs 86 800/ US$1 258 per tenement	–	–	Kshs 162 000/ US$2 347 (one tenement)
Deductions from monthly rental income	Electricity (Kshs 26 400/ US$383) Water (Kshs 9 600/US$139) Sewer blockages (Kshs 300/ US$4.34)	–	–	Caretaker (Kshs 7 000/ US$101) Municipal rates (Kshs 1 000/ US$14.5)
Net monthly income from rent (before tax)	Kshs 48 900/ US$709 per tenement	–	–	Kshs 154 000/ US$2 232

Notes: In the absence of a valuation, it was not possible to calculate return on investment for these properties.

HFCK = Housing Finance Corporation Kenya; NCC = Nairobi City Council; UIC = Umoja Inner Core

the ground floor, but not for larger shops. Unlike the tenement market in Huruma, in Umoja Inner Core landlord investors could maximize their profit by providing a higher level of finishes and fittings and charging higher rents for these units. Landlord 4's building was to be one of the 'smarter' tenements, with a central television aerial as well as bathroom tiles and fitted kitchen cabinets. Maintenance would be low, the construction cost repaid in three years (an excellent rate of recovery of investment), and a continuous source of income guaranteed. Agent 1 confirmed that one reason for the intense investment in tenements was that 'it is a good security for the future' (interview, October 21, 2005).

However, not all Umoja Inner Core investors had taken these considerations into account. Agent 3 (interview, October 22, 2005) showed us a building in this area standing vacant due to bad design (a poorly ventilated courtyard), poor workmanship (irregular steps and crooked walls) and poor maintenance (walls badly damaged by plumbing leaks). The twenty-odd two-bedroom units in this tenement could not be let, and the owner had asked the agent to sell the building. In the agent's assessment, the building should be demolished, given that any buyer would have to lay out considerable capital before the building could yield returns.

A market in completed tenements exists, although longer-term speculation with land and building value, according to Agent 1 (interview, November 1, 2005), was more common in the upper income market. Yet in the middle to low income market, owners did not only put up problematic tenements for sale. Agent 1's landlord client base also consulted him for advice on speculative investment. In a recent case, he had advised an investor to buy a rooming tenement in Mathare 4, where rents were high but property prices relatively low, and to purchase a vacant plot in Ruai, where land was expected to increase in value by 50 per cent in a matter of one year. His overall investment advice was to buy or build where demand was highest, therefore units easiest to rent out. This included the former Indian area Eastleigh, as well as the already congested Huruma. However, pragmatic limitations also determined investors' decisions on where to invest. Landlord 1 (interview, November 1, 2005) reflected that, if given another chance, he would not invest in Huruma's rooming market. After building in Huruma, he had also invested in a tenement with bedsitters in Kariobangi. He was more content with the latter investment. This had less to do with the low income character of Huruma than with the fact that the water and electricity consumption was included in the rooming rent, whereas bedsitters (whether in Kariobangi or elsewhere) were individually metered. He was looking forward to the rumored introduction of prepaid water and electricity meters for the rooming market.

The speculative chain that preceded tenement construction and pushed up prices in late 19th and early 20th century Berlin had not developed in Nairobi. However, other problems were evident in Nairobi's tenement market. Huruma's landlords, in particular, had the reputation of being interested in quick returns rather than considering longer-term investment potential. In the perception of Agent 3 (interview, October 22, 2005), Huruma's landlords would eventually abandon their investments and instead build further south-east, where new developments were taking off (his own preference was to stay clear of managing buildings in Huruma). He added that already in auctions, tenements in Huruma were not selling easily. This reinforced the landlords' focus on 'making money fast'. The auctioneer we interviewed (interview, November 1, 2005) knew of a 17-roomed tenement in Ngei II (near our Huruma sample area), which 'has been on the market for some time'. The up-market owner had defaulted on a bank loan and therefore the tenement needed to be auctioned off.

In 2000, due to insecurity in Huruma, Landlord 2 (interview, November 3, 2005) had sold a tenement that he owned in this area. He had been making a loss on the building. His brother, a 'land broker', had managed to sell the tenement 'at a good price'. With the proceeds of the sale, he had built a three-story tenement in fast-growing Githurai, where self-contained units are offered on the edges and rooming in the interior of the neighborhood. His property portfolio also included commercial space 'in town'. His observation in 2005 was that 'Huruma is safer now, I'm sorry I sold'.

In Berlin, the speculative chain in tenement production was underpinned by disturbing levels of debt. In Nairobi, all indications are that tenement investment relies to a far greater extent on surplus cash, the sources of which may not always be legitimate. In the perception of Landlord 2 (interview, November 3, 2005), 'people who grabbed money before the NARC government [came to power] are now investing in housing. They have liquid cash.' But landlords were also investing more benign capital. Mortgages required formal title, which many tenement investors did not hold. In Umoja Inner Core, the municipality had only issued title deeds for Sector Five, which is where Landlord 4 was constructing (Table 8.2). He had secured a mortgage from the Housing Finance Corporation Kenya (HFCK). Having saved with HFCK for several years, he was not required to pay a deposit or provide collateral (Landlord 4 interview, October 18, 2005). Landlord 1 (interview, November 1, 2005) had pooled family resources, having inherited the two Huruma plots from his father. Landlord 3 (interview, November 3, 2005), a *matatu* operator, had taken the *matatu* logbooks to a bank to apply for a business loan. This had been granted at 24 per cent interest. He had supplemented the loan with 'some other money' and built a tenement in Umoja Inner Core. Within a year he was able to pay back the loan, and built his second tenement with no loan. Landlord 2 (interview, November 3, 2005) had built his first tenement (in Huruma) with a 'small loan' from a cooperative. He had recovered this in three years. He had financed the construction of his second tenement (in Githurai) with a retrenchment package.

Agent 1 confirmed that some landlords were servicing loans, as they asked agents to deposit the rental income into loan accounts. The auctioneer, who was tasked by banks with selling tenements in cases where landlords had defaulted, hinted at a non-transparent (presumably corrupt) banking system – he was unwilling to divulge even the names of banks that were lending for such investments. Agents mentioned two tendencies that signaled financial distress among some landlords. One was loan defaults, which brought tenement buildings onto the market. The other was landlords asking agents for advances on their rental income, for instance to cover school fees (Agent 1 interview, October 21, 2005).

Table 8.3: Profile of the three rental agents interviewed in 2005

	Agent 1	**Agent 2**	**Agent 3**
Areas in which they were managing tenements	38 buildings in Huruma 2 buildings in UIC	Several tenements in UIC Rooming tenements in Eastleigh; bedsitters in Mathare North; self-contained units in Zimmerman (and many in other areas)	Several tenements in Umoja Upper income market
Landlord profile	Businesspeople (farming, grain/cereal traders); very few have 'office jobs'; some are women	Businesspeople (insurance, *matatu*); some invest in tenements as companies or groups of 4 (rather than as individuals); 50 per cent are women.	–
Perception of Huruma	High turnover, but ready market drawing tenants from older to newer tenements, good location.	Prefers to avoid Huruma; difficult tenants; 'thugs like to stay there' and 'people with illegal businesses'.	Would not touch Huruma; difficult to manage, high turnover, high default rate; defaulting tenants could disappear overnight; Huruma landlords think short-term.
Perception of UIC	Problems with water supply; tenants are families with children, tenants tend to take care of their flats.	Tenants are typically families with children.	People from Huruma would look in UIC when moving up the housing ladder; some landlords have made bad investments in UIC.
Commission charged to landlord	6.5 per cent	10 per cent	–

Note: UIC = Umoja Inner Core

Investor decisions in Nairobi's tenement market contribute to a pronounced spatial segregation of income groups. As already mentioned, there were only very few self-contained tenements within the predominantly rooming district of Huruma. The Huruma landlords' perception was that customers for two-bedroom units 'would want to be in a better area... In Huruma, the customers are of a certain class' (Landlord 1 interview, November 1, 2005). Landlords also were of the opinion that mixing rooming with self-contained units within the same building would not be successful, whereas bedsitters could be mixed with larger self-contained units. Investors' perceptions of the market were clearly determining a spatial segregation between customers of the rooming and self-contained apartment markets.[4]

Neither reform nor revolution: is nothing to be done about Nairobi's tenements?

With a few exceptions, Kenyan urban and housing discourse, as reflected in the published literature, has neatly skirted the multi-story tenement reality that is rapidly transforming Nairobi. I have already mentioned that the urban and housing literature has a strong bias towards the more legitimate topic of 'slums'. While much research and literature has analyzed the 'slum' problematic, it has not contributed to a solution. The state's approach to 'slums' in Nairobi remains one of government- and donor-funded redevelopment through middle class units, with few gains made in improving access to very basic services for the majority of 'slum' dwellers whom these projects have not yet displaced.

The restrictions placed on Kenyan academics over at least three decades to some extent explain the dearth of literature on Nairobi's tenements. King (1996) describes a progression from the 1970s during which foreigners still dominated academic research on Kenya, with important exceptions (apparent also from the housing literature), to the 1980s and 1990s in which Kenyans began to take the lead. However, by this time Kenyan universities had 'failed to provide a living wage. Academic research, unless funded by an external body, became a luxury that few could afford to maintain, whatever their dedication to a particular field of study' (ibid., 9). Many Kenyan academics left universities to work for donor agencies or moved abroad; others relied on 'consulting research to supplement their meagre salaries' (ibid.). With donor agencies' focus on the global 'slum' problem, consulting research in the urban field in Kenya was inevitably on this topic.

Beyond the seeming economic necessity for academics to engage in consulting work, university staff were also subjected to repression. Already in 1982, anonymous authors writing in JAM (1982, 76) referred to 'the general repression of thought, initiative, and creativity'. They expanded: 'The ruling class is mortally afraid of discussion and new ideas. It uses its control of the University administration to limit academic debate and suppress discussion' (ibid., 75). Gona (2003, 313) mentions that in the 1990s, the 'banning of scholarly activities, particularly public lectures, contributed to a state of apathy, lethargy and resignation among academics'. Furthermore, '[t]he government had to be consulted before even a modest research project was undertaken. Research became confined to areas "acceptable" and not "sensitive" to the government' (*ibid.*).

In the housing field, acceptable research boiled down to enquiries into appropriate building technology. Both the *National Housing Development Programme 2003–2007* (Ministry of Roads, Public Works and Housing 2003) and the *National Housing Policy for Kenya* (Ministry of Lands and Housing 2004) prescribe a research agenda for the Housing, and Building Research Institute (HABRI) with only one theme, namely 'building materials research', certainly a topic that is 'not sensitive' for the government.[5] The Ministry of Lands and Housing (2004, 19–21) devotes an entire chapter of the housing policy to 'building materials and research', none of which goes beyond research on building materials. Apart from the Ministry of Housing calling for (and funding) building materials research, the UN and international donor patrons of consulting academics have steered urban and housing research towards similarly non-sensitive topics, primarily surveys on 'slums'. In 1995, Kanyinga (1995, 106) observed that even NGOs had 'yet to promote the emergence of independent voices in local "civil society"'. For aid-dependent NGOs, agenda-setting by donor agencies is of course as prominent as it is for consulting academics. Kenyan academics whom I interacted with during the course of my tenement research expressed envy at the freedom that my South African university position, with sabbatical and agenda-free funding, afforded me.

It is useful at this point to return to the late 19th century discourse on Berlin's tenements. I have identified four strands of argument and action addressing Berlin's tenement reality – philanthropic development of model housing, health surveys of workers' housing, promotion of homeownership as part of a bourgeois reform agenda, and a radical Marxist dismissal of all these three, but without articulating any alternative. Although a discourse on tenements in Nairobi is not apparent as such, each of these strands has an equivalent that allows one to paint a picture of the status and orientation of engagement with the tenement reality.

At first glance, there is no direct evidence of philanthropic interventions in Nairobi's tenement market. However, two initiatives deserve discussion as they have parallels in Berlin's philanthropic attempts at housing alternatives. One is the state's NHC, the other is housing developed by the SDI-affiliated NGO Pamoja Trust. Both also promote homeownership.

Observers have attributed the drop in output of formal houses by the NHC from the 1980s to the high cost of its housing (Stren, Halfani and Malombe 1994, 189). In the past two decades, the NHC's production of multi-story apartment buildings has had to compete with the successful private tenement market. In the perception of NHC officials we interviewed in 2005, this competition is not fair, as the NHC's developments are restricted in several ways. On the one hand, new NHC projects are only for homeownership (sectional title apartments), the NHC providing the mortgage finance itself. On the other hand, the NHC has to abide by planning and building regulations. In a group interview in 2005, NHC officials explained:

> The NHC has a bone to pick with the Nairobi City Council. Council insists that NHC only builds four floors without a lift. But they seem to be allowing six to eight floors elsewhere with no lift, even on the west side of town. NHC is now trying to do five floors without a lift. (Anonymous Group J interview, October 12, 2005).

The NHC had explored single-room accommodation. However, the NARC government in 2005 (at the time of the interview with NHC officials) had insisted on a minimum standard of two-bedroom units, as reflected in the 2004 housing policy (Ministry of Lands and Housing 2004, 11). It was common knowledge across Nairobi that the NHC mortgaged most of its 600 units per year (Anonymous Group J interview, October 12, 2005) to the middle class, including Kenyans employed by foreign-funded NGOs and UN bodies with salaries that government and NHC officials themselves could only dream of. However, the NHC was also tasked with 'slum' redevelopment. Here too, a minimum standard of two-bedroom units, ownership and eighteen-year mortgage finance was politically imposed upon the NHC. In the early 1990s, the state had tasked the NHC with 'slum' redevelopment in Kibera through a similar apartment typology. All units in Kibera's Nyayo High Rise development, supposedly intended for Kibera's 'slum' dwellers, were 'allocated and/or traded to the middle class' (Huchzermeyer 2008, 21). The NHC officials explained that this was due to high-level corruption beyond the control of the NHC (Anonymous Group I interview, October 17, 2005). In accordance with zoning regulations, Nyayo High Rise is a purely residential development. However, shops had emerged informally where the slope had resulted in small ground floor rooms that could not be sold as apartments. The NHC had mortgaged these spaces (most of which had become pubs) and their owners rented them out (Anonymous Group J interview, October 12, 2005).

'Slum' redevelopment through the NHC was approached more pragmatically in the Pumwani-Majengo project. In its first phase (completed in 1989 (Muraya 2006, 124)), the NHC had allocated three-roomed apartments to 'slum' dwellers, who took in tenants to contribute to the mortgage payments. In its second phase, the NHC had adopted this approach in the planning. Referring to the standard NHC typology, the NHC officials explained that a 'three-roomed [or two-bedroom] unit can be either for a middle class family or for three rooming families', with one holding the mortgage and the other two paying rent to the mortgage holder. The NHC's hope was that once the mortgage was paid off, the owning household could 'use the entire flat, which would improve their living conditions in eighteen years' time' (Anonymous Group J interview, October 12, 2005).

From 2004 onwards, a partnership between the Nairobi-based United Nations Human Settlements Programme (UN-HABITAT) and the Kenyan government also promoted this 'innovative' housing finance approach officially in the city's high-profile Kibera-Soweto pilot project of the Kenyan Slum Upgrading Programme. In this supposed solution, 'single room tenant households are to finance the asset accumulation of a few households selected for home ownership' (Huchzermeyer 2008, 21). In the second phase of the Pumwani-Majengo project, even with the anticipated rent of Kshs 4 000 from each of the two rooms, the remaining mortgage payment of Kshs 3 000 was not within reach of Pumwani's 'slum' dwellers (*ibid.*). Here the unplanned incremental 'slum' redevelopment with multi-story rooming tenements, as in Huruma, was providing more affordable access to rooming at rents of Kshs 1 800–2 000 (the rents in 2005), though still leading to displacement of poorer 'slum' tenants.

The NGO Pamoja Trust (already mentioned in relation to its role of refocusing and supporting the 'slum' dwellers' federation *Muungano wa Wanavijiji*), has developed a more nuanced 'slum' redevelopment approach, also attempting to turn 'slum' tenants into homeowners. It has inserted compact three-roomed units, one room stacked above the other and four units attached to one another, into the Kambi Moto 'slum' area in Huruma, east of our sample area (Pamoja Trust 2005; Mutero 2007, 30). These are financed through the collective savings and credit approach promoted by SDI. Participants agreed to 'single-household occupancy' and accordingly there is an 'intimate internal staircase' connecting the three rooms inside each unit (Huchzemeyer 2008, 34). 'However, the economic attraction of landlordism is so present in the consciousness of Nairobi's residents that some of the new home-owners in this project began letting two of their three rooms soon after occupation' (*ibid.*). It resulted again in 'single-room occupation… which the project sought to eliminate' (*ibid.*). The spatial layout of the units (one room leading to the next one above it) is less suitable for subletting than the two-bedroom units of the NHC (*ibid.*).

Neither the NHC nor Pamoja Trust were seeing it as their role to engage with the reality of the tenement market. Pamoja Trust set out to demonstrate the success of an innovative adaptation of the SDI model of community mobilization and housing development around savings and credit, pioneered in India (Patel and D'Cruz 1993). The NHC's mandate, in turn, is politically limited, quite obviously, to developing well located options for middle class (two-bedroom) homeowner-ship, partly masked as housing solutions for poor tenants of well located 'slums'. Both the NHC and Pamoja Trust have been intent on inserting homeownership into the tenement market. As their focus is on individual projects, they don't articulate as such whether they believe in the 'abolition of rented dwellings'. But in promoting homeownership, their orientation is not dissimilar to that of Berlin's bourgeois reformers of late 19th and early 20th century Berlin. However, the roots of the NHC's and Pamoja Trust's homeownership emphasis differ. In the Indian initiatives that Pamoja Trust has drawn from, the intention was that land be owned collectively, and only housing units owned individually. While a theoretical lineage could be traced from an anarchist, anti-statist orientation, the Indian approach draws from more recent gender theory, while also attempting to be grounded in local circumstances (Mitlin, personal communication, June 23, 2009).[6] This is not necessarily evident for Nairobi.

Homeownership promotion by the NHC, on the other hand, is directly derived from Kenya's neoliberal housing policy, large parts of which read as off-the-shelf concepts and solutions from donor agencies, with little concern for their local applicability and few attempts at tailoring them to the Kenyan urban reality.[7] Kenya's housing policy ignores the reality of massive indigenous private investment in tenements that has bypassed planning regulation with ease. Unbelievably, it states as one of its challenges that 'investments in the housing sector since 1966… have been minimal and sporadic', and that 'stringent planning regulations… have been an impediment in the housing delivery system' (Ministry of Lands and Housing 2004, 2–3). While mentioning the trend of 'public land grabbing for speculative purposes' (*ibid.*, 15), the 2004 policy makes no mention of the widespread transgression of planning regulations and the unplanned density at which private rental housing has developed. In blatant denial of this reality, it states that 'development control will be upheld and intensified' (*ibid.*, 16)! The policy's objectives include the promotion of 'the development and ownership of housing' (*ibid.*, 5). It calls for site-and-service schemes (*ibid.*, 11) without mentioning or addressing the failed targeting of such schemes to date and their transformation into multi-story tenement districts. Orthodox off-the-shelf policy principles from donor agencies surface in the frequent references to 'enablement', 'partnership' and 'participation'. Thus, the private sector is assigned the task of '[encouraging] communities [to] improve their living environment through community participation projects' – no suggestions are made as to how this will materialize for the 84.7 per cent of Nairobi's population who are tenants, mostly of private absentee landlords whom they fear and do not know. Andreasen (1996, 365), speaking to contexts (including Kenyan cities) where tenancy is prevalent, criticizes the 'neglect of the tenant population… in most national and international housing strategies'. This neglect renders these policies 'inappropriate and hence ineffective' (*ibid.*).

In contrast to the rest of Kenya's 2004 housing policy, the 'rental market' is mentioned for the first time towards the end of the document (on page 31). Without displaying any understanding of how demand and supply operate in a private rental market, the policy assumes that 'Shelter Sector Performance Indicators… [and] Survey Statistics' will 'guide the construction of housing… in the rental market' (*ibid.*, 31). In a brief display of what clearly are the real interests served by a policy that skirts the main challenges of a tenement market, there is a statement (also towards the end of the document) that legitimizes tenement landlordism and delegitimizes tenant claims:

> People who invest in rental housing do so with the intention of getting profit just as other people who invest in other sectors... Certain sections of the Rent Restrictions Act that restrict the operations of the rental market in favour of the interests of the tenants more than those of landlords, invariably discourage investment in rental housing. (*ibid.*, 32)

The more recent *Nairobi Metro 2030* document, while harping on the challenge of 'slums' and the need to 'eradicate' them, similarly denies the existence of large tenement districts with unauthorized construction at extreme densities. It denies private investment in this housing stock and sets out to 'increase home ownership' (Ministry of Nairobi Metropolitan Development 2008, 70). Similarly, it promotes a world class public transport system without a single mention of the existence of a vibrant *matatu* industry. And yet UN-HABITAT, with its own headquarters in that very city, endorses the *Nairobi Metro 2030* vision (*UN-HABITAT News* 2008). Admittedly, the sheltered existence of its staff, into which even its Kenyan employees slip with comfort, seldom if ever leads to any knowledge, let alone understanding, of the real workings of the city.

One could argue for Kenya, as Engels did for the German Empire, that '[i]t is perfectly clear that the existing state is neither able nor willing to do anything to remedy the housing difficulty' (Engels 1887/1935, 71, as quoted in Chapter 5 above). It is likewise clear that neoliberal aid and global governance agencies are equally unable and unwilling. By endorsing the government's unrealizable plans or commissioning yet another health or living conditions survey in Nairobi's 'slums' (e.g. World Bank 2006), much money is spent on identifying what should be changed (e.g. 'to break the low-quality, high-cost trap in slum housing' (World Bank 2006, 68)), but no suggestions are made as to how these changes could be achieved. Problems are merely identified or restated, but no insight is given into their causes.

This leaves us with only one strand in Berlin's housing discourse that has no equivalent in that of present-day Nairobi, namely a Marxist position. As already mentioned, neo-Marxist academics and politicians have not enjoyed freedom under the post-independence Kenyan state. This was similar in the German Empire, where the readership of Engels' *Housing Question* increased through the state's banning of the booklet. However, the absence in this position of any urban alternative, and instead only the promotion of a revolution, contributed to the once revolutionary SPD adopting the bourgeois reform agenda which rejected tenements and promoted the complete inverse, namely light and air in a low density suburban setting, with homeownership as the dominant tenure form (capitalism quickly adjusted, to reap the benefits of this form of individual consumption). In Nairobi, there are currently neither commitments to undertake improvements to the tenement stock and moderate the excesses in the tenement market, nor a destructive discourse undermining the legitimacy of tenement investment.

A discussion on building standards and enforcement, which erupts in the media from time to time (Aron 2009a, 2009b; Owour 2009), also neatly skirts the tenement reality, focusing instead on regulatory transgression in shopping malls and commercial buildings in prominent locations such as the central business district. In this avoidance of any discussion on the city's over 10 000 tenement buildings lies an important difference between Nairobi and late 19th and early 20th century Berlin. The modern suburban town planning model still continues to enjoy legitimacy across the globe, despite considerable critique (UN-HABITAT 2009). Even where it has enjoyed little respect in the city-making process, its principles experience a revival in the convergence with visions projected by urban competitiveness such as *Nairobi Metro 2030*. The challenge is to draw attention to Nairobi's tenements without unleashing an equivalent to the destructive reform discourse which gave birth to the inordinately unsustainable ideas of the modern town planning movement at the beginning of the 20th century.

How to draw parallels with Berlin's tenement reality without undermining the legitimacy of the rented dwelling in Nairobi

Densities in Nairobi's tenement districts, while continuing to increase, already outstrip those of Berlin's densest tenement districts around 1900. This applies even in middle class Umoja Inner Core, where individual units are larger and tenements not as tall as in low income Huruma, and where almost half the plots are still undeveloped. The typology through which the densities are achieved holds parallels with Berlin's tenement types in their representation to and commercial frontage onto the street. In terms of living conditions, there are parallels in the challenges as well as the qualities that result from the high concentration of people and commercial street-level activities.

But Nairobi's tenement typology is more extreme than that of Berlin or other tenement cities of the west. The internal layout in Berlin's early tenements, with rooms along a central corridor as exemplified by Von Wülknitz's family houses, has more in common with Nairobi's rooming tenements than Berlin's subsequent typology that provided varying unit sizes with access from several stairwells, and which became dominant under the 1853 Building Ordinance. Even Von Wülknitz's family houses were only constructed once plans had been approved. Nairobi's tenement typology has evolved well beyond building regulations, though some principles from regulatory proposals are recognizable in the tenement layouts. In Berlin, it was the levels of occupation and the letting of officially uninhabitable units that displayed landlord defiance. This could be interpreted on the one hand as a pragmatic response to extreme demand, with low levels of affordability (and no option of long term self-help shack-living), or on the other hand as landlord exploitation. Either way, in Berlin as in Nairobi, some legitimacy of the tenement market and its excesses was and is pragmatically derived from the overwhelming housing need being addressed.

At the same time, tenant attachment to a particular neighborhood and neighborhood solidarity were evident, despite high levels of mobility. In Berlin, the social and retail life of the streets contributed to this. In Nairobi, streets play the same role, while a territorialized ethnic identity reinforces attachment to an area. This ethnicization has recently deepened, impacting on the functioning of the tenement market and reducing tenant choice. In Berlin, the discrimination and later extermination of Jews from the tenement market (both as landlords and as tenants) provides a tragic parallel of ethnic-racial cleansing. A further dimension of division in Berlin's tenement market followed with the political separation of East from West Berlin and abolition of private tenement ownership in the East. A much delayed restitution process, which indirectly released properties into the hands of anonymous and often globalized capitalist entities with short-term interests, complemented direct state incentives for such entities to upgrade and dispose of individual tenement units, with significant impact on the tenement market.

Landlords of both Berlin's and Nairobi's low income tenement units provided only communal taps and latrines, and in Berlin many tenement rooms lacked heating. Close on a century beyond the end of tenement production, and in the context of considerable economic and demographic change, Berlin has seen on the one hand failed and abandoned modernist mass redevelopments, and on the other hand more successful tenement renovations including participatory approaches. Today upgrading, often state-subsidized, has provided most former working class tenement units with internal bathrooms and central heating. The improvement of infrastructure and services for Nairobi's tenements seems necessary and technically possible; the recent resurfacing of roads in Huruma signals long delayed public investment. But at the same time the little remaining public open space is grabbed and developed. Ironically, water shortages are more acute in the formally planned middle income Umoja Inner Core (and unplanned middle income tenement areas such as Zimmerman) than in low income Huruma, due to their location. The advantages of location, if accompanied by superior infrastructure as well as landlord investment in tenement improvement, may well trigger a wave of displacement of Huruma's lower income tenants.

Socio-spatial segregation in the tenement market, and the spatial peripheralization of the poor or working class, was an underdeveloped concern in Berlin's late 19th century housing discourse. Strangely, James Hobrecht and Friedrich Engels stand out as two lone voices that drew on the class-segregated English counterpart. Hobrecht pointed to implications of the extreme segregation of working class housing, and Engels to the intellectual implications (for occupants) of a typology that ties each working class family to 'hearth and home' in the cottage system. Hobrecht advocated for an improved mixed income tenement. Engels defended the 'rented dwelling' or tenement against the reformers who sought its abolition, but refrained from making suggestions for a housing policy, unwilling to project beyond a revolution. Nairobi's housing discourse has not developed interest in the tenement reality. As yet, it has not been necessary to defend the rented dwelling against serious calls for its abolition. Where such threats exist, these are dealt with through untransparent formations of political patronage or increasingly through the use of vigilantism. This leaves me then, in the last chapter, to point with caution to the relevance (as well as the limits) of more recent critical urban thought for Nairobi's tenement reality. I use the comparison with Berlin to reason and make a case for a tenement future.

Endnotes

1   While not commenting specifically on rental housing and its densities, K'Akumu (2006, 40) critiques the 'general inadequacy and irrelevance' of housing statistics in Kenya.

2   Stren (1972, 86) notes that in its early years, the rent tribunal (created in 1966) was 'extremely popular among tenants, [whose interests] are almost invariably upheld against landlords'.

3   We accessed one of the landlords through the kinship of acquaintances of the research collaborator and one through a foreman on a tenement building site. The other two landlords were friends of the latter landlord.

4   We avoided the sensitive topic of ethnic segregation in the tenement market.

5   A forerunner to HABRI, the Housing, Research and Development Unit, was established in 1966 at the University College (later University of Nairobi), 'supported largely by funds allocated through the [Housing] Ministry' (Stren 1972, 87).

6   The prevalence of rental tenancy in Indian cities in 1981 was 45 per cent (UNCHS 1996, 468), substantially lower than the equivalent figure for Nairobi, although Calcutta stands out with the prevalence of rental tenancy there at 76 per cent (Andreasen 1996, 361).

7   This trend is not restricted to Kenya's capital city – 82 per cent of Kisumu's households rent (UN-HABITAT 2003a, 10). The tenant populations of Kericho, Embu, Kiambu, Nakuru and Kitale all range between 82.9 per cent and 84.8 per cent. Mavoko stands out, with 91.2 per cent of the population renting, whereas towns such as Kakamega, Garissa, Moyale, Kilifi, Wajir and Mandera have a tenant population of between 28 per cent and 59.9 per cent (Syagga 2006, 320).

Chapter 9

Conclusion: Tenements as a future

This book is a comparison across time and space. It examines how an urban phenomenon, namely a private tenement market, unfolds and dominates housing over several decades in different stages of history (see Figure 3.6 in Chapter 3 and Figure 6.2 in Chapter 6), one preceding the advent of modernism in urban spatial thinking and planning, the other superseding and defying it. In so doing, the book asks questions about the place of tenements in the urban future.

Critical urban theory gives insights that help us to consider the relevance of the Berlin-Nairobi comparison for the future of Nairobi's tenements. The urban theory literature on which I draw is primarily about cities of the north. However, '[t]he multiplex city of the North is probably no longer that different from that in the South in terms of the variety and complexity of its socio-economic circuitry. As such, it escapes management through grand projects' (Amin and Graham 1997, 426). This certainly resonates with the failed modernization of Nairobi as well as the abandonment of tenement redevelopment in Berlin. Also with relevance for Nairobi's future, the cities of the 'South' and the 'global North' will increasingly share '[t]he politics of urban emancipation', particularly where societies are 'marked by massive unemployment, historically substantial but very incomplete proletarianization, disaffection, and industrial decline as well as particularly deeply etched patterns of social and spatial fragmentation' (Mabin 2000, 564).

In this chapter I avoid drawing comparative conclusions. Where relevant, I have pointed to these in the preceding chapters and I invite the reader to explore further connections between the two cities and across the eras. Here I ask what critical urban theory may suggest about the emergence of tenement markets in Berlin and Nairobi, a century apart. Can we use history to critically engage with the future? And why is this urgent for a city like Nairobi today? What do the historical shifts in tenements' legitimacy mean for a reasoning about the future of Nairobi's tenements? What is the place of planning and regulation within this reasoning? Can one responsibly encourage tenants to mobilize and articulate their own demands? And can we draw hope from the positive aspects of both space and socialization within Nairobi's tenement streets?

Nairobi's tenement market as a triumph of space over time

In constructing the comparison in this book, I did not find the linear progression or 'development' in the historical trajectory that modernist, positivist thought and policy assumes. A 'turning of the world's geography into the world's (single) history is implicit in many visions of modernist politics, from liberal progressive to some Marxist' (Massey 2005, 68). This single history involves understanding a certain un-modern condition as 'developing' or progressing in a predictable direction. Indeed, the 'idea of chronology' itself 'is totally modern' (Lyotard 1993, 171). For the study at hand, one could assume a chronological progression from earlier forms of urban housing, including private rental establishments or tenements in an open gridiron spatial order, to modern forms of suburban homeownership (or life in residential tower blocks) in the internalized spatial order of superblocks and neighborhood units. 'In these conceptions of singular progress (of whatever hue), temporality itself is not really open. The future is already foretold; inscribed into the story' (Massey 2005, 68). Further:

> The lack of openness of the future for those 'behind' in the queue is a function of the singularity of the trajectory. Ironically, not only is this temporal convening of the geography of modernity a repression of the spatial, it is also a repression of the possibility of other temporalities... the repression of the possibility of other trajectories (other, that is, than the stately progress towards modernity/modernisation/development on the Euro-Western model). (*ibid.*, 70)

The trajectory of urban housing in Nairobi does not fit any account of 'stately progression towards modernity', although, from within the modern tradition, one may assume (as policy-makers still clearly do) that such progression will unfold in the future. However, even the tenement market and its treatment in Berlin in the post-WWII decades, rooted as it was in the urban discourse of the early 20th century, did not progress neatly towards modernity. While a modern account of this history would refer to the positions of the urban reformers as a 'constructive' rather than 'destructive' discourse, the modernist idea of mass redevelopment lost legitimacy in the 1970s, and this led to the revaluing of qualities inherent in the historic tenements. And yet, the modern ideal of homeownership (inspiring the 'abolition of the rented dwelling' (Engels 1887/1935)) is finally realized through architectural modernization and sectional titling of the old tenements in the interest of short-term profit extraction. The individual units in Berlin's former tenements are marketed no doubt with a measure of 'postmodern nostalgia', which 'constitutively plays with notions of space and time' and in this form possibly 'robs others of their histories' (Massey 2005, 124) through gentrification and economic displacement.

In Nairobi, the official discourse on the tenement market is portrayed in housing policy and more recently in the *Nairobi Metro 2030* vision. It is largely one of denial, itself a form of 'repression' of the spatial presence of tenements – just as, according to Lyotard (1993, 171), forgetting amounts to 'repression of the past'. Kenya's official housing policy reflects the donor-imposed positivist idea of an urban society progressing towards a modern tenure form, namely homeowner-ship. It is peppered with state-of-the-art policy concepts. Yet actors in Nairobi have their own ways of responding to this repression, namely through defiance. From politicians to tenants, they understand the real trajectory, one that seemingly holds a future for the tenement market in Nairobi. There is 'some degree of autonomy' (Massey 2005, 71) from the imposed modernist planning and neoliberal housing policy concepts. In this way, the unfolding of Nairobi's tenement market can be seen as 'a victory of space over time', to borrow the words Doreen Massey (*ibid.*) uses to stress that while '[t]he multiplicities of the spatial have been rendered as merely stages in the temporal queue... the opposite *has* happened, and continues to happen, and with significant effects' (emphasis in the original).

Changing legitimacies in the history of tenements and their meaning for Nairobi's future

The concern over how we engage with our past and our future is central to critical urban theory. Although one should not 'deny the extraordinary power and impor-tance of historiography as a mode of critical emancipatory insight', 'historicism' has involved 'an implicit subordination of space to time' (Soja 1993, 140). 'Historicism' in this sense refers to 'an overdeveloped historical contextualisation of social life and social theory that actively submerges and peripheralizes the geographical or spatial imagination' (*ibid.*). My approach in this book has been to use history precisely to generate emancipatory insight. In order to construct a meaningful comparison in my study of tenements across time and space, it was necessary to contextualize the emergence of tenement markets (a century apart and on different continents) within their political economies. Although urban space has been central to my analysis, I have not subordinated this space to time. I have reviewed valuable urban spatial qualities as well as distortions, excesses and deprivations produced by tenement markets, irrespective of time. The distortions, as well as the qualities, inform(ed) urban discourse. In the case of contemporary Nairobi, a critical discourse is hidden, for instance, in popular lyrics. In the case of late 19th and early 20th century Berlin, the discourse was explicit in professional and political forums and in widely distrib-uted publications. The translation of ideas into official policies, programs and interventions depends on political agency, on a moment of infusion with political power. This is often preceded by the construction of normative legitimacy of that idea, irrespective of its actual relevance (many critics of modern spatial planning questioned the relevance of this 'idea' at a time when it enjoyed wide acceptance and normative legitimacy). In Nairobi today, the idea of modern spatial city planning is normatively legitimate only among an elite of politicians and consultants. Even there, one must question the sincerity of the normative statements that are issued. However, without indulging in modern chronological thinking, one must be aware that this may change. Regional competitiveness, as articulated in the *Nairobi Metro 2030* vision, encourages East African countries to look to Nigeria's capital Abuja to their north and South African cities to their south, world class branded and aspiring African cities (Ministry of Nairobi Metropolitan Development 2008, 13) in which a land-hungry and unsustainable modern spatial order continues to be rolled out. Those evicted to make way for this spatial order can stage only a weak challenge.[1]

For Nairobi, the real danger exists that destructive modernist ideas already articulated in *Nairobi Metro 2030* find unambiguous political support, agency and funding, and out-maneuver the much delayed implementation of a constitutional democracy that ought to encompass meaningful rights to democratic representation at city level and participation in decisions over the future of the city.[2] Given the unauthorized nature of Nairobi's tenement investment and the undemocratic decision-making for the city, the future of its tenement environments depends on political patronage. With the persistence of autocratic leadership on the part of Kenyan rulers, their 'winner-take-all' approach (Mueller 2008, 186) and the violence that is readily unleashed (for instance by stoking landlord-tenant tensions) to thwart opposition, the future of Nairobi's unauthorized tenements is at best uncertain. Precisely because of this uncertainty, and the dangers inherent in the professed vision, an active and progressive engagement with this future is urgent. I argue that this engagement should learn from the past. But, taking a warning from Foucault (1993, 166), it should learn only from a thorough analysis of the past, which would protect us from any assumption that there should be a return to the past, or in Foucault's words from an 'ideology of the return'. With resonance for simplistic borrowing from the past by the early 20th century housing reformers, Foucault illustrates this argument as follows: 'A good study of peasant architecture in Europe... would show the utter vanity of wanting to return to the little individual house with its thatched roof' (*ibid.*). Foucault appeals instead to the critical thought that would ask: '*What* is this Reason that we use? What are its historical effects? What are its limits, and what are its dangers?' (*ibid.*, 165, emphasis in the original).

My interest in this book has been in the reasoning in the late 19th and early 20th century on how to deal with Berlin's tenement market, and the translation of this reasoning into policy and planning proposals, experiments, legislative change and, decades later, large-scale redevelopment programs. My interest has also been in the effects of this reasoning. It shaped normative thinking, and in so doing weakened the normative legitimacy of tenements, of their production (and of the 19th century style of tenement management), and of the typology reproduced. By 1925, it had led to a removal of the legal legitimacy of tenement production, resulting in an end to the expansion of Berlin's tenement stock and henceforth its episodic as well as gradual reduction and transformation.

Tenements in Nairobi have never enjoyed legal legitimacy. Their lack of normative legitimacy is evident in the denial of their existence in urban discourse and policy documents. This means that the future of tenements depends to a large extent on their pragmatic legitimacy, on a collective recognition of the fact that they provide shelter for large numbers of people and a source of income (legitimate or otherwise) mainly for others. Tied to the latter more than the former is the untransparent political legitimacy of landlords and their practices. This legitimacy, I have argued, is at best fragile. Once attention is drawn to the risks and inadequacies of tenement living, and once this enters the normative framework of international agencies and their expert consultants, a destructive discourse may be unleashed. Furthermore, any simplistic association of Nairobi's tenement-scape with pre-modernist urban form will antagonize the political proponents of a futuristic vision for 2030 and beyond. Instead, attention must be drawn very carefully to the reality of tenements, to their inherent qualities as well as to their dangers. Attention must also be drawn to the fact that their 19th century counterparts were recognized as upgradeable and therefore of relevance to the urban future. Even if Kenya should experience an economic growth that distributes increases in income across its different classes, Nairobi's tenements would not be rendered obsolete. If not converted into more comfortable dwellings, they would play an important role in absorbing much of the current population of single-story 'slums'. Perhaps above all, attention needs to be drawn to the access that tenements provide, today and into the future, to a city like Nairobi.

The need to acknowledge the process through which Nairobi's tenements are produced

Plan and regulation have always been hugely ineffective in guiding the way Nairobi has been built. Reform, where it was attempted, never aimed at meeting reality. Yet one may still argue that some form of regulation will be necessary in the future. On the one hand, the excesses of greedy landlords and the accompanying risks to tenants must be curbed. On the other hand, tenement investment deserves a measure of certainty through regulation. And similarly, new lower income tenement investment opportunities, once opened up and guided through appropriate planning in convenient locations, would discourage the excesses found particularly in the current lower income tenement market. One can argue that the correct form of regulation and planning would be in most people's interest. However, the challenge is to plan and regulate *with* the *de facto* city-building process, rather than to assume that this can be replaced by standard northern visioning and planning orthodoxy.

This has two implications. Firstly this process must be understood before appropriate regulation and guidance can be designed. Secondly, the real interests in the tenement market must be represented in a transparent way in decision-making on such regulation, so that it may stand a chance of being accepted politically at all levels. I return to the latter below. In terms of the existing process, many aspects of the city-building process are not transparent but are nevertheless understood by their role players, including officials. Everyone actively involved knows how the process works. Building control officials are aware of how farcical their formal functions are, when neither formal regulations nor reform initiatives bear any relation to the building process and typology that has been unfolding quite legitimately over the decades. Many officials themselves live in tenement environments and experience their density. They are aware of the benefits of such an environment – the convenience, conviviality and livelihood opportunities of street-level retail – and of the locational advantage that thousands of tenants enjoy on every hectare of well located tenement development. They also understand the burdens that unchecked densification places on tenants, and could meaningfully suggest the infrastructural improvements required. They themselves may have an untransparent interest in the tenement market, having played their part in adjusting the official rules to the real game at play. They too may own one or more tenements, and may be playing by the rules of that very game.

Nairobi's tenement districts are constructed in defiance of official plans and of the conventional role that planners would play, particularly in enforcing zoning and building regulations. Instead, a spontaneous constellation of economic benefits finds expression. It has been argued that the very fact that planners exist 'shows market society's distrust that spontaneous economic and social activity can express itself in a beautiful city, let alone a habitable or efficient one' (Mabin 2000, 557). While one would be stretching reality by calling Nairobi's tenement east 'beautiful', and while sheer density currently creates inconvenient congestion and limits habitability, it must be acknowledged that the compact built form holds possibilities for a convenient, economically vibrant and energy-efficient urban future.[3] As the threats of climate change chisel away at orthodox spatial planning norms, tenement-dominated Nairobi may be a better city than those shaped by the 'perverse and destructive' effects of '[r]ational planning in the service of humane projects', and which have led to the argument that 'if planning inflames the illness it is supposed to cure, it would seem prudent to stop planning altogether' (Hoch 1992, 207, 212, quoted in Mabin 2000, 559). This argument refers to modern planning. There are of course participatory, inclusive and emancipatory forms of planning and decision-making (UN-HABITAT 2009) that must not be dismissed. However, in a context like Nairobi they have limitations to which I briefly return below.

Real knowledge of the process at work in Nairobi's housing market is excluded from the performance acted out over the decades on the farcical (though, for some, well intentioned) stage of official policy-making, regulatory reform and planning. Here another set of actors, well paid consultants, advisors, donor employees and their counterparts in foreign-funded NGOs derive livelihoods that afford them the choice to inhabit exclusive, often walled-in parts of Nairobi. They can live in Nairobi in ignorance of the real housing process, under the illusion that their proposals for neoliberal homeownership-based policy and modernist plans and rules can in fact be implemented. While developing western- or even Asian-inspired mortgage or micro-finance systems for the homeownership that they intend for the poor, they are unaware that most of Nairobi's housing stock is miraculously built by a range of private investors with only short-term debt, if any. It is owned by and provides financial security for an undefined class of indigenous capitalists who choose to invest locally and who contribute substantially to the urban economy, unacknowledged in official statistics. Though directed at cities of the US, Amin and Graham's (1997, 427) economic argument for a 'just city' can be used to underline the importance of this indigenous entrepreneurship in Nairobi: 'a sense of place and belonging taps into hidden potential and the sources of social confidence that lie at the core of risk-taking entrepreneurial activity'. This statement speaks to the way Nairobi is built, though only with distortions of a 'just' city in the making.

Ordinary Kenyan academics, who are not part of the ethno-political academic elite, have had to choose between meager university salaries similar to those of municipal officials, and therefore a home in the tenement market, or a career as policy and research consultants, reproducing the predetermined knowledge that international donors ask for. A choice of the latter enables them financially to escape into blinkered existence. Without wanting to claim that I have done so in any significant way, it seems that few urban academics in Kenya are in a position that allows them to bridge realities, produce a critical understanding of the city (beyond building materials research called for by the Ministry of Housing or 'slum' surveys commissioned by donors) and influence an urban discourse. This is a burden that a younger generation of Kenyan urban academics is acutely aware of.

An important process that intersects with city-building (though leaving the class of advisors and consultants largely unaffected) is that of ethno-vigilantism. Its growing control over urban processes gradually undermines the indigenous urban economy, increasing the risk inherent in entrepreneurialism, while also lending raw power where demanded for political reasons or where needed to directly assert economic interests. Perhaps the most valuable insight on Nairobi's city-making process and its shifts is found among ordinary tenants, who adapt and find ways of ordering their lives around these intensifying realities.

The need to recognize the urban qualities created through Nairobi's tenement investment

The remarkable spinoff of this fraught situation is the production of a truly urban city, one with an urbanism that has no counterpart in societies that chose, like South African and other southern African cities, to adhere to Anglophone modern town planning principles. In Nairobi, an urban economic logic that involves many players and a diversity of investors is given space to play itself out. It is the same economic logic, it seems, that has underlain tenement markets wherever they have emerged in the context of unrelenting demand. When given free range, it results in excesses (ultimately self-regulated), as residential units are stacked in spatial arrangements that entail risk to health and life. At the same time, a chain of benefits are accrued in this city-building process. Space is created, imbued with economic opportunity. Access to location (shared by over 5 000 people on each hectare of the Huruma sample area and its surrounds) provides convenience, although thwarted by congestion and over-burdened services. Vulnerability arises from the danger lurking in building height, the accompanying architectural excesses along with inadequate building maintenance, and the crime that is facilitated in the anonymity of congested pedestrian traffic.

Here I need to acknowledge that my study contains a bias in the tenement areas I chose to home in on. Had I instead examined the completely unplanned, haphazardly developed and more peripherally located and therefore less convenient tenement districts of Nairobi such as Githurai, my conclusions might not have pointed to the same urban qualities and vulnerabilities. Nevertheless, the sample areas in Huruma and Umoja Inner Core represent large parts of Nairobi's compact north-east as they currently unfold. And both Huruma and Umoja Inner Core are still in the process of being shaped. There is no certainty of an end state.

In Berlin, society has revalued the urban qualities and convenience of dense residential-commercial districts. But for most younger cities, especially those in the southern hemisphere, such qualities remain thwarted by adherence to modern and more recently 'world class' city visions, plans and strategies. This is exemplified by the continental urban giant, post-apartheid Johannesburg, colossal in the land it consumes. As in Sennett's (1974, 136) description of 19th century London, Johannesburg 'smears itself' across an ever larger territory. There the city is shaped by planners playing to the investment interests of large developers, if not foreign investors, whereas the state subsidizes inconvenient homeownership on the urban periphery for the fortunate poor. The rest are left to fend for themselves in sprawling informal settlements, awaiting a turn to access and own politically legitimized urban inconvenience (Huchzermeyer 2010). In Johannesburg, bogus landlords exploit dilapidated modernist rental skyscrapers of a bygone era and convert former (abandoned) commercial skyscrapers into rental stock. This is in convenient locations, but provides quality only in the partly treed (but car-dominated), inherited streetscape and former investment in inner-city urban infrastructure. Technologically, the elevator has enabled a development height that prevents any comparison between these environments in Johannesburg and Nairobi's tenement districts, or for that matter the complex urbanism that was 'mortally wounded' (Lefebvre, 1974/1991, 312), for instance, by Haussmann's intervention in 19th century Paris.

The need to channel existing tenement interests into urban spatial decision-making

The tenement history of the west provides pointers as to how present-day tenement actors may be managed and their investment guided. Berlin's history suggests it is possible to plan spatially for a tenement market. The city's 1862 Plan was not merely the product and vision of a planner, but incorporated the interests of speculators through their direct representation in the decision-making structures. The street layout and its subsequent distortions into extremely large blocks and large properties produced some inconvenience for pedestrians. This has been moderated by an efficient public transport system, relying heavily on the compact urban form. While the 1862 Plan primarily guided land subdivision for tenement investment, it also secured generous streetscapes and attractive, visually contained open spaces, which are entirely lacking in Nairobi's east. Could the actors in Nairobi's tenement market be brought together to inform a tenement plan for that city? Could their interests be mediated by tenant representation and by careful spatial planning and regulatory proposals? Would this secure the existing investment and steer new tenement investment into areas designed and serviced with dense tenement construction in mind? Could the reproduction of excesses in this market be prevented without creating unfair advantage or privilege for the beneficiaries of the existing excesses?

Predating Berlin's 1862 Plan, the city authorities had tuned minimalist building regulations to the reality of tenement investment and construction. These regulations focused on one important dimension, namely the risk of fire. Due to their strict enforcement, they enjoyed respect from tenement investors. Once tightened, the regulations successfully reined in certain excesses in tenement design (though self-regulation was sometimes ahead of regulatory amendments) and to some extent improved living conditions in the tenements that were subsequently built. The literature gives little insight into the implications this had for landlords' returns. What we do know is that while land speculation in Berlin was extremely profitable and directly depended on anticipated rental returns that could be made on any given plot, tenement construction was nowhere as lucrative as it has been in Nairobi over the past three decades. In Nairobi, the enforcement of current building regulations would result in demolition of most of the multi-story tenement stock. Alignment of building regulations with the existing typologies would be pointless, if the purpose were not also to effectively redress and prevent the worst excesses. *Post facto* regulation in Nairobi's tenement market, if this were possible, would present a technical challenge and would call for innovation. No matter how innovative, such regulation and adjustment would interfere with entrenched economic and political interests. Any reduction in profitability would stand the danger of diverting indigenous investment into other sectors. An abandonment of existing tenement investment and slow-down in tenement construction would result in increased overcrowding and decay of existing tenements, precisely when the intention is to improve the situation. Clues for a better tenement future may more realistically lie in the existing process of self-regulation, possibly in combination with incentives, rather than in the enforcement of revised regulation. However, the question remains: who has sufficient will and power to lead such a process?

In Nairobi, indigenous capitalism, entrepreneurship and indeed tenement investment enjoy an inherent legitimacy. There, it is acceptable to be a landlord (though you might choose not to admit it) and 'it's OK to rent'. Urban property ownership, even in the form of one- or two-roomed sectional title units in a single-story condominium in Umoja II, has been recognized as a basis for tene-ment investment. Exceptions are in the controlled, gated estates (of which some are located in Nairobi's south-east) and elite suburban neighborhoods to the west. Perhaps it is fortunate that a global crisis is currently requiring policy-makers in the US, the primary promoters of the homeownership orthodoxy (cornerstone of the so-called 'American dream'), to reconsider this ideal and acknowledge that 'it's OK to rent'. In this moment, is it thinkable that decision-makers in Nairobi would stand up to their homeownership-pounding donors and policy advisors and say 'we're a rental city' or even 'a tenement city' and 'we're about to plan and regulate or create incentives for multi-story indigenous private investment in convenient, affordable and sustainable accommodation'? Or must the city rely on its politicians to continue paying lip service to donor-promoted urban concepts while allowing the city to reproduce itself according to the entrenched but unwritten rules? The latter, I argue, is a fragile option. The former requires a legitimate place for land-lord representation at the planning and decision-making table. It needs to accept the unclear position of officials in the current city-building process, and provide a place for their insights, roles and interests to be represented.

Where does this leave tenants? The adoption of a tenement plan for Nairobi may open up new, well located or well connected areas for regulated/incentiv-ized, multi-functional tenement investment that minimizes risk for all involved, incorporates safety precautions and respects the need for open spaces and public utilities. This would result in greater consumer choice for tenants, but would tenants experience this as liberating, and as allowing 'the exercise of their freedom' that Foucault (1993, 163) calls for? It may be argued that in Nairobi's context, tenant emancipation or aspiration of freedom requires rent strikes, tenant mobili-zation and agitation. Speaking to a very different context, that of Paris in the 1960s, Lefebvre (1968/1996, 179) called for the working class to take control of planning – '[u]ntil then, transformations remain superficial'. The right to the city forms part of Lefebvre's normative conceptualization. Harvey (2004, 239), considering how a right to the city might materialize, warns that

> [t]hose that now have the rights will not necessarily surrender them willingly... This does not necessarily mean violence (though, sadly, it often comes down to that). But it does mean the mobilization of sufficient power through political organisation or in the streets if necessary to change things.

Amin and Graham (1997, 423–424) call for two 'political-institutional shifts' towards achieving a just city. Firstly, 'purposeful action on the part of the state to meet basic needs as well as to encourage open and "dialogic" urban governance; and secondly, a particular civic democracy centred around creating real opportunities for communities to develop voice and self-determination'. While compelling, these ring hollow for tenants in present-day Nairobi. However, Amin and Graham (*ibid.*, 426) do not assume a 'cosy civic relationship with the state or with established economic and social associations'. They argue that where democratic structures do not exist, 'movements *are* the voice of democracy' (*ibid.*, emphasis in the original). But in Nairobi, growing ethno-vigilantism makes up a large part of civil society, expressing its interest in an un-benign manner, and certainly not as the voice of democracy. In Nairobi, tenants' demand for a substantial shift in decision-making power over the city is unlikely to be met without the opponents resorting to the violent services of vigilante gangs. Among Nairobi's tenants, the 'potentially emancipatory aspect of urban life – the ability to organise collectively' (DeFilippis and North 2004, 77) is not a given. After the 2008 post-election violence in Kenya, 'issue-based organisation [has become] more challenging' (Klopp 2008, 309). In this context, how can tenants have conferred on them 'an active right to make the city more in accord with [their] heart's desire, and to remake [themselves] thereby in a different image' (Harvey 2004, 239)?

My conclusion is that currently, it would be irresponsible to expect tenants of Nairobi's north-east to lead the demand for a change in the way the city is planned and regulated. For Nairobi today, one cannot speak lightly of promoting tenant mobilization or even tenant participation. It is only once the concerns of those with economic interests vested (legitimately or otherwise) in the tenement market are transparently represented and given a legitimate or formal outlet, that tenants can organize and constructively engage with these interests, and act to moderate them without being silenced through violent revenge. This raises the question: what about the un-benign formations of civil society, the gangs who have begun to claim their own extractive stake in the tenement-building processes, while still ambiguously offering landlords and politicians the services of tenant repression (and *vice versa*) when these are demanded? Will a constitutional state have the power to reverse and subvert this formation, or to divert it into pursuing a profitable but benign interest in a planned and regulated tenement market? Among all of this, there remains an important role for sensitive urbanists and planners in appealing to reason. Here a careful study of cities and history can inform reasoning on the future of Nairobi.

Public space and the right to the city in a critical reasoning for Nairobi's future

Jacobs (1961, 6) appeals to urban planners to learn from cities – from what she refers to as the 'immense laboratory of trial and error, failure and success' that cities represent. She argues that 'practitioners and teachers of this discipline... have ignored the study of the success and failure in real life, have been incurious about the reasons for unexpected success, and are guided instead by principles derived from... anything but cities themselves' (*ibid.*). Indeed, key principles of modern planning were derived from machines, not only in the flows and connections that the motor vehicle enabled, but also in the rather abstract idea that the city consists of separable functions and activities that are linked to one another. This is a component of Sennett's (1971/1996, 95) criticism of modern planning, which he finds rooted in the course that Haussmann set in motion for Paris. Hausmann's 'first precept' was 'that the changes in one urban sphere of activity should change other spheres of activity'. Urban planning adopted this precept in its assumption that 'the significant functioning of the city itself is found in the links between specific activities in the city' (*ibid.*). Thus for urban planning, '[it] is not what people do or experience in their own lives that counts, but the external relationship of these acts to areas of indirect experience that is the focus' (*ibid.*). Sennett likens this approach to 'the design of machines', and asks 'how can it be justified in the affairs of men?' (*ibid.*). He promotes instead a 'disordered city' that forces people 'to deal with each other'. But, while invoking this disordered city, he also distances himself from Jane Jacobs, criticizing her for wanting to see an urban condition of a past era, namely high density and mixed use and with it 'intimate relations between neighbours in city life... restored' (*ibid.*, 51). From the affluent west of the late 1960s and early 1970s, Sennett's view at the time was that '[t]his revival... shall never be; we need to find some condition of urban life appropriate for an affluent, technological era' (*ibid.*). Here he displayed both northern parochialism and modernist chronological assumptions about the urban future, assumptions that may no longer hold for the recession-struck north and certainly never have for peripheral cities like Nairobi.

If we are to learn from the 'immense laboratory' of existing cities, there is certainly more to be asked about 19th and 20th century Berlin that is of relevance to the tenement challenge in Nairobi, in other cities in Africa and elsewhere. There are many dimensions of the economy of Berlin's tenement investment over one-and-a-half centuries, including the role of ground floor retail within this economy, that could be used to develop a critical reasoning about future economic trajectories for Nairobi's mixed use tenements. Contrasting these with the economies of less densely developed cities could also challenge entrenched norms about ideal cities, as would the analysis of more and less ordered cities. In addition, the trajectory of less regulated tenement cities such as New York, and their transition from corrupt to more orderly forms of governance, are of relevance to Nairobi. Such an enquiry would raise important questions on the role of politicians and political patronage which this book does not address.

Jacobs' and Sennett's arguments were born in the 1960s in response to utopian modern planning, at the point when its post-WWII legitimacy had just begun to be challenged. They are set off by more recent calls for a return to utopianism. However, this implies a new meaning for the word 'utopia', not as the unachievable ideal, but as a positive, inspiring alternative. For instance, Harvey (2004, 237) argues that 'we cannot do without utopian ideals of justice. They are indispensible for motivation and for action. Alternative ideas coupled with outrage at injustice have long animated the quest for social change.' Pinder (2005, 264) discusses different strands in current utopian approaches to city planning. On the one hand, there are '[u]topias based on fixed urban forms', providing a 'secure picture of the future through plans that rule out change or uncertainty'. However, 'their attempt to lock in that future through closed schemes is dangerously restrictive' (*ibid.*). On the other hand, there are 'open and exploratory forms of utopianism', emerging from

> critical currents of utopian thinking... opposed to the closed, formal blueprints of traditional utopias. It is a utopianism that addresses the possibilities for shifts in consciousness and for radical change. But it is explicitly partial and accepts that struggle, conflict as well as ambiguity and flux are necessary and need to be acknowledged. (*ibid.*)

Mitchell (2003, 234, reviewing Harvey 2000) contrasts the utopia of 'spatial form' with that of 'social process', which he argues is 'a much more complex form of utopia than utopia of spatial form'. This utopia of process includes 'the dream of a full democratic and inclusive public space' (*ibid.*, 235). It is the motivating utopia of process to realize a 'right to the city' that has inspired progressive Brazilians to advance towards a legislative framework incorporating this notion, while also playing a central role in proposing and in lobbying the UN for the adoption of a 'World Charter on the Right to the City'. In his article on 'constructing the right to the city in Brazil', Fernandes (2007, 202) invites other countries to learn from the Brazilian laboratory of developing the right to the city as a 'legal right'. The Brazilian experience is relevant for Nairobi. Resonating with the Kenyan situation, in Brazil there was 'no way urban reform [could] be promoted... without the promotion of a profound legal-political reform' (*ibid.*, 204).

Mitchell (2003, 235) emphasizes the role of public space in realizing the right to the city. It 'is not only the space where the right to the city is struggled over; it is where it is implemented and represented' (*ibid.*). Amin and Graham (1997, 422) expand:

> As shared spaces, [public spaces] can play an important role in helping to develop a civic culture that combines self-belief and autonomy rooted in widespread practice of citizenship rights with the potential for tolerance and cultural exchange offered by mingling with strangers.

Nairobi, located as it is in Kenyan politics and governance, presents significant challenges for the autonomous practice of citizenship rights. At the same time, public space is always at risk of being grabbed or suffocated by relentless tenement construction. Yet it must be recognized that this very construction process, unlike that of gated estates, produces public spaces by creating a stage for 'everyday street life', which is 'the mainspring of... a shared public culture... because it is at the level of everyday social practices that social vitality and culture of socialization, talk, negotiation and understandings are produced' (Amin and Graham 1997, 422, citing Zukin 1995). This positive reality must be used as a justification for the typology, of course not for construction on land set aside for public use.

Amin and Thrift (2004) provide another positive insight, which gives value to a seemingly insignificant observation from my fieldwork in Nairobi's tenement districts. I have presented interview extracts from my discussions with a cross-ethnic group of friends who had grown up together in the mushrooming tenement environment of the Huruma sample area (see Figure 8.21 in Chapter 8). We were also told of friendship among women sharing limited tenement space and facilities. A group of 'idle friends' had started a refuse collection group. And friendships among landlords enabled our access to more than one landlord interviewee. Amin and Thrift (2004, 234) infuse this reality with some hope:

> Friendship and friendship-based associations have become an increasingly important element of the urban social glue, many of whose pleasures lie in simply relating to others. Even though the forging of the bonds of friendship may be the result of the increasing emphasis on relationship as a value in itself, such bonds also take us back to the very roots of cities as sites of association, and through this, political organisation. Thus what may seem routine, even trivial, may have all manner of political resonances that we are only just beginning to understand – and mobilize.

In Nairobi grassroots and friendship-based initiatives among tenants currently perceive landlords as preventing them from improving the standard of tenement accommodation. However, they creatively occupy tenement spaces, whether simply using balconies, corridors, streets, shops and leftover spaces to relate to one another, or doing so more formally through volunteer schools or environmental projects – the two friendship-based initiatives that I came across in the Huruma sample area. It is such groups, in addition to Nairobi's urban and public intellectuals, the many direct stakeholders in Nairobi's tenement market, and (perhaps unfairly dismissed and neglected in this book) reflective consultants and employees of bi- and multilateral agencies, who must develop a critical reasoning for Nairobi's future. I hope that they will all find the provocations in this book of help.

A critical reasoning for Nairobi's future must acknowledge the tenement reality, both in the process through which it is reproduced, with its inherent interests, and in its implicit spatial qualities. The existing interests in tenement gains have to be channeled into formal decision-making processes before one can responsibly encourage tenants to mobilize and articulate their own demands. Procedural reform towards inclusion in transparent decision-making requires the inclusion first of the powerful, then of the disempowered, before a right to the city can be formalized. However, any discussion on the right to the city in Nairobi must recognize positive aspects in space and in socialization, as well as in indigenous investment within Nairobi's tenement districts. It is the existing space and social-ization, despite ethnic division, that provides the inspiration for the procedural reforms that may secure a dense, convenient, cosmopolitan, energy-efficient and livable future for Nairobi.

Endnotes

1   Durban, Nairobi and Abuja have also been proud hosts of the African Ministerial Conference on Housing and Urban Development, since its inception in 2005.
2   *Nairobi Metro 2030* claims that consultations were held with all stakeholders (Ministry of Nairobi Metropolitan Development 2008, 12), but there is no evidence of ideas having been adopted from such consultations.
3   It is often observed that Nairobi is no longer the 'green city in the sun', the colonial-modernist ideal of a beautiful city (Nyairo 2006, 75, 88).

References

Adam, T. 2007. 'Stiften in deutschen Bürgerstädten vor dem Ersten Weltkrieg: Das Beispiel Leipzig.' *Geschichte und Gesellschaft* 33: 46–72.

Aluanga, L. 2009. 'Maasai fighting to keep the city at bay.' *East African Standard*, March 22.

Amin, A. and S. Graham. 1997. 'The ordinary city.' *Transactions of the Institute of British Geographers* 22(4): 411–429.

Amin, A. and N. Thrift. 2004. 'The "emancipatory" city?' In *The Emancipatory City? Paradoxes and Possibilities*, edited by L. Lees, 232–235 London: Sage Publications.

Amis, P. 1984. 'Squatters or tenants: The commercialisation of unauthorised housing in Nairobi.' *World Development* 12(1): 87–96.

------. 1987. 'Migration, urban poverty and the housing market: the Nairobi case.' In *Migrants, Workers and the Social Order* edited by J. Eades, 249–268. ASA Monographs 26. London: Tavistock Publications.

------. 1988. 'Commercialized rental housing in Nairobi, Kenya.' In *Spontaneous Shelter: International Perspectives and Prospects*, edited by C. Patton, 235–257. Philadelphia: Temple University Press.

------. 1996. 'Long-run trends in Nairobi's informal housing market.' *Third World Planning Review* 18(3): 271–285.

Anderson, D. 2002. 'Vigilantes, violence and the politics of public order in Kenya.' *African Affairs* 101: 531–555.

------. 2003. 'The battle of Dandora Swamp: Reconstructing the Mau Mau Land Freedom Army October 1954. In *Mau Mau & Nationhood: Arms, Authority & Narration* edited by A. Odhiambo and J. Lonsdale, 155–175. Oxford: James Currey; Nairobi: Eastern African Educational Publishers; Athens, Ohio: Ohio University Press.

Andreasen, J. 1996. 'Urban tenants and community involvement.' *Habitat International* 20(3): 359–365.

Anyang' Nyong'o, P. 2007. *A Leap into the Future: A Vision for Kenya's Socio-political Transformation*. Nairobi: African Research and Resource Forum.

Aron, M. 2009a. 'Proposed law to lock out errant contractors.' *East African Standard*, October 25.

------. 2009b. 'There are only 50 qualified urban planners.' *East African Standard*, October 25.

Aseka, E. 1990. 'Urbanisation.' In *Themes in Kenyan History*, edited by W. Ochieng, 44–67. Nairobi: Heinemann Kenya; London: James Currey; Athens, Ohio: Ohio University Press.

Barbey, G. 1984. *Wohn-Haft: Essay über die Interne Geschichte der Massenwohnung.* Braunschweig und Wiesbaden: Friedrich Vieweg und Sohn.

Becker, C. and B. Jacob. 1992. *Der Stephankiez: Ein Altbauquartier im Wandel.* Berlin: Transit Buchverlag.

Berman, B. 1992. 'Up from structuralism.' In *Unhappy Valley: Conflict in Kenya and Africa. Book One: State and Class,* edited by B. Berman and J. Lonsdale, 179–223. Nairobi: Heinemann Kenya; London: James Currey; Athens, Ohio: Ohio University Press.

Bernet, C. 2004. 'The "Hobrecht Plan" (1862) and Berlin's urban structure.' *Urban History* 31(3): 400–419.

Berning, M., M. Braun, E. Daldrup and K. Schulz. 1994. *Berliner Wohnquartiere: Ein Führer durch 60 Siedlungen in Ost und West.* Berlin: Dietrich Reimer Verlag.

Bigsten, A. 1993. 'Regulations versus price reforms in crisis management: the case of Kenya.' In *Economic crisis in Africa: Perspectives on Policy Responses,* edited by M. Blomström and M. Lundahl, 61–74. London: Routledge.

Bigsten, A. and D. Durevall. 2006. 'Openness and wage inequality in Kenya 1964–2000.' *World Development* 34(3): 465–480.

Birch, E. 1998. 'Tenement House Law of 1867.' In *The Encyclopedia of Housing,* edited by W. van Vliet, 585. London: Sage Publications.

Bodenschatz, H. 1987. *Platz Frei für das Neue Berlin! Geschichte der Stadterneuerung.* Berlin: Transit.

------. 1990. 'Die "Mietskasernenstadt" in der Kritik des 20. Jahrhunderts.' In *Berlin: Erfahrungen, Beispiele, Perspektiven,* edited by Senatsverwaltung für Bau- und Wohnungswesen, Stadterneuerung, 19–25. Berlin: Senatsverwaltung für Bau- und Wohnungswesen.

------. 2008. 'Städtebau von den neunziger Jahren des 19. Jahrhunderts bis zum Ersten Weltkrieg. 1890–1918.' In *Berlin und seine Bauten: Teil 1 – Städtebau,* edited by H. Bodenschatz, J. Düwel, N. Gutschow, and H. Stimmann, 15–112. Berlin: Dom Verlag.

------. 2010. *Berlin Urban Design: A Brief History.* Berlin: Dom Publishers.

Brockhaus. 1968. *Der Neue Brockhaus: Lexikon und Wörterbuch. Vierter Band.* Wiesbaden: F.A. Brockhaus.

Bujra, J. 1973. *Pumwani: The Politics of Property. A Study of an Urban Renewal Scheme in Nairobi, Kenya.* Report on a research project sponsored by the Social Science Research Council. Department of Anthropology and Sociology, School of Oriental and African Studies, University of London.

Bunnell, T. and A. Nah. 2004. 'Counter-global cases for place: contesting displacement in globalising Kuala Lumpur.' *Urban Studies* 14(12): 2447–2467.

Castells, M. 1983. *The City and the Grassroots.* Berkeley, CA.: University of California Press.

Central Bureau of Statistics. 2001. *1999 Population and Housing Census 'Counting People for Development'. Volume 1: Population Distribution by Administrative Areas and Urban Centres.* Nairobi: Central Bureau of Statistics, Ministry of Planning and National Development.

------. 2004. *Kenya Demographic and Health Survey (KDHS) 2003*. Nairobi and Calverton, USA: Central Bureau of Statistics, Ministry of Health, Kenya Medical Research Institute, National Council for Population and Development, Centre for Disease Control and Prevention and ORC Macro.

------. 2009. 'Population and Housing Statistics: Population Projections by Province.' Nairobi: Central Bureau of Statistics, Ministry of Planning and National Development. Accessed June 15, 2009. http://www.cbs.go.ke.

Chattopadhyay, P. 1991. 'Economic content of socialism in Lenin: Is it the same as in Marx?' *Economic and Political Weekly* 26(4): PE2–5 and PE7–8.

Cheeseman, N. 2008. 'The Kenyan elections of 2007: an introduction.' *Journal of Eastern African Studies* 2(2): 166–184.

Chege, M. 1981. 'A tale of two slums: electoral politics in Mathare and Dagoretti.' *Review of Political Economy* 20: 74–88.

Chokor, B. 2005. 'Changing urban housing form and organization in Nigeria: lessons for community planning.' *Planning Perspectives* 20: 69–96.

Clark, B. and J. Foster. 2006. 'The environmental conditions of the working class: An introduction to selections from Frederick Engels's *The Condition of the Working Class in England in 1844.*' *Organization and Environment* 19(3): 375–388.

COHRE (Centre on Housing Rights and Evictions). 2005. *Listening to the Poor? Housing Rights in Nairobi, Kenya*. Consultation Report, Fact-Finding Mission to Nairobi, Kenya. Geneva: Centre on Housing Rights and Evictions.

------. 2008, *Business as Usual? Housing Rights and Slum Eviction in Durban, South Africa*. Geneva: Centre on Housing Rights and Evictions.

COHRE and SERAC (Social and Economic Rights Action Centre). 2008. *The Myth of the Abuja Master Plan: Forced Evictions as Urban Planning in Abuja*. Geneva and Lagos: Centre on Housing Rights and Evictions and Social and Economic Rights Action Centre.

Crowder, G. 1991. *Classical Anarchism: The Political Thought of Godwin, Proudhon, Bakunin and Kropotkin*. Oxford: Clarendon Press.

Daily Nation. 1999. 'Moi blames Karura violence on hatred and tribalism.' *Daily Nation*, February 2.

------. 2009. 'Lobby calls for forum on Kenyan reforms.' *Daily Nation*, April 13.

Daunton, M. 1983. *House and Home in the Victorian City: Working Class Housing 1850–1914*. London: Edward Arnold.

Day, J. 1999. *Tenement Housing and Landlord Activism in New York City, 1890–1943*. New York: Columbia University Press.

DeFilippis, J. and P. North. 2004. 'The emancipatory community? Place, politics and collective action in cities.' In *The Emancipatory City? Paradoxes and Possibilities*, edited by L. Lees, 72–88. London: Sage Publications.

Dennis, R. 1995. 'Landlords and housing in the depression.' *Housing Studies* 10(3): 305–325.

De Troyer, F. 1991. 'Architectural Form and the Use of Resources.' International Workshop on Housing Development, Nairobi, 24 May–8 June.

Dubresson, A. 1997. Abidjan: from the public making of a modern city to urban management of a metropolis. In *The Urban Challenge in Africa: Growth and*

Management of its Large Cities, edited by C. Rakodi, 252–291. New York: United Nations University Press.

Durand-Lasserve, A. 2006. 'Market-driven evictions and displacements: implications for the perpetuation of informal settlements in developing cities.' In *Informal Settlements: A Perpetual Challenge?* edited by M. Huchzermeyer and A. Karam, 165–179. Cape Town: University of Cape Town (UCT) Press.

East African Standard. 2009. 'Officers question Mungiki leader.' *East African Standard,* May 1.

Edozie, R. 2008. 'New trends in democracy and development: democratic capitalism in South Africa, Nigeria and Kenya.' *Politikon* 35(1): 43–67.

Edwards, M. 1990. 'Rental housing and the urban poor: Africa and Latin America compared.' In *Housing Africa's Urban Poor,* edited by P. Amis and P. Lloyd, 253–272. Manchester: Manchester University Press.

Elkins, T. with B. Hofmeister. 1988. *Berlin: The Spatial Structure of a Divided City.* London and New York: Methuen.

Engels, F. 1935 (first published 1887). *The Housing Question.* London: Martin Lawrence.

Engels, F. 1958 (first published 1845). *The Condition of the Working Class in England.* Oxford: Basil Blackwell.

Etherton, D. 1971. *Mathare Valley: A Case Study of Uncontrolled Settlement in Nairobi.* Housing Research and Development Unit, University of Nairobi, Nairobi.

Fernandes, E. 2007. 'Constructing the "right to the city" in Brazil.' *Social and Legal Studies* 16(2): 201–219.

Ferudi, F. 1989. *The Mau Mau War in Perspective.* London: James Currey; Nairobi: Heinemann Kenya; Athens, Ohio: Ohio University Press.

Forsell, H. 2006. *Property, Tenancy and Urban Growth in Stockholm and Berlin 1860–1920.* Aldershot: Ashgate.

Foucault, M. 1993. 'Space, power and knowledge (interview).' In *The Cultural Studies Reader,* edited by S. During, 161–169. London: Routledge.

Fowler, D. 2008. 'Urban planning hypocrisy in the "City of Unity": forced evictions in Abuja, Nigeria.' *Trialog* 98: 10–16.

Freund, B. 1984. *The Making of Contemporary Africa. The Development of African Society since 1800.* London: Macmillan.

Gatabaki-Kamau, R. and S. Karirah-Gitau. 2004. 'Actors and interests: the development of an informal settlement in Nairobi, Kenya.' In *Reconsidering Informality: Perspectives from Urban Africa,* edited by K. Hansen and M. Vaa, 158–175. Oslo: Nordiska Afrikainstitutet.

Geist, J. and K. Kürvers. 1980. *Das Berliner Mietshaus: 1740–1862.* Munich: Prestel-Verlag.

------. 1984. *Das Berliner Mietshaus: 1862-1945.* Munich: Prestel-Verlag.

------. 1989. *Das Berliner Mietshaus: 1945-1989.* Munich: Prestel-Verlag.

Gendall, J. 2008. 'Kibera public space project by Kounkuey Design Initiative: co-designing productive parks with the poorest of Kibera, Kenya.' *Harvard Design Magazine* 28: 67–69.

Gibbon, P. 1995. 'Markets, civil society and democracy in Kenya.' In *Markets, Civil Society and Democracy in Kenya,* edited by P. Gibbon, 7–30. Uppsala: Nordic Africa Institute.

Girouard, M. 1985. *Cities and People: A Social and Architectural History*. London: Yale University Press.

Githongo, J. 2010. 'Fear and loathing in Nairobi: the challenge of reconciliation in Kenya.' *Foreign Affairs* 89(4): 2–9.

Goerke, H. 1969. 'Wohnhygiene im 19. Jahrhundert.' In *Städte-, Wohnungs- und Kleidungshygiene des 19. Jahrhunderts in Deutschland*, edited by W. Artelt, E. Hüschkel, G. Mann, and W. Rüegg, 52–69. Vorträge eines Symposiums vom 17. bis 18. Juni 1967 in Frankfurt am Main. Stuttgart: Ferdinand Enke Verlag.

Gona, G. 2003. 'Workers and the struggles for democracy in Kenya, 1963–1998.' PhD thesis, University of the Witwatersrand, Johannesburg.

Government of Kenya. 1982. *The Rent Restriction Act, Chapter 296*. Revised edition 1982 (1979). Nairobi: Government of Kenya.

------. 2004. *Kibera-Soweto Slum Upgrading Project*. Nairobi: Government of Kenya.

Hake, A. 1977. *African Metropolis: Nairobi's Self-help City*. London: Sussex University Press.

Halfani, M. 1997. 'Governance of urban development in East Africa: an examination of the institutional landscape and the poverty challenge.' In *Governing Africa's Cities*, edited by M. Swilling, 115–159. Johannesburg: Witwatersrand University Press.

Hall, P. 1990. *Cities of Tomorrow: An Intellectual History of Urban Planning and Design in the Twentieth Century*. Oxford: Blackwell.

------. 1998. *Cities in Civilization: Culture, Innovation, and Urban Order*. London: Phoenix.

Hall, T. 1997. *Planning Europe's Capital Cities: Aspects of Nineteenth Century Urban Development*. London: Taylor and Francis.

Halliman, D. and W. Morgan. 1967. 'The city of Nairobi.' In *Nairobi: City and Region*, edited by W. Morgan, 98–120. Nairobi: Oxford University Press.

Harris, J. 1972. 'A housing policy for Nairobi.' In *Urban Challenge in East Africa*, edited by J. Hutton, 39–56. Nairobi: East African Publishing House.

Harvey, D. 1974. 'Class-monopoly rent, finance capital and the urban revolution.' *Regional Studies* 8: 239–255.

------. 1985a. *Consciousness and the Urban Experience. Studies in the History and Theory of Capitalist Urbanization*. Oxford: Basil Blackwell.

------. 1985b. *The Urbanization of Capital: Studies in the History and Theory of Capitalist Urbanization*. Oxford: Basil Blackwell.

------. 1991. Afterword to *The Production of Space* by H. Lefebvre, 426–432. Oxford: Basil Blackwell.

------. 2000. *Spaces of Hope*. Berkeley, CA: University of California Press.

------. 2001. 'Possible Urban Worlds.' *Lotus International* 110: 18–22.

------. 2004. 'The right to the city.' In *The Emancipatory City? Paradoxes and Possibilities*, edited by L. Lees, 236–239. London: Sage Publications.

------. 2008. 'The right to the city.' *New Left Review* 53: 23–40.

Hauptmann, G. 1963 (first published 1892). *Die Weber*. Frankfurt: Ullstein Bücher.

Häußermann, H. and A. Kapphan. 2000. *Berlin: von der Geteilten zur Gespaltenen Stadt? Sozialräumlicher Wandel seit 1990*. Opladen: Leske und Budrich.

Häußermann, H. and W. Siebel. 1996. *Soziologie des Wohnens: Eine Einführung in Wandel und Ausdifferenzierung des Wohnens.* Weinheim and Munich: Juventa Verlag.

Hegemann, W. 1930. *Das Steinerne Berlin: Geschichte der Größten Mietskasernenstadt der Welt.* Berlin: Verlag von Gustav Kiepenheuer.

Henderson, W. and W. Chaloner. 1958. Editors' introduction to *The Condition of the Working Class in England,* by F. Engels, xxi–xxxi. Oxford: Basil Blackwell.

Heyden, M. ed. 2007. *Berlin Wohnen in Eigener Regie! Gemeinschaftsorientierte Strategien für die Mieterstadt.* Berlin: Bildungswerk Berlin der Heinrich-Böll-Stiftung.

Hirst, T. assisted by D. Lamba. 1994. *The Struggle for Nairobi: A Documentary Comic Book.* Nairobi: Mazingira Institute.

Hoch, C. 1992. 'The paradox of power in planning practice.' *Journal of Planning Education and Research* 11: 207–212.

Hochschild, A. 2002. *King Leopold's Ghost.* London: Pan Books.

Holm, A. 2006. *Die Restrukturierung des Raumes. Stadterneuerung der 90er Jahre in Ostberlin: Interessen und Machtverhältnisse.* Bielefeld: Transcript.

------. 2009. 'Baugruppen: eine Privatisierung der besonderen Art.' Interview with A. Holm conducted by K. Litschko. *Le Monde Diplomatique* 6: 24–46.

Homberger, E. with A. Hudson. 1994. *The Historical Atlas of New York City: A Visual Celebration of Nearly 400 Years of New York City's History.* New York: Henry Holt.

Horsey, M. 1990. *Tenements and Towers: Glasgow Working-Class Housing 1890–1990.* Edinburgh: The Royal Commission on the Ancient and Historical Monuments of Scotland.

Houghton-Evans, W. 1978. *Planning Cities: Legacy and Portent.* London: Lawrence and Wishart.

Huchzermeyer, M. 2007. 'Tenement city: the emergence of multi-storey districts through large-scale private landlordism in Nairobi.' *International Journal of Urban and Regional Research* 31(4): 714–732.

------. 2008. 'Slum upgrading in Nairobi within the housing and basic services market: a housing rights concern.' *Journal of Asian and African Studies* 43(1): 9–39.

------. 2010. 'Africa: where and how to house urban citizens.' In *Cities: Steering Towards Sustainability,* edited by P. Jacquet, R. Pachauri and L. Tubiana, 157–168. Delhi: TERI Press.

Jackson, K. 1957. *Marx, Proudhon and European Socialism.* London: English University Press.

Jacobs, J. 1961. *The Death and Life of Great American Cities.* London: Jonathan Cape.

JAM (Journal of African Marxists). 1982. *Independent Kenya.* Journal of African Marxists, on behalf of Kenyan authors who had to remain anonymous. London Zed Press.

Ji, L. and P. Yang. 2008. 'From family rental houses to low-rent houses.' *World Academy of Science, Engineering and Technology* 48: 402–406.

Joireman, S. and R. Vanderpoel. 2011. 'In search of order: state systems of property rights enforcement and their failings.' In *Where There Is No Government: Enforcing Property Rights in Common Law in Africa* by S. Joireman, 128–152. New York: Oxford University Press

Kagwanja P. 2005. 'Power to Uhuru: youth identity and generational politics in Kenya's 2002 elections.' *African Affairs* 105(418): 51–75.

K'Akumu, O. 2006. 'Evaluation of housing statistics in Kenya.' *Habitat International* 30 (1): 27–45.

K'Akumu, O. and W. Olima. 2007. 'The dynamics and implications of residential segregation in Nairobi.' *Habitat International* 31: 87–99.

Kanyinga, K. 1995. 'The changing development space in Kenya: Socio-political change and voluntary development activities.' In *Markets, Civil Society and Democracy in Kenya*, edited by P. Gibbon, 69–118. Uppsala: Nordic Africa Institute.

------. 2006. 'Governance institutions and inequality in Kenya.' In *Readings on Inequality in Kenya: Sectoral Dynamics and Perspectives*, edited by the Society for International Development, 345–397. Nairobi: Society for International Development.

Katumanga, M. 2005. 'A city under siege: banditry & modes of accumulation in Nairobi, 1991–2004.' *Review of African Political Economy* 106: 505–520.

Khayesi, M., H. Monheim and J. Nebe. 2010. 'Negotiating "streets for all" in urban transport planning: the case for pedestrians, cyclists and street vendors in Nairobi, Kenya.' *Antipode* 42: 104–125.

Kemper, F. 1998. 'Restructuring of housing and ethnic segregation: recent developments in Berlin.' *Urban Studies* 35(10): 1765–1789.

Kenya National Bureau of Statistics. 2010. 'Kenya 2009 population and housing census highlights.' Nairobi: Kenya National Bureau of Statistics. Accessed September 30, 2010. http://www.knbs.or.ke.

Keyder, C. 2005. 'Globalisation and social exclusion in Istanbul.' *International Journal of Urban and Regional Research* 29(1): 124–134.

Kiberenge, K. 2009. 'The pain of living in Nairobi: the city is grinding to a halt and it's not because of the jam.' *The Standard*, June 14.

King, K. 1996. *Jua Kali Kenya: Change and Development in an Informal Economy 1970–95*. London: James Currey; Nairobi: Eastern African Educational Publishers; Athens, Ohio: Ohio University Press.

Kjaer, A. 2004. ' "Old brooms can sweep too!" An overview of rulers and public sector reforms in Uganda, Tanzania and Kenya.' *The Journal of Modern African Studies* 42(3): 389–413.

Klopp, J. 2000. 'Pilfering the public: the problem of land grabbing in contemporary Kenya.' *Africa Today* 47(1): 7–26.

------. 2008. 'Remembering the destruction of Muororo: slum demolition, land and democratisation in Kenya.' *African Studies* 67(3): 295–314.

Kofman, E. and E. Lebas. 1996. 'Lost in transposition – time, space and the city.' Introduction to *Writings on Cities*, by H. Lefebvre. Oxford: Blackwell.

Kowarick, L. and C. Ant. 1994. 'One hundred years of overcrowding: slum tenements in the city.' In *Social Struggles and the City: The Case of São Paulo*, edited by L. Kowarick, 60–76. New York: Monthly Review Press.

Kristen, E. 1990. '20 Jahre Modernisierung und Rekonstruktion in Berlin-Ost.' In *Berlin: Erfahrungen, Beispiele, Perspektiven*, edited by Senatsverwaltung für Bau- und Wohnungswesen, Stadterneuerung, 73–82. Berlin: Senatsverwaltung für Bau- und Wohnungswesen.

Kumar, S. 1996. 'Landlordism in third world urban low-income settlements: a case for further research.' *Urban Studies* 33(4–5): 753–782.

Kurtz, J. 1998. *Urban Obsessions Urban Fears: The Postcolonial Kenyan Novel.* Trenton NJ: Africa World Press.

Ladd, B. 2005. 'Double restoration: rebuilding Berlin after 1945. In *The Resilient City: How Modern Cities Recover from Disaster*, edited by L. Vale and T. Campanella, 117–134. New York: Oxford University Press,.

Lafond, M. 2007. 'Experimental homes.' *Exberliner* May: 14–16.

Lee-Smith, D. 1989. 'Urban management in Nairobi: a case study of the matatu mode of public transport.' In *African Cities in Crisis: Managing Rapid Urban Growth*, edited by R. Stren and R. White, 276–304. African Modernization and Development Series. London: Westview Press.

------. 1990. 'Squatter landlords in Nairobi: a case study of Korogoho.' In *Housing Africa's Urban Poor*, edited by P. Amis and P. Lloyd, 175–187. Manchester: Manchester University Press.

Lefebvre, H. 1996 (first published 1968). *Le Droit à la Ville.* Paris: Anthopos.

------. 1991 (first published 1974). *The Production of Space.* Oxford: Blackwell.

------. 1996 (first published 1968). *Writings on Cities*, translated and edited by E. Kofman and E. Lebas. Oxford: Blackwell.

Lefèvre, A. 1990. 'Arbeiterwohnungen im Wedding – die Mietskaserne Liebenwalder Straße 40.' In *Wedding – Geschichtslandschaft Berlin, Orte und Ereignisse, Band 3*, compiled by Historische Kommission zu Berlin, 230–246. Berlin: Nicholaische Verlagsbuchhandlung.

Leo, C. 1984. *Land and Class in Kenya.* Toronto: University of Toronto Press.

Levine, M. 2004. 'Government policy, the local state, and gentrification: the case of Prenzlauer Berg (Berlin), Germany.' *Journal of Urban Affairs* 26(1): 89–108.

Leyden, F. 1995 (first published 1933). *Geographie der Weltstadt.* Berlin: Gebr. Mann Verlag.

Leys, C. 1975. *Underdevelopment in Kenya: the Political Economy of Neo-Colonialism 1964–1971.* London: Heinemann.

Liebmann, I. 2002. *Berliner Mietshaus.* Berlin: Berliner Taschenbuch Verlag.

Liedtke, P. 2006. 'From Bismarck's Pension Trap to the New Silver Workers of Tomorrow: Reflections on the German Pension Problem. Welfare and the Lengthening of the Life Cycle.' Paper no. 4. In *European Papers on the New Welfare*, 71–76. Trieste: The Risk Institute. Accessed March 27, 2009. http://eng.newwelfare.org/?p=104.

Lillteicher, J. 2007. *Raub, Recht und Restitution: Die Rückerstattung Jüdischen Eigentums in der frühen Bundesrepublik.* Göttingen: Wallstein Verlag.

Liu, Y., S. He, F. Wu and C. Webster. 2010. 'Urban villages under China's rapid urbanisation: unregulated assets and transitional neighbourhoods.' *Habitat International* 34(2): 135–144.

Loeckx, A. 1989. 'The architecture of housing in development: learning from Nairobi.' International Workshop on Housing, United Nations Centre for Human Settlements, Postgraduate Centre: Human Settlements, Katholieke Universiteit Leuven, Housing Research and Development Unit, University of Nairobi, Nairobi, January 24.

Lonsdale, J. 1992a. 'The moral economy of Mau Mau: the problem.' In *Unhappy Valley: Conflict in Kenya and Africa. Book Two: Violence and Ethnicity*, edited by B. Berman and J. Lonsdale, 265–314. London: James Currey; Nairobi: Heinemann Kenya; Athens, Ohio: Ohio University Press.

------. 1992b. 'The moral economy of Mau Mau: wealth, poverty & civic virtue in Kikuyu political thought.' In *Unhappy Valley: Conflict in Kenya and Africa. Book Two: Violence and Ethnicity*, edited by B. Berman and J. Lonsdale, 315–504. London: James Currey; Nairobi: Heinemann Kenya; Athens, Ohio: Ohio University Press.

Lubowitzki, J. 1990. *Der Hobrechtplan*. Berlin: Historical Commission of Berlin.

Lupala, J. 2002. *Urban Types in Rapidly Urbanising Cities: Analysis of Formal and Informal Settlements in Dar es Salaam, Tanzania*. Published PhD thesis, Department of Infrastructure and Planning, Division of Urban Studies, Royal Institute of Technology, Stockholm.

Lyotard, J. 1993. 'Defining the postmodern.' In *The Cultural Studies Reader*, edited by S. During, 170–173. London: Routledge.

Mabin, A. 2000. 'Varied legacies of modernism in urban planning.' In *A Companion to the City*, edited by G. Bridge and S. Watson, 555–566. Oxford: Blackwell.

Mabogunje, A. 1968. *Urbanization in Nigeria*. London: University of London Press.

MacInnes, G. 1987. *Nairobi: Two Cities Two Economies. An Ecological Analysis of a Site and Service Project*. Nairobi: Dandora Catholic Parish.

Marx, K. and F. Engels. 1964 (first published 1848). *The Communist Manifesto*. New York: Monthly Review Press.

Massey, D. 2005. *For Space*. London: Sage Publications.

Materna, I. 1997. 'Berlin – Hauptstadt des Kaiserreichs und der Weimarer Republik.' In *A Tale of Two Cities: Berlin-Kopenhagen 1650–1930*, edited by T. Riis and J. Witt, 117–129. Odense, Denmark: Odense University Press.

Mbogua, J. 1965. *Pumwani Estate Social Survey / Mbogua Report*. Nairobi: Nairobi City Council.

Mengin, C. 2007. *Guerre du Toit et Modernité Architecturale: Loger l'Employé sous la République de Weimar*. Paris: Publications de la Sorbonne.

Meredith, M. 2006. *The State of Africa: A History of Fifty Years of Independence*. Johannesburg: Jonathan Ball.

Merrifield, A. 2002. *Dialectical Urbanism: Social Struggles in the Capitalist City*. New York: Monthly Review Press.

Mifflin, E. and R. Wilton. 2005. 'No place like home: rooming houses in contemporary urban context.' *Environment and Planning A* 37: 403–421.

Miller, N. 1984. *Kenya: The Quest for Prosperity*. Boulder: Westview Press; London: Gower.

Ministry of Nairobi Metropolitan Development. 2008. *Nairobi Metro 2030: A World Class African Metropolis*. Nairobi: Ministry of Nairobi Metropolitan Development.

Ministry of Roads, Public Works and Housing. 2003. *National Housing Development Programme 2003–2007*. Nairobi: Ministry of Roads, Public Works and Housing.

Ministry of Lands and Housing 2004. *Sessional Paper No.3 on National Housing Policy for Kenya*. Nairobi: Ministry of Lands and Housing.

Mitchell, D. 2003. *The Right to the City: Social Justice and the Fight for Public Space*. New York: Guilford Press.

Mitullah, W. and K. Kibwana. 1998. 'A tale of two cities: policy, law and illegal settlements in Kenya.' In *Illegal Cities: Law and Urban Change in Developing Countries*, edited by E. Fernandes and A. Varley, 191–212. London: Zed Books.

MKP (Map Kibera Project). 2009. 'Map Kibera Project, independent open mapping project.' Accessed June 20, 2009. http://mapkiberaproject.yolasite.com/.

Montgomery, M. 2003. 'Keeping the tenants down: height restrictions and Manhattan's tenement house system, 1885–1930.' *The Cato Journal* 22(3): 495–509.

Mogan, N. and M. Daunton. 1983. 'Landlords in Glasgow: a study of 1900.' *Business History* 25(3): 264–286.

Muiruri, M. 2009a. 'Mistrust high in urban neighbourhoods.' *East African Standard*, February 27.

------. 2009b. 'Outlawed gangs terrorise urban developers.' *East African Standard*, April 13.

Müller, B. and R. Schmook. 1991. *Berlin und Brandenburg: Vom Zusammenwachsen einer Region*. Katalog zur gleichnamigen Ausstellung, im Auftrag des Presse- und Informationsamtes des Landes Berlin. Berlin: Hoch Drei.

Mueller, S. 2008. 'The political economy of Kenya's crisis.' *Journal of Eastern African Studies* 2(2): 185–210.

Mugonyi, D. and P. Kimani. 2007. 'Former MPs demand better pension.' *Daily Nation*, 31 March.

Mundia, C. and M. Aniya. 2006. Dynamics of land use/cover changes and degradation of Nairobi City, Kenya. *Land Degradation and Development* 17: 97–108.

Muraya, P. 2006. 'Urban planning and small-scale enterprises in Nairobi, Kenya.' *Habitat International* 30: 127–143.

Musyoka, R. 2006. 'Non-compliance and formalisation: mutual accommodation in land subdivision processes in Eldoret, Kenya.' *International Development Planning Review* 28(2): 235–261.

Mutero, J. 2007. *Access to Housing Finance in Africa: Exploring the Issues. Kenya*. Overview of the housing finance sector in Kenya commissioned by the FinMark Trust with support from Habitat for Humanity. Report prepared by Matrix Development Consultants, Nairobi, for FinMark Trust, Johannesburg.

Mwangi, A. 2007. 'Panic as tremors jolt Kenya.' *News*, July, 25. Geneva: International Federation of the Red Cross and Red Crescent Societies. Accessed March 14, 2009. http://www.ifrc.org/docs/news/07/07072501/.

Mwangi, I. 1997. 'The nature of rental housing in Kenya.' *Environment and Urbanisation* 9(2): 141–159.

Nairobi Informal Settlements Coordination Committee. 1997. *A Development Strategy for Nairobi's Informal Settlements*. Nairobi: Republic of Kenya.

Nairobi News. 2009. 'General: Kibera population lower than thought.' *Nairobi News*, February 17. Accessed July 30, 2009. http://nairobi.wantedinafrica.com/news/news.php?id_n=5484#.

Nairobi Urban Study Group. 1973a. *Nairobi Metropolitan Growth Strategy. Volume One: Main Report*. Nairobi: Town Planning Section, Nairobi City Council, United Nations, Colin Buchanan and Partners.

------. 1973b. *Nairobi Metropolitan Growth Strategy. Volume Two: Technical Appendices.* Nairobi: Town Planning Section, Nairobi City Council, United Nations, Colin Buchanan and Partners.

Nevanlinna, A. 1996. *Interpreting Nairobi: The Cultural Study of Built Form.* Helsinki: Suomen Historiallinen Seura.

New York Times. 1913. Skyscrapers Built in Rome in the Year A.D. 69. *New York Times,* 27 July.

Niggl, P. 1989. 'Cold as ice.' In *Stadtfront: Berlin West Berlin,* edited by G. Dietz, H. Pölking, M. Schmidt, E. Weihönig, I. Lusk and C. Zieseke, 44–67. Berlin: Elefanten Press.

Nyairo, J. 2006. '(Re)configuring the city: the mapping of places and people in contemporary Kenyan popular song texts.' In *Cities in Contemporary Africa,* edited by M. Murray and G. Myers, 71–94. New York: Palgrave Macmillan.

Obala, L. forthcoming. The relationship between land conflicts and inequity: the case of Nairobi. Draft PhD thesis, School of Architecture and Planning, University of the Witwatersrand, Johannesburg.

Obudho, R. 1997. Nairobi: national capital and regional hub. In *The Urban Challenge in Africa: Growth and Management of its Large Cities,* edited by C. Rakodi, 292–334. New York: United Nations University Press.

Ochieng, C. 2001. 'Planned housing in *Komarock* Nairobi: changes due to ten years of illegal densification.' ESN.N-AERUS Annual Workshop, Leuven, 23–26 May.

Ogot, B., 1995. The politics of populism. In *Decolonization and Independence in Kenya 1940–93,* edited by B. Ogot and W. Ochieng, 187–213. London: James Currey; Nairobi: Eastern African Educational Publishers; Athens, Ohio: Ohio University Press.

Ogot, B. and W. Ochieng, eds. 1995. *Decolonization and Independence in Kenya, 1940–93.* London: James Currey.

Okpala, D. 1984. 'Urban planning and the control of urban physical growth in Nigeria: a critique of public impact and private roles.' *Habitat International* 8(2): 73–94.

Okumu, R. 2007. 'City wide Master Plan is the solution to Nairobi's spatial planning and development control enforcement.' *The Land and Property Digest* 4: 16–17.

Omenya, A. 2006. Towards effective self-help housing delivery: contributions through network analysis in Nairobi, Kenya and Johannesburg, South Africa. PhD thesis, Faculty of Engineering and the Built Environment, University of the Witwatersrand, Johannesburg.

Osiemo, N. 1984. 'By-laws under review.' *The Standard,* May 24.

Otiso, K. 2002. 'Forced evictions in Kenyan cities.' *Singapore Journal of Tropical Geography* 23(3): 252–267.

Ott, P. 1989. Die größte Mietskasernenstadt der Welt: Wohnungselend um die Jahrhundertwende. In *Stadtfront: Berlin West Berlin,* edited by G. Dietz, H. Pölking, M. Schmidt, E. Weihönig, I. Lusk and C. Zieseke, 137–141. Berlin: Elefanten Press.

Owino, M. 1999. Review of *Decolonization and Independence in Kenya 1940–93,* edited by B.A. Ogot and W.R. Ochieng. *Journal of Asian and African Studies* 34(4): 459–462.

Owuor, M. 2009. 'Proposed building law our best chance out of the ruins.' *East African Standard,* October 22.

Özüekren, S. 1995. 'Verschwimmende Grenzen: der informelle und der formelle Wohnungssektor.' In *Self Service City: Istanbul*, edited by O. Essen and S. Lanz, 159–169. Berlin: MetroZones 4 / b.books.

Pamoja Trust. 2005. 'The Muungano Akiba Mashinani Approach to Housing.' Internal report, Pamoja Trust, Nairobi.

Patel, S. and S. D'Cruz. 1993. 'The Mahila Milan crisis credit scheme: from a seed to a tree.' *Environment and Urbanization* 5(1): 9–17.

Pieterse, E. 2008. *City Futures: Confronting the Crisis of Urban Development*. Cape Town: University of Cape Town (UCT) Press; London: Zed Books.

Pinder, D. 2005. *Visions of the City*. Edinburgh: Edinburgh University Press.

Pölking, H. 1989a. 'Die Bürger kommen: Märzrevolution in 1848 in Berlin.' In *Stadtfront: Berlin West Berlin*, edited by G. Dietz, H. Pölking, M. Schmidt, E. Weihönig, I. Lusk and C. Zieseke, 76–84. Berlin: Elefanten Press.

------. 1989b. 'Wie die ersten "Freaks" den Bürgern die rote Fahne zeigen.' In *Stadtfront: Berlin West Berlin*, edited by G. Dietz, H. Pölking, M. Schmidt, E. Weihönig, I. Lusk and C. Zieseke, 74–75. Berlin: Elefanten Press.

Potts, D. 2006. 'City life in Zimbabwe at a time of fear and loathing: urban planning, urban poverty, and Operation Murambatsvina.' In *Cities in Contemporary Africa*, edited by M. Murray and G. Myers, 265–288. New York: Palgrave Macmillan.

Presse- und Informationsamt Berlin. 1993. *Berlin in Brief*. Berlin: Presse- und Informationsamt des Landes Berlin.

Purcell, M. 2002. 'Excavating Lefebvre: the right to the city and the politics of the inhabitant.' *GeoJournal* 58: 99–108.

Rajab R. and A. Kanina. 2009. 'Architects warn of impending disaster.' *East African Standard*, October 17.

Rakodi, C. 1995. 'Rental tenure in the cities of developing countries.' *Urban Studies* 32(4–5): 791–811.

------. 2001. 'Forget planning, put politics first? Priorities for urban management in developing countries.' *International Journal for Applied Earth Observation and Geoinformation Sciences* 3(3): 209–223.

Read, S., J. Rosemann and J. Eldijk, eds. 2005. *Future City*. London: Spon Press.

Rasmussen, J. 2010. 'Mungiki as youth movement: revolution, gender and generational politics in Nairobi, Kenya.' *Young: Nordic Journal of Youth Research* 18(3): 301–319.

Reimann, B. 1997. 'The transition from people's property to private property: consequences of the restitution principle for urban development and urban renewal in East Berlin's inner-city residential areas.' *Applied Geography* 17(4): 301–314.

Reinoß, H. 1988. *Das Neue Zille-Buch*. Hannover: Fackelträger-Verlag.

Republic of Kenya. 2010. *The Constitution of Kenya*. Nairobi: Republic of Kenya.

Richie, A. 1998. *Faust's Metropolis. A History of Berlin*. London: HarperCollins.

Ritzer, G. 1996. *Sociological Theory*. Fourth Edition. Singapore: McGraw-Hill.

Robinson, J. 2004. *Ordinary Cities: Between Modernity and Development*. London: Routledge.

Robinson, P. 2005. 'Edinburgh – a tenement city?' In *Edinburgh: The Making of a Capital City*, edited by B. Edwards and P. Jenkins, 103–125. Edinburgh: Edinburgh University Press.

Rodenstein, M. 1988. *'Mehr Licht, Mehr Luft': Gesundheitskonzepte im Städtebau seit 1750.* Fankfurt and New York: Campus Verlag.

Rodger, R. 1989. *Housing in Urban Britain 1780–1914.* Studies in Economic and Social History. Basingstoke: MacMillan Education.

Rolnick, R. 1994. 'São Paulo in the early days of industrialisation: space and politics.' In *Social Struggles and the City: The Case of São Paulo*, edited by L. Kowarick, 60–76. New York: Monthly Review Press.

Rüdiger, R. 1985. 'Zur Geschichte der örtlichen Arbeiterbewegung und Betriebsgeschichte: die Tätigkeit der Arbeitersanitätskommission in Berlin (1892–1903).' *Beiträge zur Geschichte der Arbeiterbewegung* 27(1): 94–103.

Ruteere, M. and M. Pommerolle. 2003. 'Democratizing security or decentralising repression? The ambiguities of community policing in Kenya.' *African Affairs* 102: 587–604.

Sacchetti, M. 2009. 'Risks grow with spread of illegal apartments: Cities intensify crackdowns.' *The Boston Globe*, March 27.

Schäche, W. 1989. 'Die faschistische "Reichshauptstadtplanung".' In *Stadtfront: Berlin West Berlin*, edited by G. Dietz, H. Pölking, M. Schmidt, E. Weihönig, I. Lusk and C. Zieseke, 132–135. Berlin: Elefanten Press.

Senator für Stadtentwicklung und Umweltschutz. 1986. *Städtebauliche Entwicklung Berlins von 1650 bis Heute.* Beiheft zum Kartenwerk und zur Ausstellung. Berlin: Der Senator für Stadtentwicklung und Umweltschutz.

Sennett, R. 1974. *The Fall of Public Man.* London: Cambridge University Press.

Sennett, R. 1996 (first published 1971). *The Uses of Disorder: Personal Identity and City Life.* London: Faber and Faber.

Shihembetsa, L. 1989. 'Brief notes on Dandora.' International Workshop on Housing, United Nations Centre for Human Settlements, Postgraduate Centre: Human Settlements, Katholieke Universiteit Leuven, Housing Research and Development Unit, University of Nairobi, Nairobi, January 25.

------. 1991. 'Short notes on Nairobi's dwelling environments.' International Workshop on Housing, United Nations Centre for Human Settlements, Postgraduate Centre: Human Settlements, Katholieke Universiteit Leuven, Housing Research and Development Unit, University of Nairobi, Nairobi, May 24 – June 8.

Sims, D. 2003. *The case of Cairo, Egypt.* Urban Slums Report. Understanding Slums: Case Studies for the Global Report on Human Settlements 2003. Cairo: GTZ.

Soja, E., 1968. *The Geography of Modernization in Kenya: A Spatial Analysis of Social, Economic, and Political Change.* Syracuse Geographical Series No. 2. Syracuse: Syracuse University Press.

------. 1979. 'The geography of modernisation – a radical reappraisal.' In *The Spatial Structure of Development: A Study of Kenya*, edited by R. Obudho and D. Taylor, 28–45. Boulder: Westview Press.

------. 1993. 'History: geography: modernity.' In *The Cultural Studies Reader*, edited by S. During, 135–150. London: Routledge.

Souza, M. 2003. 'Alternative urban planning and management in Brazil: instructive examples for other countries in the south?' In *Confronting Fragmentation: Housing and Urban Development in a Developing Society*, edited by P. Harrison,

M. Huchzermeyer and M. Mayekiso, 190–208. Cape Town: University of Cape Town (UCT) Press.

------. 2009. 'Social movements in the face of criminal power: the socio-political fragmentation of space and "micro-level warlords" as challenges for emancipative urban struggles.' *City* 13(1): 27–52.

Steffek, J. 2003. 'The legitimation of international governance: a discourse approach.' *European Journal of International Relations* 9(2): 249–274.

Stren, R. 1972. 'The evolution of housing policy in Kenya.' In *Urban Challenge in East Africa*, edited by J. Hutton, 57–96. Nairobi: East African Publishing House.

------. 1978. *Housing the Urban Poor in Africa: Policy, Politics, and Bureaucracy in Mombasa.* Berkeley, CA: Institute of International Studies, University of California.

------. 1989. 'The administration of urban services.' In *African Cities in Crisis: Managing Rapid Urban Growth*, edited by R. Stren and R. White, 37–67. London: Westview Press.

Stren, R., M. Halfani and J. Malombe. 1994. 'Coping with urbanization and urban policy.' In *Beyond Capitalism vs. Socialism in Kenya and Tanzania*, edited by J. Barkan, 175–200. Boulder: Lynne Rienner Publishers.

Syagga, P. 2006. 'Land ownership and use in Kenya: policy prescriptions from an inequality perspective.' In *Readings on Inequality in Kenya: Sectoral Dynamics and Perspectives*, edited by the Society for International Development, 289–344. Nairobi: Society for International Development.

Syagga, P., W. Mithulla and S. Karirah-Gitau. 2001. *Nairobi Situation Analysis Consultative Report.* Collaborative Nairobi Slum Upgrading Initiative, Government of Kenya and United Nations Centre for Human Settlements, Nairobi.

------. 2002. *Nairobi Situation Analysis Supplementary Study: A Rapid Economic Appraisal of Rents in Slums and Informal Settlements.* Collaborative Nairobi Slum Upgrading Initiative, Government of Kenya and United Nations Human Settlements Programme, Nairobi.

Taut, B. 1920. *Die Auflösung der Städte.* Hagen: Folkwang-Verlag. http://www.tu-cottbus.de/Theo/D_A_T_A/Architektur/20.Jhdt/BrunoTaut/DieAufloesung/Aufloesung1.htm

Temple, F. and N. Temple. 1980. 'The politics of public housing in Nairobi.' In *Politics and Policy Implementation in the Third World*, edited by M. Grindle, 224–249. Princeton, NJ: Princeton University Press.

Teschner, K. 2008. 'Die unerträgliche Leichtigkeit der Vertreibung – Muster der Legitimation von Gewalt gegen städtische Arme.' *Trialog* 98: 4–9.

The Interministerial Task Force, n.d. *Building By-laws and Planning Regulations, Final Report. A Strategy for Disseminating and Implementing the Revised Building Code as it Applies to Low Cost Housing.* Nairobi: Ministry of Lands and Housing, Ministry of Local Government, Ministry of Health, Solicitor General.

Treue, W. 1969. 'Haus und Wohnung im 19. Jahrhundert.' In *Städte-, Wohnungs- und Kleidungshygiene des 19. Jahrhunderts in Deutschland*, edited by W. Artelt, E. Hüschkel, G. Mann und W. Rüegg, 34–51. Vorträge eines Symposiums vom 17. bis 18. Juni 1967 in Frankfurt am Main. Stuttgart: Ferdinand Enke Verlag.

Tuhus-Dubrow, R. 2009. 'Rethinking rent: Maybe we should stop trying to be a nation of homeowners.' *The Boston Globe*, March 22.

Tuts, T. 1996. 'Cost modelling for appropriate building and planning standards in Kenya.' *Habitat International* 20(4): 607–523.

UNCHS (United Nations Centre for Human Settlements). 1996. *An Urbanising World. Global Report on Human Settlements 1996*. Nairobi: United Nations Centre for Human Settlements.

UN-HABITAT (United Nations Human Settlements Programme). 2003a. *Rental Housing: An Essential Option for the Urban Poor in Developing Countries*. Nairobi: United Nations Human Settlements Programme.

------. 2003b. *The Challenge of Slums. Global Report on Human Settlements 2003*. Nairobi: United Nations Human Settlements Programme; London: Earthscan.

------. 2008. *The State of African Cities 2008: A Framework for Addressing Urban Challenges in Africa*. Nairobi: United Nations Human Settlements Programme.

------. 2009. *Planning Sustainable Cities. Global Report on Human Settlements 2009*. Nairobi: United Nations Human Settlements Programme.

UN-HABITAT News. 2008. 'Nairobi slum residents to benefit from new toilet and bathroom facilities.' *UN-Habitat News*, November 26. Accessed May 20, 2009. http://www.unhabitat.org/content.asp?cid=6080&catid=5&typeid=6&subMenuId=0.

Van Vliet, W. 1998. *Encyclopaedia of Housing*. London: Sage Publications.

Von Saldern, A. 1997. 'Im Hause, zu Hause. Wohnen im Spannungsfeld von Gegebenheiten und Aneignungen.' In *Geschichte des Wohnens, Band 3, 1800–1918. Das Bürgerliche Zeitalter*, edited by J. Reulecke, 145–332. Stuttgart: Verlag DVA.

Von Siemens, W. 1986 (written in 1889). *Lebenserinnerungen*. Munich: Prestel-Verlag.

Waki, P. 2008. *Kenya: Waki Commission of Enquiry into the Post-Election Violence Following the December 2007 General Election*. October 15. Nairobi: Republic of Kenya.

Wang, Y.P., Y.L. Wang and J. Wu. 2009. 'Urbanization and informal development in China: urban villages in Shenzhen.' *International Journal of Urban and Regional Research* 33(4): 957–973.

Wanjohi Consulting Engineers, Mutiso Menezes International, African Development & Economic Consultants, Westconsult and John L. Aluoch & Associates. 1983. Umoja Phase 2 Project, Draft: Project Definition Report. Prepared for the City Council of Nairobi, Nairobi.

Warah, R. 2004. 'Nairobi's silent majority fights back.' *People and Cities*, May 11. Accessed April 20, 2009. http://www.peopleandplanet.net/doc.php?id=2217.

------. 2010. 'How numbers game turned Kibera into "the biggest slum in Africa".' *Daily Nation*, September 12.

Watson, V. 2009. '"The planned city sweeps the poor away...": urban planning and 21st century urbanisation.' *Planning in Progress* 72: 151–193.

Weiglin, P. 1942. *Berliner Biedermeier: Leben, Kunst und Kultur in Alt-Berlin zwischen 1815 und 1948*. Bielefeld: Belhagen und Kalsing.

Weinreb, A. 2001. 'First politics, then culture: accounting for ethnic differences in demographic behaviour in Kenya.' *Population and Development Review* 27(3): 437–467.

Weisner, T. 1976. 'Kariobangi: the case history of a squatter resettlement scheme in Kenya.' In *A Century of Change in Eastern Africa*, edited by W. Arens, 76–99. The Hague: Mouton.

Werlin, H. 1966. 'The Nairobi City Council: a study in comparative local government.' *Comparative Studies in Society and History* 8(2): 181–198.

Weru, J. 2004. 'Community federations and city upgrading: the work of Pamoja Trust and Muungano in Kenya.' *Environment and Urbanization* 16(1): 47–62.

White, L. 1990. *The Comforts of Home: Prostitution in Colonial Nairobi*. London: University of Chicago Press.

White, L., L. Silberman and P. Anderson. 1948. *Nairobi Master Plan for a Colonial Capital: A Report Prepared for the Municipal Council of Nairobi*. London: His Majesty's Stationery Office.

Wiedenhoeft, R. 1985. *Berlin's Housing Revolution: German Reform in the 1920s*. Michigan: UMI Research Press.

Wietog, J. 1981. 'Der Wohnungsstandard der Unterschichten in Berlin: Eine Betrachtung anhand des Mietsteuerkatasters 1848–1871 und der Wohnungsaufnahmen 1861–1871.' In *Arbeiterexistenz im 19. Jahrhundert: Lebensstandard und Lebensgestaltung Deutscher Arbeiter und Handwerker*, edited W. Conze and U. Engelhardt, 114–137. Stuttgart: Klett-Cotta.

Wimpey, R. 2004. 'Lessons from self-help housing in Sao Paulo.' *Architecture South Africa* May/June: 22–24.

Wischermann, C. 1997. 'Mythen, Macht und Mängel: Der deutsche Wohnungsmarkt im Urbanisierungsprozeß.' In *Geschichte des Wohnens, Band 3, 1800–1918. Das Bürgerliche Zeitalter*, edited by J. Reulecke, 335–636. Stuttgart: Verlag DVA.

World Bank. 2006. *Kenya – Inside Informality: Poverty, Jobs, Housing and Services in Nairobi's Slums*. Report No. 36347-KE. Washington D.C.: Water Unit 1, Africa Region, The World Bank.

Wrong, M. 2009. *It's Our Turn to Eat: The Story of a Kenyan Whistle Blower*. London: Fourth Estate.

Yahya, S. 1987. *Review of Building Codes and Regulations: A Manual Based on Kenya's Experience*. Nairobi: Housing Research and Development Unit, University of Nairobi.

------. 1990. 'Residential urban land markets in Kenya.' In *Housing Africa's Urban Poor*, edited by P. Amis and P. Lloyd, 157–173. Manchester: Manchester University Press.

Zukin, S. 1995. *The Culture of Cities*. Oxford: Blackwell.

Cited interviews

Anonymous officials in Nairobi City Council and public agencies

Anonymous A. October 25, 2005 and October 27, 2005. Official, Housing Development Department, Dandora, Nairobi City Council, Nairobi.

Anonymous B. October 13, 2005. Senior Official, Physical Planning, Nairobi City Council, Nairobi.

Anonymous C. May 26, 2008. Senior Official, Physical Planning, Nairobi City Council, Nairobi.

Anonymous D. October 5, 2005. Senior Official, Development Control, Nairobi City Council, Nairobi.

Anonymous E. October 27, 2005. Engineer, Nairobi Water and Sewerage Company, Nairobi.

Anonymous F. November 2, 2005. Official, Development Control, Nairobi City Council, Nairobi.

Anonymous G. October 31, 2005. Town Planner, Forward Planning, Nairobi City Council, Nairobi.

Anonymous H. October 5, 2005. Town Planner, Forward Planning, Nairobi City Council, Nairobi.

Anonymous Group I. October 17, 2005. Official supervising meter reading, and Regional Commercial Coordinator, Eastleigh Office of the Nairobi Water and Sewerage Company, Nairobi.

Anonymous Group J. October 12, 2005. Chief Architect, Senior Architect and Architect, National Housing Corporation, Nairobi.

Officials of Central Bureau of Statistics

Mwando, Mr. November 2, 2005. Central Bureau of Statistics, Nairobi.

Mushiri, Mr. November 2, 2005. Central Bureau of Statistics, Nairobi.

Estate agents and auctioneers

Agent 1. October 21, 2005 and November 1, 2005. Bonage Properties, Nairobi.

Agent 2. October 17, 2005 and October 26, 2005. Metrocosmo, Nairobi.

Agent 3. October 22, 2005. Sparrow Property Services, Nairobi.

Auctioneer. November 1, 2005. Garam Auctioneers, Nairobi.

Landlords and owner

Landlord 1. November 1, 2005. Experienced landlord owning two tenements in Huruma and two in Kariobangi Light Industries. Interview at his downtown grain business, Nairobi.

Landlord 2. November 3, 2005. Experienced landlord who owned, but later disposed of, a tenement in Huruma. Now owns buildings in several other areas. Interview at his downtown taxi business, Nairobi.

Landlord 3. November 3, 2005. Experienced landlord owning two buildings in Umoja Inner Core. Interview at his downtown taxi business, Nairobi.

Landlord 4. October 18, 2005. First-time landlord constructing a tenement in Umoja Inner Core. Interview at his building site in Umoja Inner Core, Nairobi.

Umoja II condominium unit owner. Interview in her condominium unit. October 26, 2005. Umoja Inner Core, Nairobi.

Tenants

Tenant 1. October 25, 2005; October 29, 2005; May 25, 2008; May 28, 2008; June 15, 2009; February 9, 2010 (by e-mail). Husband and father of a young family, in formal skilled employment. Grew up in Huruma. Interview in his family's tenement room, Huruma, Nairobi.

Tenant 2. October 25, 2005. Housewife in a two-bedroom flat in one of the few tenements in Huruma that do not exclusively provide rooming. Interview in her family's flat, Huruma, Nairobi.

Tenant 3. October 25, 2005. Housewife and young mother of two in a rooming tenement. Interview on the balcony in front of her family's room, Huruma, Nairobi.

Tenant 4. October 31, 2005. Husband and father of three living in a tenement room in Huruma, self-employed in one of the local garbage collection cartels. Interview in a tenement room of a friend, Huruma, Nairobi.

Tenant 5. May 28, 2008. Husband, grew up in Huruma, has lived in the same tenement since 2000 (longest-renting tenant in his building). Interview with his friends, in the open space outside his tenement, Huruma, Nairobi.

Tenant 6. May 28, 2008. Husband and father of a small baby. Grew up in Huruma, lives in a two-story tenement owned by his father, who has moved into Council housing. Runs a small pub in the building and organizes a group of traditional dancers. Interview in his tenement room, Huruma, Nairobi.

Shop attendant. October 31, 2005. General dealer, Umoja Inner Core. Interview in the shop, Nairobi.

Personal communication with academics and consultants

Agevi, E. October 24, 2005. Urban/housing consultant, Nairobi.

Mitlin, D. June 23, 2009. Senior Lecturer, Institute for Development Policy and Management, School of Environment and Development, University of Manchester and International Institute for Environment and Development, London (via telephone).

Obala, L. September 3, 2010. Lecturer, Department of Real Estate and Construction Economics, University of Nairobi, Nairobi.

Omenya, A. June 14, 2009. Lecturer, Department of Architecture and Building Science, University of Nairobi, Nairobi.

Index